BREATHTURN INTO TIMESTEAD

BREAT
INTO
TIMES

Paul Celan

THE COLLECTED LATER POETRY

A BILINGUAL EDITION

TRANSLATED FROM THE GERMAN AND
WITH COMMENTARY BY PIERRE JORIS

FARRAR STRAUS GIROUX   NEW YORK

FARRAR, STRAUS AND GIROUX
18 West 18th Street, New York 10011

First edition, 2014

Library of Congress Cataloging-in-Publication Data
Celan, Paul, author.
    [Poems. Selections. English]
    Breathturn into timestead : the collected later poetry :
a bilingual edition / Paul Celan ; translated by Pierre Joris.
      pages cm
    Includes bibliographical references and index.
    ISBN 978-0-374-60803-3
    I. Joris, Pierre, translator. II. Title.

PT2605.E4 A2 2014
831'.914—dc23

                                    2014020543

Designed by Quemadura

Farrar, Straus and Giroux books may be purchased for educational, business,
or promotional use. For information on bulk purchases, please contact the
Macmillan Corporate and Premium Sales Department at 1-800-221-7945,
extension 5442, or write to specialmarkets@macmillan.com.

www.fsgbooks.com
www.twitter.com/fsgbooks
www.facebook.com/fsgbooks

P1

Contents

FADENSONNEN | THREADSUNS

III

EINGEDUNKELT | TENEBRAE'D

LICHTZWANG | LIGHTDURESS

I

SCHNEEPART | SNOWPART

ZEITGEHÖFT | TIMESTEAD

I

Introduction

Since his death in 1970, Paul Celan's reputation, though already firmly established during his lifetime, has grown exponentially. He is now considered the major German-language poet of the period after 1945, and by some (George Steiner, for example) even as the major European poet of that period. Only Rilke, among last century's German-language poets, can conceivably match his fame and impact on German and world poetry. Despite the difficulties the work presents (or maybe because of them), the usual postmortem eclipse, so often visited upon poets well-known and influential during their lifetimes, did not touch Celan: the flow of essays, commentaries, and books on his work has not only continued unabated, but has picked up speed and grown to flood-tide proportions—an informed guess would put it at some six-thousand-plus items worldwide by now. Translations of his work into a wide range of foreign languages are myriad. A benchmark of limit-possibilities for many younger poets in Europe, America, and beyond, Celan's work has also proved a major attraction for contemporary philosophy. As Hölderlin functioned for the late Heidegger, so does Celan represent a lodestone pointing to directions "north of the future" for philosophers and thinkers as diverse as Otto Pöggeler, Maurice Blanchot, Jacques Derrida, Hans-Georg Gadamer, Philippe Lacoue-Labarthe, Jean Bollack, Anne Carson, and Peter Szondi, who have all devoted at least one book to his work.

At the same time, the publication of Celan's work has progressed apace so that we now have the oeuvre available nearly in toto (with the exception, mainly, of personal diaries and notebooks) in a variety of forms. Thus the slightly fewer than a thousand poems are distributed over eleven individual volumes, and are gathered in several collected works editions, including an annotated collected poems, different selected works volumes, and in two major critical-historical editions based on the individual volumes. Beyond the poetry proper, we have some two hundred fifty pages of prose available, and nearly seven hundred pages of poetry translated by Celan from eight languages and assembled in two volumes. To date, some fifteen volumes of correspondence have been published, if only a few of these in English translation so far. Though we do not yet have an official or reliable and exhaustive biography (except for Israel Chalfen's *Paul Celan: Biography of His Youth*), the two-volume edition of the annotated correspondence between Paul Celan and Gisèle Celan-Lestrange[1] can stand in for such a book (although available right now only in French and German—and in an updated 2008 Spanish edition—it is, however, in the process of being translated into English as of this writing). Besides several volumes that gather historical, archival, and critical materials—one on the Goll affair, others on his stay in Vienna and on his hometown, Czernowitz, as well as one on his activities as a translator—there is also an annotated volume of Celan's philosophical library inventorying some five hundred books in six languages (German, French, ancient Greek, English, Latin, and Russian) and reproducing all the text extracts underlined or marked by Celan, as well as his handwritten marginalia. At the end of this book the reader will find a selected bibliography of critical texts on Celan's work available in English.

1. "DEATH IS A MASTER FROM GERMANY"

Celan's life is inseparable from the fate of the Jewish people in the twentieth century. The Shoah is thus core to the life and work, even if Celan did his best to make sure that neither would be overdetermined by or become reducible to those events. He is a survivor of *khurbn* (to use Jerome Rothenberg's "ancient and dark word"), and his work is a constant bearing witness to those atrocities; even when it imagines a world beyond those historical limits, it remains *eingedenk* (to use Hölderlin's word), that is, mindful, conscious of said events. Born Paul Antschel in Czernowitz (today Chernivtsi, in Ukraine), the capital of the Bukovina, a province of the Habsburg Empire that fell to Romania in 1920, the year of his birth, Celan was raised in a Jewish family that insisted both on young Paul receiving the best secular education—with the mother inculcating her love of the German language and culture—and on his Jewish roots: both his parents came from Orthodox and, on one side, Hasidic family backgrounds. The languages were multiple: besides the usual Czernowitz languages—Romanian, Ukrainian, and Yiddish—the family at home spoke High German, somewhat different from the Czernowitzian dialectical German with "its Austrian informality and Slavic breadth, and interwoven with Yiddish idioms."[2] Following his father's Zionist ideals, young Paul attended the local Hebrew grade school, Safah-Ivriah, for three years, though moving eventually to the Romanian high school, where he showed great interest in botany and French. Because of growing anti-Semitism, he moved to another state high school, where he added Italian, Latin, and ancient Greek to his studies. As a German-speaking student, he studied primarily the classics of German literature, supported in this by his mother and from 1937 on by his friend Edith Horowitz, whose father, a scholar of German literature, had a library very rich in this field. After his Bar Mitzvah Paul stopped studying Hebrew and began distancing himself from his father's ideological leanings. At this time he also began to take part in meetings of communist youth groups, got involved in antifascist activities, and read intensely in the classics of socialist literature.[3]

Celan, always reticent of speaking of private matters, left little autobiographical information, and the only somewhat expansive statement concerning his homeland occurs in the so-called Bremen speech, where he writes:

> The region from which I come to you—with what detours! but then, is there such a thing as a detour?—will be unfamiliar to most of you. It is the home of many of the Hassidic stories which Martin Buber has retold in German. It was—if I may flesh out this topographical sketch with a few details which are coming back to me from a great distance—it was a landscape where both people and books lived. There, in this former province of the Habsburg monarchy, now dropped from history, I first encountered the name of Rudolf Alexander Schröder while reading Rudolf Borchardt's "Ode with Pomegranate" . . . Within reach, though far enough, what I could aim to reach, was Vienna. You know what happened, in the years to come, even to this nearness.[4]

On November 9, 1938, the night that came to be known as Kristallnacht and that saw the first major Nazi pogrom against Jews in Germany and parts of Austria, Paul Celan traveled by train through Germany, an occasion remembered in the poem "La Contrescarpe," where he writes: "Via Kraków / you came, at the Anhalter / railway station / a smoke flowed toward your glance, / it already belonged to tomorrow." He was on his way via Paris to Tours, France, to study medicine at the local university, obedient to his parents' wishes. During this year in France he came in contact with a range of contemporary French literature and, in fact, spent much time on literary matters while slowly turning away from his premed studies. He had already started to write poetry a few years earlier, and in the summer of 1939, after returning to Czernowitz, and unable to return to Tours and his medical studies because of the outbreak of the war, Celan decided on a major career change, enrolling in Romance studies at his hometown's university. The oldest surviving poems date from 1939 but would be published only posthumously.

The following year Soviet troops occupied his hometown, only to be replaced in 1941 by Romanian and German Nazi troops—specifically, Einsatzgruppe D, led by SS-Brigadeführer Ohlendorf, which reached Czernowitz on July 6. The SS had one essential job to fulfill—"Energisch durchgreifen, die Juden liquidieren" (to energetically liquidate the Jews), as they didn't trust the Romanians to do the job thoroughly enough. On July 7, the Great Temple went up in flames and for the next three days the hunt was open: 682 Jews were murdered. By late August, Ohlendorf triumphantly reported to Berlin that more than 3,000 had been killed. On October 11, the ghetto was created—the first one in the history of the Bukovina and of Czernowitz. Then began the *Umsiedlung* (relocation) of most Jews to Transnistria. The Romanians managed to argue with the Germans and to retain 15,000 Jews in Czernowitz to keep the city functioning. The Antschel family were among those who, at least for the time being, remained in the ghetto. Paul was ordered to forced labor on construction sites. Then, in June 1942, a new wave of arrests and deportations began, taking place primarily on Saturday nights. With the help of his friend Ruth Lackner, Paul had found a large and comfortable hideout, but his parents refused adamantly to take refuge there, preferring to remain in their own house—where Celan's mother did prepare rucksacks in case they should be deported. On one of those nights, disobeying his parents' orders, Paul left the house and decided to spend the night in the hideout. When he returned the next morning he found his home sealed off: his parents had been deported.

Celan continued to work in forced labor camps, where in the late fall of 1942 he learned that his father, physically broken by the slave labor he was subjected to, had been killed by the SS. Later that winter the news reached him that his mother too had been shot. These killings, especially that of his mother, were to remain the core experience of his life. He was released in February 1944, when the labor camps were closed. In April, Soviet troops occupied Czernowitz without a fight. Celan was put to work as a medical auxiliary in a psychiatric clinic and made one trip as an ambulance assistant to Kiev. He remained in Czernowitz for one more year, enrolled at the now Ukrainian-Russian university there, studying English literature while working as a translator for local newspapers. In February 1944 he had put together a first typescript of poems, expanding it in the fall of that year to include the poems written during his labor camp days. He entrusted this manuscript to his friend Ruth Kraft, who took it with her to Bucharest to present it to the poet Alfred Margul-Sperber. (This book would be published posthumously in 1986 as *Gedichte 1938–1944*, with a foreword by Ruth Kraft.) In April 1945 he left his hometown, Czernowitz, never to return. But the Bukovinian "meridian" (to use one of his favorite lines of orientation) would always be present; he mentioned "my (Czernowitz) meridian" in a letter to Gideon Kraft as late as 1968,[5] as he spoke of Gustav Landauer and Leon Kellner, two elder Bukovinians who had been important to him. As one commentator put it: "Celan's poetry transforms the main characteristic of Bukovina's culture into a structural principle. It is the legendary Bukovinian receptivity to heterogeneous ethnic traditions with which Celan infuses the rich intertextuality of his entire oeuvre."[6]

For two years he settled in Bucharest, making a living as a translator (mainly from Russian into Romanian) and working at becoming a poet, remaining true to his mother's language, German, as he would do all his life, but also trying his hand briefly at poems in Romanian. He was clear about this choice, stating on a number of occasions that there is no such thing as bilingual poetry, that the poet has to write in his mother tongue. The strongest formulation of this conviction was reported by Ruth Lackner, to whom he said: "Only in the mother tongue can one speak one's own truth, in a foreign language the poet lies."[7] It is, however, in Bucharest and in a Romanian translation by his friend Petre Solomon that the poem that would make his fame—"Todesfuge" (Death-fugue)—was first published in May 1947, in the magazine *Contemporanul*, as "Tangoul Mortii" (Tango of death). It is also here that Paul Antschel, who signed many of the translations of that time with various pseudonyms, decided to change his name and anagrammatically transformed the Romanian spelling of Antschel, Ançel, into Celan.

But Vienna, the old Hapsburg capital, which the German-cultured Bukovinians and Czernowitzians had always looked up to as *their* cultural center, beckoned, and in December 1947 Celan clandestinely crossed over to Austria via Hungary—from the little information we have, an arduous journey but one made necessary by the tightening of the Iron Curtain. The only German-speaking place the poet was ever to live in, the Vienna of those years[8]—Orson Welles's *The Third Man* comes close to what it must have felt like to Celan—

was relatively hospitable to the young poet, though the minimal and superficial denazification program it had submitted itself to must have left the survivor uneasy, to say the least. Through an introduction from Margul-Sperber he met Otto Basil, the editor of the avant-garde literary magazine *Der Plan*, in which he would publish a number of poems, and at some point he went to meet Ludwig von Ficker, who had been a close friend of Georg Trakl's, and who celebrated the young Bukovinian poet as "heir to Else Lasker-Schüler." A meeting with the surrealist painter Edgar Jené led to the writing of the first essay by Celan that we have, "Edgar Jené and the Dream of the Dream," composed as a foreword to a Jené exhibition catalogue. He also met a number of people who would remain lifelong friends, among them Nani and Klaus Demus, and maybe most important, the young poet Ingeborg Bachman, who even after their early love affair faded was to remain a close friend and a staunch defender in the later, darker days of the Goll affair. It was also in Vienna that Celan readied his first book, *Der Sand aus den Urnen* (The sand from the urns), for publication—though he would recall the book and have it destroyed, judging that the many typos and mistakes lethally disfigured his work.

From Hölderlin's hallucinatory walk to the Bordelais and back, to von Horvath's strange death (a branch severed by lightning killed him on the Champs-Élysées), France has always proved a point of focal, not to say fatal, attraction—and certainly often enough, a point of rupture—for poets and writers of the German language: suffice it to add in this context the names of Heinrich Heine, Rainer Maria Rilke, and Walter Benjamin. For most of these, their stays in France were limited, and freely chosen. But often also they were a matter of political and/or intellectual exile. Few of them, however, had as symbiotic and long-term a relationship with France as Paul Celan. The latter clearly had not found what he was looking for in Vienna, and after less than a year—and even before his first book came out—he left Austria to head for Paris, where he arrived in July 1948. The city by the Seine, the *ville lumière*, was to remain his home until his death in late April 1970. It was not easy for him to adapt and make a living at first, but while doing this he never lost sight of his and poetry's aim: he worked tirelessly at getting his poetry published and known in the German-language areas, be it Austria or Germany. In early 1952 he was invited by the already well-known Gruppe 47 to read in their yearly gathering in Niendorf, and this started a pattern of forays into Germany that would continue until just a few months before his death. His first major volume of poems, *Mohn und Gedächtnis* (Poppy and memory), was published later that year by the German publisher DVA (Deutsche Verlags-Anstalt) in Stuttgart, and brought instant recognition, as well as a measure of fame, due in no small part to what was to become one of the best-known and most-anthologized poems of the post-war era, the "Todesfuge." A new volume of poems followed roughly every four years, with that rhythm accelerating, as we shall see, during the last years of his life.

In Paris, he made contact with the literary scene and soon met a number of writers who were to stay important for him. Among them was the poet Yves Bonnefoy, who recalls Celan in those days:

> His gestures, above all in the first years after Vienna—at the time of the room in *rue des Ecoles*, of the cheap university restaurants, of the archaic typewriter with a Greek-temple peristyle, of destitution—had nonchalance, and his head had a graceful movement towards the shoulder: as if to accompany, for a stretch, along the summer streets after a lively night's conversation, the friend being left for a whole day.[9]

It was Bonnefoy who introduced Celan, on the latter's insistence, to Yvan Goll in November 1949. This encounter would much later produce terrible results: festering throughout the fifties, the "Goll affair"—in which Claire Goll, the poet's widow, falsely accused Celan of plagiarism, and, shockingly, a range of German newspapers and reviews uncritically accepted and spread those false accusations—broke in 1960 and does indeed mark a traumatic turning point.[10]

Celan does not seem ever to have seriously thought about moving elsewhere, and certainly not after meeting the French graphic artist Gisèle Lestrange in the fall of 1951, and marrying her in late 1952. He became a naturalized French citizen in 1955, and it was as a French citizen and a Parisian literary person that he spent the rest of his life, employed as a teacher of German language and literature at the École Normale Supérieure on the rue d'Ulm, summering from 1962 on in the little farmhouse the Celans bought in Normandy. A first child, François, died shortly after birth in 1953, but 1955 saw the birth of his son Eric, with whom Celan would be very close. The last years brought a separation from his wife and son, and from 1967 to 1970 Celan lived alone in Paris.

During this final decade of his life, his latent psychic troubles had come to the fore, exacerbated by the false accusations of plagiarism leveled by the widow Goll. Celan the survivor's already tenuous psychic health was seriously endangered, and would increasingly necessitate medical attention. He had been in self-imposed psychiatric care sometime around May 1965, and was forcibly put in psychiatric confinement in November 1965 after a life-threatening knife attack on his wife. Further hospitalizations followed from December 1965 to early June 1966. The following year started ominously with the chance encounter on January 25 at a literary event at the Paris Goethe Institute with the widow Goll, triggering deep psychic turmoil. Five days later, on January 30, Celan, after threatening the life of his wife, who then demanded a separation, tried to kill himself with a knife—or a letter opener—that missed his heart by an inch. Saved by his wife in extremis, he was transported to the Hôpital Boucicaut and operated on immediately, as his left lung was gravely wounded. He was in and out of psychiatric institutions from February 1967 to October of that year, even though by the middle of May he had started teaching again at the École Normale. These stays involved drug and shock therapy, and old friends who saw him during or after those days reported major changes in the man. Thus Petre Solomon, visiting Paris that summer, found Celan "profoundly altered, prematurely aged, taciturn, frowning . . . 'They are doing experiments on me,' he said in a stifled voice, interrupted by sighs."[11] One can hear this "stifled" voice, deeper though no less resonant—and perceive behind it the psychic pain probably muffled by medication—by listening to the 1967 recordings of poems from *Threadsuns.*[12]

Despite all this, Celan's last years were extremely active ones: the writing—contrary to a widespread belief that he came close to a *Verstummen*, a falling silent—kept on unabated with long productive periods that saw the composition of poems on a near-daily basis, with a number of days that brought several poems. He kept traveling: to Switzerland for holidays and meetings with old friends; to Germany for readings, recordings, and encounters (with the philosopher Martin Heidegger, among others); and to Israel in 1969—though he broke that trip off after two weeks to return precipitately to Paris.[13] He had moved from his small studio apartment on rue Tournefort in the fifth arrondissement to an apartment on the avenue Émile Zola in late 1969, and on the night of April 19–20, 1970, he succumbed to his psychic demons: the Pont Mirabeau, close to his apartment at the end of avenue Émile Zola, is probably where he decided to put an end to his life by going into the Seine. His body was found farther downstream on May 1. He was buried in the Thiais cemetery on the outskirts of Paris, where his son François already rested and where his wife, Gisèle, would join him in December 1991.

On his desk Paul Celan had left Wilhelm Michael's biography of Hölderlin, *Das Leben Friedrich Hölderlins*, lying open to page 464. He had underlined the following sentence from a letter by Clemens Brentano: "Sometimes this genius goes dark and drowns in the bitter well of his heart."

2. "LESESTATIONEN IM SPÄTWORT"

In the early sixties, that is, midway through Paul Celan's writing career, a radical change, a poetic *Wende*, or turn, occurred, later inscribed in the title of the volume *Atemwende | Breathturn*, heralding the poetics he was to explore for the rest of his life. His poems, which had always been highly complex but rather lush, with an abundance of near-surrealistic imagery and sometimes labyrinthine metaphoricity—though he vehemently denied the critics' suggestion that his was a "hermetic" poetry—were pared down, the syntax grew tighter and more spiny, and his trademark neologisms and telescoping of words increased, while the overall composition of the work became much more serial in nature. That is, rather than insisting on individual, titled poems, he moved toward a method of composition by cycles and volumes.

Borrowed from a poem in the volume *Lichtzwang | Lightduress*, the title of this section—*Lesestationen im Spätwort*—translates as "reading stations in the late-word." I have written elsewhere[14] on the idea of the individual poem as being, for the reader, a momentary stopping point, a temporary "station" in a (though not religious, even if the term is used in both Christian and Sufi thinking) circumambulation of marked spaces. In Celan's late work, individual poems are such markers in the ongoing flux of the cycles and volumes, and the reader is well counseled to keep eye and ear on the continuity of this flux, while homing in on, or honing, individual poems as "reading-stations," as necessary stops at the knotty difficulties the work presents, yet also and simultaneously as restorative moments of rest, of refreshment and nourishment. The place suggested by Celan as such a point of entry, maybe the one most immediately visible and available to the reader is, in fact, infra-poem, that is, a smaller unit inside the individual poem: it is in front of the word that the poet tells us to stop and knock—or beg—for entry. To grasp what is at stake we have to hear what has been erased and simultaneously kept alive in the neologism "Spätwort," "late-word," namely the term *Spätwerk*, "late work." To get to the "late work," we have to stop in front of the "late-word," we have to come to terms with the development away from a poetry of flowing musical lines and lyric melody, as they reign supreme in the early collections, to one consisting of terse, often single-word or -syllable verse structures, thus from a predominantly horizontal to an ever more vertiginously vertical axis. It is singular words, extracted, it is true, from a vast array of rich language-veins that now carry the weight of the poem. George Steiner suggests that "such words must be quarried from far and stony places. They lodge in the 'wall of the heart' . . . Their authority is, in the true sense, radical, of the root (etymological). Or it springs from fusion, from the poet's right and need to weld neologisms."[15]

Celan seems to have signaled as far back as 1958 that a change in his poetics was taking place, when he suggested that for him poetry was no longer a matter of "transfiguring" (*verklären*). The statement came in a short text written as a reply to a questionnaire from the Librairie Flinker in Paris, and needs quoting more fully, as it shows Celan already thinking through changes that will be implemented only in the poetry of the sixties, and which the volume *Sprachgitter | Speechgrille*, to be published the following year, foreshadows without fully developing. Given "the sinister events in its memory," writes Celan, the language of German poetry has to become "more sober, more factual . . . 'grayer.'" This greater factuality checks a core impulse of the lyrical tradition—in German the common word for poetry is *Lyrik*—and its relation to the lyre, to music: "it is . . . a language which wants to locate even its 'musicality' in such a way that it has nothing in common with the 'euphony' which more or less blithely continued to sound alongside the greatest horrors." The direct effect of giving up this "euphony" is to increase the accuracy of the language: "it does not transfigure or render 'poetical'; it names, it posits, it tries to measure the area of the given and the possible."[16]

Celan underscores this turning point, this *Wende,* when he uses the word in the title of the volume that incarnates the turn and opens the book underhand: *Atemwende | Breathturn*—an unusual title in the general economy of the naming of his books, at least until this period. Contrary to the titles of the previous volumes, it is neither a phrase, such as *Mohn und Gedächtnis | Poppy and Memory*, nor a compound word extracted from a poem and set above the whole collection as title, such as *Sprachgitter | Speechgrille.* Unable to link the title directly to a specific poem in the collection, one finds it difficult to determine or control its meaning by contextualizing it thematically or tropically within the book—hence the sense that the title is programmatic for the poetics of the work rather than evocative of a specific poetic content. And indeed, the word *Atemwende* does occur elsewhere in Celan's writings—namely, in the Meridian speech (delivered on the occasion of receiving the Georg Büchner Prize in Darmstadt, October 22, 1960), which is his most important and extended statement on poetics. It is here that we have to look for the theoretical base of the changes from the early to the late work.

In the speech, Celan addresses the question of art through the work of Georg Büchner, specifically the play *Danton's Death* and the prose novella *Lenz*. He defines Lucile's final exclamation in the play—"Long live the king!"—as "a word against the grain, the word which cuts the 'string,' which does not bow to the 'bystanders and old warhorses of history.' It is an act of freedom. It is a step." In short, it is what Celan calls a *Gegenwort*, a "counterword," and thus the word of poetry. But, he goes on, there is an even fiercer *Gegenwort*, and that is Lenz's silence: "Lenz—that is, Büchner—has gone a step farther than Lucile. His 'Long live the king' is no longer a word. It is a terrifying falling silent, it takes away his—and our—breath and words." It is in the next sentence that Celan introduces the term *Atemwende*:

Poetry: that can mean an *Atemwende*, a breathturn. Who knows, perhaps poetry travels this route—also the route of art—for the sake of such a breathturn? Perhaps it will succeed, as the strange, I mean the abyss and the Medusa's head, the abyss and the automatons, seem to lie in one direction—perhaps it will succeed here to differentiate between strange and strange, perhaps it is exactly here that the Medusa's head shrinks, perhaps it is exactly here that the automatons break down—for this single short moment? Perhaps here, with the I—with the estranged I set free *here* and *in this manner*—perhaps here a further Other is set free?

Perhaps the poem is itself because of this . . . and can now, in this art-less, art-free manner, walk its other routes, thus also the routes of art—time and again?

Perhaps.[17]

I have quoted this passage at length not only because it may be the one that most closely defines Celan's thinking about poetry, but also to give a sense of its rhetorical texture, its tentative, meditative, one could say groping, progress. The temptation—and many critics have not resisted it—would be to extract from the passage the definitive, affirmative statement "Poetry is a breathturn," but in the process one would have discarded the series of rhetorical pointers, the ninefold repetition of the word *vielleicht*, "perhaps," which turns all the sentences into questions. The passage is, however, not an isolated rhetorical formula in the speech; indeed, one could argue that the whole of the Meridian speech is a putting into question of the possibilities of art, in Celan's own words, "eine radikale In-Frage-Stellung der Kunst," which all of poetry (and art in general) has to submit to today if it wants to be of essential use. Gerhard Buhr, in an essay analyzing the Meridian speech from exactly this angle, comments on Celan's expression "eine radikale In-Frage-Stellung der Kunst" as follows:

> The phrase "radikale In-Frage-Stellung der Kunst" (radical putting-into-question of art) has a double meaning given the two ways the genitive can read: Art, with "everything that belongs and comes to it" . . . has to be radically questioned; and it [art] puts other things, such as man or poetry, radically into question. That is exactly why the question of poetry, the putting-into-question of poetry is not exterior to art —: The nature of art is rather to be discussed and clarified in connection with the nature of the question itself.[18]

Celan, a careful poet not given to rhetorical statements or linguistic flourishes, who in his late poems will castigate himself and his own early work for an overuse of such "flowers," needs to be taken quite literally here: he is groping, experimenting, questioning, trying to find his way to a new possibility in poetry. It is a slow process: the term *Atemwende*, coined in this speech of 1960, will reemerge as the title of a volume only seven years later.

The last book published before the Meridian speech had been *Sprachgitter*, which had come out the previous year and already points to some of the directions the late work will take. For the first time Celan uses a single compound word as a title, something he will do for all subsequent volumes; for the first time it contains poems, albeit only five, devoid of individual titles—something that will become the norm in the late work; the language has now given up nearly completely the long dactylic lines and the rhymes of the first three books, while the brief, foreshortened, often one-word lines have become more frequent. Most important, some of the poems are clearly what has been called *Widerrufe*: attempts at retracting, countermanding, disavowing previous poetics—those of other poets, but also his own earlier stance. The poem "Tenebrae," for example, is a carefully constructed refutation of Hölderlin's "Patmos" hymn, which, as Götz Wienold has shown,[19] negates the (Christian/pagan) hope for salvation expressed in Hölderlin's lines "Nah ist / Und schwer zu fassen der Gott. / Wo aber Gefahr ist, wächst / Das Rettende auch" (Close / and difficult to grasp is God. / But where danger lurks, that which saves / also grows); simultaneously the poem inverts and negates the (Judaic) hopes regarding God's promises as expressed in the psalms, specifically Psalm 34, and in other places in the Bible that are alluded to, mainly Isaiah 43:20 and Leviticus 17.

In a similar vein, the title poem, "Sprachgitter," takes issue both with Gottfried Benn's famous essay *Probleme der Lyrik* and with the optimism of Psalm 126.

However, Celan's *Widerrufe* are not only addressed to German poetry and the scriptures. He also calls into question his own earlier poetics. One can thus read "Engführung," the great poem that concludes *Sprachgitter*, as a rewriting with different poetics of the "Todesfuge," as Hans Mayer[20] and others have done. This critical stance toward his early poetics remains perceptible in several poems of the late work and is thematized in the opening stanza of a poem in *Breathturn*:

> WEGGEBEIZT vom
> Strahlenwind deiner Sprache
> das bunte Gerede des An-
> erlebten – das hundert-
> züngige Mein-
> gedicht, das Genicht.

> ERODED by
> the beamwind of your speech
> the gaudy chatter of the pseudo-
> experienced—the hundred-
> tongued perjury-
> poem, the noem.

The neologism "Meingedicht" is based on the German word *Mein-eid*, "perjury," but because Celan breaks the word the way he does, one cannot but also hear in the prefix the possessive *mein*, "my." As Jerry Glenn has suggested,[21] this "allude[s] to Celan's own early attempts to come to terms with the past in elaborate, colorful metaphors." The new language of the addressed "you," which here seems to be the poet himself, his new "beamwind"-language, aims to erode the "gaudy chatter" of the early work, and lead into a bare northern landscape of snow and ice: *nordwahr*, "northtrue," as another poem puts it, where the true "unalterable testimony" which it is the poet's job to create can be found, located deep in the ice, as an *Atemkristall*, a "breath-crystal."

What all of Celan's *Widerrufe* seem to have in common is a deep dissatisfaction with traditional (and that includes modernist) poetics, and a need to push toward a new vision of writing and the world, and of the relationship between those two. For Celan, art no longer harbors the possibility of redemption, in that it can neither lead back to or bring back the gods, as Hölderlin suggested, nor can it constitute itself as an independent, autonomous aesthetic sphere of *Artistik*, "artistry," as Gottfried Benn sees it, and behind Benn, the tradition that starts with Mallarmé. It is this new poetics tentatively proposed in the Meridian speech that is implemented throughout the late work.

3. "LINE THE WORD-CAVES"

The Meridian speech thus points the way, with many "perhaps"es to the late work, but how to read these obviously difficult poems remains a problem. Happily, besides the *Widerrufe* poems, Celan has written a number of programmatic metapoems, showing how the poet envisaged the act of writing, thus how he would have liked his work to be read and understood. Let me give a somewhat detailed reading of one such poem from *Fadensonnen* | *Threadsuns*.

KLEIDE DIE WORTHÖHLEN AUS
mit Pantherhäuten,

erweitere sie, fellhin und fellher,
sinnhin und sinnher,

gib ihnen Vorhöfe, Kammern, Klappen
und Wildnisse, parietal,

und lausch ihrem zweiten
und jeweils zweiten und zweiten
Ton.

In my translation:

LINE THE WORDCAVES
with panther skins,

widen them, hide-to and hide-fro,
sense-hither and sense-thither,

give them courtyards, chambers, drop doors
and wildnesses, parietal,

and listen for their second
and each time second and second
tone.

Following Celan's own suggestions, I have already insisted on the importance of the *word* in the late poetry. This poem thematically foregrounds the point, yielding insights not only into Celan's writing process, but also into the reading process. The work of poetry is to be done on the word itself, the word that is presented here as hollow, as a cave—an image that suggests immediately a range of connections with similar topoi throughout the oeuvre, from prehistoric caves to Etruscan tombs. The word is nothing solid, diorite, or opaque, but a formation with its own internal complexities and crevasses—closer to a geode, to extend the petrological imagery so predominant in the work from *Breathturn* on. In the context of this first stanza, however, the "panther skins" seem to point more toward the image of a prehistoric cave, at least temporarily, for the later stanzas retroactively change this reading, giving it the multiperspectivity so pervasive throughout the late work.

These words need to be worked, transformed, enriched, in order to become meaningful. In this case the poem commands the poet to "line" them with animal skins, suggesting that something usually considered as an external covering is brought inside and turned inside out. The geometry of this inversion makes for an ambiguous space, like that of a Klein bottle, where inside and outside become indeterminable or interchangeable. These skins, pelts, hides, or furs also seem to be situated *between* something, to constitute a border of some sort, for the next stanza asks for the caves to be enlarged in at least two, if not four, directions: "hide-to and hide-fro, / sense-hither and sense-thither." This condition of being between is indeed inscribed in the animal chosen by Celan, via a multilingual pun (though he wrote in German, Celan lived in a French-speaking environment, while translating from half a dozen languages he mastered perfectly): "between" is *entre* in French, while the homophonic rhyme-word *antre* refers to a cave; this *antre*, or cave, is inscribed and can be heard in the animal name "Panther." (One could of course pursue the panther image in other directions, for example, into

Rilke's poem—and Celan's close involvement with Rilke's work is well documented.) Unhappily, the English verb "line" is not able to render the further play on words rooted in the ambiguity of the German *auskleiden*, which means to line, to drape, to dress with, and to undress.

These "Worthöhlen," in a further echo of inversion, call to mind the expression *hohle Worte*—"empty words." (The general plural for *Wort* is *Wörter*, but in reference to specific words you use the plural *Worte*.) Words, and language as such, have been debased, emptied of meaning—a topos that can be found throughout Celan's work—and in order to be made useful again the poet has to transform and rebuild them, creating in the process those multiperspectival layers that constitute the gradual, hesitating, yet unrelenting mapping of Celan's universe. The third stanza thus adds a further stratum to the concept of "Worthöhlen" by introducing physiological terminology, linking the wordcaves to the hollow organ that is the heart. These physiological topoi appear with great frequency in the late books and have been analyzed in some detail by James Lyon,[22] who points out the transfer of anatomical concepts and terminology, and, specifically in this poem, how the heart's atria become the poem's court-yards, the ventricles, chambers, and the valves, drop doors. The poem's "you," as behooves a programmatic text, is the poet exhorting himself to widen the possibilities of writing by adding attributes, by enriching the original wordcaves. The poem's command now widens the field by including a further space, namely "wildnesses," a term that recalls and links back up with the wild animal skins of the first stanza. Celan does not want a linear transformation of the word from one singular meaning to the next, but the constant presence of multiple layers of meaning accreting in the process of the poem's composition. The appearance in the third stanza of these

wildnesses also helps to keep alive the tension between a known, or-
dered, constructed world and the unknown and unexplored, which
is indeed the Celanian *Grenzgelände*, that marginal borderland into
which, through which, and from which language has to move for the
poem to occur.

But it is not just a question of simply adding and enlarging, of a
mere constructivist activism: the poet also has to listen. The last
stanza gives this command, specifying that it is the second tone that
he will hear that is important. The poem itself foregrounds this:
"tone" is the last word of the poem, constituting a whole line by it-
self, while simultaneously breaking the formal symmetry of the text
which had so far been built on stanzas of two lines each. Given the
earlier heart imagery, this listening to a double tone immediately
evokes the systole/diastole movement. The systole corresponds to
the contraction of the heart muscle when the blood is pumped
through the heart and into the arteries, while the diastole repre-
sents the period between two contractions of the heart when the
chambers widen and fill with blood. The triple repetition on the
need to listen to the second tone thus insists that the sound produced
by the diastole is what interests the poet.

The imagery of the heart and of the circulation of the blood is, of
course, a near-classical topos in poetry; Celan, however, transforms
it in such a way that it becomes vital poetic imagery at the end of his
century. In no way is it readable as a kind of postmodernist (in the
aesthetical-architectural sense) citation or pastiche of classical po-
etic/decorative topoi. Numerous other poems take up, develop, and
transform this and related imagery. Here, as one example, is a poem
that appears a few pages after "Line the wordcaves" and that speaks
of this second movement, though this time from an anatomical po-
sition slightly above, though still near, the heart:

NAH, IM AORTENBOGEN,
im Hellblut:
das Hellwort.

Mutter Rahel
weint nicht mehr.
Rübergetragen
alles Geweinte.

Still, in den Kranzarterien,
unumschnürt:
Ziv, jenes Licht.

NEAR, IN THE AORTIC ARCH,
in the light-blood:
the light-word.

Mother Rachel
weeps no more.
Carried over:
all the weepings.

Quiet, in the coronary arteries,
unconstricted:
Ziv, that light.

This poem centers around both historical and kabbalistic Judaic motifs (*Ziv* is Hebrew for "light" and refers to the mystical light of the Shekinah, the female aspect of God, and also to various symbolic accretions, such as the figure of Sophia/Wisdom, and connects to that of Rachel, as maternal figure/personification of Zion), though the place it opens out from and which grounds it—"the aortic arch" of the "coronary arteries"—clearly links it to the biological/anatomical topos of "Line the wordcaves." More could be said of this poem and its topoi, but let's return briefly to the first poem and close this excursus by presenting another, additive reading of some of the complexities of "Line the wordcaves." In a brilliant essay, Werner Hamacher discusses the movement of the figure of inversion as central to the poetics of late Celan, using a poem from *Speechgrille*, "Stimmen," and concentrating on the line "sirrt die Sekunde" (the second buzzes) where he de- and reconstructs the expression "die Sekunde" (the second) as "diese Kunde" (this message, this conduit of information). In a footnote he includes a brief analysis of "Line the wordcaves," which I will cite and let stand as conclusion to my own analysis, if only to show how the polyperspectivity of a Celan poem permits multiple approaches, all of which help to shed light on the wordcaves these late poems are. Having also picked up on the sound pun of *antre*, and the transference of the animal's outer layer into the word's inside, Hamacher writes:

> Here too we have an inversion of familiar ideas . . . Sense is only one—and indeed an alien, second—skin, an inner mask. Tone, as "that which is always second," is in each case distanced further than the audible tone, infinitely secondary; it too a *second*. Celan's later poems are written out of this second and for its sake; they are *dated*, as finite language, on the second. The inversion of the secondary into the "primary," of the outer into the "inner," is always effected in them so that they expand the character of the secondary, *in fine*, instead of domesticating it. Thus, as he himself stressed, we can only "understand" his texts "from a distance."
>
> In addition, *auskleiden* is one of the possible meanings of *auslegen* (to interpret). Insofar as the poem takes on this—second—

sense in the image, in the clothing, in the pelt, it itself practices the hermeneutic operation it recommends: the whole becomes feline, *fellhin und fellher*, although not without falling into what would count as failure for a normative understanding.[23]

For Hamacher, the tropes and images of Celan's poetry are thus "not metaphors for representations but metaphors for metaphorization, not images of a world but images of the generation of images, not the transcription of voices but the production of the etched voices of the poem itself."

4. "... ABOVE THE GRAYBLACK WASTES"

Breathturn, which so forcefully marks the entrance into the late work, includes a poem titled "Fadensonnen" | "Threadsuns." Celan will reuse this title to name his next volume of poems. It should therefore prove useful to read the poem closely as it may not only help with clarifying some of Celan's poetological thinking but also throw light beyond that on his philosophical outlook—if these two can, in fact, be separated.

FADENSONNEN
über der grauschwarzen Ödnis.
Ein baum-
hoher Gedanke
greift sich den Lichtton: es sind
noch Lieder zu singen jenseits
der Menschen.

THREADSUNS
above the grayblack wastes.

> A tree-
> high thought
> grasps the light-tone: there are
> still songs to sing beyond
> mankind.

A desolate landscape, truly "north of the future," as Celan writes in another poem. But also one that lets us formulate exactly where and how the late poetry of Paul Celan settles—even as it unsettles. Neither utopia nor dystopia, Celan's topos is a visionary-realistic land- and language-scape mapping the second half of the twentieth century, from the devastating aporia constituted by World War II, with its extermination camps and nuclear wastelands, and reaching beyond Celan's own dates through that fin de siècle into the mauled dawn of the twenty-first century. Today, nearly fifty years after the composition of these poems, their readability has opened up, making the very difficulties they present not a stumbling block but a gate to anyone attentive to the times and the words. This gate may be narrow; indeed, it needs to be narrow—it is an *Engführung*, a "straightening," a "leading into the narrows," as Celan calls an earlier poem that rewrites the "Todesfuge"—if only as an index to the irreducible complexity of the age and to the effort needed to crack—"à la pointe acérée" (with the sharpened tip) of pen and thought—the husk humanity frantically consolidates, thickening around the kernel of whatever truth there may be. And Celan believed in being, in working, at all costs, in a realm where clarity was law.

Celan insisted, and rightly so, I believe, on the fact that his poetry was directly linked to, and arose from, the real. This insistence is important to keep in mind today, here in the United States, even though it was first formulated in the narrower focus of an answer to the early

German critics who wanted to dismiss the work as just "surreal," that is, as imaginary/fictive imagery, or, even worse, as psychotic ravings, and did so in order to cover up their own inability and actual refusal to acknowledge the lethal reality (and German responsibility for it) from which Celan wrote himself into the present.[24] This is shared reality—thus not only Celan's landscape but ours too, even if we are often unwilling to acknowledge the starkness and the darkness of the place in which we live. For indeed, we no longer live, as the plural of the poem's title immediately makes clear, under the cozy reassurance of a world held in place, centered around *a* or *the* sun, *our* sun, Helios, as it was called under an older dispensation. We have had to acknowledge, at least at the macrocosmic level, the fiction of the one star from which we have been able metaphorically to derive the (to us) reassuring though fictitious conditions of a single belonging, a single origin, a single fate—a realization that traverses Celan's work: In a poem from the 1963 volume, *Die Niemandsrose*, there is "eine Sonne"—a, one, one could nearly say "some," sun—that comes along "swimming." The prose *récit* "Conversation in the Mountains" opens with the sentence "Eines Abends, die Sonne, und nicht nur sie, war untergegangen" (One evening, the sun, and not only the sun, had set), where "untergegangen" (to set), especially because the sun is accompanied in this action by something else ("and not only the sun"), also clearly carries its further meanings of "to perish," "to disappear," "to sink," "to founder," "to drown," etc. Ezra Pound lamented in the Cantos that "the center does not hold"—Celan knows that this is so because there is no single center, no single sun that can hold it all up, that, in fact, there has always been only a decentered multiplicity of centers.

But not only have the centers multiplied (or maybe because of that), the shape of our certainties has also altered radically. That most reassuring of shapes, the circle, the sphere, the form of perfection, the unalterable, unbreachable, unanswerable form of the truth, which we had derived from the single sun as source of our world, that form too has, under the pressure of the multiple and the many, been changed, has ex- or imploded: these suns are threads now, thin, elongated—lines of flight. And there is doubt how much light, if any, such suns may shed—clearly the scape beneath or against which these suns appear is barren, desert, a wilderness—*eremiai anthrôpôn*. Threads are fragile, they can break: we can no longer barter our own finitude for the possible transcendental infinitude of the sun-circle, Helios, or Jahve, or however he was named. Our, man and woman's, finitude is our measure—and, as the expression has it, it hangs, we hang, by a thread. The thread spun by the Fates, or their Norse counterparts, the Norns—these latter dwell, as it happens, in a northern scape, a place, in Celan's phrase, "north of the future."

Yet all is not loss. These "Fadensonnen," these threadsuns fold into the word that gives their elongation—the *Faden*, the thread—something more, something which in English is still there in the word "fathom," which comes to us via the Indo-European root *pet* and Germanic *fathmaz*: "the length of two arms stretched out." The thread is thus a way of measuring space, or of "sounding" depth (the poem also speaks of a "Lichtton," a "light-tone" or sound), and, maybe, of a measure, or a new measure for the world and for poetry. If the first volume that announced the late work and its radically innovative poetics was called *Breathturn*, to indicate that a turn, a change, was needed—had, in fact, taken place—then the title of the next volume spoke of a new measure, of new measures, to be accurate: of those new measures needed in a world seen as "grayblack wastes" to link the above and the below, the inside and the outside, the tree-high thought and the wastes, because, Celan goes on, "there are / still songs to be sung," poems to be written even under the duress—*Lightduress* will be the title of the next collection—of the present condition. Even if these poems are "beyond mankind"— beyond any older humanistic category of aesthetics. (As he told Esther Cameron at this time: "But I don't give a damn for aesthetic construction."[25]) His writing had moved toward such a postaestheic, posthumanist condition nearly from the start, even if early work, say the "Todesfuge," achieves this only through an acidly sarcastic use of a traditional aesthetic form. The late work would realize this condition, exactly.

5. ". . . EACH POEM HAS ITS OWN '20 JANUARY' INSCRIBED IN IT."

Always mindful of dates—those of history as well as those of his own story, inscribed as often as not in the poems—Celan wrote a poem on November 23, 1965, his forty-fifth birthday ("All deine Siegel erbrochen? Nie." | "All your seals broken open? Never."), and on the manuscript added the following motto, taken from Psalm 45 in the Buber-Rosenzweig translation of the Bible: "Reite für die Treue."[26] Although the King James version gives this as "ride prosperously because of truth," in this context it would be better to translate the motto as "ride for the Truth" or "ride for the Faith." John Felstiner comments: "The Psalmist, having said 'My tongue is the pen of a ready writer,' was urging his king to ride forth righteously. The poet, for whom certain dates and dates as such held more than natural significance, was marking his birthday with an ancient motto that renewed his task."[27] For Celan, this truth or faith he was willing to ride for should, however, not be seen as theologically based. In 1960 he had told Nelly Sachs, after she had indicated that she was a believer, that he "hoped to be able to blaspheme until the end"— a stance that comes through in many of the poems of the late work, which show (while hiding, in a very Celanian fashion) a biting sarcasm often overlooked by critics, who tend to approach the work all too piously.

The conditions of the writing of the poems of this period, the midsixties on to the end, were difficult ones, as already mentioned. If the "Reite für die Treue" motto points to Celan's wish for movement, for the poet's desire, maybe, to be that "figure of outward" (as Charles Olson put it) this movement is never a simple, linear, one-to-one relation and interaction with some immutable outside, especially if the basic position from which the "traveler" moves is already exilic. It is then rather a nomadic line of flight over mutable, friable terrain: in one poem Celan speaks of phosphorous "detour-maps" pointing toward movements the temporal and spatial coordinates of which did not, could not, follow any straight two- or even three-dimensional map, but had to happen in accordance with other, at times controllable, and at times uncontrollable, modes of displacement, willed and unwilled *dérives*, drifts. Even the dates—which on the surface would seem to anchor at least the temporal coordinates— are caught up in movement, as he puts it a few lines later in the Meridian speech: "But don't we all write ourselves from such dates? And toward what dates do we write ourselves?" This is not the place to analyze the question of the date(s) further, but I would like to refer the reader interested in this central Celanian topos to Jacques Derrida's superb essay "Shibboleth: For Paul Celan."[28] That essay, like other critical writings about Celan, investigates a line, seen as of core importance to the poetics, from the Meridian speech, which says "perhaps one can say that each poem has its own '20 January' inscribed in it" and which refers to the fact that in Georg Büchner's novella *Lenz*, the poet Lenz is said to have set off for the mountains on a twentieth of January. This date then gets linked to further events in Celan's life and to other historical occasions. Celan followed that sentence by this one: "Perhaps what's new in the poems written today is exactly this: theirs is the clearest attempt to remain mindful of such dates." Which Derrida glosses as follows: "Let us not believe that what thus becomes readable would be the date *itself*; rather, it is only the poetic experience of the date, that which a date, *this one*, ordains in our relation to it, a certain poetic seeking."

The concept of "dated" poems is, however, not just a useful and elegant way of thinking theoretically through the historical or philosophical dimensions of Celan's polyverse. In a very practical sense we have to be mindful of the dates of the poems in the compositional procedure of the late work—especially as Celan carefully erased them from the books as such, even if he had inscribed the manuscript just as carefully with the dates of composition—if we want to understand the cyclical nature of these books. It is this serial mode of composition that suggests the need, neglected in the various selected poems editions, for publishing translations of the exact and complete volumes Celan himself had published—or, as far as the posthumous work goes, readied for publication—rather than excerpting a few "translatable" poems from this or that book. As all his worksheets were dated, we can reconstruct in exact detail the chronological composition of the late volumes and determine the grounds they were built on. Such analysis corroborates what earlier had been only an intuition, namely, that these volumes were essentially composed chronologically with a sense of serial/cyclical composition as core structuring device. I have therefore given the dates of composition of the individual poems in the commentaries at the end of this book, as these dates were gathered and established by Barbara Wiedemann in her commented edition of the complete poems.[29] Thus Jean Bollack, who knew Celan well, writes of Celan's poems' compositional process: "Their composition is each time conceived as an instant of life, of plenitude or emptiness, the instant of the act of writing (that is the only *parousia*, his—of a word: his) [instant de l'écriture en acte (c'est l'unique parousie, la sienne—d'un verbe: le sien)]; the texts give themselves as such, present themselves more and more in that biographical form, like poetic notes inscribed in an open 'journal'; it opens and continues in discontinuity."[30]

This organization into series of cycles building up to individual volumes can be seen, using a musical analogy, as sections that are *durchkomponiert*, "through-composed," and then assembled into larger coherences. This has been shown for some of the cycles, especially as concerns the one most attentively studied so far, *Atemkristall* | *Breathcrystal*, comprising the twenty-one poems that open *Breathturn*, though we know it to be true of later cycles, as well. This is important to keep in mind, as it helps us understand the serial/cyclical nature of late Celan—which in turn will play a central role in how we approach the translation of those books, as well as being essential to any serious hermeneutical or theoretical reading of the work.

Such research and textual clarification concerning the sequence of books starting with *Breathturn* also helps to dispel any notion of a *Verstummen*, a falling silent by the poet, which had been one of the alibis used to dismiss the late work: Celan, or so this fallacious argument went, in the last however many years of his life, because of illness or some other unexplained cause, had either nothing left to say, or only incoherencies, as is obvious from the poems' growing smaller and more gnarled and incomprehensible—this dismissive argument even attempted to bring to bear the poet's suicide as alleged proof of his desperate rush toward a *Verstummen*, a "becoming mute." A quick accounting will tell us that it is not so. Between 1948 and 1963, Celan published five collections of poems, the publication of each volume separated by roughly four years. With *Breathturn*, this pattern changes drastically: published in 1967 (again four years after the publication of the previous volume), it is the largest single volume up to then, containing seventy-eight poems, while the average number of poems in the previous collections was fewer than fifty. *Fadensonnen | Threadsuns*, the largest single collection, with 105 poems, follows in rapid succession; it is published in 1968, while *Lichtzwang | Lightduress* appears in the spring of 1970, shortly after the poet's suicide. *Schneepart | Snowpart*, published in 1971, contains poems written in 1967 and 1968, thus at times preceding, or often overlapping with, or composed just after those in *Fadensonnen | Threadsuns* and *Lichtzwang | Lightduress*. During 1967 and 1968 Celan had also published two limited editions of poems later gathered in *Lightduress*, and four volumes of translations. To talk of *Verstummen* in the case of such high, not to say hectic, productivity is simply nonsense—or a malevolent attempt at out-of-hand dismissal; it is a wrongheaded reading based on critics comparing the size and word count of individual poems and speaks more to their own bafflement and shortsightedness than to the actual facts. Rather than falling silent, Celan became truly voluble in those, the last years of his life. The present volume gathers this great, rich late harvest in its fullness.

6. "POETRY IS BY NECESSITY A UNIQUE INSTANCE OF LANGUAGE."

Indeed, so unique, that a number of practitioners and commentators have concluded that therefore poetry is untranslatable. Celan's work, given its supposed and much vaunted hermeticism, given the actual and unarguable linguistic and hermeneutic difficulties it presents, has often been held up as exemplary of just such untranslatability. And yet Celan's own practice, including as it does an immense oeuvre of translation of very difficult poetry from more than a half-dozen languages, certainly intimates nothing of the kind. A good translation presupposes a certain complicity between original poem and translator—something Celan expressed in a letter to Vittorio Sereni, editor and translator at the Italian publishing house Mondadori, in relation to a projected translation of his work into Italian: "Among the problems that remain to be resolved there is before all— and it is a major one—that of the translator. Personally, in matters of poetry, I have only ever tried to translate something that did, as one says in my language, *speak* to me (was mich anspricht), and I imagine that your own experiences must be similar to mine."[31]

Celan's poetry does exactly that—it speaks to me, has, in fact, spoken to me since I first heard it read aloud when I was fifteen (I have written of this in more detail elsewhere), and has accompanied me for some fifty years now. I too—obviously—believe in the possibility of translating poetry, would even call it a necessity, even if such faith is at times sorely questioned. Or maybe exactly because of this very dynamic: to question the possibility of translation means to question the very possibility of literature, of writing, of language, which is always already a translation, that is, is both an act of translation and the result of such an act. In the half century I have by now spent in the practice of poetry, both writing it and translating it, a sense has emerged suggesting that a poem is not only the one version printed in a book, but also all its other (possible) printed versions— context changing or adding to or subtracting from meaning(s)— plus all the possible oral and/or visual performances, as well as the totality of translations it gives rise to. The printed poem is, in fact, only a score for all subsequent readings (private or public) and performative transformations, be they through music, dance, painting, or foreign-language translation. Such a view is bound to destabilize any concept of the poem as some fixed and absolute artifact, readable (understandable, interpretable) once and for all. This is also how I hear Celan's line in the Meridian speech: "The absolute poem—no, it certainly does not, cannot exist."

I started translating *Atemwende*, the volume that opens this compilation, in 1967, the year of its publication. I did so not with the immediate intention of having it published (though I certainly did not want to exclude that possibility, even then), but rather as the only way I saw of entering into an apprenticeship with the poet to whose work I owed my own turn to poetry, what I can only describe as the epiphanic experience that, six years earlier, had opened the realm of poetry as possible place of a life's quest and fulfillment. In the spring of 1969 I completed the first translation of *Breathturn* in the context of an undergraduate thesis at Bard College, where I had the subtle and immensely enriching advice of the poet and scholar Robert Kelly to help me along the way. Four or five years later—by then I was living in London—Asa Benveniste, the poet and publisher of Trigram Press, proposed to print *Breathturn*. I revised the book carefully, but despite all his efforts Trigram was unable to secure the rights from the German publishers and the project came to nothing. Between 1976 and 1979, living in Constantine, Algeria—and with much free time on my hands—I yet again went over the early translations while starting work on *Threadsuns* and *Lightduress*. Upon my return to London—and even more so after moving to Paris in the early eighties—I became friends with Gisèle Celan-Lestrange, the poet's widow, a friendship that proved a further spur and kept me working on Celan, reading, rereading, thinking about, and writing on the oeuvre—when I was not translating. When I moved back to the United States in 1987, I brought along a near complete translation of all of late Celan, starting with *Breathturn*. Between 1988 and 1991, I reworked all of these translations yet again for a Ph.D. dissertation at SUNY Binghamton—an occasion that gave me the leisure and ability to catch up on the vast amount of secondary Celan literature that had accrued over the years. Three volumes— *Breathturn*, *Threadsuns*, and *Lightduress*—were published between 1995 and 2005, work I followed up with my translation of the scholarly edition of *The Meridian*—a book it took me nearly seven years to complete and that was published in 2011. I then set to work on preparing this volume, gathering and reworking all the poems from *Breathturn* on, adding the cycle *Eingedunkelt | Tenebrae'd*, as well as the commentaries the reader will find at the end of this book.

The detailed narrative of the various stages of this project is not meant to propose the count of years and the accumulation of versions as proof of quality—to the contrary: it is meant to relativize the very notion of a definitive, final translation. Any given stage was as definite a translation as I could make at that time, and next year's version would no doubt be—even if only ever so slightly—different from this one. (On the ontogenetic level, this tale of successive versions of translations repeats the phylogenetic need for all great poems—and maybe the less great need this even more so—to be re-translated, generation after generation, to be of use. The accumulation of these readings, for that is what translations are, constitutes the [after]life of a poem.) The presentation of the Celan translations (and of most other such work of *meta-phorein* I've done) that I would prefer has always been linked to the time I studied medicine: namely, to those wonderful textbook inserts consisting of a series of transparent plastic sheets, each of which had a part or layer of the anatomy printed on it, making for a palimpsest one could leaf through backward and forward. All books of translations should be such palimpsests, for if there can be a definite original text—which we know is not true, though it may be a necessary fiction from the translator's perspective—there can be only layers upon layers of unstable, shifting, tentative, other-languaged versions, even if a given one may be the most fitting and thus the "best" one for its moment and place. But this synchronic or symphonic presentation of the versions is not a practical possibility; we will have to make do with the tale of the diachrony of the work and hope that the narrative of the process will permit these versions to be seen as just that: versions, momentary stopping points, and configurations in an unending process of transmutation.

7. SOME FURTHER NOTES ON THE TRANSLATION

There are specific problems that make translating Celan a difficult undertaking. Among them is the extremely complex, not to say complicated, relationship Celan had to the language in which he wrote. His German strongly distances itself from any use that language was put to, both in literature and as vehicle for spoken communication, either before or during the poet's lifetime. It is truly an invented German. A translator thus first has to locate the language, or rather the languages, from which Celan has "translated" or "transcribed" his poetry into German. The sources are manifold, and the commentators have laid some of these bare: to "cleanse" his language "of historical political dirt" (Steiner), Celan has often gone to earlier forms of German, so that medieval or late medieval words and etymologies enter the poems and need to be tracked down. Similarly, rare or dialectical (such as north and south German, as well as Austrian) words no longer in current use, or known only to dialect speakers, make frequent appearances, baffling even native German speakers. Celan was an assiduous reader and user of the Grimm Brothers' monumental *Deutsches Wörterbuch*, probably the most important dictionary and reference book for coming, literally, to (the) terms with (of) his language.

For the same reasons Celan has mined other politically uncontaminated vocabularies (uncontaminated at least by the plague of thirties' and forties' Germany), such as those of botany, ornithology, and entomology, but also geology, mineralogy, geography, chemistry, crystallography, nuclear physics, contemporary and Space Age technology, hunting, anatomy, physiology, and medicine, with the latter gaining in importance in the late work. But even the ability to determine the origin of a given word rarely resolves the translator's problem. In German, most of the technical and scientific terms, are composite forms of common German words; in Celan's use of the terms, those common word-roots shine through and create multiple levels of meaning. In English, such vocabularies are based mainly on Greek or Latin roots, which severs their use from any vernacular connection to the language, reducing the multilevel play of meanings. One such term, a traditional technological description of a machine, can be found in the poem "Hafen" | "Harbor" [p. 38]: in the expression "Laufkatze Leben" Celan clearly wants the reader to hear the compound word made up by the words *Katze* (cat) and *Lauf* (run) as descriptive of *Leben* (life), but the word *Laufkatze* is also, and unavoidably in the poem's harbor geography, the technical apparatus called in English a "trolley" or "trolley hoist." Unable to find an English equivalent that would render this meaning-complex in a satisfactory manner, I have, in this particular instance, tried to play with a paratactic juxtaposition of both meanings, combined with the use of the female pronoun "she" rather than the expected "it."

To complicate matters further, Celan often creates neologisms based on analogical word constructions, in which it is essential to hear (or see) the original word. Maybe the best-known one—because the philospher Hans-Georg Gadamer gave a far-fetched and hotly contested metaphorical interpretation of it—is the word *Schläfenzange* (temple-tongs or -clamps) [p. 10], constructed by analogy with the word *Geburtszange* (obstetric forceps), with the baby's temples being indeed the place where the obstetrician tries to apply the forceps. Celan does this also in nonspecialized vocabulary areas, creating puns and wordplays that get lost in the process of translation. In paronomastic formations such as *rauchdünn* (smoke-thin) one hears the common expression *hauchdünn* (paper-thin; literally, breath-thin); similarly, one hears *Morgenrot* ("the red of dawn," literally, "morning-red") in Celan's "Morgen-Lot" (morning-sounder or -plumb). Such exempla could be extended ad infinitum.

Another area that informs Celan's language is that of Jewish mysticism. While not generally creating new words or word combinations (though some Hebrew word and grammar usages are on occasion adapted by Celan), his interweaving of mystical themes lays further strata of meaning on some of the most common words in the language, such as "light" or "sister," as already mentioned above when discussing the poem "Near, in the aortic arch." The abundant use of such specialized vocabularies and their interweaving with frequent neologisms poses problems even for the native reader. Seasoned commentators have been caught claiming a given word as a neologism when, in fact, a quick look into the Grimms' *Wörterbuch* would have shown it to have once been a common German word, even if no longer in use. Conversely, one often comes across a word that looks and feels like a "real" German word, but when trying to trace it one realizes that it is a Celan "invention." The effect of this manipulation of vocabularies is to create a linguistic minefield through which the reader—and a fortiori the translator—has to move with extreme care (and great delight at the poet's endless inventive and combinatory powers). I have put the word "invention" between quotation marks with respect to Celan's own reported claim: "At bottom my word formations are not inventions. They belong to the very oldest layers of language." This statement may be philosophically true for its author, but it does not bring philological solace to the translator.

One also has to take into account the influence of other languages, as Celan's early acquisition of and familiarity with a number of these has inflected his own writing. Romanian would be one example, though it is likely that Russian will eventually be shown to have had a more conscious influence, not the least through Celan's very strong identification with Osip Mandelstam—one commentator speaking of the "slavification" of certain grammatical moments in Celan. French, which was the language environment Celan functioned in during the last twenty-two years of his life, has in all probability had some influence. However, little work has been done on this as yet, except for a few commentators pointing out some rather obvious homophonic occurrences. The most often cited of these examples comes from a poem where the German word *Neige* (decrease) sees its French homonym meaning "snow" appear as the German *Schnee* in the next line. Another concerns Celan's use of the word *Kommissur* in a poem that plays on the German meaning that refers to an anatomical aspect of the brain and on the French expression *commissure des lèvres*. In English the word "commissure" happily carries both meanings and for once the polysemy is not lost in the translation.

If knowledge of these and similar complexities in Celan's language has anything to tell the translator it is essentially this: Celan's language, though German on the surface, is a foreign language even for native speakers. Although German was his *mother* tongue and the *Kultursprache* of his native Bukovina, it was also, and in an essential way, his *other* tongue. Celan's German is an eerie, nearly ghostly, language: it is both mother tongue, and thus firmly anchored in the realm of the dead, and a language the poet has to make up, to re-create, to reinvent, to bring back to life. One could say that Celan raids the German language—and I use the military metaphor advisedly, for there seems to me to run through Celan's life if not a desire for assault on Germany and revenge for the death of his parents (or of his mother before all), then at least a constant, unrelenting sense of being on a war footing, of being under attack and needing to counter this attack. The Celanian dynamic is, however, not simple-minded or one-directional: it involves a complex double movement—to use the terms of Empedocles—of *philotes* (love) for his mother('s tongue) and of *neikos* (strife) against her murderers, who are the originators and carriers of that same tongue.

This profound alienation in relation to his writing language is the very ground upon which and against which Celan works, or, to use the Heraclitian formula: Celan is estranged from that which is most familiar. In his answer to the questionnaire sent out by the Librairie Flinker, he wrote: "Reality is not simply there; it must be searched for and won." Reality for Celan, maybe more so than for any other poet of his century, came to its deepest richness in the word, in language, while, to deturn Marx's line that "all that is solid melts into air" (including the bodies of the Jews gone up in smoke in the extermination camps), only what is caught in, (re)created by, a purified, reconstructed language becomes real and is simultaneously able to retain its relationship to the actual world. Radically dispossessed of any other reality, Celan had to set out to create his own language— a language as absolutely exiled as he was himself. To try to translate it as if it was current, commonly spoken or available German—that is, to find a similarly current English or American *Umgangssprache*, or vernacular—would be to miss an essential aspect of the poetry, that of a linguistic undermining and displacement creating a multiperspectival mirroring that reticulates the polysemous meanings of the work.

Celan's "language," as I have tried to show, is really a number of dismantled and re-created languages. This dismantling and rewelding, this semantic and syntactical wrenching, uses as its substratum a German language that offers itself relatively willingly to such linguistic surgery. Other languages do not have that flexibility, or else have it to a much lesser degree. French, for example, basically does not permit such word creations and is also resistant to the syntactical wrenchings so characteristic of late Celan—which is why, despite his many years in France and his relations with some of the best French poets of his generation, it took so long to have good translations of Celan in that language. In English, the telescoping of multiple words, though more available than in French, remains problematic at a number of levels. Noun-composita of two elements, such as "Wortwand" | "wordwall" or "Eisdorn" | "Icethorn," often can be rendered as such in English, while those made up of more than two root words, such as "Rundgräberschatten" | "roundgraveshadow" or "Knochenstabritzung" | "bone-rod-incisions," tend to be unwieldy and inelegant and often demand to be broken up. The major formal problems posed by Celan's verbal grafts, however, concern his play with prefixes and affixes, especially the use of spatial adverbs and prepositions. Word formations such as "weggebeizt" | "eroded" and "weggesackt" | "sagged away," which sound quite natural in German, or those like "auseinandergebrannt" | "asunder-burned" and "hinüberdunkeln" | "darken over," which sound clearly artificial, invented, even in German, usually cannot be rendered by an English compound word and require circumlocutions or simplifications, that is, entail loss in translation. There are a number of more complex and stranger-sounding word creations, such as "verunewigt" or "unentworden," that are so artificial in the original that they both give permission for and require similar constructions in English: "de-eternalized" or, possibly, "diseternalized" and "undebecome" try to approach the oddity of the German. Many of Celan's neologisms employ verbal or adjectival root elements that are turned into nouns. The capitalization of nouns in German helps the reader identify such formations much more easily than is possible in English. There are, finally, no hard and fast linguistic rules the translator could apply across the board concerning these word formations. Solutions will tend to be local and dependent on context and on the eventual readability of the English term.

Even more problematic than the vocabulary, however, are certain syntactical possibilities of German lacking in English, foremost the fact that in German it is possible to have nouns preceded by complete qualifying clauses. In the late poems, many of which are made up of long single sentences, Celan makes ample use of this possibility, thereby giving the poem a structure of suspense by deferring resolution of what or who is being addressed or modified until the end of the sentence. In a poem from *Breathturn* [p. 28], consisting in all of two sentences, this problem arises several times:

ÜBER DREI im meer-
trunkenen Schlaf
mit Braunalgenblut
bezifferte Brust-
warzensteine

stülp deinen sich
von der letzten
Regenschnur los-
reißenden Himmel.

Und laß
deine mit dir hierher-
gerittene Süßwassermuschel

all das hinunter-
schlürfen, bevor
du sie ans Ohr
eines Uhrschattens hältst,
abends.

Standard English syntax for the first sentence (making up the first two stanzas) would suggest a fourfold reversal of Celan's construction, and would read something like this: "Clap your sky which is breaking away from the last raincord over three breast-nipple stones

that are ciphered with brown-algae blood in sea-drunken sleep."
Trying to keep the movement of Celan's sentence alive, so that "sky"
can appear as the last word in the sentence, produces the following
translation:

> OVER THREE in sea-
> drunken sleep
> with brownalgae-blood
> ciphered breast-
> nipplestones
>
> clap your
> from the last
> raincord breaking
> loose sky.

There is no doubt that the twisted syntax sounds more strained in
English than in German, especially the clause qualifying the sky in
the second stanza. One could try to make the stanza more readable
in English by altering the visual organization of the lines, possibly as
follows:

> clap
> your from the last
> raincord breaking loose
> sky.

But this does not remove the strain completely while falsifying the
dense rhythmic movement of the original. The third stanza presents
a similar though even more intractable problem. Keeping Celan's
syntax would give the following translation:

And let

your ridden with you to this place

freshwatermussel . . .

This is clearly nonsensical in English and needs to be altered so as
to read something like:

And let

your freshwatermussel that rode

with you to this place . . .

Again, any solution is bound to be local, as the translator cannot rely
on a generally applicable rule but has to try to reproduce, wherever
possible, the movement of Celan's language, while deciding how
much strain it is reasonable to impose on the target language.

But there is yet another problem facing the translator of Celan
into English. It concerns what I like to call the present episteme of
American poetry, that is, the set of presuppositions, linguistic and
historical, that determine to a great extent how we hear and what
we recognize as "good" poetry and, by extension, good transla-
tions. This episteme, so revivifying for American poetry since World
War II, is in part inherited from such great modernists as William
Carlos Williams, Ezra Pound, and others, but goes back at least as far
as Walt Whitman. It demands that the language of poetry be as close
as possible to the spoken, colloquial language of today. As a reaction
to the genteel tradition of the British poetry of the Victorian and Ed-
wardian eras (and its American equivalents), this has meant avoiding
rhetorical flourishes and most traditional "poetic" effects. In relation
to translating Celan into English, this can all too often induce the
temptation to oversimplify the original poem, by giving short shrift
to the oddities of the word constructions and by ironing out the

twists and quirks of Celan's syntax, in a doomed attempt to make the language sound "natural." Yet the development of Celan's poetry away from the traditional metrics and rhymes still present in the early work toward a line based on different units (breath, syllable, word) brings to mind certain developments in American poetry—one need only think of Charles Olson's injunctions in the "Projective Verse" essay concerning a new breath-based metrics or compare the tight vowel-leading poetics of Louis Zukofsky's poem "*A*" with similar attentions in Celan.

In my versions I have drawn on every possible scrap of information I could garner concerning the poems and on all possible poetic knowledge I have been able to gather in English. My first aim has not been to create elegant, easily readable, and accessible American versions of these German (under erasure) poems. The aim has been to get as much of the complexity and multiperspectivity of Celan's work into American English as possible, and if elegant moments or stretches of *claritas* occur, all the better. Any translation that makes a poem sound more accessible than (or even as accessible as) it is in the original will be flawed. I have doubtlessly not achieved what Hölderlin did with his translations from the Greek—to write Greek in German, and thus to transform the German, though that must remain the aim of any translator, just as it is the aim of any poet to transform his or her language.

Paul Celan himself spoke to the difficulties in his work and suggested that they were inherent to a poetry that dealt with experiencing the actual world: "Imagination and experience, experience and imagination make me think, in view of the darkness of the poem today, of a darkness of the poem qua poem, a constitutive, thus a congenital darkness. In other words: the poem is born dark; it comes, as the result of a radical individuation, into the world as a language fragment, thus, as far as language manages to be world, freighted with world."[32] But such darkness is not hermeticism, which would be willed obscurity for the sake of obscurity; it corresponds to the real darkness that surrounds us and that is inside us as much as it is inside the outside world. The poem thus does not try to throw some "light" (or fake "light-ness") on either inside or outside worlds. This darkness should not, however, discourage us, but should remind us to read Celan with negative capability, that is, with what Keats defined as the needed ability to be "in uncertainties, Mysteries, doubts without any irritable reaching after fact and reason."

For me as translator, and, I believe, for anyone coming to his work, Celan's own suggestion as to how to read the work is still the best: "Lesen sie! Immerzu nur lesen, das Verständnis kommt von selbst." (Just read and keep on reading! Understanding will come by itself.)

There are too many who have contributed in one way or another to this work over the past forty-five years for me to be able to acknowledge them all here individually. May they all be thanked, because without them this project would never have come to fruition—or with a much different and no doubt poorer result. Of course, it is I who am responsible for any and all remaining errors.

NOTES TO THE INTRODUCTION

1. For the relationship between Celan and his wife, Gisèle Celan-Lestrange, as well as for all the biographical details of his life as a poet in Paris (1948–1970), see Paul Celan and Gisèle Celan-Lestrange, *Correspondance (1951–1970)*, ed. Bertrand Badiou with Eric Celan (Paris: Seuil, 2001).

2. Israel Chalfen, *Paul Celan: A Biography of His Youth* (New York: Persea Books, 1991), p. 13.

3. Much detail here is taken from *Celan Handbuch: Leben, Werk, Wirkung*,

ed. Markus May, Peter Goßens, and Jürgen Lehmann (Stuttgart: J. B. Metzler, 2008), pp. 7–9.

4. *Paul Celan: Collected Prose*, trans. Rosmarie Waldrop (Manchester: Carcanet Press, 1986), pp. 33–34.

5. Chalfen, *Paul Celan*, p. 180.

6. Amy D. Colin, "Paul Celan," in *Holocaust Literature: An Encyclopedia of Writers and Their Work*, ed. S. Lillian Kremer (New York: Routledge, 2003), 1:216.

7. Chalfen, *Paul Celan*, p. 184.

8. For a detailed account of those years, see *"Displaced": Paul Celan in Wien, 1947–1949*, ed. Peter Goßens and Marcus G. Patka (Frankfurt am Main: Suhrkamp Verlag, 2001).

9. Yves Bonnefoy, "Paul Celan," in *Translating Tradition: Paul Celan in France*, ed. Benjamin Hollander, *ACTS, a Journal of New Writing* 8/9 (1988): 12.

10. For a full treatment of this affair, see Barbara Wiedemann, *Paul Celan: Die Goll-Affäre* (Frankfurt am Main: Suhrkamp Verlag, 2000).

11. In Felstiner's citation and translation in *Paul Celan: Poet, Survivor, Jew* (New Haven, Conn.: Yale University Press, 1995), p. 243.

12. See especially side 3 of the double cassette edition of Paul Celan's readings *Ich hörte sagen: Gedichte und Prosa* (Munich: Der Hörverlag, 1977).

13. For more details regarding the intersections between the life and the work, see the introductions to the various volumes of poems in the commentaries section at the end of this book; see also the introduction to my *Paul Celan: Selections* (Berkeley: University of California Press, 2005).

14. Pierre Joris, *A Nomad Poetics: Essays* (Middletown, Conn.: Wesleyan University Press, 2003), p. 47.

15. George Steiner, "A Terrible Exactness," *The Times Literary Supplement*, June 11, 1976, pp. 709–10.

16. *Paul Celan: Collected Prose*, pp. 15–16.

17. Paul Celan, *The Meridian: Final Version—Drafts—Materials*, ed. Bernhard Böschenstein and Heino Schmull; trans. Pierre Joris. (Palo Alto, Calif.: Stanford University Press, 2011), pp. 7–8.

18. Gerhard Buhr, "Von der radikalen In-Frage-Stellung der Kunst in Celans Rede 'Der Meridian,'" *Celan Jahrbuch* 2 (1988): 169–208.

19. Götz Wienold, "Paul Celans Hölderlin-Widerruf" (Paul Celan's Hölderlin Revocation), *Poetica* 2, no. 2 (April 1968): 216–28.

20. Hans Mayer, "Erinnerung an Paul Celan," *Merkur* 24 (1970): 1160.

21. Jerry Glenn, *Paul Celan* (New York: Twayne Publishers, 1973), p. 141.

22. James K. Lyon, "Die (Patho-)Physiologie des Ichs in der Lyrik Paul Celans," *Zeitschrift für Deutsche Philologie* 106, no. 4 (1987b): 591–608.

23. Werner Hamacher, "The Second of Inversion: Movements of a Figure Through Celan's Poetry," *Yale French Studies* 69 (1985): 276–314; reprinted in *Word Traces: Readings of Paul Celan*, edited by Aris Fioretos (Baltimore: Johns Hopkins University Press, 1994), pp. 219–63.

24. See, for example, the essay on Celan's relation to the Gruppe 47 in *Ingeborg Bachmann und Paul Celan: Poetische Korrespondenzen*, ed. Bernhard Böschenstein and Sigrid Weigel (Frankfurt am Main: Suhrkamp Verlag, 1997).

25. Esther Cameron, "Erinnerung an Paul Celan," in Werner Hamacher and Winfried Menninghaus, eds., *Paul Celan* (Suhrkamp Verlag, 1988), p. 339.

26. This, and much other information in this section, is taken from volume 8, part 2, of the *Historisch-kritische Ausgabe*, prepared by Bonner Arbeitsstelle für die Celan-Ausgabe (Frankfurt am Main: Suhrkamp Verlag, 1991).

27. John Felstiner, *Paul Celan: Poet, Survivor, Jew* (New Haven, Conn.: Yale University Press, 1995), p. 228.

28. Jacques Derrida, "Shibboleth: For Paul Celan," in *Sovereignties in Question: The Poetics of Paul Celan*, ed. Thomas Dutoit and Outi Pasanen (Bronx, N.Y.: Fordham University Press, 2005), 1–64.

29. *Die Gedichte: Kommentierte Gesamtausgabe in einem Band*, ed. Barbara Wiedemann (Frankfurt am Main: Suhrkamp Verlag, 2003). This is the edition used throughout the present volume.

30. Jean Bollack, "Pour une lecture de Paul Celan," *Lignes* 1 (November 1987): 147–61.

31. Paul Celan, letter to Vittorio Sereni (Mondadori), February 22, 1962 (copy), Deutsches Literaturarchiv Marbach, D.90.1.3096.

32. Celan, *Meridian*, p. 73.

Atemwende

Breathturn

I

DU DARFST mich getrost
mit Schnee bewirten:
sooft ich Schulter an Schulter
mit dem Maulbeerbaum schritt durch den Sommer,
schrie sein jüngstes
Blatt.

———————————————

VON UNGETRÄUMTEM geätzt,
wirft das schlaflos durchwanderte Brotland
den Lebensberg auf.

Aus seiner Krume
knetest du neu unsre Namen,
die ich, ein deinem
gleichendes
Aug an jedem der Finger,
abtaste nach
einer Stelle, durch die ich
mich zu dir heranwachen kann,
die helle
Hungerkerze im Mund.

———————————————

IN DIE RILLEN
der Himmelsmünze im Türspalt

I

YOU MAY confidently
serve me snow:
as often as shoulder to shoulder
with the mulberry tree I strode through summer,
its youngest leaf
shrieked.

BY THE UNDREAMT etched,
the sleeplessly wandered-through breadland
casts up the life mountain.

From its crumb
you knead anew our names,
which I, an eye
similar
to yours on each finger,
probe for
a place, through which I
can wake myself toward you,
the bright
hungercandle in mouth.

INTO THE FURROWS
of the heavenscoin in the doorcrack

preßt du das Wort,
dem ich entrollte,
als ich mit bebenden Fäusten
das Dach über uns
abtrug, Schiefer um Schiefer,
Silbe um Silbe, dem Kupfer-
schimmer der Bettel-
schale dort oben
zulieb.

IN DEN FLÜSSEN nördlich der Zukunft
werf ich das Netz aus, das du
zögernd beschwerst
mit von Steinen geschriebenen
Schatten.

VOR DEIN SPÄTES GESICHT
allein-
gängerisch zwischen
auch mich verwandelnden Nächten,
kam etwas zu stehn,
das schon einmal bei uns war, un-
berührt von Gedanken.

---

you press the word
from which I rolled,
when I with trembling fists
the roof over us
dismantled, slate for slate,
syllable for syllable, for the copper-
glimmer of the begging-
cup's sake up
there.

IN THE RIVERS north of the future
I cast the net, which you
hesitantly weight
with shadows stones
wrote.

BEFORE YOUR LATE FACE,
a loner
wandering between
nights that change me too,
something came to stand,
which was with us once already, un-
touched by thoughts.

DIE SCHWERMUTSSCHNELLEN HINDURCH,
am blanken
Wundenspiegel vorbei:
da werden die vierzig
entrindeten Lebensbäume geflößt.

Einzige Gegen-
schwimmerin, du
zählst sie, berührst sie
alle.

DIE ZAHLEN, im Bund
mit der Bilder Verhängnis
und Gegen-
verhängnis.

Der drübergestülpte
Schädel, an dessen
schlafloser Schläfe ein irr-
lichternder Hammer
all das im Welttakt
besingt.

WEGE IM SCHATTEN-GEBRÄCH
deiner Hand.

DOWN MELANCHOLY'S RAPIDS
past the blank
woundmirror:
There the forty
stripped lifetrees are rafted.

Single counter-
swimmer, you
count them, touch them
all.

THE NUMBERS, in league
with the images' doom
and counter-
doom.

The clapped-on
skull, at whose
sleepless temple a will-
of-the-wisping hammer
celebrates all that in
worldbeat.

PATHS IN THE SHADOW-BREAK
of your hand.

Aus der Vier-Finger-Furche
wühl ich mir den
versteinerten Segen.

WEISSGRAU aus-
geschachteten steilen
Gefühls.

Landeinwärts, hierher-
verwehter Strandhafer bläst
Sandmuster über
den Rauch von Brunnengesängen.

Ein Ohr, abgetrennt, lauscht.

Ein Aug, in Streifen geschnitten,
wird all dem gerecht.

MIT ERDWÄRTS GESUNGENEN MASTEN
fahren die Himmelwracks.

In dieses Holzlied
beißt du dich fest mit den Zähnen.

Du bist der liedfeste
Wimpel.

From the four-finger-furrow
I root up the
petrified blessing.

WHITEGRAY of
shafted, steep
feeling.

Landinward, hither
drifted sea oats blow
sand patterns over
the smoke of wellchants.

An ear, severed, listens.

An eye, cut in strips,
does justice to all this.

WITH MASTS SUNG EARTHWARD
the sky-wrecks drive.

Onto this woodsong
you hold fast with your teeth.

You are the songfast
pennant.

SCHLÄFENZANGE,
von deinem Jochbein beäugt.
Ihr Silberglanz da,
wo sie sich festbiß:
du und der Rest deines Schlafs –
bald
habt ihr Geburtstag.

BEIM HAGELKORN, im
brandigen Mais-
kolben, daheim,
den späten, den harten
Novembersternen gehorsam:

in den Herzfaden die
Gespräche der Würmer geknüpft –:

eine Sehne, von der
deine Pfeilschrift schwirrt,
Schütze.

STEHEN, im Schatten
des Wundenmals in der Luft.

Für-niemand-und-nichts-Stehn.
Unerkannt,

TEMPLECLAMPS,
eyed by your malar bone.
Its silverglare there
where they gripped:
you and the rest of your sleep—
soon
will be your birthday.

NEXT TO THE HAILSTONE, in
the mildewed corn-
cob, home,
to the late, the hard
November stars obedient:

In the heartthread, the
knit of worm-talk—:

a bowstring, from which
your arrowscript whirrs,
archer.

TO STAND, in the shadow
of the stigma in the air.

Standing-for-no-one-and-nothing.
Unrecognized,

für dich
allein.

Mit allem, was darin Raum hat,
auch ohne
Sprache.

DEIN VOM WACHEN stößiger Traum.
Mit der zwölfmal schrauben-
förmig in sein
Horn gekerbten
Wortspur.

Der letzte Stoß, den er führt.

Die in der senk-
rechten, schmalen
Tagschlucht nach oben
stakende Fähre:

sie setzt
Wundgelesenes über.

MIT DEN VERFOLGTEN in spätem, un-
verschwiegenem,
strahlendem
Bund.

for you
alone.

With all that has room in it,
even without
language.

YOUR DREAM, butting from the watch.
With the wordspoor carved
twelve times
helically into its
horn.

The last butt it delivers.

In the ver-
tical narrow
daygorge, the upward
poling ferry:

it carries
sore readings over.

WITH THE PERSECUTED in late, un-
silenced,
radiating
league.

Das Morgen-Lot, übergoldet,
heftet sich dir an die mit-
schwörende, mit-
schürfende, mit-
schreibende
Ferse.

FADENSONNEN
über der grauschwarzen Ödnis.
Ein baum-
hoher Gedanke
greift sich den Lichtton: es sind
noch Lieder zu singen jenseits
der Menschen.

IM SCHLANGENWAGEN, an
der weißen Zypresse vorbei,
durch die Flut
fuhren sie dich.

Doch in dir, von
Geburt,
schäumte die andre Quelle,
am schwarzen
Strahl Gedächtnis
klommst du zutag.

The morning-plumb, gilded,
hafts itself to your co-
swearing, co-
scratching, co-
writing
heel.

THREADSUNS
above the grayblack wastes.
A tree-
high thought
grasps the light-tone: there are
still songs to sing beyond
mankind.

IN THE SERPENTCOACH, past
the white cypress,
through the flood
they drove you.

But in you, from
birth,
foamed the other spring,
up the black
ray memory
you climbed to the day.

HARNISCHSTRIEMEN, Faltenachsen,
Durchstich-
punkte:
dein Gelände.

An beiden Polen
der Kluftrose, lesbar:
dein geächtetes Wort.
Nordwahr. Südhell.

WORTAUFSCHÜTTUNG, vulkanisch,
meerüberrauscht.

Oben
der flutende Mob
der Gegengeschöpfe: er
flaggte – Abbild und Nachbild
kreuzen eitel zeithin.

Bis du den Wortmond hinaus-
schleuderst, von dem her
das Wunder Ebbe geschieht
und der herz-
förmige Krater
nackt für die Anfänge zeugt,
die Königs-
geburten.

SLICKENSIDES, fold-axes,
rechanneling-
points:
your terrain.

On both poles
of the cleftrose, legible:
your outlawed word.
Northtrue. Southbright.

WORDACCRETION, volcanic,
drowned out by searoar.

Above,
the flooding mob
of the contra-creatures: it
flew a flag—portrait and replica
cruise vainly timeward.

Till you hurl forth the word-
moon, out of which
the wonder ebb occurs
and the heart-
shaped crater
testifies naked for the beginnings,
the kings-
births.

(ICH KENNE DICH, du bist die tief Gebeugte,
ich, der Durchbohrte, bin dir untertan.
Wo flammt ein Wort, das für uns beide zeugte?
Du – ganz, ganz wirklich. Ich – ganz Wahn.)

WEGGEBEIZT vom
Strahlenwind deiner Sprache
das bunte Gerede des An-
erlebten – das hundert-
züngige Mein-
gedicht, das Genicht.

Aus-
gewirbelt,
frei
der Weg durch den menschen-
gestaltigen Schnee,
den Büßerschnee, zu
den gastlichen
Gletscherstuben und -tischen.

Tief
in der Zeitenschrunde,
beim
Wabeneis
wartet, ein Atemkristall,
dein unumstößliches
Zeugnis.

(I KNOW YOU, you are the deeply bowed,
I, the transpierced, am subject to you.
Where flames a word, would testify for us both?
You—all, all real. I—all delusion.)

ERODED by
the beamwind of your speech
the gaudy chatter of the pseudo-
experienced—the hundred-
tongued perjury-
poem, the noem.

Evorsion-
ed,
free
the path through the men-
shaped snow,
the penitent's snow, to
the hospitable
glacier-parlors and -tables.

Deep
in the timecrevasse,
in the
honeycomb-ice
waits, a breathcrystal,
your unalterable
testimony.

II

VOM GROSSEN
Augen-
losen
aus deinen Augen geschöpft:

der sechs-
kantige, absageweiße
Findling.

Eine Blindenhand, sternhart auch sie
vom Namen-Durchwandern,
ruht auf ihm, so
lang wie auf dir,
Esther.

―――――――――――――――――――――――――――――――――――――――

SINGBARER REST – der Umriß
dessen, der durch
die Sichelschrift lautlos hindurchbrach,
abseits, am Schneeort.

Quirlend
unter Kometen-
brauen
die Blickmasse, auf
die der verfinsterte winzige

II

BY THE GREAT
Eye-
less
scooped from your eyes:

the six-
edged, denialwhite
erratic.

A blind man's hand, it also starhard
from name-wandering,
rests on him, as
long as on you,
Esther.

SINGABLE REMNANT—the outline
of him, who through
the sicklescript broke through unvoiced,
apart, at the snowplace.

Whirling
under comet-
brows
the gaze's bulk, toward
which the eclipsed, tiny

Herztrabant zutreibt
mit dem
draußen erjagten Funken.

– Entmündigte Lippe, melde,
daß etwas geschieht, noch immer,
unweit von dir.

FLUTENDER, groß-
zelliger Schlafbau.

Jede
Zwischenwand von
Graugeschwadern befahren.

Es scheren die Buchstaben aus,
die letzten
traumdichten Kähne –
jeder mit einem
Teil des noch
zu versenkenden Zeichens
im
geierkralligen Schlepptau.

ZWANZIG FÜR IMMER
verflüchtigte Schlüsselburg-Blumen
in deiner schwimmenden linken
Faust.

heart-satellite drifts
with the
spark caught outside.

—Disenfranchised lip, announce,
that something happens, still,
not far from you.

FLOWING, big-
celled sleepingden.

Each
partition traveled
by graysquadrons.

The letters are breaking formation,
the last
dreamproof skiffs—
each with
part of the still
to be sunken sign
in
the towrope's vulturegrip.

TWENTY FOREVER
evaporated Schlüsselburg-primroses
in your swimming left
fist.

In die Fisch-
schuppe geätzt:
die Linien der Hand,
der sie entwuchsen.

Himmels- und Erd-
säure flossen zusammen.
Die Zeit-
rechnung ging auf, ohne Rest. Es kreuzen
– dir, schnelle Schwermut, zulieb –
Schuppe und Faust.

KEINE SANDKUNST MEHR, kein Sandbuch, keine Meister.

Nichts erwürfelt. Wieviel
Stumme?
Siebenzehn.

Deine Frage – deine Antwort.
Dein Gesang, was weiß er?

Tiefimschnee,
      Iefimnee,
         I – i – e.

Into the fish-
scale etched:
the lines of the hand
from which they grew.

Heaven- and earth-
acid flowed together.
The time-
reckoning worked out, without remainder. Cruising
—for your, quick melancholy, sake—
scale and fist.

NO SANDART ANYMORE, no sandbook, no masters.

Nothing in the dice. How
many mutes?
Seventen.

Your question—your answer.
Your chant, what does it know?

Deepinsnow,
      Eepinno,
          I—i—o.

HELLIGKEITSHUNGER – mit ihm
ging ich die Brot-
stufe hinauf,
unter die Blinden-
glocke:

sie, die wasser-
klare,
stülpt sich über
die mitgestiegene, mit-
verstiegene Freiheit, an der
einer der Himmel sich sattfraß,
den ich sich wölben ließ über
der wortdurchschwommenen
Bildbahn, Blutbahn.

ALS UNS DAS WEISSE ANFIEL, nachts;
als aus dem Spendekrug mehr
kam als Wasser;
als das geschundene Knie
der Opferglocke den Wink gab:
Flieg! –

Da
war ich
noch ganz.

BRIGHTNESSHUNGER—with it
I walked up the bread-
step, under
the blindness-
bell:

it, water-
clear,
claps itself over
the freedom that climbed with
me, that misclimbed
too high, on which
one of the heavens gorged itself,
that I let vault above
the worddrenched
image orbit, blood orbit.

WHEN WHITENESS ASSAILED US, at night;
when from the libation-ewer more
than water came;
when the skinned knee
gave the sacrificebell the nod:
Fly!—

Then
I still
was whole.

HOHLES LEBENSGEHÖFT. Im Windfang
die leer-
geblasene Lunge
blüht. Eine Handvoll
Schlafkorn
weht aus dem wahr-
gestammelten Mund
hinaus zu den Schnee-
gesprächen.

ÜBER DREI im meer-
trunkenen Schlaf
mit Braunalgenblut
bezifferte Brust-
warzensteine

stülp deinen sich
von der letzten
Regenschnur los-
reißenden Himmel.

Und laß
deine mit dir hierher-
gerittene Süßwassermuschel

all das hinunter-
schlürfen, bevor

Hollow lifehomestead. In the windtrap
the lung
blown empty
flowers. A handful
sleepcorn
drifts from the mouth
stammered true
out toward the snow-
conversations.

Over three in sea-
drunken sleep
with brownalgae-blood
ciphered breast-
nipplestones

clap your
from the last
raincord breaking
loose sky.

And let
your freshwatermussel that rode
with you to this place

lap all that
up, before

du sie ans Ohr
eines Uhrschattens hältst,
abends.

AM WEISSEN GEBETRIEMEN – der
Herr dieser Stunde
war
ein Wintergeschöpf, ihm
zulieb
geschah, was geschah –
biß sich mein kletternder Mund fest, noch einmal,
als er dich suchte, Rauchspur
du, droben,
in Frauengestalt,
du auf der Reise zu meinen
Feuergedanken im Schwarzkies
jenseits der Spaltworte, durch
die ich dich gehn sah, hoch-
beinig und
den schwerlippigen eignen
Kopf
auf dem von meinen
tödlich genauen
Händen
lebendigen Körper.

Sag deinen dich
bis in die Schluchten hinein-
begleitenden Fingern, wie

you hold her to the ear
of a clock's shadow,
evenings.

ON THE WHITE PHILACTERY—the
Lord of this hour
was
a wintercreature, for his
sake
happened what happened—
my climbing mouth bit in, once more,
when it looked for you, smoketrace
you, up there,
in woman's shape,
you on the journey to my
firethoughts in the blackgravel
beyond the cleftwords, through
which I saw you walk, high-
legged and
the heavylipped own
head
on the by my
deadly accurate
hands
living body.

Tell your fingers
accompanying you far in-
side the crevasses, how

ich dich kannte, wie weit
ich in dich ins Tiefe stieß, wo
dich mein bitterster Traum
herzher beschlief, im Bett
meines unablösbaren Namens.

ERBLINDE schon heut:
auch die Ewigkeit steht voller Augen –
darin
ertrinkt, was den Bildern hinweghalf
über den Weg, den sie kamen,
darin
erlischt, was auch dich aus der Sprache
fortnahm mit einer Geste,
die du geschehn ließt wie
den Tanz zweier Worte aus lauter
Herbst und Seide und Nichts.

ENGHOLZTAG unter
netznervigem Himmelblatt. Durch
großzellige Leerstunden klettert, im Regen,
der schwarzblaue, der
Gedankenkäfer.

Tierblütige Worte
drängen sich vor seine Fühler.

I knew you, how far
I pushed you into the deep,
where my most bitter dream
slept with you heart-fro, in the bed
of my inextinguishable name.

Go BLIND today already:
eternity too is full of eyes—
wherein
drowns, what helped the images
over the path they came,
wherein
expires, what took you too out of
language with a gesture
that you let happen like
the dance of two words of just
autumn and silk and nothingness.

LATEWOODDAY under
netnerved skyleaf. Through
bigcelled idlehours clambers, in rain,
the blackblue, the
thoughtbeetle.

Animal-bloodsoming words
crowd before its feelers.

HEUTE:
Nächtliches, wieder, feuergepeitscht.
Glosender
Nacktpflanzenreigen.

(Gestern:
über den rudernden Namen
schwebte die Treue;
Kreide ging schreibend umher;
offen lag es und grüßte:
das wassergewordene Buch.)

Den Eulenkiesel erlost –
vom Schlafsims
blickt er herunter
aufs Fünfaug, dem du verfielst.

Sonst?
Halb- und Viertel-
verbündete auf
der Geschlagenen-Seite. Reichtümer an
verloren-vergällter
Sprache.

Wenn sie den letzten
Schatten pfählen,
brennst du die schwörende Hand frei.

TODAY:
nightthings, again, fire whipped.
Glowing
naked-plants-dance.

(Yesterday:
above the rowing names
floated faithfulness;
chalk went around writing;
open it laid and greeted:
the turned-to-water book.)

The owl-pebble raffled—
from the sleep-cornice
he looks down
upon the five-eye, to whom you devolved.

Otherwise?
Half- and quarter-
allies on
the side of the beaten. Riches of
lost-soured
language.

When they impale
the last shadow,
you burn the vowing hand free.

MITTAGS, bei
Sekundengeflirr,
im Rundgräberschatten, in meinen
gekammerten Schmerz
– mit dir, Herbei-
geschwiegene, lebt ich
zwei Tage in Rom
von Ocker und Rot –
kommst du, ich liege schon da,
hell durch die Türen geglitten, waagrecht –:

es werden die Arme sichtbar, die dich umschlingen, nur sie. Soviel
Geheimnis
bot ich noch auf, trotz allem.

UNTER DIE HAUT meiner Hände genäht:
dein mit Händen
getrösteter Name.

Wenn ich den Klumpen Luft
knete, unsere Nahrung,
säuert ihn der
Buchstabenschimmer aus
der wahnwitzig-offenen
Pore.

MIDDAY, with
seconds' flurry,
in the roundgraveshadow, into my
chambered pain
—with you, hither-
silenced, I lived
two days in Rome
on ocher and red—
you come, I already lie there,
gliding light through the doors, horizontal—:

the arms holding you become visible, only they. That much
secrecy
I still summoned, in spite of all.

SOWN UNDER the skin of my hands:
your name comforted
by hands.

When I knead the lump
of air, our nourishment,
it is leavened by the
letters' shimmer from
the lunatic-open
pore.

DAS STUNDENGLAS, tief
im Päonienschatten vergraben:

Wenn das Denken die Pfingst-
schneise herabkommt, endlich,
fällt ihm das Reich zu,
wo du versandend verhoffst.

HAFEN

Wundgeheilt: wo-,
wenn du wie ich wärst, kreuz-
und quergeträumt von
Schnapsflaschenhälsen am
Hurentisch

– würfel
mein Glück zurecht, Meerhaar,
schaufel die Welle zuhauf, die mich trägt, Schwarzfluch,
brich dir den Weg
durch den heißesten Schoß,
Eiskummerfeder –,

wo-
hin
kämst du nicht mit mir zu liegen, auch
auf die Bänke

THE HOURGLASS, deep
in paeony shadow, buried:

When Thinking comes down
the Pentecost-lane, finally,
it inherits that empire,
where you, mired, test the wind.

HARBOR

Sorehealed: where—,
when you were like me, criss-
and crossdreamt by
schnappsbottlenecks at the
whore table

—cast
my happiness aright, Seahair,
heap up the wave, that carries me, Blackcurse,
break your way
through the hottest womb,
Icesorrowpen—,

where-
to
didn't you come to lie with me, even
on the benches

bei Mutter Clausen, ja sie
weiß, wie oft ich dir bis
in die Kehle hinaufsang, heidideldu,
wie die heidelbeerblaue
Erle der Heimat mit all ihrem Laub,
heidudeldi,
du, wie die
Astralflöte von
jenseits des Weltgrats – auch da
schwammen wir, Nacktnackte, schwammen,
den Abgrundvers auf
brandroter Stirn – unverglüht grub
sich das tief-
innen flutende Gold
seine Wege nach oben –,

        hier,
mit bewimperten Segeln,
fuhr auch Erinnrung vorbei, langsam
sprangen die Brände hinüber, ab-
getrennt, du,
abgetrennt auf
den beiden blau-
schwarzen Gedächtnis-
schuten,
doch angetrieben auch jetzt
vom Tausend-
arm, mit dem ich dich hielt,

at Mother Clausen's, yes, she
knows, how often I sang all
the way up into your throat, hey-diddle-doo,
like the bilberryblue
alder of homeland with all its leaves,
hey-doodle-dee,
you, like the
astral-flute from
beyond the worldridge—there too
we swam, nakednudes, swam,
the abyssverse on
the fire-red forehead—unconsumed by
fire the deep-
inside flooding gold
dug its paths upward—,

                    here,
with eyelashed sails,
remembrance too drove past, slowly
the conflagration jumped over, cut
off, you,
cut off on
the two blue-
black memory-
barges,
but driven on now also
by the thousand-
arm, with which I held you,

kreuzen, an Sternwurf-Kaschemmen vorbei,
unsre immer noch trunknen, trinkenden,
nebenweltlichen Münder – ich nenne nur sie –,

bis drüben am zeitgrünen Uhrturm
die Netz-, die Ziffernhaut lautlos
sich ablöst – ein Wahndock,
schwimmend, davor
abweltweiß die
Buchstaben der
Großkräne einen
Unnamen schreiben, an dem
klettert sie hoch, zum Todessprung, die
Laufkatze Leben,
den
baggern die sinn-
gierigen Sätze nach Mitternacht aus,
nach ihm
wirft die neptunische Sünde ihr korn-
schnapsfarbenes Schleppseil,
zwischen
zwölf-
tonigen Liebeslautbojen
– Ziehbrunnenwinde damals, mit dir
singt es im nicht mehr
binnenländischen Chor –
kommen die Leuchtfeuerschiffe getanzt,
weither, aus Odessa,

die Tieflademarke,
die mit uns sinkt, unsrer Last treu,

they cruise, past starthrow-dives,
our still drunk, still drinking
byworldly mouths—I name only them—,

till over there at the timegreen clocktower
the net-, the numberskin soundlessly
peels off—a delusion-dock,
swimming, before it,
off-world-white the
letters of the
tower cranes write
an unname, along which
she clambers up, to the deathjump, the
cat, the trolley, life,
which the sense-
greedy sentences dredge up, after midnight,
at which
neptunic sin throws its corn-
schnapps-colored towrope,
between
twelve-
toned lovesoundbuoys
—draw well winch back then, with you
it sings in the no-longer-
inland choir—
the beaconlightships come dancing,
from afar, from Odessa,

the loadline,
which sinks with us, true to our burden,

eulenspiegelt das alles
hinunter, hinauf und – warum nicht? *wundgeheilt, wo-,*

                                                      wenn –

herbei und vorbei und herbei.

III

SCHWARZ,
wie die Erinnerungswunde,
wühlen die Augen nach dir
in dem von Herzzähnen hell-
gebissenen Kronland,
das unser Bett bleibt:

durch diesen Schacht mußt du kommen –
du kommst.

Im Samen-
sinn
sternt dich das Meer aus, zuinnerst, für immer.

Das Namengeben hat ein Ende,
über dich werf ich mein Schicksal.

---

owlglasses all this
downward, upward, and why not? *sorehealed, where—,*

when—

hither and past and hither.

III

BLACK,
like the memory-wound,
the eyes dig toward you
in the by heart-teeth light-
bitten crownland,
that remains our bed:

through this shaft you have to come—
you come.

In seed-
sense
the sea stars you out, innermost, forever.

The namegiving has an end,
over you I cast my lot.

HAMMERKÖPFIGES, im
Zeltgang,
neben uns her, der doppelten,
langsam strömenden Rotspur.

Silbriges:
Hufsprüche, Schlaflied-
gewieher – Traum-
hürde und -wehr –: niemand
soll weiter, nichts.

Dich unter mir, kentaurisch
gebäumt,
münd ich in unsern hinüber-
rauschenden Schatten.

LANDSCHAFT mit Urnenwesen.
Gespräche
von Rauchmund zu Rauchmund.

Sie essen:
die Tollhäusler-Trüffel, ein Stück
unvergrabner Poesie,
fand Zunge und Zahn.

Eine Träne rollt in ihr Auge zurück.

Die linke, verwaiste
Hälfte der Pilger-

ANVILHEADEDNESS, at
palfrey pace,
alongside us, of the double
slowly streaming redtrack.

Silvery:
Hoofsayings, lullaby-
neighing—dream-
hurdle and -weir—: no one
shall go farther, nothing.

You under me, centaurishly
rearing,
I empty into our across-
roaring shadow.

LANDSCAPE with urnbeings.
Conversations
from smokemouth to smokemouth.

They eat:
the bedlamite's truffle, a piece
unburied poetry,
found tongue and tooth.

A tear rolls back into its eye.

The left, orphaned
half of the pilgrim-

muschel – sie schenkten sie dir,
dann banden sie dich –
leuchtet lauschend den Raum aus:

das Klinkerspiel gegen den Tod
kann beginnen.

DIE GAUKLERTROMMEL,
von meinem Herzgroschen laut.

Die Sprossen der Leiter, über
die Odysseus, mein Affe, nach Ithaka klettert,
rue de Longchamp, eine Stunde
nach dem verschütteten Wein:

tu das zum Bild,
das uns heimwürfelt in
den Becher, in dem ich bei dir lieg,
unausspielbar.

WENN DU IM BETT
aus verschollenem Fahnentuch liegst,
bei blauschwarzen Silben, im Schneewimperschatten,
kommt, durch Gedanken-
güsse,
der Kranich geschwommen, stählern –
du öffnest dich ihm.

mussel—they gave it to you,
then they bound you—
listening it illuminates the space:

the clinker game against death
can begin.

THE JUGGLERDRUM,
from my heartpenny loud.

The rungs of the ladder, up
which Ulysses, my monkey, clambers toward Ithaca,
rue de Longchamp, one hour
after the spilled wine:

add that to the image,
which casts us home into
the dice-cup, where I lie by you,
unplayable.

WHEN YOU LIE
in the bed of missing bunting,
by blueblack syllables, in
the shadow of snowlashes,
through thought-showers the steely
crane comes swimming—
you open yourself to him.

Sein Schnabel tickt dir die Stunde
in jeden Mund – in jeder
glöcknert, mit glutrotem Strang, ein Schweige-
Jahrtausend,
Unfrist und Frist
münzen einander zutode,
die Taler, die Groschen
regnen dir hart durch die Poren,
in
Sekundengestalt
fliegst du hin und verrammelst
die Türen Gestern und Morgen, – phosphorn,
wie Ewigkeitszähne,
knospt deine eine, knospt auch die
andere Brust,
den Griffen entgegen, unter
den Stößen –: so dicht,
so tief
gestreut
ist der sternige
Kranich-
Same.

HINTERM KOHLEGEZINKTEN Schlaf
– man kennt unsre Kate –,
wo uns der Traumkamm schwoll, feurig, trotz allem,
und ich die Goldnägel trieb in unser
nebenher sargschön
schwimmendes Morgen,

His bill ticks you the hour
into each mouth—in each
chimes, with bloodred bell-rope, a silence-
millennium,
the hour and the reprieve
coin each other to death,
the taler, the groschen
rain hard through your pores
in
the shape of a second
you fly there and barricade
the doors Yesterday and Tomorrow,—phosphorous
like eternity-teeth,
buds your one, then your other
breast,
toward the grips, under
the strokes—: so tightly,
so deeply
sown
is the starry
crane-
seed.

BEHIND COALMARKED sleep
—our cottage is known—
where our dreamcrest swelled, fiery, despite all,
and I drove the goldnails into our
coffin-beautiful morning
swimming alongside,

da schnellten die Ruten königlich vor unserm Aug,
Wasser kam, Wasser,
bissig
gruben sich Kähne voran durch die Großsekunde Gedächtnis,
es trieb das Getier mit den Schlamm-Mäulern um uns
– so viel
fing noch kein Himmel –,
was warst du, Zerrissene, doch
wieder für eine Reuse! –, trieb das Getier, das Getier,

Salzhorizonte
bauten an unsern Blicken, es wuchs ein Gebirg
weit hinaus in die Schlucht,
in der meine Welt die deine
aufbot, für immer.

IN PRAG

Der halbe Tod,
großgesäugt mit unserm Leben,
lag aschenbildwahr um uns her –

auch wir
tranken noch immer, seelenverkreuzt, zwei Degen,
an Himmelssteine genäht, wortblutgeboren
im Nachtbett,

there the rods dipped royally before our eye,
water came, water,
savagely
the skiffs bit through the grand-second memory,
the mud-muzzled beasts drifted around us
—that much
no heaven caught yet—,
what a weir, torn one,
you were, once again!—, the beasts, the beasts, adrift,

salthorizons
were building on our glances, a mountain grew
far outward into the ravine,
where my world summoned
yours, forever.

IN PRAGUE

Half-death,
suckled on our life,
lay ash-image-true around us—

we too
kept on drinking, soul-crossed, two swords,
stitched to heavenstones, born of wordblood,
in the nightbed,

größer und größer
wuchsen wir durcheinander, es gab
keinen Namen mehr für
das, was uns trieb (einer der Wieviel-
unddreißig
war mein lebendiger Schatten,
der die Wahnstiege hochklomm zu dir?),

ein Turm,
baute der Halbe sich ins Wohin,
ein Hradschin
aus lauter Goldmacher-Nein,

Knochen-Hebräisch,
zu Sperma zermahlen,
rann durch die Sanduhr,
die wir durchschwammen, zwei Träume jetzt, läutend
wider die Zeit, auf den Plätzen.

VON DER ORCHIS HER –
geh, zähl
die Schatten der Schritte zusammen bis zu ihr
hinterm Fünfgebirg Kindheit –,
von ihr her, der
ich das Halbwort abgewinn für die Zwölfnacht,
kommt meine Hand dich zu greifen
für immer.

larger and larger
we grew, intergrafted, there was
no name left for
what urged us on (one of thirty-
and-how-many
was my living shadow,
who climbed up the delusion-stairs to you?),

a tower,
the half-one built into the Whither,
a Hradčany
all of goldmaker's No,

bone-Hebrew,
ground to sperm,
ran through the hourglass,
through which we swam, two dreams now, tolling
against time, on the squares.

STARTING FROM THE ORCHIS—
go, count
the shadows of the steps up to it
behind the five-mountain childhood—,
from it, I win
the half-word for twelfth-night, from it
comes my hand to grab you
forever.

Ein kleines Verhängnis, so groß
wie der Herzpunkt, den ich
hinter dein meinen Namen
stammelndes Aug setz,
ist mir behilflich.

        Du kommst auch,
wie über Wiesen,
und bringst das Bild einer Kaimauer mit,
da würfelten, als
unsre Schlüssel, tief im Verwehrten,
sich kreuzten in Wappengestalt,
Fremde mit dem, was
wir beide noch immer besitzen
an Sprache,
an Schicksal.

HALBZERFRESSENER, masken-
gesichtiger Kragstein,
tief
in der Augenschlitz-Krypta:

Hinein, hinauf
ins Schädelinnre,
wo du den Himmel umbrichst, wieder und wieder,
in Furche und Windung
pflanzt er sein Bild,
das sich entwächst, entwächst.

A little doom, as big
as the heartdot I set
behind your my name
stammering eye,
is helpful to me.

        You also come,
as if over meadows,
and bring along the image of a quaywall,
there—when
our keys, deep in the refused,
crossed each other heraldically—
strangers play dice with what
we both still own
of language,
of destiny.

HALFGNAWED, mask-
miened corbel stone,
deep
in the eyeslit-crypt:

Inward, upward
into skull's inside,
where you break up heaven, again and again,
into furrow and convolution
he plants his image,
which outgrows, outgrows itself.

AUS FÄUSTEN, weiß
von der aus der Wortwand
freigehämmerten Wahrheit,
erblüht dir ein neues Gehirn.

Schön, durch nichts zu verschleiern,
wirft es sie, die
Gedankenschatten.
Darin, unverrückbar,
falten sich, heut noch,
zwölf Berge, zwölf Stirnen.

Die auch von dir her stern-
äugige Streunerin Schwermut
erfährts.

SCHWIRRHÖLZER fahren ins Licht, die Wahrheit
gibt Nachricht.

Drüben die Ufer-
böschung schwillt uns entgegen,
ein dunkler
Tausendglanz – die
auferstandenen Häuser! –
singt.

Ein Eisdorn – auch wir
hatten gerufen –
versammelt die Klänge.

FROM FISTS, white
from the truth hammered
free of the wordwall,
a new brain blooms for you.

Beautiful, to be veiled by nothing,
it casts them, the
thoughtshadows.
Therein, immovable,
fold up, even today,
twelve mountains, twelve foreheads.

Vagabond Melancholy, also star-
eyed by way of you,
hears of it.

———————————————————————————————

BULLROARERS whizz into the light, truth
sends word.

Yonder, the shore's
slope swells toward us,
a dark
thousand-brightness—the
ressurected houses!—
sings.

An icethorn—we too
had called—
gathers the tones.

ABENDS, in
Hamburg, ein
unendlicher Schuhriemen – an
ihm
kauen die Geister –
bindet zwei blutige Zehen zusammen
zum Wegschwur.

BEI DEN ZUSAMMENGETRETENEN
Zeichen, im
worthäutigen Ölzelt, am Ausgang
der Zeit,
hellgestöhnt
ohne Laut
– du, Königsluft, ans
Pestkreuz genagelte, jetzt
blühst du –,
porenäugig,
schmerzgeschuppt, zu
Pferde.

DAS AUFWÄRTSSTEHENDE LAND,
rissig,
mit der Flugwurzel, der
Steinatem zuwächst.

EVENING, in
Hamburg, an
endless shoelace—at
which
the ghosts gnaw—
binds two bloody toes together
for the road's oath.

AT THE ASSEMBLED
signs, in the
wordmembraned oiltent, at the outlet
of time,
groaned into brightness
soundlessly
—you, royal air, nailed
to the plague-cross, now
you bloom—,
pore-eyed,
pain-scaly, on
horseback.

THE UPWARD-STANDING COUNTRY,
cracked,
with the flightroot, to which
stonebreath accrues.

Auch hier
stürzen die Meere hinzu, aus der Steilschlucht,
und dein sprach-
pockiger, panischer
Ketzer
kreuzt.

DAS UMHERGESTOSSENE
Immer-Licht, lehmgelb,
hinter
Planetenhäuptern.

Erfundene
Blicke, Seh-
narben,
ins Raumschiff gekerbt,
betteln um Erden-
münder.

ASCHENGLORIE hinter
deinen erschüttert-verknoteten
Händen am Dreiweg.

Pontisches Einstmals: hier,
ein Tropfen,
auf

Here also
the seas rush in, out of the steep ravine,
and your speech-
pocked, panic
heretic
cruises.

THE PUSHED-AROUND
ever-light, loam yellow,
behind
planetheads.

Invented
looks, see-
scars,
carved into the spaceship,
beg for earth-
mouths.

ASHGLORY behind
your shaken-knotted
hands at the threeway.

Pontic erstwhile: here,
a drop,
on

dem ertrunkenen Ruderblatt,
tief
im versteinerten Schwur,
rauscht es auf.

(Auf dem senkrechten
Atemseil, damals,
höher als oben,
zwischen zwei Schmerzknoten, während
der blanke
Tatarenmond zu uns heraufklomm,
grub ich mich in dich und in dich.)

Aschen-
glorie hinter
euch Dreiweg-
Händen.

Das vor euch, vom Osten her, Hin-
gewürfelte, furchtbar.

Niemand
zeugt für den
Zeugen.

the drowned rudder blade,
deep
in the petrified oath,
it roars up.

(On the vertical
breathrope, in those days,
higher than above,
between two painknots, while
the glossy
Tatarmoon climbed up to us,
I dug myself into you and into you.)

Ash-
glory behind
you threeway
hands.

The cast-in-front-of-you, from
the East, terrible.

No one
bears witness for the
witness.

IV

DAS GESCHRIEBENE höhlt sich, das
Gesprochene, meergrün,
brennt in den Buchten,

in den
verflüssigten Namen
schnellen die Tümmler,

im geewigten Nirgends, hier,
im Gedächtnis der über-
lauten Glocken in – wo nur?,

wer
in diesem
Schattengeviert
schnaubt, wer
unter ihm
schimmert auf, schimmert auf, schimmert auf?

CELLO-EINSATZ
von hinter dem Schmerz:

die Gewalten, nach Gegen-
himmeln gestaffelt,
wälzen Undeutbares vor
Einflugschneise und Einfahrt,

I V

THE WRITTEN hollows itself, the
spoken, seagreen,
burns in the bays,

in the
liquified names
the dolphins dart,

in the eternalized Nowhere, here,
in the memory of the over-
loud bells in—where only?,

who
pants
in this
shadow-quadrat, who
from beneath it
shimmers, shimmers, shimmers?

CELLO-ENTRY
from behind pain:

The powers, escheloned
as the counterheavens,
roll inexplicables before
approach lane and arrival,

der
erklommene Abend
steht voller Lungengeäst,

zwei
Brandwolken Atem
graben im Buch,
das der Schläfenlärm aufschlug,

etwas wird wahr,

zwölfmal erglüht
das von Pfeilen getroffene Drüben,

die Schwarz-
blütige trinkt
des Schwarzblütigen Samen,

alles ist weniger, als
es ist,
alles ist mehr.

FRIHED

Im Haus zum gedoppelten Wahn,
wo die Steinboote fliegen
überm

the
scaled evening
stands full of lungbranches,

two
blaze-clouds of breath
dig in the book
which the temple-din opened,

something comes true,

twelve times glows
the arrow-riddled yonder,

she, black-
biled, drinks
the blackbiled's seed,

all is less, than
it is,
all is more.

FRIHED

In the house of the doubled delusion,
where the stone boats fly
over

Weißkönigs-Pier, den Geheimnissen zu,
wo das endlich
abgenabelte
Orlog-Wort kreuzt,

bin ich, von Schilfmark Genährte,
in dir, auf
Wildenten-Teichen,

ich singe –

was sing ich?

Der Mantel
des Saboteurs
mit den roten, den weißen
Kreisen um die
Einschuß-
stellen
– durch sie
erblickst du das mit uns fahrende
frei-
sternige Oben –
deckt uns jetzt zu,

der Grünspan-Adel vom Kai,
mit seinen Backstein-Gedanken
rund um die Stirn,
häuft den Geist rings, den Gischt,

Whiteking's pier, toward the secrets,
where finally with
cut cord the
man-of-war-word cruises,

I, reed-pith nourished, am
in you, on
wild ducks' ponds,

I sing—

what do I sing?

The saboteur's
coat
with the red, with the white
circles around the
bullet
holes
—through them
you sight the with us driving
free-
starry Above—
covers us now,

the verdigris-nobility from the quay,
with its burned-brick thoughts
round about the forehead,
heaps the spirit round, the spindrift,

schnell
verblühn die Geräusche
diesseits und jenseits der Trauer,

die näher-
segelnde
Eiterzacke der Krone
in eines Schief-
geborenen Aug
dichtet
dänisch.

DEN VERKIESELTEN SPRUCH in der Faust,
vergißt du, daß du vergißt,

am Handgelenk schießen
blinkend die Satzzeichen an,

durch die zum Kamm
gespaltene Erde
kommen die Pausen geritten,

dort, bei
der Opferstaude,
wo das Gedächtnis entbrennt,
greift euch der Eine
Hauch auf.

---

quick
the noises wither
this side and that side of mourning,

the crown's
closer-
sailing pus-prong
in the eye of one
born crooked
writes poems
in Danish.

THE SILICIFIED SAYING in the fist,
you forget that you forget,

blinking, the punctuation marks
crystallize at the wrist,

through the earth
cleft to the crest
the pauses come riding,

there, by
the sacrifice-bush,
where memory catches fire,
the One Breath
seizes you.

Wo?
In den Lockermassen der Nacht.

Im Gramgeröll und -geschiebe,
im langsamsten Aufruhr,
im Weisheitsschacht Nie.

Wassernadeln
nähn den geborstenen
Schatten zusammen – er kämpft sich
tiefer hinunter,
frei.

KÖNIGSWUT, steinmähnig, vorn.

Und die verrauchten
Gebete –
Hengste, hinzu-
geschmerzt, die
unbezähmbar-gehorsame
Freischar:

psalmhufig, hinsingend über
auf-, auf-, auf-
geblättertes Bibelgebirg,
auf die klaren, mit-
klirrenden,
mächtigen Meerkeime zu.

WHERE?
In night's friable matter.

In grief-debris and -drift,
in slowest uproar,
in the wisdom-shaft Never.

Waterneedles
sew the burst
shadow together—it fights its way
deeper down,
free.

KING'S RAGE, stonemaned, up front.

And the prayers,
gone up in smoke—
stallions, pain-
accrued, the
untamable-obedient
irregulars:

psalm-hoofed, singing across
open-, open-, open-
leafed Biblemountains,
toward the clear, also
clattering,
mighty seagerms.

SOLVE

Entosteter, zu
Brandscheiten zer-
spaltener Grabbaum:

an den Gift-
pfalzen vorbei, an den Domen,
stromaufwärts, strom-
abwärts geflößt

vom winzig-lodernden, vom
freien
Satzzeichen der
zu den unzähligen zu
nennenden un-
aussprechlichen
Namen aus-
einandergeflohenen, ge-
borgenen
Schrift.

COAGULA

Auch deine
Wunde, Rosa.

Und das Hörnerlicht deiner
rumänischen Büffel

SOLVE

De-easterned tomb-
tree, split into
firebrands:

past the Poison-
Palatinates, past the cathedrals,
upstream, down-
stream rafted

by the tiny-flaring, by the
free
punctuation mark of the
script salvaged and dis-
solved into the count-
less to-be-
named un-
pronounceable
names.

COAGULA

Your wound
too, Rosa.

And the hornslight of your
Romanian buffaloes

an Sternes Statt überm
Sandbett, im
redenden, rot-
aschengewaltigen
Kolben.

SCHÄDELDENKEN, stumm, auf der Pfeilspur.

Dein hohes
Lied, in den harten
Februarfunken verbißner,
halbzertrümmerter
Kiefer.

Die eine, noch
zu befahrende Meile
Melancholie.

Von Erreichtem umbuscht jetzt, zielblau,
aufrecht im Kahn,
auch aus dem knirschenden Klippen-
segen entlassen.

OSTERQUALM, flutend, mit
der buchstabenähnlichen
Kielspur inmitten.

in star's stead above the
sandbed, in the
talking, red–
ember-mighty
alembic.

SKULLTHINKING, dumb, on the arrowtrace.

Your song of
song, into the hard
February-spark clamped,
half-shattered
jaw.

The one, still
to be traveled mile
Melancholy.

Ambushed now by the achieved, aimblue,
upright in the skiff,
also from the gnashing crag–
blessings released.

EASTERSMOKE, flooding, with
the letterlike
keeltrack amidst.

(Niemals war Himmel.
Doch Meer ist noch, brandrot,
Meer.)

Wir hier, wir,
überfahrtsfroh, vor dem Zelt,
wo du Wüstenbrot bukst
aus mitgewanderter Sprache.

Am äußersten Blickrand: der Tanz
zweier Klingen übers
Herzschattenseil.

Das Netz darunter, geknüpft
aus Gedanken-
enden – in welcher
Tiefe?

Da: der zerbissene
Ewigkeitsgroschen, zu uns
heraufgespien durch die Maschen.

Drei Sandstimmen, drei
Skorpione:
das Gastvolk, mit uns
im Kahn.

(Never was heaven.
But sea still is, fire red,
sea.)

We here, we,
glad for the passage, before the tent,
where you baked desertbread
from wandered-along language.

At the farthest sight-edge: the dance
of two blades across the
heartshadowcord.

The net underneath, knotted
from thought-
ends—at what
depth?

There: the bitten through
eternity-penny, spat
up to us through the meshes.

Three sandvoices, three
scorpions:
the guest-people, with us
in the skiff.

KAIMAUER-RAST, rittlings,
im Schatten der
von obenher auf-
gefächerten Trümpfe –

deine
abgegriffenen
Hände, gröber als je,
greifen anderswohin.

Die schöpfende, wieder
und wieder
überschwappende, um-
zugießende Schale voll Galle.

Die leicht
herübergeneigten,
flußaufwärts gesteuerten
Wandergefäße, dicht
an deinem Knieschorf vorbei.

Quader, reit.

Grauglaube neben mir,
trink
mit.

QUAYWALL-REST, astride,
in the shadow of the
trumps fanned open
from above—

your
worn-out
hands, coarser than ever,
reach elsewhere.

The scooping, again
and again
slopping over, to be
spilled, cup full of bile.

The slightly
hither-bent,
upstream-steered
wander-vessels, passing
hard by your kneescab.

Ashlar, ride.

Grayfaith next to me,
drink
up.

ERHÖRT
von den umgebetteten Funken
der Feuerduft um
den Leuchterstachel.

Alle
Bahnen sind frei.

Mehrere Erden
spiel ich dir zu im Erblinden –
die beiden
weißen behältst du, eine
in jeder Hand.

Die Un-
bestatteten, ungezählt, droben,
die Kinder,
sind absprungbereit –

Dir,
Quellnächtige, war
ich nicht ähnlich:
dich Freudige, wie
du jetzt schwebst,
pfählt der unsichtbare, zweite,
stehende Brand.

ANSWERED
by the transferred sparks
the fire-fragrance around
the pricket.

All
orbits are free.

Several earths
I lob to you while going blind—
the two
white ones you keep, one
in each hand.

The un-
buried, uncounted, up there,
the children,
are ready to jump—

You,
source-nightly, I
did not resemble:
you, joyous as
you now hover, are
impaled by the invisible, second,
standing firebrand.

SCHAUFÄDEN, SINNFÄDEN, aus
Nachtgalle geknüpft
hinter der Zeit:

wer
ist unsichtbar genug,
euch zu sehn?

Mantelaug, Mandelaug, kamst
durch alle die Wände,
erklimmst
dieses Pult,
rollst, was dort liegt, wieder auf –

Zehn Blindenstäbe,
feurig, gerade, frei,
entschweben dem eben
geborenen Zeichen,

steh
über ihm.

Wir sind es noch immer.

—————————————————————————

EIN DRÖHNEN: es ist
die Wahrheit selbst
unter die Menschen

SIGHT THREADS, SENSE THREADS, from
nightbile knitted
behind time:

who
is invisible enough
to see you?

Mantle-eye, almondeye, you came
through all the walls,
climb
on this pulpit,
roll, what lies there, up again—

Ten blindstaffs,
fiery, straight, free,
float from the just
born sign,

stand
above it.

It is still us.

A ROAR: it is
truth itself
stepped among

getreten,
mitten ins
Metapherngestöber.

IRRENNÄPFE, vergammelte
Tiefen.

Wär ich – –

Nun ja, wär ich
die – wohin gebogene? –
Esche draußen,

ich wüßte dich zu begleiten,
leuchtendes Graugericht mit
dem dich durchwachsenden, schnell
herunterzuwürgenden Bild
und dem eng-
gezogenen, flackernden
Denkkreis um euch
beide.

LICHTENBERGS ZWÖLF mit dem Tischtuch
ererbte Mundtücher – ein
Planetengruß an
die Sprachtürme rings
in der totzuschweigenden Zeichen-
Zone.

mankind,
right into the
metaphor-flurry.

LUNATIC-BOWLS, rotten
depths.

Were I— —

Well, yes, were I
the—whither bent?—
ashtree outside,

I would know how to accompany you,
shining graydish with the
quickly-to-be-gulped
down image, marbling you,
and the tightly
drawn, flickering
thought-circle around you
both.

LICHTENBERG'S TWELVE with the tablecloth
inherited napkins—a
planet-greeting to
the language-towers everywhere
in the to-be-silenced-to-death sign-
zone.

Sein

– kein Himmel ist, keine
Erde, und beider
Gedächtnis gelöscht
bis auf den einen
eschengläubigen Blauspecht –,

sein
vom Stadtwall gepflückter
weißer Komet.

Eine Stimmritze, ihn
zu bewahren,
im All.

Das Rotverlorene eines
Gedanken-
fadens. Die laut-
gewordenen Klagen
darüber, die Klage
darunter – wessen
Laut?

Damit – frag nicht,
wo –
wär ich fast –
sag nicht wo, wann,wieder.

Being

—no heaven is, no
earth, and the
memory of both extinguished
but for the one
ashtree-believing nuthatch—,

his
from the city-ramparts gathered
white comet.

A voice-rift, to
preserve him, in
the universe.

The redlorn of a
thought-
thread. The bur-
geoned laments
about it, the lament
below it—whose
sound?

With it—don't ask
where—
I nearly—
don't say where, when, again.

GIVE THE WORD

Ins Hirn gehaun – halb? zu drei Vierteln? –,
gibst du, genächtet, die Parolen – diese:

„Tartarenpfeile".
        „Kunstbrei".
                „Atem".

Es kommen alle, keiner fehlt und keine.
(Sipheten und Probyllen sind dabei.)

Es kommt ein Mensch.

Weltapfelgroß die Träne neben dir,
durchrauscht, durchfahren
von Antwort,
        Antwort,
                Antwort.
Durcheist – von wem?

„Passiert", sagst du,
           „passiert",
                „passiert".

Der stille Aussatz löst sich dir vom Gaumen
und fächelt deiner Zunge Licht zu,
                Licht.

GIVE THE WORD

Cut to the brains—half? three quarters?—,
you give, benighted, the passwords—these:

"Tatararrows."

              "Artpap."

                        "Breath."

All are coming, no one's missing.
(Siphets and probyls are among them.)

A man comes.

Worldapplesize, the teardrop beside you,
swept through, crossed
by answer,

           answer,

                answer.
Iced-through—by whom?

"Pass," you say,

              "pass,"

                   "pass."

The quiet lepra peels off your palate
and fans light to your tongue,

                  light.

VOM ANBLICK DER AMSELN, abends,
durchs Unvergitterte, das
mich umringt,

versprach ich mir Waffen.

Vom Anblick der Waffen – Hände,
vom Anblick der Hände – die längst
vom flachen, scharfen
Kiesel geschriebene Zeile

– Welle, du
trugst ihn her, schliffst ihn zu,
gabst dich, Un-
verlierbare, drein,
Ufersand, nimmst,
nimmst auf,
Strandhafer, weh
das Deine hinzu –,

die Zeile, die Zeile,
die wir umschlungen durchschwimmmen,
zweimal in jedem Jahrtausend,
all den Gesang in den Fingern,
den auch die durch uns lebendige,
herrlich-undeutbare
Flut uns nicht glaubt.

FROM BEHOLDING THE BLACKBIRDS, evenings,
through the unbarred, that
surrounds me,

I promised myself weapons.

From beholding the weapons—hands,
from beholding the hands—the long ago
by the sharp, flat
pebble written line

—Wave, you
carried it hither, honed it,
gave yourself, un-
losable, up,
shoresand, you take,
take in,
sea oats, blow
yours along—,

the line, the line,
through which we swim, entwined,
twice each millennium,
all that singing at the fingers,
that even the through us living,
magnificent-unexplainable
flood does not believe us.

V

GROSSE, GLÜHENDE WÖLBUNG
mit dem sich
hinaus- und hinweg-
wühlenden Schwarzgestirn-Schwarm:

der verkieselten Stirn eines Widders
brenn ich dies Bild ein, zwischen
die Hörner, darin,
im Gesang der Windungen, das
Mark der geronnenen
Herzmeere schwillt.

Wo-
gegen
rennt er nicht an?

Die Welt is fort, ich muß dich tragen.

SCHIEFERÄUGIGE, von
der schreitenden Gegenschrift am
Tag nach der Blendung erreicht.

Lesbare Blutklumpen-Botin,
herübergestorben, trotz allem,
von wissenden Stacheldrahtschwingen
über die unverrückbare
Tausendmauer getragen.

V

GREAT, GLOWING VAULT
with the
outward- and away-
burrowing black-constellation swarm:

into the silicified forehead of a ram
I burn this image, between
the horns, therein,
in the singing of the coils, the
marrow of the curdled
heartseas swells.

What
doesn't he
butt against?

The world is gone, I have to carry you.

SLATE-EYED ONE, reached
by the striding counterscript the
day after the blinding.

Readable bloodclot-messenger,
hither-died, despite all,
carried by knowing barbedwire-wings
over the undisplaceable
thousand-wall.

Du hier, du: verlebendigt
vom Hauch der im frei-
geschaufelten Lungengeäst
hängengebliebenen
Namen.

Zu
Entzifferende du.

Mit dir,
auf der Stimmbänderbrücke, im
Großen Dazwischen,
nachtüber.

Mit Herztönen beschossen,
von allen Weltkanzeln her.

SCHLICKENDE, dann
krautige Stille der Ufer.

Die eine Schleuse noch. Am
Warzenturm, mit
Brackigem übergossen,
mündest du ein.

Vor dir, in
den rudernden Riesensporangien,
sichelt, als keuchten dort Worte,
ein Glanz.

You here, you: quickened
by the breath of the
names
caught in the free-
shoveled lungbranches.

To–
be-deciphered you.

With you,
on the vocalcords' bridge, in the
great Inbetween,
nightover.

Shot at with hearttones,
from all the world-pulpits.

Oozy, then
weedy silence of the shores.

The one sluice yet. At
the warttower, doused
with brackish,
you empty into.

Before you, in
the rowing giant sporangia,
as if words panted there, a
luster sickles.

Du, das mit dem hell-
sehenden Hochschlaf von
der Lippe genommene Haar:
durchs Goldöhr der
zurechtgesungenen Aschen-
nadel gefädelt.

Du, der mit dem Einen
Licht aus dem Hals
gerissene Knoten:
durchstoßen von Nadel und Haar,
unterwegs, unterwegs.

Eure Umschwünge, immerzu, um
die sieben-
fingrige Kußhand hinterm
Glück.

DER MIT HIMMELN GEHEIZTE
Feuerriß durch die Welt.

Die Wer da?-Rufe
in seinem Innern:

durch dich hier hindurch
auf den Schild
der Ewigen Wanze gespiegelt,
umschnüffelt von Falsch und Verstört,

YOU, THE hair taken from
the lip with the bright-
seeing highsleep:
threaded through the goldeye
of the sung-aright ash-
needle.

You, the knot torn out
of the throat with
the One Light:
run through by needle and hair,
under way, under way.

Your reversals, incessantly, round
the seven-
fingered kisshand behind
happiness.

THE WITH HEAVENS HEATED
firefissure through the world.

The Who's there?—calls
inside it:

mirror-cast through you here
onto the shield
of the Eternal Bug,
sniffed around by False and Bewildered,

die unendliche Schleife ziehend, trotzdem,
die schiffbar bleibt für die un-
getreidelte Antwort.

DUNSTBÄNDER-, SPRUCHBÄNDER-AUFSTAND,
röter als rot,
während der großen
Frostschübe, auf
schlitternden Eisbuckeln, vor
Robbenvölkern.

Der durch dich hindurch-
gehämmerte Strahl,
der hier schreibt,
röter als rot.

Mit seinen Worten
dich aus der Hirnschale schälen, hier,
verscharrter Oktober.

Mit dir das Gold prägen, jetzt,
wenns herausstirbt.

Mit dir den Bändern beistehn.

Mit dir das glasharte Flugblatt vertäuen
am lesenden Blutpoller, den
die Erde durch diesen
Stiefpol hinausstieß.

looping the unending loop, nevertheless,
which stays navigable for the un-
towed answer.

VAPORBAND-, BANDEROLE-UPRISING,
redder than red,
during the great
frost-thrusts, on
sliding ice-bucklings, before
seal nations.

The beam hammered all
the way through you,
that writes here,
redder than red.

With its words
to shuck you out of the brainshell, here,
hastily buried October.

With you to coin the gold, now,
when it dies out of.

With you to assist the banderoles.

With you to moor the glasshard leaflet
to the blood-bollard, that
the earth pushed out
through this step-pole.

RUH AUS IN DEINEN WUNDEN,
durchblubbert und umpaust.

Das Runde, klein, das Feste:
aus den Blicknischen kommts
gerollt, nahebei,
in keinerlei Tuch.

(Das hat
– Perle, so schwer
wars durch dich –,
das hat sich den Salzstrauch ertaucht,
drüben, im Zweimeer.)

Ohne Licht rollts, ohne
Farbe – du
stich die Elfenbeinnadel hindurch
– wer weiß nicht,
daß der getigerte Stein, der dich ansprang,
an ihr zerklang? –,
und so – wohin fiel die Erde? –
laß es sich drehen zeitauf,
mit zehn Nagelmonden im Schlepptau,
in Schlangennähe, bei Gelbflut,
quasistellar.

Rest in your wounds,
blubbered out, lulled.

The round, small, the firm:
from the gazeniches it comes
rolling, nearby,
into no kind of cloth.

(It has
—Pearl, it was
so difficult through you—,
it has, diving, won the saltbush,
over there, in the Twosea.)

Without light it rolls, without
color—you,
stick the ivory needle through it
—who doesn't know
that the tigered stone, that jumped you,
rang out on it?—,
and so—whither fell earth?—
let it turn time-up,
with ten nailmoons on the towrope,
in serpent-nearness, at yellow-flood,
quasistellar.

VI

Einmal,
da hörte ich ihn,
da wusch er die Welt,
ungesehn, nachtlang,
wirklich.

Eins und Unendlich,
vernichtet,
ichten,

Licht war. Rettung.

VI

ONCE,
I did hear him,
he did wash the world,
unseen, nightlong,
real.

One and unending,
annihilated,
I'ed.

Light was. Salvation.

Fadensonnen

Threadsuns

I

AUGENBLICKE, wessen Winke,
keine Helle schläft.
Unentworden, allerorten,
sammle dich,
steh.

FRANKFURT, SEPTEMBER

Blinde, licht-
bärtige Stellwand.
Ein Maikäfertraum
leuchtet sie aus.

Dahinter, klagegerastert,
tut sich Freuds Stirn auf,

die draußen
hartgeschwiegene Träne
schießt an mit dem Satz:
„Zum letzten-
mal Psycho-
logie."

I

EYE-GLANCES, whose winks,
no brightness sleeps.
Undebecome, everywhere,
gather yourself,
stand.

FRANKFURT, SEPTEMBER

Blind, light-
bearded partition.
A cockchaferdream
floodlights it.

Behind it, complaint-rastered,
Freud's forehead opens up,

the tear, hard-
silenced outside,
links on with the sentence:
"For the last
time psycho-
logy."

Die Simili-
Dohle
frühstückt.

Der Kehlkopfverschlußlaut
singt.

GEZINKT DER ZUFALL, unzerweht die Zeichen,
die Zahl, vervielfacht, ungerecht umblüht,
der Herr ein Flüchtignaher, Regnender, der zuäugt,
wie Lügen sieben-
                    lodern, Messer
                              schmeicheln, Krücken
Meineid schwören, U-
unter
        dieser
                Welt
wühlt schon die neunte,
                    Löwe,
sing du das Menschenlied
von Zahn und Seele, beiden
Härten.

WER

HERRSCHT?

Farbenbelagert das Leben, zahlenbedrängt.

The imitation
jackdaw
breakfasts.

The glottal stop
sings.

CHANCE, MARKED—the signs, unscattered,
the number, multiplied, unjustly flowered around,
the Lord someone fugitive-close, raining, who looks,
as lies seven-
        blaze, knives
              flatter, crutches
perjure themselves, U-
under
    this
      world
the ninth already burrows,
          lion,
you sing the humansong
of tooth and soul, both
hardnesses.

WHO
RULES?

Thronged by colors, life, harried by numbers.

Die Uhr
stiehlt sich die Zeit beim Kometen,
die Degen
angeln,
der Name
vergoldet die Finten,
das Springkraut, behelmt,
beziffert die Punkte im Stein.

Schmerz, als Wegschneckenschatten.
Ich höre, es wird gar nicht später.
Fad und Falsch, in den Sätteln,
messen auch dieses hier aus.

Kugellampen statt deiner.
Lichtfallen, grenzgöttisch, statt
unsrer Häuser.

Die schwarzdiaphane
Gauklergösch
in unterer
Kulmination.

Der erkämpfte Umlaut im Unwort:
dein Abglanz: der Grabschild
eines der Denkschatten
hier.

The watch
steals its time from the comet,
the swords
fish,
the name
gilds the ruses,
the touch-me-not, helmeted,
ciphers the periods in the stone.

Pain, as slugshadow.
I hear, it won't become later.
Fay and false, in the saddle,
gauge this here too.

Globelamps instead of yours.
Lighttraps, border-idolatrish, instead
of our houses.

The black-diaphanous
juggler jaws
in lower
culmination.

The hard-won umlaut in the unword:
your reflection: the tombshield
of one of the wordshadows
here.

DIE SPUR EINES BISSES im Nirgends.

Auch sie
mußt du bekämpfen,
von hier aus.

IN DER EWIGEN TEUFE: die Ziegel-
münder
rasen.

Du brennst ein Gebet ab
vor jedem.

Buchstabentreu, auf dem Notsteg,
stehen Hinauf und Hinunter,
den Mischkrug voll blasigen
Hirns.

SICHTBAR, bei Hirnstamm und Herzstamm,
unverdunkelt, terrestrisch,
der Mitternachtsschütze, morgens,
jagt den Zwölfgesang durch
das Mark von Verrat und Verwesung.

THE TRACE OF A BITE in the nowhere.

It too
you have to fight,
from here on out.

IN THE ETERNAL DEPTH: the brick-
mouths
rave.

You blow up a prayer
before each.

Letterfaithful, on the emergency trail,
stand Up and Down,
the krater full of bubbly
brain.

VISIBLE, by brainstem and heartstem,
undarkened, terrestrial,
the midnight marksman, mornings,
chases the twelvesong through
the marrow of treason and putrefaction.

UMWEG-
KARTEN, phosphorn,
weit hinter Hier von lauter
Ringfingern geschlagen.

Reiseglück, schau:

Das Fahrtgeschoß, zwei
Zoll vorm Ziel,
kippt
in die Aorta.

Das Mitgut, zehn
Zentner
Folie à deux,
erwacht
im Geierschatten,
in der siebzehnten Leber, am Fuß
des stotternden
Informationsmasts.

Davor,
im geschieferten Wasserschild die
drei stehenden Wale
köpfeln.

Ein rechtes Auge
blitzt.

DETOUR-
MAPS, phosphorous,
far behind Here by sheer
ring-fingers beaten.

Travelluck, look:

The tripdart, two
inches from the target,
topples
into the aorta.

The shared goods, ten
hundredweight
folie à deux,
wake up
in the vultureshadow,
in the seventeenth liver, at the foot
of the stuttering
information mast.

Before it,
in the slated watershield, the
three standing whales
head the ball.

A right eye
flashes.

SACKLEINEN-GUGEL, turmhoch.

Sehschlitze
für das Entsternte
am Ende der Gramfibrille.

Die Wimpernaht, schräg
zu den Gottesbränden.

In der Mundbucht die Stelle
fürs rudernde
Kaisergetschilp.

Das. Und das Mit-ihm-
Gehn übers rauchblaue,
blanke
Tafelland, du.

SPASMEN, ich liebe dich, Psalmen,

die Fühlwände tief in der Du-Schlucht
frohlocken, Samenbemalte,

Ewig, verunewigt bist du,
verewigt, Unewig, du,

hei,

SACKCLOTH-MOLD, tower-high.

Eye slot
for the destarred
at the end of the grief-fibril.

The eyelash-seam, at a slant
to the god-blazes.

In the mouthbay the place
for the rowing
Kaisertwitter.

The. And the Going-with-
him across smokeblue,
blank
tableland, you.

⁂

SPASMS, I love you, psalms,

the feeling-walls deep in the you-ravine
rejoice, seedpainted one,

Eternal, de-eternalized you are
eternalized, Uneternal, you,

hey,

in dich, in dich
sing ich die Knochenstabritzung,

Rotrot, weit hinterm Schamhaar
geharft, in den Höhlen,

draußen, rundum
der unendliche Keinerlei-Kanon,

du wirfst mir den neunmal
geschlungenen, triefenden
Grandelkranz zu.

DEINE AUGEN IM ARM,
die
auseinandergebrannten,
dich weiterwiegen, im fliegen-
den Herzschatten, dich.

Wo?

Mach den Ort aus, machs Wort aus.
Lösch. Miß.

Aschen-Helle, Aschen-Elle – ge-
schluckt.

Vermessen, entmessen, verortet, entwortet,

into you, into you
I sing the bone-rod-incisions

Redred, far behind the pubic hair
harped, in the caves,

outside, all around
the unending none-whatsoever-canon,

you throw me the nine times
twined, dripping
eyetooth-circlet.

YOUR EYES IN THE ARM
the
asunder-burned,
to go on rocking you, in the fly-
ing heartshadow, you.

Where?

Arrange the place, arrange the word.
Extinguish. Measure.

Ash-brightness, ash-ell—swal-
lowed.

Mismeasure, unmeasure, misplaced, unworded,

entwo

Aschen-
Schluckauf, deine Augen
im Arm,
immer.

HENDAYE

Die orangene Kresse,
steck sie dir hinter die Stirn,
schweig den Dorn heraus aus dem Draht,
mit dem sie schöntut, auch jetzt,
hör ihm zu,
eine Ungeduld lang.

PAU, NACHTS

Die Unsterblichkeitsziffer, von Heinrich
dem Vierten in
den Schildkrötenadel gewiegt,
höhnt eleatisch
hinter sich her.

---

unwo

ash-
hiccup, your eyes
in the arm,
always.

HENDAYE

The orange pepperwort,
stick it behind your forehead,
silence the barb out of the wire,
with which she flatters, even now,
listen to it,
for the span of an impatience.

PAU, BY NIGHT

The immortality cypher, by Henry
the Fourth rocked in
to tortoise-nobility,
sneers eleatically
behind itself.

PAU, SPÄTER

In deinen Augen-
winkeln, Fremde,
der Albigenserschatten –

nach
dem Waterloo-Plein,
zum verwaisten
Bastschuh, zum
mitverhökerten Amen,
in die ewige
Hauslücke sing ich
dich hin:

daß Baruch, der niemals
Weinende
rund um dich die
kantige,
unverstandene, sehende
Träne zurecht-
schleife.

DER HENGST mit dem blühenden Docht,
levitierend, in Paß-
höhe,
Kometenglanz auf
der Kruppe.

PAU, LATER

In the corner of
your eyes, stranger,
the Albigenses-shadow—

after
the Waterloo-Plein,
toward the orphaned
raffia shoe, toward
the also bartered Amen,
into the eternal
housegap I
sing you:

so that Baruch, he who never
weeps,
may grind aright
all around you the
angular,
ununderstood, seeing
tear.

THE STALLION with the flowering wick,
levitating, at pass-
height,
comet brilliance on
the rump.

Du, in den mit-
verschworenen Wildbächen Auf-
geschlüsselte, die
hüpfenden Brüste im scharfen
Versspangen-Joch,
stürzt mit mir durch
Bilder, Felsen, Zahlen.

DIE UNZE WAHRHEIT tief im Wahn,

an ihr
kommen die Teller der Waage
vorübergerollt,
beide zugleich, im Gespräch,

das kämpfend in Herz-
höhe gestemmte Gesetz,
Sohn, siegt.

IN DEN GERÄUSCHEN, wie unser Anfang,
in der Schlucht,
wo du mir zufielst,
zieh ich sie wieder auf, die
Spieldose – du
weißt: die unsichtbare,
die
unhörbare.

You, in the con-
spirationary torrents un-
locked, the
bouncing breasts in the sharp
verse-fibula-yoke,
fall with me through
images, rocks, numbers.

THE OUNCE OF TRUTH deep inside delusion,

past it
the trays of the balance
roll,
both together, in conversation,

the law, raised in struggle to heart-
level,
son, wins.

IN THE NOISES, like our beginning,
in the ravine,
where you fell to me,
I wind it up again, the
musical box—you
know: the invisible,
the
inaudible one.

LYON, LES ARCHERS

Der Eisenstachel, gebäumt,
in der Ziegelsteinnische:
das Neben-Jahrtausend
fremdet sich ein, unbezwingbar,
folgt
deinen fahrenden Augen,

jetzt,
mit herbeigewürfelten Blicken,
weckst du, die neben dir ist,
sie wird schwerer,
schwerer,

auch du, mit allem
Eingefremdeten in dir,
fremdest dich ein,
tiefer,

die Eine
Sehne
spannt ihren Schmerz unter euch,

das verschollene Ziel
strahlt, Bogen.

LYON, LES ARCHERS

The iron spike, reared,
in the brickniche:
the co-millennium
instranges itself, unconquerable,
follows
your driving eyes,

now,
with glances cast here by dice
you wake, who is beside you,
she becomes heavier,
heavier,

you too, with all
the instrangedness in you,
instrange yourself,
deeper,

the One
string
tenses its pain between you,

the missing target
radiates, bow.

DIE KÖPFE, ungeheuer, die Stadt,
die sie baun,
hinterm Glück.

Wenn du noch einmal mein Schmerz wärst, dir treu,
und es käm eine Lippe vorbei, diesseitig, am
Ort, wo ich aus mir herausreich,

ich brächte dich durch
diese Straße
nach vorn.

WO BIN ICH
heut?

Die Gefahren, alle,
mit ihrem Gerät,
bäurisch verhumpelt,

forkenhoch
die Himmelsbrache gehißt,

die Verluste, kalkmäulig – ihr
redlichen Münder, ihr Tafeln! –
in der entwinkelten Stadt,
vor Glimmerdroschken gespannt,

– Goldspur, entgegengestemmte
Goldspur! –,

THE HEADS, monstrous, the city,
they are building,
behind happiness.

If once more you were my pain, faithful to you,
and a lip came by, this side, at the
place, where I reach out of myself,

I would bring you through
this street
up front.

WHERE AM I
today?

The dangers, all,
with their appliance,
hickishly gamey,

pitchfork-high
the heavensfallow hoisted,

the losses, chalkmouthed—you
upright mouths, you tables!—
in the disangled town,
harnessed to glimmerhackneys,

—goldtrace, counterheaved
goldtrace!—,

die Brücken, vom Strom überjauchzt,

die Liebe, droben im Ast,
an Kommend-Entkommendem deutelnd,

das Große Licht,
zum Funken erhoben,
rechts von den Ringen
und allem Gewinn.

DIE LÄNGST ENTDECKTEN
flüstern sich Briefworte zu,
flüstern das Wort ohne Blatt, das umspähte,
groß wie dein Taler,

hör auch
mein starkes
Du-
weißt-wie,

das hohe Herbei, die Umarmung
ist mit uns, ohne Ende,
auf der Treppe
zum Hafen,

der Stechschritt erlahmt,
Odessitka.

---

the bridges, overjoyed by the stream,

love, up there in the branch,
niggling at the coming-escaping,

the Great Light,
elevated to a spark,
on the right of the rings
and all gain.

THE LONG DISCOVERED
whisper letterwords to each other,
whisper the word without leaf, the peeked-around,
the size of your taler,

hear also
my strong
You-
know-how,

the high hither, the embrace
is with us, without end,
on the staircase
to the harbor,

the goose step falters,
Odessitka.

ALL DEINE SIEGEL ERBROCHEN? NIE.

Geh, verzedere auch
sie, die brief-
häutige, elf-
hufige Tücke:

daß die Welle, die honig-
ferne, die milch-
nahe, wenn
der Mut sie zur Klage bewegt,
die Klage zum Mut, wieder,

daß sie nicht auch
den Elektronen-Idioten
spiegle, der Datteln
verarbeitet für
menetekelnde
Affen.

***

II

SCHLAFBROCKEN, Keile,
ins Nirgends getrieben:
wir bleiben uns gleich,
der herum-
gesteuerte Rundstern
pflichtet uns bei.

ALL YOUR SEALS BROKEN OPEN? NEVER.

Go, cedarize it
too, the letter-
skinned, eleven-
hoofed guile:

so that the wave, honey-
distant, milk-
close, when
courage moves it to complaint,
complaint to courage, again,

so that it not also
mirror the electron-
idiot, who processes
dates for
portentous
apes.

———————————————————————————

II

SLEEPMORSELS, wedges,
driven into the nowhere:
we remain equal to ourselves,
the turned-
about roundstar
agrees with us.

DIE WAHRHEIT, angeseilt an
die entäußerten Traumrelikte,
kommt als ein Kind
über den Grat.

Die Krücke im Tal,
von Erdklumpen umschwirrt,
von Geröll, von
Augensamen,
blättert im hoch
oben erblühenden Nein – in der
Krone.

AUS DEN NAHEN
Wasserschächten
mit unerweckten
Händen heraufgeschaufeltes Graugrün:

die Tiefe
gibt ihr Gewächs her, unhörbar,
widerstandslos.

Auch das noch
bergen, ehe
der Steintag die Menschen-

TRUTH, roped to
the relinquished dreamrelics,
comes as a child
over the ridge.

The crutch in the valley,
whirred about by earthclods,
by gravel, by
eyeseed,
leafs through the high-
up flowering No—in the
crown.

OUT OF THE NEAR
waterpits
graygreen shoveled
upward with unawakened hands:

the depth
gives up its growth, inaudible,
without resistance.

To recover that
too, before
the stoneday blows the men-

und Tierschwärme leerbläst, ganz wie
die vor die Münder, die Mäuler getretne
Siebenflöte es fordert.

AUSGESCHLÜPFTE
Chitin-
sonnen.

Die Panzerlurche
nehmen die blauen Gebetmäntel um, die sand-
hörige Möwe
heißt es gut, das lauernde
Brandkraut
geht in sich.

EWIGKEITEN, über dich
hinweggestorben,
ein Brief berührt
deine noch un-
verletzten Finger,
die erglänzende Stirn
turnt herbei
und bettet sich in
Gerüche, Geräusche.

---

and animal-swarms empty, exactly as
the sevenflute, fronting the mouths, the
maws, demands it.

HATCHED
chitin-
suns.

The armored amphibians
wrap the blue prayercoats around themselves, the sand-
enthralled gull
sanctions it, the lurking
lampwick
goes into itself.

ETERNITIES, died
over and above you,
a letter touches
your still un-
wounded fingers,
the shining forehead
vaults hither
and beds itself in
odors, noises.

DER PUPPIGE STEINBRECH
in der Fliesenfuge
des leer-
gebeteten, treibhaus-
haften Asyls,

ein horniger Blick
schläft sich ins halb-
offene Tor ein,

schlaksig
kommt eine über-
mündige Silbe geschritten,

ein erwachter
Blindenstab weist ihr
den Ort zu hinter
den Schimmelmähnen.

———————————————————————————

DIE ZWISCHENEIN-
gehagelte Hilfe
wächst,

der Namenbau
setzt aus,

die Gletschermilch karrt
die Vollwüchsigen durch

THE PERTY SAXIFRAGE
in the tile's joint
of the empty-
prayed, hothouse-
like asylum,

a ceratose gaze
sleeps itself into the half-
open gate,

gangly,
a more than
major syllable comes walking,

an awakened
blindman's staff points it
to the place behind
the whitehorsemanes.

THE BETWEEN-WHILES
hailed aid
grows,

the name-edifice
pauses,

the glacier milk carts
the fully grown through

das schwimmende Ziel
ihrer unbeirrbaren
Brände.

DER GEGLÜCKTE
Mumiensprung übers
Gebirge.

Das vereinzelte Riesen-
blatt der Paulownia,
das ihn vermerkt.

Ungepflückt die großen
Spielzeug-
welten. Keinerlei Dienst
am Gestirn.

In den Kontrolltürmen hämmern
die hundert silbernen Hufe
das verbotene
Licht frei.

AUF ÜBERREGNETER FÄHRTE
die kleine Gauklerpredigt der Stille.

Es ist, als könntest du hören,
als liebt ich dich noch.

the swimming target
of its unwavering
blazes.

THE SUCCESSFUL
mummy-leap across
the mountain.

The singular giant-
leaf of the paulownia,
that records it.

Unpicked, the large
toy-
worlds. No service whatsoever
in the constellation.

In the controltowers the hundred
silver hoofs hammer
the forbidden
light free.

ON THE RAINED-OVER SPOOR
silence's little juggler sermon.

It is, as if you could hear,
as if I still loved you.

WEISSGERÄUSCHE, gebündelt,
Strahlen-
gänge
über den Tisch
mit der Flaschenpost hin.

(Sie hört sich zu, hört
einem Meer zu, trinkt es
hinzu, entschleiert
die wegschweren
Münder.)

Das Eine Geheimnis
mischt sich für immer ins Wort.
(Wer davon abfällt, rollt
unter den Baum ohne Blatt.)

Alle die
Schattenverschlüsse
an allen den
Schattengelenken,
hörbar-unhörbar,
die sich jetzt melden.

DIE TEUFLISCHEN
Zungenspäße der Nacht
verholzen in deinem Ohr,

WHITESOUNDS, bundled,
ray-
passages
over the table
with the bottle post hither.

(It listens to itself, listens
to a sea, drinks it
too, unveils
the roadheavy
mouths.)

The One Secret
butts forever into the word.
(Who falls off that, rolls
under the leafless tree.)

All the
shadowclasps
on all the
shadowjoints,
audible-inaudible,
that announce themselves now.

THE DEVILISH
tonguejokes of night
lignify in your ear,

mit den Blicken Rückwärts-
gesträhltes
springt vor,

die vertanen
Brückenzölle, geharft,
durchmeißeln die Kalkschlucht vor uns,

der meerige Lichtsumpf
bellt an uns hoch –
an dir,
irdisch-unsichtbare
Freistatt.

DIE DUNKEL-IMPFLINGE, auf
ihrer unbeirrbaren Kreisbahn
rund um die Wunde,
nadelig,
jenseits von Zahl und Unzahl,
auf Botengang, unermüdlich,

die glasharten
Schleifgeräusche der Schrift,

an beiden Säumen
das aufgeforstete
Hände-Revier (du halber
Schein, alabastern),

what the glances
beamed back,
jumps forward,

the wasted
bridgetolls, harped,
chisel through the chalkravine before us,

the sea-ish lightswamp
barks up at us—
at you,
earthly-invisible
sanctuary.

THE DARK VACCINATION CANDIDATES, on
their unwavering orbit
around the wound,
needly,
beyond number and host,
running errands, indefatigable,

the glasshard
grinding sounds of writing,

on both seams
the afforested
hand-district (you half
sheen, alabaster),

in der wintrigen Schonung
spricht eine Kiefer sich frei.

DIE ZWEITE
Nesselnachricht
an den
tuckernden
Schädel:

Weggesackt
der lebendige
Himmel. Unter
der jaulenden
Düse,
mitten im ewigen
Blinkspiel,
beiß dich als Wort in den wissenden,
sternlosen
Halm.

DAS AUSGESCHACHTETE HERZ,
darin sie Gefühl installieren.

Großheimat Fertig-
teile.

in the wintery preserve
one pine absolves itself.

THE SECOND
nettle-message
to the
chugging
skull:

Sagged away,
the living
sky. Under
the yowling
nozzle,
amidst the eternal
blinker game,
bite yourself as word into the knowing,
starless
stalk.

THE EXCAVATED HEART,
wherein they install feeling.

Wholesale homeland pre-
fabricated parts.

Milchschwester
Schaufel.

DIE FLEISSIGEN
Bodenschätze, häuslich,

die geheizte Synkope,

das nicht zu enträtselnde
Halljahr,

die vollverglasten
Spinnen-Altäre im alles-
überragenden Flachbau,

die Zwischenlaute
(noch immer?),
die Schattenpalaver,

die Ängste, eisgerecht,
flugklar,

der barock ummantelte,
spracheschluckende Duschraum,
semantisch durchleuchtet,

die unbeschriebene Wand
einer Stehzelle:

Milksister
shovel.

THE INDUSTRIOUS
mineral resources, homey,

the heated syncope,

The not-to-be-deciphered
jubilee,

The completely glassed-in
spider-altars in the all-
overtowering low building,

the intermediate sounds
(even yet?),
the shadowpalavers,

the anxieties, icetrue,
flightclear,

the baroquely cloaked,
language-swallowing showerroom,
semantically floodlit,

the uninscribed wall
of a standing-cell:

hier

leb dich
querdurch, ohne Uhr.

DIE KOLLIDIERENDEN Schläfen,
nackt, im Maskenverleih:

hinter der Welt
wirft die ungebetene Hoffnung
die Schlepptrosse aus.

An den meerigen Wundrändern landet
die atmende Zahl.

EINGEHIMMELT in Pest-
laken. Am
entnachteten
Ort.

Die Lidschlagreflexe während
der üppigen
Traumstufe
null.

---

here

live yourself
straightthrough, without clock.

THE COLLIDING temples,
naked, in the mask-rental:

behind the world
unbidden hope casts
out the towropes.

On the sea-ish woundborders lands
the breathing number.

IN-HEAVENED in plague-
shrouds. At
the disnighted
place.

The eyeblinkreflexes during
the luxuriant
dreamlevel
null.

WENN ICH NICHT WEISS, NICHT WEISS,
ohne dich, ohne dich, ohne Du,

kommen sie alle,
die
Freigeköpften, die
zeitlebens hirnlos den Stamm
der Du-losen
besangen:

Aschrej,

ein Wort ohne Sinn,
transtibetanisch,
der Jüdin
Pallas
Athene
in die behelmten
Ovarien gespritzt,

und wenn er,

er,

foetal,

karpatisches Nichtnicht beharft,

dann spitzenklöppelt die
Allemande

WHEN I DON'T KNOW, DON'T KNOW,
without you, without you, without a You,

they all come,
the
freebeheaded, who
lifelong brainlessly sang
of the tribe
of the You-less:

Ashrei,

a word without meaning,
trans-Tibetan,
injected into the
Jewess
Pallas
Athena's
helmeted ovaries,

and when he,

he,

fetally,

harps Carpathian nono,

then the Allemande
bobbins her lace for

das sich übergebende un-
sterbliche
Lied.

EINGEWOHNT-ENTWOHNT,

einentwohnt,

die gehorsame Finsternis: drei
Blutstunden hinterm
Blickquell,

die Kaltlicht-Ozellen,
ummuttert von Blendung,

das dreizehn-
lötige Nichts:
über dich, mit
der Glückshaut,
stülpt sichs

während
der Auffahrt.

RIESIGES,
wegloses, baum-

the vomiting im-
mortal
song.

ACCLIMATIZED-DISCLIMATIZED,

adisclimatized,

the obedient darkness: three
bloodhours behind the
gaze-spring,

the coldlight-ocellae, s-
mothered by blinding,

the thirteen-
carat Nothing:
over you, with
the luckskin,
it folds itself

during
the ascent.

GIANT,
pathless, tree-

bewürfeltes
Hand-
gelände,

Quincunx.

Die Äste, nervengesteuert,
machen sich über
die schon
angeröteten Schlagschatten her,
einen Schlangenbiß vor
Rosen-
aufgang.

GEWIEHERTE TUMBAGEBETE,

Bluthufe scharren
die Denksträuße zusammen,

ein Aschen-Juchhe
blättert die Singstimmen um,
hängt die zerstrahlten Topase
hoch in den Raum,

die gewitterpflichtigen
Leichensäcke
richten sich aus,

die-cast
hand-
scape,

quincunx.

The branches, nerve-piloted,
fall upon
the already
reddened harsh shadows,
a snakebite before
rose-
rise.

Neighed tombprayers,

bloodhoofs paw
the thoughtbouquets together,

an ash-hooray
turns over the vocal parts,
hangs the irradiated topazes
high up in space,

the storm-compulsary
corpse bags
line up,

im Trauerkondukt
grinst unwiderstehlich
das Königreich
Bemen.

DIE EWIGKEITEN TINGELN
im abgebeugten Strahl,

ein Gruß steht kopf, zwischen zweien,

der dunkelblütige, sich
mitverschweigende
Muskel
kammert den Namen ein, den er mittrug,

und pflanzt sich fort

durch Knospung.

MÜLLSCHLUCKER-CHÖRE, silbrig:

Das Frieselfieber
läuft und läuft um das Schachtgrab,

wer

in the funeral procession
the kingdom of
Bohemia grins
irresistably.

THE ETERNITIES HONKYTONK
in the bent beam,

a greeting goes wild, twixt two,

the darkblood
muscle, it too
concealing itself,
encapsulates the name it carried along,

and reproduces itself

through budding.

TRASHSWALLOWER-CHOIRS, silvery:

Miliary fever
runs and runs around the pit-tomb,

whoever

diesen Dezember denkt, dem
feuchtet ein Blick
die redende Stirn.

III

ENTTEUFELTER NU.
Alle Winde.

Die Gewalten, ernüchtert,
nähn den Lungenstich zu.
Das Blut stürzt in sich zurück.

In Bocklemünd, über die vordere, die
Leichtschrift,
auch über dich,
tieferer Mitbruder Buchstab,
eilt, unendlichkeitsher,
der Hammerglanz hin.

HÜLLEN im Endlichen, dehnbar,
in jeder
wächst eine andre Gestalt fest

Tausend ist
noch nicht einmal Eins.

thinks that December, a
gaze will wet his
talking forehead.

III

DEDEVILED INSTANT.
All winds.

The powers, sobered,
sow the lungstitch shut.
The blood collapses back upon itself.

In Bocklemünd, across the one in front,
the lightscript,
but also across you,
deeper confrère letter,
eternity-hither the
hammershine hurries.

SHELLS inside Finitude, stretchable,
in each
another figure grows itself fast

A thousand
is not even yet One.

Jeden Pfeil, den du losschickst,
begleitet das mitgeschossene Ziel
ins unbeirrbar-geheime
Gewühl.

DIE LIEBE, zwangsjackenschön,
hält auf das Kranichpaar zu.

Wen, da er durchs Nichts fährt,
holt das Veratmete hier
in eine der Welten herüber?

DU WARST mein Tod:
dich konnte ich halten,
während mir alles entfiel.

ZUR RECHTEN – wer? Die Tödin.
Und du, zur Linken, du?

Die Reise-Sicheln am außer-
himmlischen Ort
mimen sich weißgrau
zu Mondschwalben zusammen,
zu Sternmauerseglern,

Each arrow you loose
is accompanied by the sent-along target
into the unerringly-secret
tumult.

LOVE, straitjacket-pretty,
bears in on the pair of cranes.

Who, given that he drives through the void,
does the disbreathed here
bring across into one of the worlds?

YOU WERE my death:
you I could hold on to,
while all fell from me.

TO THE RIGHT—who? Shedeath.
And you, to the left, you?

The travel-sickles at the outer-
heavenly place
mime themselves whitegray
into moonswallows,
into starswifts.

ich tauche dorthin
und gieß eine Urnevoll
in dich hinunter,
hinein.

DIE ABGEWRACKTEN TABUS,
und die Grenzgängerei zwischen ihnen,
weltennaß, auf
Bedeutungsjagd, auf
Bedeutungs-
flucht.

WUTPILGER-STREIFZÜGE durch
meerisches Draußen und Drinnen,
Conquista
im engsten
untern Ge-
herz.
(Niemand entfärbt, was jetzt strömt.)

Das Salz einer hier
untergetauchten
Mit-Träne
müht sich die hellen
Logbüchertürme
aufwärts.

I dive over there
and pour an urnfull
down, into,
you.

THE DISMANTLED TABOOS,
and the bordercrisscrossing between them,
worldwet, on a
meaning chase, on a
meaning
flight.

RAGE-PILGRIM RAIDS across
a sea-ish Outside and Inside,
Conquista
in the narrowest
bottom heart-
vitals.
(Nobody discolors what now streams.)

The salt of a co-
tear here
submerged
struggles up
the light
logbooktowers.

Bald
blinkt es uns an.

STILLE, Fergenvettel, fahr mich durch die Schnellen.
Wimpernfeuer, leucht voraus.

DIE EINE eigen-
sternige
Nacht.

Aschendurchfadmet
stundaus, stundein,
von den Lidschatten zu-
gefallener Augen,

zusammengeschliffen
zu pfeildünnen
Seelen,
verstummt im Gespräch
mit luftalgenbärtigen
krauchenden Köchern.

Eine erfüllte
Leuchtmuschel fährt
durch ein Gewissen.

Soon
it flashes at us.

SILENCE, old hag, ride me through the rapids.
Lids' fires, light up the way.

THE ONE self-
starred
night.

Threathed through by ashes,
hour-hither hour-yonder,
by the lidshadows of shut-
down eyes,

ground down
to arrowthin
souls,
silenced in conversation
with airalgae-bearded
crawling quivers.

A fulfilled
lightconch drives
through a conscience.

BEI GLÜH- UND MÜHWEIN, nekronym
lang vor der Zeit,
laß ich die Gläserwelt – und nicht nur sie –
Revue passieren

und roll mich in ein steifes Segel, mastenstark,
die Enden tief im Hohlzahn eines Ankers,

und leg mir einen Nabel zu, zwischen den Mitten,
aus unter fetten Sternen
in der gerunzelten Flut,
die sie um-eist,
rotgehurtem
Kork.

SCHIEF,
wie uns allen,
sitzt dir die Eine
Hörklappe auf,
frei,

und das Gehörlose an dir,
drüben, beim Schläfenfirn,
blüht sich jetzt aus, mit Narren-
schellen an jedem
Kelchblatt.

OVER MULLED AND TOILED WINE, necronymic
long before time,
I muster the glassworld—and not it alone—
for inspection

and roll myself into a stiff sail, mast-strong,
the ends deep in an anchor's hollow tooth,

and get myself a navel, between the middles,
made of, below fat stars
in the wrinkled flood
icing them in,
redwhored
cork.

ASLANT,
as for us all,
the single hearing-flap
perches on you,
free,

and the deafness in you,
over there, by the temple-firn,
ceases to bloom now, with fool's
bells on each
sepal.

DIE HERZSCHRIFTGEKRÜMELTE Sichtinsel
mittnachts, bei kleinem
Zündschlüsselschimmer.

Es sind zuviel
zielwütige Kräfte
auch in dieser
scheinbar durchsternten
Hochluft.

Die ersehnte Freimeile
prallt auf uns auf.

UNVERWAHRT.
Schräggeträumt aneinander.

Das Öl rings –
verdickt.

Mit ausgebeulten Gedanken
fuhrwerkt der Schmerz.

Die koppheistergegangene Trauer.

Die Schwermut, aufs neue geduldet,
pendelt sich ein.

THE HEARTSCRIPTCRUMBLED vision-isle
at midnight, in feeble
ignition key glimmer.

There are too many
goalcrazed powers
even in this
seemingly starstudded
highair.

The longed for freemile
crashes into us.

UNKEPT.
Dreamed aslant, joined.

The oil around—
thickened.

With bulging thoughts
pain busies itself.

Mourning, gone awry.

Melancholy, put up with anew,
finds its level.

DAS UNBEDINGTE GELÄUT
hinter all der gemanschten Tristesse.

Hilfsgestänge, gedrungen,
im zeitgeschwärzten Emblem.
Frostfurchen der
Devise entlang.

All das bei halbem
Muttermal-Licht.

DIE EWIGKEIT altert: in
Cerveteri die
Asphodelen
fragen einander weiß.

Mit mummelnder Kelle,
aus den Totenkesseln,
übern Stein, übern Stein,
löffeln sie Suppen
in alle Betten
und Lager.

SPÄT. Ein schwammiger Fetisch
beißt sich die Zapfen vom Christbaum,

THE UNCONDITIONAL CHIMING
behind the masticated tristesse.

Guiding rods, compact,
in the time-blackened emblem.
Frostfurrows along
the motto.

All that in the
birthmark's half-light.

ETERNITY ages: in
Cerveteri the
asphodels
question each other white.

With mumbling ladle,
from the deads' cauldrons,
o'er the stone, o'er the stone,
they spoon soups
into all the beds
and camps.

LATE. A spongy fetish
bites off the cones of the Christmas tree,

aufgerauht von
Frostsprüchen
hüpft ein Wunsch ihnen nach,

das Fenster fliegt auf, wir sind draußen,

nicht ebenzubringen
der Hubbel Dasein,

eine kopflastige,
tiefenfreudige Wolke
kutschiert uns auch darüber
hin.

DIE SÄMLINGE – causa secunda – pachten
das übergewisse
pupillenhörige
Nichts,
das deine – warum nur? – auch heute
hochzuckende Braue
noch säumt, wenn ich hinseh,
um des darunter
veilleicht noch zu leistenden
Augenschwurs willen.

---

roughened up by
frostsayings
a wish bobs after them,

the window flies open, we're outside,

unplaneable,
the lump Being,

a nose-heavy,
depth-enjoying cloud
chauffeurs us even over
that.

THE SEEDLINGS—causa secunda—lease
the overcertain
pupil-enslaved
nothing,
which still skirts your—why
only?—even still today up-
twitching brow,
when I look at it, for the
sake of the maybe
still to be given
eye-oath below it.

DIE HÜGELZEILEN ENTLANG
die niedlichen Streckfoltern zwischen
Bäumchen und Bäumchen,
geißblattumrankt,

Dum-dum-Horizonte, davor,
vertausendfacht, ja,
dein
Hör-Silber,
Spinett,

Tagnacht voll schwirrender Lungen,

die
entzweigten Erzengel schieben
hier Wache.

KOMM, wir löffeln
Nervenzellen
– die Entengrütze, multipolar,
der leergeleuchteten Teiche –
aus den
Rauten-
gruben.

Zehn Fasern ziehn
aus den noch erreichbaren Zentren
Halberkennbares nach.

ALONG THE HILL LINES
the pretty torture racks between
treeling and treeling,
honeysuckled in,

Dumdum horizons, before them,
milliplied, yes,
your
Hear-Silver,
spinet,

daynight full of whirring lungs,

the
disbranched archangels stand
guard here.

COME, we're ladling
nerve cells
—the duck's porridge, multipolar,
of the light-emptied ponds—
from the
rhomboid
fossas.

Ten tendons draw forth
half-recognizables
from the still reachable centers.

ENTSCHLACKT, entschlackt.

Wenn wir jetzt Messer wären,
blankgezogen wie damals
im Laubengang zu Paris, eine Augenglut lang,

der arktische Stier
käme gesprungen
und bekrönte mit uns seine Hörner
und stieße zu, stieße zu.

SEELENBLIND, hinter den Aschen,
im heilig-sinnlosen Wort,
kommt der Entreimte geschritten,
den Hirnmantel leicht um die Schultern,

den Gehörgang beschallt
mit vernetzten Vokalen,
baut er den Sehpurpur ab,
baut ihn auf.

ANRAINERIN Nacht.
Zwerg- und riesenwüchsig, je
nach dem Schnitt in der Fingerbeere,
nach dem,
was aus ihm tritt.

DESLAGGED, deslagged.

If we were knives now,
unsheathed like back then
in the pergola in Paris, the time of an eye-ember,

the arctic bull
would leap in
would crown his horns with us
would thrust, would thrust.

SOULBLIND, behind the ashes,
in the holy-meaningless word,
the disrhymed comes walking,
his cerebral mantle draped lightly over the shoulders,

the ear canal irradiated
with reticulated vowels,
he deconstructs the visual purple,
reconstructs it.

BORDERESS: night.
Vigorous dwarf- and giant-growth, de-
pending on the cut in the fingertip,
on what
emerges from it.

Überäugig zuweilen,
wenn bikonkav
ein Gedanke hinzugetropft kommt,
nicht von ihr her.

MÖWENKÜKEN, silbern,
betteln den Altvogel an:
den Rotfleck am Unter-
schnabel, der gelb ist.

Schwarz – eine Kopf-
attrappe führt es dir vor –
wär ein stärkerer Reiz. Auch Blau
ist wirksam, doch nicht
die Reizfarbe machts:
es muß eine
Reizgestalt sein, eine ganze,
komplett
konfiguriert,
ein vorgegebenes Erbe.

. . . .

Freund,
teerübergoßner Sackhüpfer du,
auch hier, auf diesem
Gestade gerätst du

Too many-eyed at times,
when, biconcavely,
a thought adds its drop,
not from her.

GULLCHICKS, silvery,
beg the adult bird:
the red spot on the lower
beak, which is yellow.

Black—a decoy
head demonstrates it for you—
was a stronger stimulus. Blue also
works, but it is not
the color stimulus that does it:
it has to be a
stimulus-figure, a whole,
completely
configured,
a pregiven inheritance.

. . . .

Friend,
you tardrenched sackracer,
here also, on this
shore, you go down

beiden, Zeit und Ewigkeit, in die
falsche
Kehle.

IV

IRISCH

Gib mir das Wegrecht
über die Kornstiege zu deinem Schlaf,
das Wegrecht
über den Schlafpfad,
das Recht, daß ich Torf stechen kann
am Herzhang,
morgen.

DIE STRICKE, salzwasserklamm:
der weiße
Großknoten – diesmal
geht er nicht auf.

Auf der Schütte Seegras daneben,
im Ankerschatten,
neckt ein Name das
entzwillingte
Rätsel.

both time and eternity's
wrong
pipe.

- -

IV

IRISH

Give me the right of way
across the grain ladder into your sleep,
the right of way
across the sleep trail,
the right, for me to cut peat
along the heart's hillside,
tomorrow.

- -

THE ROPES, salt-water-clammy:
the white
topknot—this time
it does not come undone.

On the seagrass chute next to it,
in anchor's shadow,
a name teases the
untwinned
riddle.

TAU. Und ich lag mit dir, du, im Gemülle,
ein matschiger Mond
bewarf uns mit Antwort,

wir bröckelten auseinander
und bröselten wieder in eins:

der Herr brach das Brot,
das Brot brach den Herrn.

ÜPPIGE DURCHSAGE
in einer Gruft, wo
wir mit unsern
Gasfahnen flattern,

wir stehn hier
im Geruch
der Heiligkeit, ja.

Brenzlige
Jenseitsschwaden
treten uns dick aus den Poren,

in jeder zweiten
Zahn-
karies erwacht
eine unverwüstliche Hymne.

DEW. And I lay with you, thee, in the rubble,
a mushy moon
pelted us with answer,

we crumbled apart
we brittled back together:

the Lord broke the bread,
the bread broke the Lord.

LAVISH MESSAGE
in a crypt, where
we flap with
our gasflags,

we stand here
in the odor
of sanctity, yep.

Singed
vapor waves of the beyond
thickly drift from our pores,

in each second
tooth-
cavity an un-
destructable hymn wakes up.

Den Batzen Zwielicht, den du uns reinwarfst,
komm, schluck ihn mit runter.

AUSGEROLLT dieser Tag:
der vieltausendjährige Teig
für den späteren
Hunnenfladen,

ein ebensoalter
Kiefer, leicht verschlammt,
gedenkt aller Frühzeit
und bleckt gegen sie und sich selber,

Huf-
schläge des Vorgetiers zum
Hefen-Arioso:
es geht, fladenschön-singbares Wachstum,
immer noch aufwärts,

ein schatten-
loser Geist, ent-
einsamt, ein
unsterblicher,
bibbert
selig.

The clump of twilight you throw down to us,
come, swallow it too down.

THIS DAY, rolled out:
the many-thousand-years-old dough
for the later
hunic flat cake,

a just-as-old
jaw, somewhat oozy,
commemorates all early times,
and bares its teeth against them and itself,

hoof-
beats of the protoanimal to the
yeast-arioso:
it goes, flat-cake beautiful singable growth,
still and always upward,

a shadow-
less spirit, dis-
lonelied, an
immortal,
shivers
blissfully.

ÖLIG still
schwimmt dir die Würfel-Eins
zwischen Braue und Braue,
hält hier
inne, lidlos,
schaut mit.

IHR MIT DEM
im Dunkelspiegel Geschauten,

du Einer
mit der erblickten
stofflosen Leuchtspiegelfläche zuinnerst:

durchs zehn-
türmige Wüstentor tritt
euer Boten-Selbst vor euch, steht,
einen Dreivokal lang,
in der hohen
Röte,

als wär das Volk in den Fernen
abermals um euch geschart.

AUS ENGELSMATERIE, am Tag
der Beseelung, phallisch

OILY still
the die's One swims
between brow and brow,
stops here,
lidless, follows
your gaze.

YOU WITH THE
in the darkglass gazed at,

you One
with the beheld
substanceless light-mirror-surface innermost:

through the ten-
towered desert gate your
messenger-self steps before you, stands,
for the length of a trivowel,
in the high
redness,

as if the people in the distances
were once again gathered around you.

OUT OF ANGEL-MATTER, on the day
of the ensouling, phallically

vereint im Einen
– Er, der Belebend-Gerechte, schlief dich mir zu,
Schwester –, aufwärts
strömend durch die Kanäle, hinauf
in die Wurzelkrone:
gescheitelt
stemmt sie uns hoch, gleich-ewig,
stehenden Hirns, ein Blitz
näht uns die Schädel zurecht, die Schalen
und alle
noch zu zersamenden Knochen:

vom Osten gestreut, einzubringen im Westen, gleich-ewig –,

wo diese Schrift brennt, nach dem
Dreivierteltod, vor
der herumwälzenden Rest-
seele, die sich
vor Kronenangst krümmt,
von urher.

DIE FREIGEBLASENE LEUCHTSAAT
in den unter Weltblut
stehenden Furchen.

Eine Hand mit dem Schimmer des Urlichts
wildert jenseits
der farnigen Dämme:

united in the One
—He, the Enlivening-Just, slept you toward me,
sister—, upward
streaming through the channels, up
into the rootcrown:
parted
she hoists us up, equal-eternal,
with standing brain, a bolt of lightning
sews our skulls aright, the pans
and all
the still-to-be-dissemened bones:

strewn from the East, to be harvested in the West: equal-eternal—,

where this script burns, after the
threequarter-death, before
the rolling around remainder-
soul, which
writhes in crownfear,
since ur-ever.

THE FREE-BLOWN LIGHTCROP
in the under worldblood
standing furrows.

A hand with the shimmer of the urlight
poaches beyond
the ferny dams:

als hungerte noch
irgendein Magen,
als flügelte noch
irgendein zu
befruchtendes Aug.

KLEIDE DIE WORTHÖHLEN AUS
mit Pantherhäuten,

erweitere sie, fellhin und fellher,
sinnhin und sinnher,

gib ihnen Vorhöfe, Kammern, Klappen
und Wildnisse, parietal,

und lausch ihrem zweiten
und jeweils zweiten und zweiten
Ton.

DIE HOCHWELT – verloren, die Wahnfahrt, die Tagfahrt.

Erfragbar, von hier aus,
das mit der Rose im Brachjahr
heimgedeutete Nirgends.

---

as if there still starved
any stomach,
as if there fluttered
any still-to-be-
fertilized eye.

LINE THE WORDCAVES
with panther skins,

widen them, hide-to and hide-fro,
sense-hither and sense-thither,

give them courtyards, chambers, drop doors
and wildnesses, parietal,

and listen for their second
and each time second and second
tone.

THE HIGHWORLD—lost, the delusion-ride, the day-ride.

Ascertainable, from here on out,
the with the rose in the fallow year
home-sensed Nowhere.

DIE BRABBELNDEN
Waffen-
pässe.

Auf der übersprungenen
                    Stufe
räkeln sich die
              Sterbereien.

. . . AUCH KEINERLEI
Friede.

Graunächte, vorbewußt-kühl.
Reizmengen, otterhaft,
auf Bewußtseinsschotter
unterwegs zu
Erinnerungsbläschen.

Grau-in-Grau der Substanz.

Ein Halbschmerz, ein zweiter, ohne
Dauerspur, halbwegs
hier. Eine Halblust.
Bewegtes, Besetztes.

Wiederholungszwangs-
Camaïeu.

THE MUTTERING
arms-
passes.

On the leaped over
                step
the deathdoodads
                diddle.

. . . THOUGH NO KIND OF
peace.

Graynights, preconscious-cool.
Stimuli-quanta, otterlike,
over consciousness-gravel
on the way to
memory-vesicles.

The grisaille of matter.

A halfpain, a second, without
permanent trace, halfway
here. A halfpleasure.
The moved. The cathexed.

Repetition-compulsion-
monochrome.

NAH, IM AORTENBOGEN,
im Hellblut:
das Hellwort.

Mutter Rahel
weint nicht mehr.
Rübergetragen
alles Geweinte.

Still, in den Kranzarterien,
unumschnürt:
Ziw, jenes Licht.

———

WIRF DAS SONNENJAHR, an dem du hängst,
über den Herzbord
und rudere zu, hungre dich fort, kopulierend:

zwei Keimzellen, zwei Metazoen,
das wart ihr,

das Unbelebte, die Heimat,
fordert jetzt Rückkehr –:

später, wer weiß,
kommt eins von euch zwein
gewandelt wieder herauf,
ein Pantoffeltierchen,
bewimpert,
im Wappen.

Near, in the aortic arch,
in the light-blood:
the light-word.

Mother Rachel
weeps no more.
Carried over:
all the weepings.

Quiet, in the coronary arteries,
unconstricted:
Ziv, that light.

Throw the solar year, to which you cling,
over the heart railings
and row to, starve yourself away, copulating:

two germ cells, two metazoons,
that's what you were,

the inanimate, the homeland,
now requests return—:

later, who knows,
one of you two, transformed,
may reemerge,
a slipper animalcule,
ciliated,
in the shield.

WEIL DU DEN NOTSCHERBEN FANDST
in der Wüstung,
ruhn die Schattenjahrhunderte neben dir aus
und hören dich denken:

Vielleicht ist es wahr,
daß hier der Friede zwei Völker besprach,
aus Tongefäßen.

ES IST GEKOMMEN DIE ZEIT:

Die Hirnsichel, blank,
lungert am Himmel,
umstrolcht von Gallengestirn,

die Antimagneten, die Herrscher,
tönen.

LIPPEN, SCHWELLGEWEBE der Du-Nacht:

Steilkurvenblicke kommen geklettert,
machen die Kommissur aus,
nähn sich hier fest –:
Zufahrtsverbote, Schwarzmaut.

Es müßte noch Leuchtkäfer geben.

BECAUSE YOU FOUND THE WOE-SHARD
in the deserted settlement,
the shadow-centuries relax by your side
and hear you think:

Maybe it is true
that here peace debated two peoples,
from clay pots.

IT HAS COME THE TIME:

The brainsickle, unsheathed,
lounges in the sky,
rumbled by gallstars,

the antimagnets, the rulers,
sound off.

LIPS, ERECTILE-TISSUE of the You-night:

Hairpincurve-glances are climbing up,
making out the commissure,
sew themselves fast here—:
No admittance! Blacktoll.

There should still be glowworms.

V

MÄCHTE, GEWALTEN.

Dahinter, im Bambus:
bellende Lepra, symphonisch.

Vincents verschenktes
Ohr
ist am Ziel.

TAGBEWURF: die
lichtdurchlässige Dorn–
schläfe
grapscht sich noch ein
einziges taufrisches
Dunkel.

An der Herzspitze kommt
eine Muskelfaser
sinnend zu Tode.

V

PRINCIPALITIES, POWERS.

Back of them, in the bamboo:
yelping lepra, symphonic.

Vincent's offered
ear
has reached its goal.

DAYBOMBARDMENT: the
light-permeable thorn-
temple
grabs just one
more dewfresh
darkness.

At the heart's apex a
musclefiber comes
musing to death.

REDEWÄNDE, raumeinwärts –
eingespult in dich selber,
grölst du dich durch bis zur Letztwand.

Die Nebel brennen.

Die Hitze hängt sich in dich.

VERWAIST im Gewittertrog
die vier Ellen Erde,

verschattet des himmlischen
Schreibers Archiv,

vermurt Michael,
verschlickt Gabriel,

vergoren im Steinblitz
die Hebe.

BEIDER entnarbte Leiber,
beider Todesblatt über der Blöße,
beider entwirklichtes Antlitz.

An Land gezogen von
der weißesten Wurzel
des weißesten
Baums.

SPEECHWALLS, space inward—
spooled in upon yourself,
you holler yourself through all the way to the lastwall.

The fogs are burning.

The heat hangs itself inside you.

ORPHANED in the stormtrough
the four ells of earth,

shadowed in, the heavenly
writer's archives,

moored in, Michael
mired in, Gabriel

fermented in the stone lightning,
the share.

OF BOTH: the de-scarred bodies,
of both: the deathleaf over their nakedness,
of both: the de-realized faces.

Pulled onto land by
the whitest root
of the whitest
tree.

FORTGEWÄLZTER Inzest-Stein.

Ein Auge, dem Arzt
aus der Niere geschnitten,
liest an Hippokrates Statt
das Meineid-make up.

Sprengungen, Schlafbomben, Goldgas.

Ich schwimme, ich schwimme

ALS FARBEN, gehäuft,
kommen die Wesen wieder, abends, geräuschvoll,
ein Viertelmonsum
ohne Schlafstatt,
ein Prasselgebet
vor den entbrannten
Lidlosigkeiten.

DIE RAUCHSCHWALBE stand im Zenith, die Pfeil-
schwester,

die Eins der Luft-Uhr
flog dem Stundenzeiger entgegen,
tief hinein ins Geläut,

ROLLED-AWAY incest-stone.

An eye, cut from
the doctor's kidney,
reads in Hippocrates's stead
the perjured oath's makeup.

Explosions, sleepbombs, goldgas.

I swim, I swim

AS COLORS, piled up,
the beings return, evenings, clamorously,
a quartermonsoon
without sleeping place,
a patterprayer
before the ignited
lidlessnesses.

THE CHIMNEY SWALLOW stood at the zenith, the arrow-
sister,

the One of the air-clock
flew toward the hour hand,
deep into the chiming,

der Hai
spie den lebenden Inka aus,

es war Landnahme-Zeit
in Menschland,

alles
ging um,
entsiegelt wie wir.

WEISS, weiß, weiß
wie Gittertünche,
reihn die Gesetze sich ein
und marschieren
einwärts.

UNBEDECKTE. Ganz und gar
Brüstende du.
Entflochten der Brodem vor dir,
im Angesicht aller.
Keines
Atem wächst nach, Un-
umkleidbare.

Der Steinmützenkönig vorn
stürzt von der Steineselskruppe,

the shark
spat out the living Inca,

it was conquest-time
in Manland,

everything
went about,
unsealed like us.

WHITE, white, white
like lattice whitewash
the laws fall into line
and march
inward.

BARE ONE. Udderly
chest-thumping you.
Your funk wafted,
in the face of all.
No one's
breath regrowths, un-
redressable one.

The stonecap-king up front
falls from the stone donkey's rump,

die Hände klamm
vorm tittenbeschrieenen
Antlitz.

DER SCHWEIGESTOSS gegen dich,
die Schweigestöße.

Küstenhaft
lebst du dich fort
in den Umschlaghäfen der Zeit,
in Pistenpaar-Nähe,
wo die kegelköpfige Eis-Crew
die Abstellplätze behimmelt.

HAUT MAL

Unentsühnte,
Schlafsüchtige,
von den Göttern Befleckte:

deine Zunge ist rußig,
dein Harn schwarz,
wassergallig dein Stuhl,

du führst,
wie ich,
unzüchtige Reden,

clammy hands
over the tit-lashed
face.

THE SILENCE-BUTT against you,
the silence-butts.

Coastlike
you survive yourself
in time's transshipment ports,
in paired paths' nearness,
where the pinheaded ice-crew
beheavens the stockrooms.

HAUT MAL

Unexpiated,
narcoleptic,
stained by the gods:

your tongue is smutty,
your urine black,
watery-bilious your stool,

you hold forth,
as I do,
lubriciously,

du setzt einen Fuß vor den andern,
legst eine Hand auf die andre,
schmiegst dich in Ziegenfell,

du beheiligst
mein Glied.

DAS TAUBENEIGROSSE GEWÄCHS
im Nacken:
ein Denkspiel,
mitrechnerisch-göttlich,
für die Allonge-
Perücke,

ein Ort,
zukunftsenthüllend,
stahlfiberfroh,
zur Erprobung
des ein-
maligen Herzstichs.

ANGEWINTERTES Windfeld: hier
mußt du leben, körnig, granatapfelgleich,
aufgeharscht von
zu verschweigendem Vorfrost,
den Schriftzug der Finsterung mitten

you put one foot before the other,
put one hand on the other,
cuddle up in goatfur,

you hallow
my member.

THE PIGEON-EGG-SIZE GROWTH
on the nape:
a thoughtgame,
inclusively-godly,
for the full-bottomed
wig,

a place,
future-baring,
steelfibergay,
for the testing
of the one-
off heartstab.

BEWINTERED windfield: here
you must live, granular, pomegranate-like,
hardpacked by
the not-to-be-mentioned prefrost,
darkening's handwriting amidst

im goldgelben Schatten – doch nie
warst du nur Vogel und Frucht –
der sternbespieenen
Überschall-Schwinge,
die du
ersangst.

DRAUSSEN. Quittengelb weht
ein Stück Halbabend von
der driftenden Gaffel,

die Schwüre,
graurückig, seefest,
rollen
auf die Galion zu,

eine
Henkers-
schlinge, legt sich die Zahl
um den Hals der noch sicht-
baren Figur.

Die Segel braucht keiner zu streichen,

ich Fahrensmann
geh.

---

the goldyellow shadow—yet never
were you only bird and fruit—
of the star-bespat
supersonic wing,
you won
through song.

OUTSIDE. Quince-yellow a piece
of half-evening blows from
the drifting gaff,

the oaths,
graybacked, seaworthy,
roll
toward the galleon,

a
hangman's
noose, the number drapes itself
around the neck of the still visi-
ble figure.

Nobody needs to take in the sails,

I journeyman
go.

WER GAB DIE RUNDE AUS?

Es war sichtiges Wetter, wir tranken

und grölten den Aschen-Shanty
auf die große Sonnwend-Havarie.

HEDDERGEMÜT, ich kenn
deine wie Kleinfische wimmelnden
Messer,

härter als ich
lag keiner am Wind,

keinem wie mir
schlug die Hagelbö durch
das seeklar gemesserte
Hirn.

KEIN NAME, der nennte:
sein Gleichlaut
knotet uns unters
steifzusingende
Hellzelt.

WHO STOOD THE ROUND?

The weather was clear, we drank

and hollered the ash-chantey
about the great midsummer-average.

DYSPOSITION, I know
your knives swarming like
minnows,

closer to the wind than I
nobody sailed,

nobody more than I
was cut by the hail squall
to the seaclear knived
brain.

NO NAME, that would name:
its consonance
knots us under the
in song to be stiffened
lighttent.

DENK DIR

Denk dir:
der Moorsoldat von Massada
bringt sich Heimat bei, aufs
unauslöschlichste,
wider
allen Dorn im Draht.

Denk dir:
die Augenlosen ohne Gestalt
führen dich frei durchs Gewühl, du
erstarkst und
erstarkst.

Denk dir: deine
eigene Hand
hat dies wieder
ins Leben empor-
gelittene
Stück
bewohnbarer Erde
gehalten.

Denk dir:
das kam auf mich zu,
namenwach, handwach
für immer,
vom Unbestattbaren her.

IMAGINE

Imagine:
the moorsoldier from Masada
teaches himself homeland, in
the most inextinguishable way,
against
all barbs in the wire.

Imagine:
the eyeless without shape
lead you free through the throng, you
grow stronger and
stronger.

Imagine: your
own hand
has held once
more this
into life re–
suffered
piece of
inhabitable earth.

Imagine:
that came toward me,
awake to the name, awake to the hand,
forever,
from what cannot be buried.

Eingedunkelt

Tenebrae'd

BEDENKENLOS,
den Vernebelungen zuwider,
glüht sich der hängende Leuchter
nach unten, zu uns

Vielarmiger Brand,
sucht jetzt sein Eisen, hört,
woher, aus Menschenhautnähe,
ein Zischen,

findet,
verliert,

schroff
liest sich, minutenlang,
die schwere,
schimmernde
Weisung.

NACH DEM LICHTVERZICHT:
der vom Botengang helle,
hallende Tag.

Die blühselige Botschaft,
schriller und schriller,
findet zum blutenden Ohr.

Unscrupulously,
against the obfuscations,
the hanging candlestick glows itself
downward, toward us

Manyarmed torch,
now searches for its iron, hears,
where from, from human skincloseness,
a hissing,

finds,
loses,

harsh
it reads, minutes long,
the heavy,
shimmering
behest.

After the lightwaiver:
the day, bright, re-
sounding from the errand.

The flowersome message,
shriller and shriller,
finds to the bleeding ear.

DEUTLICH, weithin, das offne
Umklammerungszeichen,

Entlassen die Liebenden,
auch aus der Ulmwurzel-Haft,

Schwarz-
züngiges, reif, am Sterben,
wird abermals laut, Beglänztes
rückt näher.

VOM HOCHSEIL herab-
gezwungen, ermißt du,
was zu gewärtigen ist
von soviel Gaben,

Käsig-weißes Gesicht
dessen, der über uns herfällt,

Setz die Leuchtzeiger ein, die Leucht-
ziffern,

Sogleich, nach Menschenart,
mischt sich das Dunkel hinzu,
das du herauserkennst

aus all diesen
unbußfertigen, unbotmäßigen
Spielen.

EXPLICIT, wide, the open
parenthesishug,

Release the lovers
also from the elmroot-arrest

Black–
tongued, ripe, at agony
becomes loud again, the quickening
draws closer.

———————————————————————————

FORCED OFF the high
wire, you fathom out
what's to be expected
from so many gifts,

cheesy-white face
of the one who pounces on us,

Deploy the lightpointers, the light-
ciphers,

Immediately, as humans do,
darkness mixes in,
which you distinguish

among all these
unrepentent insubordination
games.

ÜBER DIE KÖPFE
hinweggewuchtet
das Zeichen, traumstark entbrannt
am Ort, den es nannte.

Jetzt:
Mit dem Sandblatt winken,
bis der Himmel
raucht.

WIRFST DU
den beschrifteten
Ankerstein aus?

Mich hält hier nichts,

nicht die Nacht der Lebendigen,
nicht die Nacht der Unbändigen,
nicht die Nacht der Wendigen,

Komm, wälz mit mir den Türstein
vors Unbezwungene Zelt.

HEAVED FAR OVER
the heads:
the sign, dreamstrong, ablaze
at the place it named.

Now:
Wave with the sandleaf
until the sky
smokes.

DO YOU THROW
the written upon
anchor stone?

Nothing holds me here,

not the night of the living,
not the night of the intractable,
not the night of the nimble,

Come, together let's roll the doorstone
in front of the untamed tent.

ANGEFOCHTENER STEIN,
grüngrau, entlassen
ins Enge.

Enthökerte Glutmonde
leuchten
das Kleinstück Welt aus:

das also warst du
auch.

In den Gedächtnislücken
stehn die eigenmächtigen Kerzen
und sprechen Gewalt zu.

EINGEDUNKELT
die Schlüsselgewalt.
Der Stoßzahn regiert,
von der Kreidespur her,
gegen die Welt-
sekunde.

FÜLL DIE ÖDNIS in die Augensäcke,
den Opferruf, die Salzflut,

komm mit mir zu Atem
und drüber hinaus.

CONTESTED STONE,
graygreen, discharged
into the narrow.

Unhuckstered glowmoons
floodlight
the small matter Earth:

so you too were
that.

In the memory fissures
the autonomous candles stand
and adjudge power.

TENEBRAE'D
the keypower.
The tusk rules,
up from the chalktrace,
against the world-
second.

SHOVEL THE VOID into the eyebags,
the sacrificecall, the saltflood,

come with me to breath
and out beyond.

EINBRUCH des Ungeschiedenen
in deine Sprache,
Nachtglast,

Sperrzauber, stärker.

Von fremdem, hohem
Flutgang unterwaschen
dieses
Leben.

MIT UNS, den
Umhergeworfenen, dennoch
Fahrenden:

der eine
unversehrte,
nicht usurpierbare,
aufständische
Gram.

IRRUPTION of the undifferentiated
into your language,
nightshimmer,

counterspell, stronger.

By a foreign, high
floodflow washed out—
this
life.

WITH US, the
tossed about, yet
traveling:

the one
unharmed,
not usurpable,
rebellious
grief.

Lichtzwang

Lightduress

I

HÖRRESTE, SEHRESTE, im
Schlafsaal eintausendundeins,

tagnächtlich
die Bären-Polka:

sie schulen dich um,

du wirst wieder
er.

IHN RITT DIE NACHT, er war zu sich gekommen,
der Waisenkittel war die Fahn,

kein Irrlauf mehr,
es ritt ihn grad –

Es ist, es ist,
         als stünden im Liguster die Orangen,
als hätt der so Gerittene nichts an
als seine
erste
muttermalige, ge-
heimnisgesprenkelte
Haut.

I

Soundscraps, visionscraps, on
ward onethousandandone,

daynightly
the Bear Polka:

they retrain you,

you again become
he.

—

Night rode him, he had come to,
the orphan's frock as flag,

no more false runs
it rode him straight—

It is, it is,
                as though oranges stood in the privet,
as though the thus ridden wore nothing
but his
first
birthmarked, se-
cret-speckled
skin.

MUSCHELHAUFEN: mit
der Geröllkeule fuhr ich dazwischen,
den Flüssen folgend in die ab-
schmelzende Eis-
heimat,
zu ihm, dem nach wessen
Zeichen zu ritzenden
Feuerstein im
Zwergbirkenhauch.

Lemminge wühlten.

Kein Später.

Keine
Schalenurne, keine
Durchbruchscheibe,
keine Sternfuß-
Fibel.

Ungestillt,
unverknüpft, kunstlos,
stieg das Allverwandelnde langsam
schabend
hinter mir her.

MIT DER ASCHENKELLE GESCHÖPFT
aus dem Seinstrog,

MUSSELHEAP: with
the screemace I drove inbetween,
following the rivers to the
melting ice-
homeland,
toward it, the firestone,
to be incised according
to whose sign, in
the dwarfbirchbalm.

Lemmings burrowed.

No Later.

No
bowl urn, no
pierced necklace,
no starfoot–
fibula.

Unappeased,
unconnected, artless,
the all-transforming slowly
scraping
climbed after me.

SCOOPED WITH THE ASHLADLE
from the Beingtrough,

seifig, im
zweiten
Ansatz, auf-
einanderhin,

unbegreiflich geatzt jetzt,
weit
außerhalb unser und schon – weshalb? –
auseinandergehoben,

dann (im dritten
Ansatz?) hinters
Horn geblasen, vor das
stehende
Tränentrumm,
einmal, zweimal, dreimal,

aus unpaariger,
knospend-gespaltener,
fahniger
Lunge.

MIT MIKROLITHEN gespickte
schenkend-verschenkte
Hände.

Das Gespräch, das sich spinnt
von Spitze zu Spitze,

soapy, at
the second
try, toward
each other,

incomprehensibly fed now,
far
outside our and already—wherefore?—
heaved asunder,

then (at the third
try?) blown
behind the horn, before the
standing
tear-brink,
once, twice, thrice,

from unpaired,
budding-cleft
flaggy
lung.

LARDED WITH MICROLITHS,
giving-given away
hands.

The conversation, spinning itself
from tip to tip,

angesengt von
sprühender Brandluft.

Ein Zeichen
kämmt es zusammen
zur Antwort auf eine
grübelnde Felskunst.

IN DIE NACHT GEGANGEN, helferisch,
ein stern-
durchlässiges Blatt
statt des Mundes:

es bleibt
noch etwas wild zu vertun,
bäumlings.

WIR LAGEN
schon tief in der Macchia, als du
endlich herankrochst.
Doch konnten wir nicht
hinüberdunkeln zu dir:
es herrschte
Lichtzwang.

---

singed by
spraying blaze-air.

A sign
combs it together
as answer for a
brooding rockart.

GONE INTO THE NIGHT, helperish,
a star-
permeable leaf
instead of the mouth:

something remains
for wild wasting,
treeward.

WE ALREADY LAY
deep in the underbrush, when you
finally crept along.
But we could not
darken over toward you:
there reigned
lightduress.

TRETMINEN auf deinen linken
Monden, Saturn.

Scherbenversiegelt
die Umlaufbahnen dort draußen.

Es muß jetzt der Augenblick sein
für eine gerechte
Geburt.

WER SCHLUG SICH ZU DIR?
Der lerchengestaltige
Stein aus der Brache.
Kein Ton, nur das Sterbelicht trägt
an ihm mit.

Die Höhe
wirbelt sich
aus, heftiger noch
als ihr.

ABGLANZBELADEN, bei den
Himmelskäfern,
im Berg.

CONTACT MINES on your left
moons, Saturn.

Shardsealed
the orbits out there.

Now must be the moment
for a just
birth.

WHO SIDED WITH YOU?
The lark-shaped
stone from the fallow.
No sound, only the deathwatchlight lends
a hand.

The height
whirls itself
out, more fiercely even
than you.

REFLECTION-LADEN, by the
heavensbeetles,
in the mountain.

Den Tod,
den du mir schuldig bliebst, ich
trag ihn
aus.

FREIGEGEBEN auch dieser
Start.

Bugradgesang mit
Corona.

Das Dämmerruder spricht an,
deine wach-
gerissene Vene
knotet sich aus,

was du noch bist, legt sich schräg,
du gewinnst
Höhe.

BAKEN-
sammler, nächtlings,
die Hucke voll,
am Fingerende den Leitstrahl,

The death
you owed me, I
carry it
out.

—————————————————————————————

CLEARED, this start
also.

Bow-wheelchant with
fermata.

The duskrudder responds,
your torn-
awake vein
unknots itself,

what's left of you, slants,
you gain
altitude.

—————————————————————————————

BEACON-
collector, nightly,
a bellyful,
at finger's tip the guide beam,

für ihn, den einen an-
fliegenden
Wortstier.

Baken-
meister.

AUS VERLORNEM Gegossene du,
maskengerecht,

die Lid-
falte entlang
mit der eignen
Lidfalte dir nah sein,

die Spur und die Spur
mit Grauem bestreun,
endlich, tödlich.

WAS UNS
zusammenwarf,
schrickt auseinander,

ein Weltstein, sonnenfern,
summt.

---

for him, the single lan-
ding
wordbull.

Beacon-
master.

A YOU, cast in lost matter,
accurate to the mask,

along the lid-
crease with
one's own
lidcrease to be near you,

the trace and the trace
to strew it with gray,
final, deathly.

WHAT THREW
us together,
scare-scatters,

a worldstone, sun-distant,
hums.

II

EINMAL, der Tod hatte Zulauf,
verbargst du dich in mir.

BEILSCHWÄRME
über uns,

Gespräche
mit Tüllenäxten im Tiefland –

Inselflur du,
mit der dich
übernebelnden
Hoffnung.

VORGEWUSST blutet
zweimal hinter dem Vorhang,

Mitgewußt
perlt

II

ONCE, death was much in demand,
you hid in me.

HATCHETSWARMS
above us,

conversations
with socket-axes in the lowland—

Islandpasture, you,
with the hope
fogging you
in.

PRECOGNITION bleeds
twice behind the curtain,

Cognizance
pearls

BEI BRANCUSI, ZU ZWEIT

Wenn dieser Steine einer
verlauten ließe,
was ihn verschweigt:
hier, nahebei,
am Humpelstock dieses Alten,
tät es sich auf, als Wunde,
in die du zu tauchen hättst,
einsam,
fern meinem Schrei, dem schon mit-
behauenen, weißen.

WO ICH mich in dir vergaß,
wardst du Gedanke,

etwas
rauscht durch uns beide:
der Welt erste
der letzten
Schwingen,

mir wächst
das Fell zu überm
gewittrigen
Mund,

TWO AT BRANCUSI'S

If one among these stones
were to tell
what conceals it:
here, nearby,
on the old man's crutch-stick,
it would open, as a wound,
into which you'd have to dive,
lonely,
far from my scream, the already also
hewn, white one.

WHERE I forgot myself in you,
you became thought,

something
rushes through us both:
the world's first
of the last
wings,

the hide
spreads over my
storm-riddled
mouth,

du
kommst nicht
zu
dir.

SEIT LANGEM bestiegener Schlammkahn.

Ein ab-
gesprungener
Knopf
tüftelt an jeder Ranunkel,

die Stunde, die Kröte,
hebt ihre Welt aus den Angeln.

Wenn ich die Karrenspur fräße,
wär ich dabei.

TODTNAUBERG

Arnika, Augentrost, der
Trunk aus dem Brunnen mit dem
Sternwürfel drauf,

in der
Hütte,

you
come not
to
you.

LONG AGO boarded mudskiff.

A but-
ton, come
off,
nitpicks every buttercup,

the hour, the toad,
takes its world off the hinges.

If I gulped down the cartrut,
I'd be there too.

TODTNAUBERG

Arnica, eyebright, the
draft from the well with the
star-die on top,

in the
Hütte,

die in das Buch
– wessen Namen nahms auf
vor dem meinen? –,
die in dies Buch
geschriebene Zeile von
einer Hoffnung, heute,
auf eines Denkenden
kommendes
Wort
im Herzen,

Waldwasen, uneingeebnet,
Orchis und Orchis, einzeln,

Krudes, später, im Fahren,
deutlich,

der uns fährt, der Mensch,
der's mit anhört,

die halb-
beschrittenen Knüppel-
pfade im Hochmoor,

Feuchtes,
viel.

———————————————————————

SINK mir weg
aus der Armbeuge,

written in the book
—whose name did it record
before mine?—,
in this book
the line about
a hope, today,
for a thinker's
word
to come,
in the heart,

forest sward, unleveled,
orchis and orchis, singly,

raw exchanges, later, while driving,
clearly,

he who drives us, the mensch,
he also hears it,

the half-
trod log-
trails on the highmoor,

humidity,
much.

SINK away from
the crook of my arm,

nimm den Einen
Pulsschlag mit,

verbirg dich darin,
draußen.

JETZT, da die Betschemel brennen,
eß ich das Buch
mit allen
Insignien.

EINEM BRUDER IN ASIEN

Die selbstverklärten
Geschütze
fahren gen Himmel,

zehn
Bomber gähnen,

ein Schnellfeuer blüht,
so gewiß wie der Frieden,

eine Handvoll Reis
erstirbt als dein Freund.

---

take the One
pulse beat along,

hide yourself in it,
outside.

Now, that the prayerstools burn,
I eat the book
with all the
insignia.

TO A BROTHER IN ASIA

The auto-transfigured
cannons
drive toward heaven,

ten
bombers yawn,

a running fire blooms,
as surely as peace,

a handful of rice
expires as your friend.

ANGEREMPELT beim Wahngang
von einem, der las:
Grind und Schorf. Schorf und Grind.

In die Schlafgrätsche gehn, o einmal.

WIE DU dich ausstirbst in mir:

noch im letzten
zerschlissenen
Knoten Atems
steckst du mit einem
Splitter
Leben.

HIGHGATE

Es geht ein Engel durch die Stube –:
du, dem unaufgeschlagenen Buch nah,
sprichst mich
wiederum los.

Zweimal findet das Heidekraut Nahrung.
Zweimal erblaßts.

JOSTLED along the delusion-run
by someone who read:
Scab and scurf. Scurf and scab.

To vault the sleep-buck, O once.

HOW YOU die out in me:

even in the last
threadbare
breath-knot
you stick with one
splinter
life.

HIGHGATE

An angel walks through the room—:
you, close to the unopened book,
absolve me
once again.

Twice the heather finds nourishment.
Twice it pales.

BLITZGESCHRECKT, unverwandelt, kaum
gesträubt:
        Géricaults
           Pferd,
              schon
von deinen Nadelblicken geheilt
über und über.

Noch hier in diesem
Gewitter
reitest du's zu.

Ein Trittstein, noch fern deinem Fuß,
winkt mit der einen
rötlichen
Strähne aus meinem Bart.

———————————————

III

WURFSCHEIBE, mit
Vorgesichten besternt,

wirf dich

aus dir hinaus.

———————————————

BY LIGHTNING SCARED, untransformed, barely
balking:
       Géricault's
             horse,
                  already
healed by your needle-glances
over and over.

Even here in this
thunderstorm
you break it in.

A stepstone, still far from your foot,
waves with the one
reddish
strand from my beard.

III

DISCUS, bestarred
with pre-faces,

throw yourself

out of yourself.

KLOPF die
Lichtkeile weg:

das schwimmende Wort
hat der Dämmer.

———————————————————————————

DIE ENTSPRUNGENEN
Graupapageien
lesen die Messe
in deinem Mund.

Du hörsts regnen
und meinst, auch diesmal
sei's Gott.

———————————————————————————

IN DEN DUNKELSCHLÄGEN erfuhr ichs:

du lebst auf mich zu, dennoch,
im Steigrohr,
im
Steigrohr.

———————————————————————————

STREUBESITZ, staub-
unmittelbar.

KNOCK the
lightwedges off:

dusk has
the swimming word.

THE ESCAPED
gray parrots
say mass
in your mouth.

You hear the rain
and guess, this time too
it's God.

IN THE DARKCLEARINGS I learned it:

you live toward me, nevertheless,
in the standpipe,
in the
standpipe.

SCATTERED PROPERTY, dust-
immediate.

Abend um Abend schweben
die den Gedanken entzognen
Botschaften ein,
königshart, nachthart,
in die Hände der Klage-
vögte:

aus dem Knick
ihrer Lebens-
linien
tritt lautlos die Antwort:
der eine ewige
Tropfen
Gold.

DER VON DEN UNBESCHRIEBENEN
Blättern
abgelesene Brief,

der Totstell-Reflexe
grausilberne Kette darauf,
gefolgt von drei silbernen
Takten.

Du weißt: der Sprung
geht über dich, immer.

Evening after evening
the messages, withdrawn from
the thoughts, drift in,
king-hard, night-hard,
into the hands of the grievance-
reeves:

from the break
of their life-
lines
the answer steps soundless:
the one eternal
drop of
gold.

THE LETTER READ FROM
the unwritten
pages,

the play-dead reflex's
graysilver chain on it,
followed by three silver
beats.

You know: the leap
goes over you, always.

SCHNEID DIE GEBETSHAND
aus
der Luft
mit der Augen-
schere,
kapp ihre Finger
mit deinem Kuß:

Gefaltetes geht jetzt
atemberaubend vor sich.

WAS ES AN STERNEN BEDARF,
schüttet sich aus,

deiner Hände laubgrüner Schatten
sammelt es ein,

freudig zerbeiß ich
das münzenkernige
Schicksal.

ICH KANN DICH NOCH SEHEN: ein Echo,
ertastbar mit Fühl-
wörtern, am Abschieds-
grat.

CUT THE PRAYERHAND
from
the air
with the eye-
scissors,
lop off its fingers
with your kiss:

What's folded now happens
breathtakingly.

WHAT'S REQUIRED AS STARS
pours itself out,

your hands' leafgreen shadow
gathers it in,

joyously I crunch
the coin-pithy
destiny.

I CAN STILL SEE YOU: an echo,
palpable with feel-
words, at the departure-
ridge.

Dein Gesicht scheut leise,
wenn es auf einmal
lampenhaft hell wird
in mir, an der Stelle,
wo man am schmerzlichsten Nie sagt.

―――――――――――――――――――――

LAUTER
Einzelkinder
mit leisen, moorigen
Muttergerüchen im Hals,
zu Bäumen – zu Schwarz-
erlen – erkoren,
duftlos.

―――――――――――――――――――――

IM LEEREN
wo sich die Kuttel rankt
mit der Bregen-
Blüte,
warf ich mich Steinen zu,
die fingen mich auf
und bekrönten ein Rund
mit dem, was ich wurde.

―――――――――――――――――――――

Your face shies quietly,
when all at once
lamplike it lights up
inside me, at that place
where one most painfully says Never.

NOTHING BUT
single children
with faint, moory
mothersmells in the throat,
as trees—as black-
alders—elected,
scentless.

IN THE VOID
where the chitlins wind
around the brains-
blossom,
I threw myself toward stones,
they caught me
and crowned a round
with what I became.

DIE LEHMIGEN OPFERGÜSSE,
von Schnecken umkrochen:

das Bild der Welt,
dem Himmel entgegengetragen
auf einem Brombeerblatt.

DAS WILDHERZ, verhäuslicht
vom halbblinden Stich

in die Lunge,

Veratmetes sprudelt,

langsam, blutunterwaschen
konfiguriert sich
das selten verheißne
rechte
Neben-
leben.

IV

DIE EWIGKEITEN fuhren
ihm ins Gesicht und drüber
hinaus,

THE LOAMY SACRIFICE DOWNPOURS,
circled by snails:

the image of the world,
carried heavenward
on a blackberry-leaf.

THE WILDHEART, dishoused
by the halfblind stab

in the lung,

disbreathed bubbles,

slowly, bloodunderwashed
the rarely promised
right
by-
life
configures itself.

IV

THE ETERNITIES went
for his face and beyond
it,

langsam löschte ein Brand
alles Gekerzte,

ein Grün, nicht von hier,
umflaumte das Kinn
des Steins, den die Waisen
begruben und wieder
begruben.

HERZSCHALL-FIBELN, eingezäunt,

das Kranichpaar
denkt sich dir vor,

aspektral
verschenkt sich das Licht deiner Blume,

dem Fangbein der Mantis
begegnet dein über-
sterniges
Immer.

ANEINANDER
müde geworden,
randgängerisch,
mündig,

slowly a blaze put out
everything candled,

a green, not from here,
bedowned the chin of
the stone, which the orphans
buried and again
buried.

HEARTSOUND-FIBULAS, fenced in,

the pair of cranes
thinks itself before you,

aspectral
the light of your flower bestows itself,

the mantis's trapleg
meets your over-
starry
Always.

GROWN WEARY
of each other,
roaming the margins,
come of age,

Luft
schaufelt sich zu, auch
Wasser,

die Kartenschlägerin klebt
erschlagen hinterm
Herz-As.

EIN EXTRA-SCHLAG NACHT
ist das Teil
des von fernher un-
versehrt
gefangengenommenen
Sohnes.

Eine Stimme, inmitten,
erkräht ein Gesicht.

HINTER FROSTGEBÄNDERTEN KÄFERN
ballert das fahrende
Leuchtglück,

eine hilflose
Bauchfratze, Freund,
schläfert dich
ein.

---

air
shovels itself up, water
too,

the fortune-teller, slain, she
sticks to the back of the
ace of hearts.

AN EXTRA DOLLOP OF NIGHT
is the share
of the from afar un-
damaged
captured
son.

A voice, amidst,
a-crows a face.

BEHIND FROSTSTREAKED BEETLES
the driving lighthappiness
bangs away,

a helpless
belly-grimace, friend,
lulls you to
sleep.

DIE IRIN, die abschiedsgefleckte,
beliest deine Hand,
schneller als
schnell.

Ihrer Blicke Bläue durchwächst sie,
Verlust und Gewinn
in einem:

du,
augenfingrige
Ferne.

DIE MIR HINTERLASSNE
balkengekreuzte
Eins:

an ihr soll ich rätseln,
während du, im Rupfengewand,
am Geheimnisstrumpf strickst.

VERWORFENE, not-
freundliche,
kunkelbeinige
Göttin:

THE IRISHWOMAN, farewell-stained,
reads into your hand,
faster than
fast.

Her gaze's blue marbles it,
loss and gain
in one:

you,
eye-fingery
distance.

THE LEFT-TO-ME
beamcrossed
One:

I am to puzzle it out,
while you, in sackcloth,
knit at the secretstocking.

REPUDIATED, need-
friendly,
distaff-legged
goddess:

Wo du dich auftust, im Kniesitz,
dreht sich ein wissendes Messer
um seine Achse,
im Gegenblut-
Sinn.

FERTIGUNGS-
HALLE:

Blendeffekte, im Dämmer,

– auf dir, denk,
ruhte die heilende Hand unterm auf-
zuckenden Schein –

das Schutzwort
im Überdruckhelm,
ein Zeichen im Satz
als Frischluftgerät.

Schweißung der Seelen, Kurzlicht.

In den Boxen:
Beatmung
des reimigen, schönen
Metallbalgs.

Where you open up, in the kneeseat,
a knowing knife turns
on its axis,
in counterblood-
sense.

PRODUCTION-
HANGAR:

Glare-effects, at dusk,

—on you, imagine,
rested the healing hand under the flash-
ing sheen—

the guardian-word
in the overpressure-helmet,
a sign in the sentence
as fresh-air-machine.

Welding of the souls, shortlight.

In the blast bays: application of
artificial respiration to
the rhymy, beautiful
metal bellows.

IN DER BLASENKAMMER erwacht
das Entatmete, der
gefährliche Keimling,

an seinem Krater-
ende
springt das Drittauge auf
und speit
Porphyr, auch
Pein.

MAGNETISCHE BLÄUE im Mund,
erkeuchst du Pol um Pol,

gesömmerter Schnee
wirft sich drüber,

bald hängt der taumlige Star
im doppelten Liedschwarm.

VORFLUT
kämmt deine Algen zusammen,
legt sie
um dich.
Eingedämmt wuchert,
was du noch hast.

IN THE VESICLE CHAMBER the
disbreathed wakes up, the
dangerous embryo,

at its crater–
end
sprouts the thirdeye
and spits
porphyry, also
pain.

MAGNETIC BLUE in mouth,
you gasp-gain pole after pole,

summered snow
throws itself on top,

soon the staggering starling hangs
in the double songswarm.

OUTFALL
combs your algae together,
lays them
around you.
What you still have
grows rampant, dammed in.

Ein weißer Stirnsplitter geht
für dich über die Grenze.

DIE MANTIS, wieder,
im Nacken des Worts,
in das du geschlüpft warst –,

muteinwärts
wandert der Sinn,
sinneinwärts
der Mut.

KEIN HALBHOLZ mehr, hier
in den Gipfelhängen,
kein mit-
sprechender
Thymian.

Grenzschnee und sein
die Pfähle und deren
Wegweiser-Schatten
aushorchender, tot-
sagender
Duft.

A white forehead-splinter goes
for you across the border.

THE MANTIS, again,
in the nape of the word
into which you had slipped—,

courage-inward
wanders meaning,
meaning-inward,
courage.

No HALFWOOD anymore, here,
on the peakslopes,
no con-
versing
thyme.

Bordersnow and
—sounding
out, death-
saying the stakes and their
waypost-shadows—its
odor.

SCHWIMMHÄUTE zwischen den Worten,

ihr Zeithof –
ein Tümpel,

Graugrätiges hinter
dem Leuchtschopf
Bedeutung.

ANREDSAM
war die ein-
flüglig schwebende Amsel,
über der Brandmauer, hinter
Paris, droben,
im
Gedicht.

V

ORANIENSTRASSE 1

Mir wuchs Zinn in die Hand,
ich wußte mir nicht
zu helfen:
modeln mochte ich nicht,
lesen mocht es mich nicht –

WEBBING between the words,

their timehalo—
a slough,

graycrestedness behind
the lightmane
meaning.

———————————————————

ADDRESSABLE
was the one-
winged soaring blackbird,
above the firewall, behind
Paris, up there,
in the
poem.

———————————————————

V

ORANIENSTRASSE 1

Tin grew in my hand
I didn't know how
to help myself:
I didn't want to mold,
it didn't want to read me—

Wenn sich jetzt
Ossietzkys letzte
Trinkschale fände,
ließ ich das Zinn
von ihr lernen,

und das Heer der Pilger-
stäbe
durchschwiege, durchstünde die Stunde.

BRUNNEN-
artig
ins Verwunschne getieft,
mit doppelt gewalmten
Tagträumen drüber,

Quader-
ringe
um jeden Hauch:

die Kammer, wo ich dich ließ, hockend,
dich zu behalten,

das Herz befehligt
den uns leise bestrickenden Frost
an den geschiedenen
Fronten,

If now
Ossietzky's last
drinking bowl
could be found,
I'd let the tin
learn from it,

and the host of pilgrims'
staffs
would ensilence, endure the hour.

WELL-
like
depthed into the enchanted,
with double-hipped
daydreams above,

ashlar-
rings
around each breath:

the chamber, where I left you, crouching,
to keep you,

the heart commands
the frost quietly fascinating us
at the separate
fronts,

du wirst keine Blume sein
auf Urnenfeldern
und mich, den Schriftträger, holt
kein Erz aus der runden
Holz-Lehm-Hütte, kein
Engel.

MIT TRAUMANTRIEB auf der Kreisbahn,
an-
geschwelt,

zwei Masken statt einer,
Planetenstaub in den gehöhlten
Augen,

nachtblind, tagblind,
weltblind,

die Mohnkapsel in dir
geht irgendwo nieder,
beschweigt
einen Mitstern,

die schwimmende Trauerdomäne
vermerkt einen weiteren Schatten,

es helfen dir alle,

you'll be no flower
in urnfields
and me, the scriptbearer, no
ore, no arch takes me from the round
wood-mud-hut, no
angel.

WITH DREAMPROPULSION in orbit,
smolder-
singed,

two masks instead of one,
planetdust in the caved
eyes,

nightblind, dayblind,
worldblind,

the poppy head in you
lands somewhere,
besilences
an also-star,

the swimming mourning-domain
records a further shadow,

they all help you,

der Herzstein durchstößt seinen Fächer,
keinerlei
Kühle,

es helfen dir alle,

du segelst, verglimmst und verglost,

Augenschwärme passieren die Enge,
ein Blutkloß schwenkt ein auf die Bahn,
Erdschwärme sprechen dir zu,
das Wetter im All
hält Ernte.

FÜR DEN LERCHENSCHATTEN
brachgelegt das Verborgne,

un-
verhärtet
eingebracht die erfahrene
Stille, ein Acker, inslig,
im Feuer,

nach der
abgesättigten Hoffnung,
nach allem
abgezweigten Geschick:

the heartstone pierces its fan,
no kind of
coolness,

they all help you,

you sail, smolder, and die down,

eyeswarms pass the narrows,
a blood clump swings into the orbit,
earthswarms encourage you,
the weather in outer space
begins to harvest.

FOR THE LARKSHADOW
laid fallow: the hidden

un-
hardened,
brought in: the experienced
stillness, a field, islandy,
in the fire,

after the
saturated hope,
after all
branched off fate:

die unbußfertig ersungenen
Moosopfer, wo du

mich suchst, blindlings.

DER DURCHSCHNITTENE Taubenkordon,
die gesprengten
Blütengewalten,

die tatverdächtige
Fundsache Seele.

FAHLSTIMMIG, aus
der Tiefe geschunden:
kein Wort, kein Ding,
und beider einziger Name,

fallgerecht in dir,
fluggerecht in dir,

wunder Gewinn
einer Welt.

---

the unrepentant, sung up
moss-victims, where you

search for me, blindly.

THE CUT-THROUGH dove-cordon,
the blasted
blossom-powers,

the suspected
found object, soul.

WAN-VOICED, ha-
rassed from the deep:
not a word, not a thing,
and of both the single name,

fall-true in you,
flight-true in you,

sore gain
of a world.

SCHALLTOTES SCHWESTERGEHÄUS,
laß die Zwerglaute ein,
die ausgefragten:
sie mummeln das Großherz zusammen
und tragen es huckepack zu
jeder Not, jeder Not.

WETTERFÜHLIGE HAND,
die Moorlache weist ihr den Weg,
nachts, durch den Bruchwald.

Lumineszenz.

Wer jetzt die Bälge der Torforgel tritt, ein-
beinig, der
gewinnt einen Starkstrahl
Verlust.

IM ZEITWINKEL SCHWÖRT
die entschleierte Erle
still vor sich hin,

auf dem Erdrücken, handspannenbreit,
hockt die durchschossene
Lunge,

SOUNDDEAD SISTERSHELL,
let the dwarftones in,
the interrogated:
they mumble the greatheart together
and carry it piggyback to
every plight, every plight.

WEATHERSENSING HAND,
the moorpool shows it the way,
at night, through the fenwood.

Luminescence.

Who now works the bellows of the peatorgan, one-
legged, will
win a strongstream
loss.

IN TIME'S CORNER the
unveiled alder swears
under its breath,

on earth's back, wide as a hand,
crouches the shot-through
lung,

an der Flurgrenze pickt
die Flügelstunde das Schneekorn
aus dem eigenen Steinaug,

Lichtbänder stecken mich an,
Kronschäden flackern.

AUCH MICH, den wie du Geborenen, hält keine Hand,
und keine wirft mir ein Glück in die Stunde, nicht anders als dir,
dem wie ich in Stierblut Getauchten,

doch stehen die Zahlen bereit, der Träne zu leuchten,
die in die Welt schnellt
aus unserm Nabel,

doch geht in die große Silbenschrift ein,
was uns nah kam, einzeln,

und die Mandelhode
gewittert
und blüht.

DIE RÜCKWÄRTSGESPROCHENEN
Namen, alle,

at the field's boundary the
winghour picks the snowcorn
from its own stone-eye,

lightbands set me afire,
crown-damages flicker.

ME TOO, who am born like you, no hand holds,
and none throws me a happiness into the hour, no different from you,
dipped like I into bull's blood,

yet the numbers stand ready to light the tear,
leaping into the world
from our navel,

yet what came near us, singly,
enters the great syllable-script,

and the almond-testicle
thunders
and blooms.

THE BACKWARDSPOKEN
names, all,

der äußerste, zum
König gewiehert
vor Rauhreifspiegeln,

umlagert, umstellt
von Mehrlingsgeburten,

der Zinnenriß durch ihn,
der dich Vereinzelten
mitmeint.

ALLMÄHLICH CLOWNGESICHTIG,
nichtsgespiegelt,

die Schminke Wahrheit blaugefrorn
im Winkelmund,

Frostpollen Puder auf dem blanken Überschädel,
rund um die dünne Fragelocke Schwarz,

die Brauen, Brauen: wachsend,
zwei Riesenfühlerkämme, zwei,
– du großgestrählte,
großgespürte Rauhnacht Immerimmer –,
schon fortgeschwungen aus der Flocke Welt,
nicht hin, nicht her.

the outmost, whinnied
into kinghood
before hoarfrost-mirrors,

beleaguered, besieged
by multiple births,

the merlon-cleft through it,
which means you, isolato,
also.

GRADUALLY CLOWNFACED
nothingmirrored,

the cosmetics, truth, frozen blue
in the angle-mouth,

frostpollen powder on the blank superskull,
round about the thin questionlock Black,

the brows, the brows: growing,
two giant feelercombs, two
—you, tall-streaked,
large-felt roughnight Alwaysalways—,
already swung away from the flake world,
not to, not fro.

SPERRTONNENSPRACHE, Sperrtonnenlied.
Die Dampfwalze wummert
die zweite
Ilias
ins aufgerissene
Pflaster,

sandgesäumt
staunen die alten
Bilder sich nach, in die Gosse,

ölig verbluten die Krieger
in Silberpfützen, am Straßen-
rand, tuckernd,

Troja, das staubbekrönte,
sieht ein.

UNTER DER FLUT
fliegen, an
gehöhten schwarzen
Opfersteinen vorbei,

die unendlich geerdete Schwermut
in den
Fahrwerkschächten,

berauschte Flugschreiber im
Sehnsuchtsgehänge,

ROADBLOCKBUOY LANGUAGE, roadblockbuoy song.
The steamroller thrumps
the second
Iliad
into the torn-up
pavement,

sandseamed
the old images
surprise themselves, into the gutter,

the warriors bleed to death oily
in silver puddles, on the road-
side, thudding,

Troy, dust-crowned,
gets it.

TO FLY UNDER
the flood, past
raised black
sacrifice stones,

unendingly earthed melancholy
in the
undercarriage shafts,

drunken flightwriters on
the yearning-slope,

künftige Fundstücke, silbrig,
im
schädligen Cockpit,

Sichttunnels, in
den Sprachnebel geblasen,

Selbstzündblumen
an allen Kabeln,

im großen, unausgefahrenen
Felgenring deinen
genabten Schatten,
Saturn.

VI

WAHNGÄNGER-AUGEN: in euch
münden die übrigen Blicke.

Eine einzige
Flut
schwillt an.

Bald glänzt ihr
den Felsen zutode, auf den sie

future found objects, silvery,
in
the cockpit's skullery,

sight tunnels, blown
into the speechfog,

self-sparkflowers
on all cables,

in the great, unextended
rimring your
hubbed shadow,
Saturn.

VI

DELUSIONSTALKER EYES: in you
end up the rest of the gazes.

A single
flood
swills up.

Soon you brighten
the rock to death, on which they

gesetzt
haben, wider
sich selbst.

SPERRIGES MORGEN,
ich beiße mich in dich, ich schweige mich an dich,

wir tönen,
allein,

pastos
vertropfen die Ewigkeitsklänge,
durchquäkt
von heutigem
Gestern,

wir fahren,

groß
nimmt uns der letzte
Schallbecher auf:

den beschleunigten Herzschritt
draußen
im Raum,
bei ihr, der Erd-
achse.

have
bet, against
themselves.

UNWIELDY MORROW,
I bite myself into you, I silence myself at you,

we resound,
alone,

the pastose
eternity-chimes drip away,
squawked through
by today's
yesterday,

we drive,

grandly
does the last soundbell
take us in:

the accelerated heartstep
outside
in space,
near her, the earth–
axis.

MERKBLÄTTER-SCHMERZ,
beschneit, überschneit:

in der Kalenderlücke
wiegt ihn, wiegt ihn
das neugeborene
Nichts.

STREU OCKER in meine Augen:
du lebst nicht
mehr drin,

spar
mit Grab-
beigaben, spar,

schreite die Steinreihen ab,
auf den Händen,

mit ihrem Traum
streich über die
ausgemünzte
Schläfenbeinschuppe,

an der
großen
Gabelung er-
zähl dich dem Ocker
dreimal, neunmal.

NOTEPAPER-PAIN,
besnowed, oversnowed:

in the calendargap
he's cradled, he's cradled
by the newborn
nothing.

—————————

STREW OCHER into my eyes:
you no longer
live there,

save
on the tomb-
furnishings, save,

pace off the stonerows,
on your hands,

with their dream
paint over the
stamped-out
temporal bone's squama,

at the
great
bifurcation re-
count yourself to the ocher
three times, nine times.

SCHWANENGEFAHR,
Lappentaucher-
Bedrohung,

der Eisbewimperte mit
Kraken-
armen,

du, bekrallter
Jakuten-
Puschkin:

Hei, Chebeldei, Chebeldei.

SCHALTJAHRHUNDERTE, Schalt-
sekunden, Schalt-
geburten, novembernd, Schalt-
tode,

in Wabentrögen gespeichert,
bits
on chips,

das Menoragedicht aus Berlin,

SWANDANGER,
grebe-
threat,

the icelashed with
kraken-
arms,

you, clawed
Yakut–
Pushkin:

Hei, Chebeldei, Chebeldei.

LEAPCENTURIES, leap-
seconds, leap-
births, novembering, leap-
deaths,

stocked in honeycomb-troughs,
bits
on chips,

the menorah-poem from Berlin,

(Unasyliert, un-
archiviert, un-
umfürsorgt? Am
Leben?),

Lesestationen im Spätwort,

Sparflammenpunkte
am Himmel,

Kammlinien unter Beschuß,

Gefühle, frost-
gespindelt,

Kaltstart –
mit Hämoglobin.

QUELLPUNKTE, nachts,
auf den Fernstrecken,
göttergewärtig,

deine Ausläufer, Hirnberg,
im Herz-Du,
von ihnen
umschäumt.

(Unasylumed, un–
archived, un–
cared for? A
-live?),

reading stations in the late-word,

dotted pilotlights line
the sky,

crestlines under fire,

feelings, frost–
spindled,

cold start—
with hemoglobin.

SOURCEPOINTS, at night,
on the expressways,
expectant of the gods,

your foothills, Brainmountain,
in the heart-you,
by them
foamed around.

TRECKSCHUTENZEIT,
die Halbverwandelten schleppen
an einer der Welten,

der Enthöhte, geinnigt,
spricht unter den Stirnen am Ufer:

Todes quitt, Gottes
quitt.

DU SEI WIE DU, immer.

*Stant up Jherosalem inde
erheyff dich*

Auch wer das Band zerschnitt zu dir hin,

*inde wirt
erluchtet*

knüpfte es neu, in der Gehugnis,

Schlammbrocken schluckt ich, im Turm,

Sprache, Finster-Lisene,

*kumi
ori.*

TREKSCOWTIME,
the halftransformed pull
at one of the worlds,

the diselevated one, interiorized,
speaks under the foreheads on the bank:

Quits with death, quits with
God.

YOU BE LIKE YOU, always.

Stant up Jherosalem inde
erheyff dich

Even he who cut the band with you,

inde wirt
erluchtet

tied it anew, in the gehugnis,

mudclots I swallowed, in the tower,

language, dark pilaster strip,

kumi
ori.

WIRK NICHT VORAUS,
sende nicht aus,
steh
herein:

durchgründet vom Nichts,
ledig allen
Gebets,
feinfügig, nach
der Vor-Schrift,
unüberholbar,

nehm ich dich auf,
statt aller
Ruhe.

DO NOT WORK AHEAD,
do not send out,
stand
inward:

transgrounded by the void,
free of all
prayer,
fine-fugued, according to
Writ's pre-Script,
not overtakable,

I take you in,
instead of any
rest.

Schneepart

Snowpart

I

UNGEWASCHEN, UNBEMALT,
In der Jenseits-
Kaue:

da,
wo wir uns finden,
Erdige, immer,

ein
verspätetes
Becherwerk geht
durch uns Zerwölkte hindurch,
nach oben, nach unten,

aufrührerisch
flötets darin, mit Narren-
beinen,

der Flugschatten im
irisierenden Rund
heilt uns ein, in der Sieben-
höhe,

eiszeitlich nah
steuert das Filzschwanenpaar
durch die schwebende
Stein-Ikone

I

UNWASHED, UNPAINTED,
in Hereafter's
pithead:

there
where we find ourselves,
Earthy, always,

a
belated
bucket conveyor pierces
us cloudtorn,
upward, downward,

seditious
piping inside, on Fool's
legs,

the flightshadow in
the iridescing round
heals us in, into seven-
heighth,

ice-age-close
the feltswan pair steers
through the hovering
stone-icon

DU LIEGST im großen Gelausche,
umbuscht, umflockt.

Geh du zur Spree, geh zur Havel,
geh zu den Fleischerhaken,
zu den roten Äppelstaken
aus Schweden –

Es kommt der Tisch mit den Gaben,
er biegt um ein Eden –

Der Mann ward zum Sieb, die Frau
mußte schwimmen, die Sau,
für sich, für keinen, für jeden –

Der Landwehrkanal wird nicht rauschen.
Nichts
      stockt.

LILA LUFT mit gelben Fensterflecken,

der Jakobsstab überm
Anhalter Trumm,

Kokelstunde, noch nichts
Interkurrierendes,

YOU LIE in the great listening,
ambushed, snowed in.

Go to the Spree, go to the Havel,
go to the butcher hooks,
to the red apple stakes
from Sweden—

Here comes the table with the presents,
he turns around an Eden—

The man became a sieve, the woman
had to swim, the sow,
for herself, for none, for everyone—

The Landwehr canal will not roar.
Nothing
        stalls.

LILAC AIR with yellow windowstains,

Orion's belt above the
Anhalter ruin,

flamehour, nothing
intercurrent yet,

von der
Stehkneipe zur
Schneekneipe.

BRUNNENGRÄBER im Wind:

es wird einer die Bratsche spielen, tagabwärts, im Krug,
es wird einer kopfstehn im Wort Genug,
es wird einer kreuzbeinig hängen im Tor, bei der Winde.

Dies Jahr
rauscht nicht hinüber,
es stürzt den Dezember zurück, den November,
es gräbt seine Wunden um,
es öffnet sich dir, junger
Gräber-
brunnen,
Zwölfmund.

DAS ANGEBROCHENE JAHR
mit dem modernen Kanten
Wahnbrot.

Trink
aus meinem Mund.

---

from
standing bar to
snow bar.

WELLDIGGER in the wind:

someone will play the viola, day downward, in the alehouse,
someone will stand on his head in the word Enough,
someone will hang crosslegged in the gateway, next to the winch.

This year
does not roar across,
it throws back December, November,
it turns up its wounds,
it opens up to you, young
grave-
well,
twelvemouth.

THE BREACHED YEAR
with the moldering crust
delusion bread.

Drink
from my mouth.

UNLESBARKEIT dieser
Welt. Alles doppelt.

Die starken Uhren
geben der Spaltstunde recht,
heiser.

Du, in dein Tiefstes geklemmt,
entsteigst dir
für immer.

HURIGES SONST. Und die Ewigkeit
blutschwarz umbabelt.

Vermurt
von deinen lehmigen Locken
mein Glaube.

Zwei Finger, handfern,
errudern den moorigen
Schwur.

WAS NÄHT
an dieser Stimme? Woran
näht diese
Stimme
diesseits, jenseits?

UNREADABILITY of this
world. Everything doubles.

The strong clocks
agree with the fissure-hour,
hoarsely.

You, wedged into your deepest,
climb out of yourself
forever.

WHORISH ELSE. And eternity
bloodblack circumbabeled.

Mudflood-swamped
by your loamy locks,
my faith.

Two fingers, far from the hand,
a-row the moory
oath.

WHAT SEWS
at this voice? On what
does this
voice
sew
hither, beyond?

Die Abgründe sind
eingeschworen auf Weiß, ihnen
entstieg
die Schneenadel,

schluck sie,

du ordnest die Welt,
das zählt
soviel wie neun Namen,
auf Knien genannt,

Tumuli, Tumuli,
du
hügelst hinweg, lebendig,
komm
in den Kuß,

ein Flossenschlag,
stet,
lichtet die Buchten,
du gehst
vor Anker, dein Schatten
streift dich ab im Gebüsch,

Ankunft,
Abkunft,

ein Käfer erkennt dich,
ihr steht euch

The chasms are
sworn in on White, from them
arose
the snowneedle,

swallow it,

you order the world,
that counts
as much as nine names,
named on knees,

tumuli, tumuli,
you
hill away, alive,
come
into the kiss,

a flip of the fin,
steady,
lights up the bays,
you drop
anchor, your shadow
strips you off on the bush,

arrival,
descent,

a chafer recognizes you,
you approach

bevor,
Raupen
spinnen euch ein,

die Große
Kugel
gewährt euch den Durchzug,

bald
knüpft das Blatt seine Ader an deine,
Funken
müssen hindurch,
eine Atemnot lang,

es steht dir ein Baum zu, ein Tag,
er entziffert die Zahl,

ein Wort, mit all seinem Grün,
geht in sich, verpflanzt sich,

folg ihm

ICH HÖRE, DIE AXT HAT GEBLÜHT,
ich höre, der Ort ist nicht nennbar,

ich höre, das Brot, das ihn ansieht,
heilt den Erhängten,
das Brot, das ihm die Frau buk,

each other,
caterpillars
spin you in,

the Great
Sphere
grants you passage through,

soon
the leaf buttons its vein to yours,
sparks
have to cross through
for the length of a breathdistress,

you are entitled to a tree, a day,
it decodes the number,

a word with all its green
enters itself, transplants itself,

follow it

I HEAR THE AXE HAS BLOSSOMED,
I hear the place is unnamable,

I hear the bread that looks at him
heals the hanged man,
the bread the woman baked for him,

ich höre, sie nennen das Leben
die einzige Zuflucht.

MIT DER STIMME DER FELDMAUS
quiekst du herauf,

eine scharfe
Klammer,
beißt du dich mir durchs Hemd in die Haut,

ein Tuch,
gleitest du mir auf den Mund,
mitten in meiner
dich Schatten beschwerenden
Rede.

IN ECHSEN-
häute, Fall-
süchtige,
bett ich dich, auf den Simsen,
die Giebel-
löcher
schütten uns zu, mit Lichtdung.

I hear they call life
the only shelter.

WITH THE VOICE OF THE FIELDMOUSE
you squeak up,

a sharp
clamp,
you bite through the shirt into my skin,

a cloth,
you slide across my mouth,
midway through my
words weighing you, shadow,
down.

IN LIZARD-
skins, Epi-
leptic one,
I bed you, on the cornices,
the gable-
holes
bury us, with lightdung.

SCHNEEPART, gebäumt, bis zuletzt,
im Aufwind, vor
den für immer entfensterten
Hütten:

Flachträume schirken
übers
geriffelte Eis;

die Wortschatten
heraushaun, sie klaftern
rings um den Krampen
im Kolk.

II

DIE NACHZUSTOTTERNDE WELT,
bei der ich zu Gast
gewesen sein werde, ein Name,
herabgeschwitzt von der Mauer,
an der eine Wunde hochleckt.

DU MIT DER FINSTERZWILLE,
du mit dem Stein:

SNOWPART, arched, to the last,
in the updraft, before
the forever dewindowed
huts:

flatdreams skip
over the
chamfered ice;

to carve out
the wordshadows, to stack them
around the cramp
in the crater.

II

THE TO-BE-RESTUTTERED WORLD,
whose guest I
will have been, a name,
sweated down the wall,
up which a wound licks.

YOU WITH THE DARKNESS SLINGSHOT,
you with the stone:

Es ist Überabend,
ich leuchte hinter mir selbst.
Hol mich runter,
mach mit uns
Ernst.

EINGEJÄNNERT
in der bedornten
Balme. (Betrink dich
und nenn sie
Paris.)

Frostgesiegelt die Schulter;
stille
Schuttkäuze drauf;
Buchstaben zwischen den Zehen;
Gewißheit.

SCHLUDERE, Schmerz,
schlag ihr nicht ins Gesicht,
erpfusch dir
die Sandknubbe im
weißen Daneben.

---

it is overevening,
I light behind myself.
Take me down,
be serious about
us.

ENJANUARIED
in the thorned
rockshelter. (Get drunk
and call it
Paris.)

The shoulder, freezesealed;
immobile
tawdry owls on it;
letters between the toes;
certainty.

BE SLOPPY, Pain,
don't slap her face
you yourself botch
the sand boil in
the white Beside.

STÜCKGUT gebacken,
groschengroß, aus
überständigem Licht;

Verzweiflung hinzugeschippt,
Streugut;

ins Gleis gehoben die volle
Schattenrad-Lore.

VON QUERAB
komm ein, als die Nacht,
das Notsegel
bauscht sich,

eingeschreint
an Bord
ist dein Schrei,
du warst da, du bist unten,

unterhalb bist du,

ich geh, ich geh mit den Fingern
von mir,
dich zu sehn,
mit den Fingern, du Untre,

die Armstrünke wuchern,

PARCELED GOODS baked,
groschen-size, from
over-ripe light;

desperation thrown in,
scatter-grit;

lifted up onto the rail, the full
shadow-wheel truck.

FROM ABEAM
come in, as the night,
the jury rig
billows,

enshrined
aboard
is your scream,
you were there, you are below,

down below you are,

I go, I go with the fingers
from me,
to see you,
with the fingers, you, the One Below,

the arm stumps run riot,

das Leuchtfeuer denkt
für den ein-
sternigen Himmel,

mit dem Schwertkiel
les ich dich auf.

HOLZGESICHTIGER,
schlackermäuliger
Narr überm Tretrad:

am Ohrlappen hängt
dir das Aug
und hüpft
begrünt.

LARGO

Gleichsinnige du, heidegängerisch Nahe:

über-
sterbens-
groß liegen
wir beieinander, die Zeit-
lose wimmelt
dir unter den atmenden Lidern,

the beacon thinks
for the single-
star sky,

with the sword keel
I pick you up.

WOODFACED,
slackmawed
fool above the treadwheel:

from your earlobe
hangs and
hops your eye,
greened.

LARGO

Thought-sister, heath stroll close:

sur-
dying-
large we
lie next to each other, fall
crocus swarms
under your breathing lids,

das Amselpaar hängt
neben uns, unter
unsern gemeinsam droben mit-
ziehenden weißen

Meta-
stasen.

ZUR NACHTORDNUNG Über-
gerittener, Über-
geschlitterter, Über-
gewitterter,

Un-
besungener, Un-
bezwungener, Un-
umwundener, vor
die Irrenzelte gepflanzter

seelenbärtiger, hagel-
äugiger Weißkies-
stotterer.

MIT DEN SACKGASSEN sprechen
vom Gegenüber,
von seiner
expatriierten
Bedeutung –:

the pair of blackbirds hangs
out near us, under our
together up there
drifting along white

meta-
stases.

TO NIGHTORDER ridden-
over, sledded-
over, stormed-
over,

un-
sung, un-
vanquished, un-
entwined, planted in
front of the insanity tents

soulbearded, hailstone-
eyed whitepebble-
stutterer.

TO SPEAK WITH the blind alleys
of the opposite,
of its
expatriated
meaning—:

dieses
Brot kauen, mit
Schreibzähnen.

ETWAS WIE NACHT, scharf-
züngiger als
gestern, als morgen;

etwas wie einer
Fischmäuligen Gruß
übern Jammer-
tresen;

etwas Zusammengewehtes
in Kinderfäusten;

etwas aus meinem
und keinerlei Stoff.

III

WARUM DIESES JÄHE ZUHAUSE, mittenaus, mittenein?
Ich kann mich, schau, in dich senken, gletschrig,
du selbst erschlägst deine Brüder:
eher als sie
war ich bei dir, Geschneete.

to chew
this bread, with
writing-teeth.

SOMETHING LIKE NIGHT, sharper-
tongued than
yesterday, than tomorrow;

something like her
fishmouthed greeting
over the sorrow-
bar;

something blown together
in children's fists;

something of my
and of no substance.

III

WHY THIS SUDDEN AT-HOMENESS, all-out, all-in?
I can, look, sink myself into you, glacierlike,
you yourself slay your brothers:
earlier than they
I was with you, Snowed One.

Wirf deine Tropen
zum Rest:
einer will wissen,
warum ich bei Gott
nicht anders war als bei dir,

einer
will drin ersaufen,
zwei Bücher an Stelle der Lungen,

einer, der sich in dich stach,
beatmet den Stich,

einer, er war dir der nächste,
geht sich verloren,

einer schmückt dein Geschlecht
mit deinem und seinem Verrat,

vielleicht
war ich jeder

WARUM AUS DEM UNGESCHÖPFTEN,
da's dich erwartet, am Ende, wieder
hinausstehn? Warum,
Sekundengläubiger, dieser
Wahnsold?

Throw your tropes
in with the rest:
Someone wants to know,
why with God I
was no different than with you,

someone
wants to drown in that,
two books instead of lungs,

someone who stabbed himself into
you, bebreathes the cut,

someone, he was the one closest to you,
gets lost to himself,

someone adorns your sex
with your and his betrayal,

maybe
I was both

———————————————————————

WHY, FROM THE UNCREATED,
given that, in the end, its awaits you again,
stand out? Why,
believer in seconds, these
delusion wages?

Metallwuchs, Seelenwuchs, Nichtswuchs.
Merkurius als Christ,
ein Weisensteinchen, flußaufwärts,
die Zeichen zuschanden-
gedeutet,

verkohlt, gefault, gewässert,

unoffenbarte, gewisse
Magnalia.

MAPESBURY ROAD

Die dir zugewinkte
Stille von hinterm
Schritt einer Schwarzen.

Ihr zur Seite
die
magnolienstündige Halbuhr
vor einem Rot,
das auch anderswo Sinn sucht –
oder auch nirgends.

Der volle
Zeithof um
einen Steckschuß, daneben, hirnig.

Metalgrowth, soulgrowth, nothinggrowth.
Mercurius as Christ,
a philosopher's pebble, upriver
the sign interpreted
to shreds,

carbonized, rotted, watered,

unrevealed, certain
magnalia.

MAPESBURY ROAD

Waved toward you,
the quiet from behind
the step of a black woman.

By her side
the
magnolia-houred half-watch
of a red,
that also searches for meaning elsewhere—
or maybe nowhere.

The full
timehalo around
a lodged bullet, next to it, brainish.

Die scharfgehimmelten höfigen
Schlucke Mitluft.

Vertag dich nicht, du.

DER ÜBERKÜBELTE ZURUF: dein
Gefährte, nennbar,
neben dem abgestoßenen Buchrand:

komm mit dem Leseschimmer,
es ist
die Barrikade.

HERVORGEDUNKELT, noch einmal,
kommt deine Rede
zum vorgeschatteten Blatt-Trieb
der Buche.

Es ist
nichts herzumachen von euch,
du trägst eine Fremdheit zu Lehen.

Unendlich
hör ich den Stein in dir stehn.

The sharply heavened spacy
sips sharedair.

You—do not adjourn yourself.

—————

THE OVERLOADED CALL: your
companion, nameable,
next to the dinged bookedge:

come with the reading shimmer,
it is
the barricade.

—————

DARKENED FORTH, once more
your talk reaches
the foreshadowed leaf-shoot of
the beech tree.

Nothing can
be done or gotten from you
you are enfied to a strangeness.

Endlessly
I hear the stone stand in you.

—————

MIT DIR DOCKE kungeln, es kommt
der Lumpenkarren daher-
gejazzt, mit uns
wills dahin,

die gestopfte
Trompete
haucht uns zeitauf,
ins härteste
Ohr dieser Welt,

auch so
klemmts uns Rot-
holzige zwischen
Zulieb und Zuleid,

dann,
wenn es uns loshakt,
sackst du mir mitten
ins Sein.

AUCH DER RUNIGE wechselt die Fahrbahn:
mitten
im Greiftrupp
schabt er
sich Greifend-Gegriffenen rot,

Mohrrübe, Schwester,
mit deinen Schalen

WITH YOU, RAGDOLL, to fiddle, the
ragman's cart comes a-
jazzing, it's over there
we want,

the muted
trumpet
breathes us time-up,
into the hardest
ear of this world,

then also
jams red-
wood between our
for-pleasure and for-harm,

then,
when it hoes us free,
you crumble plumb into
my being.

THE RUNIC ONE TOO changes lanes:
amidst
the arrest-squad
he scrapes him-
self, arresting-arrested, red,

carrot, sister,
with your peels

pflanz mich Moorigen los
aus seinem
Morgen,

in den
Hochkörben, beim
abgerufenen Zündschwamm,
hinauf-
gestiegen ins phallische
Hirntransplantat, übertagt
der für immer geheutigte
Wundstein.

———————————————

DEINEM, AUCH DEINEM
fehldurchläuteten Schatten
gab ich die Chance,

ihn, auch ihn
besteinigt ich mit mir
Gradgeschattetem, Grad-
geläutetem – ein
Sechsstern,
dem du dich hinschwiegst,

heute
schweig dich, wohin du magst,

Zeitunterheiltes schleudernd,
längst, auch ich, auf der Straße,

plant me, the moory one, free
from his
Tomorrow,

in the
high buckets, near
the recalled tinder-sponge,
as–
cended into the phallic
braintransplant, overdays
the forever daily'd
woundstone.

YOUR, EVEN YOUR
falsenotes-suffused shadow
I gave a chance,

him, him too
I stoned with my
straightshadowed, straight-
pealed me——a
six-star,
toward which you silenced yourself,

today
silence yourself, whereto you want,

hurling what time undersanctified,
long since, me too, in the street,

tret ich, kein Herz zu empfangen,
zu mir ins Steinig-Viele
hinaus.

MAUERSPRUCH

Entstellt – ein Engel, erneut, hört auf –
kommt ein Gesicht zu sich selber,

die Astral-
waffe mit
dem Gedächtnisschaft:
aufmerksam grüßt sie
ihre
denkenden Löwen.

FÜR ERIC

Erleuchtet
rammt ein Gewissen
die hüben und drüben
gepestete Gleichung,

I step, not to receive a heart,
toward me out into the
stony-many.

WALLSLOGAN

Disfigured—an angel, anew, stops dead—
a face comes to itself,

the astral-
weapon with
the memoryshaft:
attentively it greets
its
thinking lions.

FOR ERIC

Illuminated
a conscience rams
the hither and thither
plague-ridden equation,

später als früh: früher
hält die Zeit sich die jähe
rebellische Waage,

ganz wie du, Sohn,
meine mit dir pfeilende
Hand.

WER PFLÜGT NICHTS UM?
Er. Diesmal.
Unverackert
steht sein Land in den Sinn seiner Sonnen-
nächte.
Er nennt uns.

Ja, er kätnert.
Ja, er heißt gut, er belehmigt,
was du verhüttest
vor Ort,
hinter Ort,
über Ort, brach,
gegen die Erze,
zuunterst,
lebendig.

---

later than early: earlier
time holds the brusk
rebellious scales,

just as you, son,
hold my with you arrowing
hand.

WHO DOESN'T PLOUGH UP SOMETHING?
He. This time.
Untilled
his land stands into the sense of his sun-
nights.
He names us.

Yes, he roustabouts.
Yes, he approves, he beloams,
what you smelt
pre-site,
post-site,
above-site, fallow,
against the ores,
at the very bottom,
alive.

LEVKOJEN, katzenbemündigt.
Beweibt
rechts von dir dieser Rasen.

Stab- und Mondsichel-Patt.

Du sollst nicht, so, gleich dir, hinterm Gitter, damals,
der
maltesische Jude, groß-
lippig – ihn
sprang der Knochen an, jäher
als dich, der Knochen,
den ein schon Morgiger warf –,
du
sollst nicht
aufsehn zum Himmel, du ließest
ihn denn, wie er dich,
im Stich, neben-
lichtig.
·   ·   ·   ·   ·   ·   ·   ·   ·   ·   ·   ·   ·
Schwester Kastanie, Vielblatt,
mit deinem blanken
Hiedrüben.

_____

DU DURCHKLAFTERST
Farbenstoß, Zahlwurf, Verkenntnis,

viele
sagen:

GILLYFLOWERS, cat-enfranchised.
With wife
on your right, this lawn.

Rod- and moonsickle-stalemate.

You shouldn't, thus, like you, behind bars, back then,
the
Maltese Jew, big-
lipped—him
the bone jumped, abrupter
than I, the bone
that someone already from tomorrow threw—,
you
should not
look up to heaven, you left
him then, as he you,
stranded,
side-lit.
. . . .
Sister chestnut, multifoliate,
with your blank overhither.

YOU TRANSFATHOM
colorpush, numbertoss, misconception,

many
say:

du bists, wir verwissens,
viele verneinen sich an dir,
der du sie dir einzeln
erjast,
aufständisch wie
der dem Handgesagten geschenkte
Steinmut,
der sich hinhob zur Welt
am Saum des gewendeten Schweigens
und aller Gefahr.

FÜR ERIC

In der Flüstertüte
buddelt Geschichte,

in den Vororten raupen die Tanks,

unser Glas
füllt sich mit Seide,

wir stehn.

DEIN BLONDSCHATTEN, auf
Schwimmtrense gezäumt,
schwenkt die Wasserschabracke,

it's you, we disknow it,
many negate themselves on you,
you who affirm them one by
one for yourself,
insurrectionary like
the stonecourage,
given as present to the handsaid,
who raised himself to the world
at the seam of the turned silence
and of all danger.

FOR ERIC

In the megaphone
history excavates,

in the suburbs the tanks crawl,

our glass
fills up with silk,

we stand.

YOUR BLONDSHADOW, swim-
snaffle bridled,
waves the watershabrack,

– auch du
hättest ein Recht auf Paris,
würdest du deiner
bitterer inne –,

dein Hankenmal, farblos
skizziert es die halb-
nahe Levade.

DIE ABGRÜNDE STREUNEN: Summkies –:

dem kommst du bei
mit Taubheitsgefühlen
und Unschlaf,

und kämen – die Lockstoffe geistern
den Fahnenmast hoch –,
kämen auch hier
die Albembleme geflattert,
du wärst, dich erplündernd,
gebieterisch-gleich
ihr Entzwei.

DEIN MÄHNEN-ECHO
– ihm wusch ich den Stein aus –,
mit Rauhreif beschlagen,

—you too
would have a right to Paris,
if more bitter you
innered yourself—,

your haunchmark, colorless
it sketches the half-
near levade.

THE ABYSSES ROAM: humgravel—:

you can sort that out
with feelings of numbness
and unsleep,

and if—the baits haunt
the flagpole to the top—,
if here too the
nightmare-emblems fluttered by,
you would be, plundering yourself,
domineeringly-even,
their fission.

YOUR MANE-ECHO
—I rinsed its stone—,
studded with hoarfrost,

mit entsiegelter
Stirn beleu-
mundet
von mir.

IV

DAS IM-OHRGERÄT treibt eine Blüte,
du bist ihr Jahr, dich beredet
die Welt ohne Zunge,
das weiß
jeder sechste.

DER HALBZERFRESSENE Wimpel
frißt alle Länder vom Meer fort,
alle Meere vom Land,

ein weiterer Name
– du, du beleb dich! –
muß eine Ziffer
dulden,

Unzählbarer du:
um ein Un-

with unsealed
forehead be-
famed
by me.

IV

THE IN-EAR-DEVICE sprouts a bloom,
you are its year, you are dis-
cussed by the tongueless world,
one in six
knows this.

THE HALFGNAWED pennant
devours all lands away from the sea,
all seas away from the land,

a further name
—hey, you, animate yourself!—
has to endure
a cipher,

uncountable you:
you are one un-

zeichen
bist du ihnen allen
voraus.

EIN BLATT, baumlos,
für Bertolt Brecht:

Was sind das für Zeiten,
wo ein Gespräch
beinah ein Verbrechen ist,
weil es soviel Gesagtes
mit einschließt?

PLAYTIME: die Fenster, auch sie,
lesen dir alles Geheime
heraus aus den Wirbeln
und spiegelns
ins gallertäugige Drüben,

doch
auch hier,
wo du die Farbe verfehlst, schert ein Mensch aus, entstummt,
wo die Zahl dich zu äffen versucht,
ballt sich Atem, dir zu,

gestärkt
hält die Stunde inne bei dir,

sign
ahead of them
all.

A LEAF, treeless,
for Bertolt Brecht:

What times are these
when a conversation
is nearly a crime,
because it includes so much
that's already been said.

PLAYTIME: the windows, they too,
read you all that secrecy
from your whirls
and mirror it
in the jelly-eyed beyond,

but
here too,
where you miss the color, a human sheers off, unmuted,
where the number tries to ape you,
breath clots, toward you,

strengthened
the hour stops next to you,

du sprichst,
du stehst,
den vergleichnisten Boten
aufs härteste über
an Stimme
an Stoff.

AUS DER VERGÄNGNIS
stehen die Stufen,

das ins Ohr Geträufelte
mündigt die Vorzeit darin,

Fjorde
sind Dochte,

nüchtern Erzähltes
träumt,

du berührst es, ein Tag-
verschworner.

OFFENE GLOTTIS, Luftstrom,
der
Vokal, wirksam,
mit dem einen
Formanten,

you speak,
you stand,
most firm above
the parabelized messengers
by voice
by matter.

OUT OF FUTURE–PAST FATE
stand the steps,

what's poured in the ear
emancipates prehistory in it,

fjords
are wicks,

what's recounted on an empty stomach
dreams,

you touch it, a day-
conspirator.

OPEN GLOTTIS, airstream,
the
vowel, effective,
with the one
formant,

Mitlautstöße, gefiltert
von weithin
Ersichtlichem,

Reizschutz: Bewußtsein,

unbesetzbar
ich und auch du,

überwahr-
heitet
das augen-, das
gedächtnisgierige rollende
Waren-
zeichen,

der Schläfenlappen intakt,
wie der Sehstamm.

AUS DEM MOORBODEN ins
Ohnebild steigen,
ein Häm
im Flintenlauf Hoffnung,
das Ziel, wie Ungeduld mündig,
darin.

Dorfluft, rue Tournefort.

---

consonant-thrusts, filtered
by clarity clear
from afar,

protection shield: consciousness

uncathectable
I and you too,

overtruth-
ed
the eye-,
the memory-greedy rolling
commodity
sign,

the temporal lobe intact,
like the visionstem.

FROM THE MOORFLOOR to
climb into the sans-image,
a hemo
in the gun barrel hope,
the aim, like impatience, of age,
in it.

Village air, rue Tournefort.

HOCHMOOR, uhrglas-
förmig (einer hat Zeit),

soviel Ritter, sonnentausüchtig,

aus dem
Lagg
stehen die Sabbatkerzen nach oben,

Schwingmoor, wenn du vertorfst,
entzeigere ich
den Gerechten.

ERZFLITTER, tief im
Aufruhr, Erzväter.

Du behilfst dir
damit,
als sprächen, mit ihnen,
Angiospermen
ein offenes
Wort.

Kalkspur Posaune.

Verlorenes findet
in den Karstwannen
Kargheit, Klarheit.

HIGHMOOR, watch-glass-
shaped (someone has time),

so many knights, sundewaddicted,

from the
lagg
the Sabbath candles rise up,

swingmoor, when you peatify,
I'll unhand
the Just One.

OREGLITTER, deep in
turmoil, urfathers.

You help yourself
thus,
as if
angiosperms spoke
a clear word,
with them.

Chalktrace trombone.

In the karst depression
the lost finds
sparseness, clarity.

EINKANTER: Rembrandt,
auf du und du mit dem Lichtschliff,
abgesonnen dem Stern
als Bartlocke, schläfig,

Handlinien queren die Stirn,
im Wüstengeschiebe, auf
den Tischfelsen
schimmert dir um den
rechten Mundwinkel der
sechzehnte Psalm.

MIT REBMESSERN, bei
Gebethub,
alle Marssegel spleißen,

herkämpfend, stehend, hinter
der Wimper, im Ölrock,
von Güssen gesalbt,

den Kalmengürtel schnüren
um deine Ulkspake, Beiboot
Welt.

LÖSSPUPPEN: also
hier steints nicht,

EINKANTER: Rembrandt
on easy terms with the lightcut,
sunned off the star
as beardlock, templish,

handlines cross the forehead,
in the desertshifts, on
the pedestal boulders
around your right
commissure shimmers
the sixteenth psalm.

WITH PRUNING HOOKS, at
prayer's tidal range,
to splice all topsails,

afighting, standing, behind
the eyelash, in oilskin,
anointed by showers,

to tie the calmbelt
around your joke-spike, dinghy
world.

LOESSDOLLS: thus,
here it doesn't petrify,

nur Landschneckenhäuser,
unausgeblasen,
sagen zur Wüste: du
bist bevölkert –:

die Wildpferde stoßen
in Mammut-
hörner:

Petrarca
ist wieder
in Sicht.

V

STAHLSCHÜSSIGER SEHSTEIN, umstirnter,
dies hier:

die Palmfarne, jetzt,
in Castrup: ein
metallischer Vortrupp
des nächsten
Urjahrhunderts,

eine Flughaut, lippig,
du
durchstößt sie,

only landsnailshells,
not blown empty,
say to the desert: you
are inhabited—:

the wild horses blow
into mammouth-
horns:

Petrarch
is in sight
again.

V

STEELUGINOUS VISIONSTONE, bestarred,
this here:

The palm ferns, now,
in Castrup: a
metallic vanguard troop
of the next
ur-century,

a flightskin, big-lipped,
you
push through it,

die bildersüchtige blanke
Rolltreppe
kann dich nicht spiegeln.

UND KRAFT UND SCHMERZ
und was mich stieß
und trieb und hielt:

Hall-Schalt-
Jahre,

Fichtenrausch, einmal,

dein Typhus, Tanja,

die wildernde Überzeugung,
daß dies anders zu sagen sei als
so.

MITERHOBEN
von den Geräuschen,
forderst du – Glas
feindet an, was immer
undurchdringlicher dein ist –,
forderst du alles
in seine Aura,

the image-addicted, blank
escalator
cannot mirror you.

AND STRENGTH AND PAIN
and what rammed me
and pushed and held:

jubilee-leap-
years,

spruceroar, once,

your typhus, Tanja,

the wilding conviction
that this is to be said differently than
so.

RAISED TOGETHER
by the noises,
you push—glass
agresses, what is ever
more impenetrably yours—,
you push everything
into his aura,

das Quentchen Mut
bittert sich ein,
wachsam:
es weiß, daß du weißt.

STEINSCHLAG hinter den Käfern.
Da sah ich einen, der log nicht,
heimstehn in seine Verzweiflung.

Wie deinem Einsamkeitssturm
glückt ihm die weit
ausschreitende Stille.

ICH SCHREITE deinen Verrat aus,
Fußspangen an
allen Seins-
gelenken,

Krümelgeister
kalben
aus deinen gläsernen
Titten,

mein Stein ist gekommen zu dir,
selbstentgittert, du inwendig
Ottern-
befrachtete,

the quantum courage
bitters itself in,
watchful:
it knows that you know.

FALLING ROCKS behind the beetles.
There I saw one, he didn't lie,
home-standing into his desperation.

As the solitude-storm did for you
so does wide-striding silence
succeed for him.

I STRIDE ACROSS your treason,
anklets clasping
all Being-
articulations,

crumghosts
calf
from your glass-
tits,

my stone came to you,
selfdebarred, you otter-
cargoed,
inside

du verhebst dich
an meinem leichtesten Schmerz,

du wirst sichtbar,

irgendein Toter, ganz bei sich,
setzt Lee über Luv.

LEUCHTSTÄBE, deren
Gespräch,
auf Verkehrsinseln,
mit endlich beurlaubten
Wappen-Genüssen,

Bedeutungen
grätschen im aufgerissenen Pflaster,

das Küken
Zeit, putt, putt, putt,
schlüpft in den Kraken-Nerv,
zur Behandlung,

ein Saugarm holt sich
den Jutesack voller
Beschlußmurmeln aus
dem Klöten-ZK,

die Düngerrinne herauf und herunter
kommt Evidenz.

you hurt yourself
lifting my lightest pain,

you become visible,

a, any, dead one, all for himself,
changes tack.

────────────────────

LIGHTRODS, whose
conversation,
on traffic islands,
with armory-delights finally
given leave,

meanings
straddle the ripped-up pavement,

the chick
Time, putt, putt, putt,
slips into the octopus-nerve,
for treatment,

a tentacle grabs
the jutebag full of
decision marbles from the
ballocks-ZK,

up and down the dunggutter
comes the evidence.

EIN LESEAST, einer,
die Stirnhaut versorgend,

eine Lichtquelle, von dir
schläfrig geschluckt,
passiert das hungrige
Wirtsgewebe,

Sehhilfe, streifig,
über mondbefahrene
Rückstreu-Sonden. Im großen: im kleinen.

Erden, immer noch, Erden.
Hornhautüber-
zogner Basalt,
raketengeküßt:
kosmisches
Umlauf-Geschau, und doch:
Binnenland-Horizonte.

Terrestrisch, terrestrisch.

Ein Leseast, einer,
die Stirnhaut versorgend – als schriebst du
Gedichte –,
er trifft auf den Kartengruß auf,
damals, vorm
Blutklumpenort, auf der Lungen-

ONE READING BRANCH, one,
feeding the forehead skin,

one light source, sleepily
swallowed by you,
passes the hungry
host-tissue,

visual aid, striated,
over moon scouring
backscatter-probes. On a large: on a small scale.

Earths, still and always, earths.
Cornea-covered
basalt,
rocket-kissed:
cosmic
circulation-gawking, and yet:
landlocked horizons.

Terrestrial, terrestrial.

One reading branch, one,
feeding the forehead skin—as if you wrote
poems—,
it comes to the postcard greeting,
back then, before
the bloodclotplace, on the lung-

schwelle, jahrhin, aus Pilsen,
jahrüber,
zeitwild von soviel
Leisegepreßtem:

Bon vent, bonne mer,

ein flackernder
Hirnlappen, ein
Meerstück,
hißt, wo du lebst,
seine Hauptstadt, die
unbesetzbare.

ZERR DIR den Traum vom Stapel,
pack deinen Schuh rein,

Rauschelbeeräugige, komm,
schnür zu.

KALK-KROKUS, im
Hellwerden: dein
steckbriefgereiftes
Von-dort-und-auch-dort-her,
unspaltbar,

threshold, yearward, from Pilsen,
yearover,
ensavaged from so much
pressed into muteness:

Bon vent, bonne mer,

a flickering
brainlobe, a
seapiece,
there, where you live,
its capital, the un-
occupiable.

TEAR YOUR dream from the launchpad,
pack your shoe into it,

mezery-eyed one, come,
lace it up.

CHALK-CROCUS, in
the clearing: your
wanted-poster-ripened
from-there-and-from-there-too,
unsplittable,

Sprengstoffe
lächeln dir zu,
die Delle Dasein
hilft einer Flocke
aus sich heraus,

in den Fundgruben
staut sich die Moldau.

Es sind schon die Kabel gelegt
zum Glück hinter dir
und zu dessen
munitionierten
Bereitstellungslinien,

in den Entlastungs-
städten,
dir zugewandt,
wo sie Gesundheitserreger versprühen,
melden melodische
Antitoxine
den Rennfahrerspurt
durch dein Gewissen.

In den Einstiegluken zur Wahrheit
beten die Spürgeräte,

Explosives
smile at you,
the Dasein Dent
helps a flake
get out of itself,

in the treasure troves
the Moldau collects itself.

THE CABLES ARE already laid
to the happiness behind you
and to its
munitioned
attack lines,

in the decongestion
cities
turned toward you,
where they vaporize health agents,
melodious
antitoxins
announce the racedriversprint
through your conscience.

IN THE ACCESS HATCHES to truth
the detectors pray,

bald kommen die Mauern geflogen
zu den Verhandlungstischen,

die Embleme palavern
sich Blut ab,

eine Krähe setzt
ihren halbgesichtigen
Peil-Flügel auf
halbmast.

UND JETZT, bei strategischer
Großlage, klauen-
signiertes
Gesinnungs-Lametta,

eine Wortlitze, rot-
gefüttert,
näht sich den Mündern
gesamtbarock in die
wund-
geschwiegene
Kommissur.

Schimmelbrothelle
eckt an,
abgekämpfte
Gedanken, was sonst,
stellen sich quer.

soon the walls come flying
to the negotiation tables,

the emblems palaver
away the blood,

a crow sets
its half-faced
radar-wing to
halfmast.

AND NOW, in a major strategic
situation, claw-
signed
conviction-tinsel,

a wordbraid, red-
lined,
sews itself to the mouths
all-baroque in the
wound-
silenced
commissure.

Breadmildewclarity
gives offense,
exhausted
ideas, what else,
set themslves against.

SCHNELLFEUER-PERIHEL.

Reite dein Staubkorn zu,
ihr müßt mit,
mahnt das Flugblatt.

(Du, Akosmische, als ich.)

Eines Knödels Trabanten, klug,
auf den Geister-Pawlatschen.

WIR ÜBERTIEFTEN, geeinsamt
in der Gefrornis.
Jedes Hängetal karrt eine Wimper
an den Augenabdruck
und seinen Steinkern
heran.

HINTER SCHLÄFENSPLITTERN,
im notfrischen
Holzwein,

(der Ort, wo du herkommst,
er redet sich finster, südwärts),

Rapidfire-perihelion.

Break in your dustmote,
you have to come along,
warns the flyer.

(You, acosmic, as I.)

A knödel's satellites, keen,
on the ghost-pawlatschen.

We the overdeepened, aloned
in the permafrost.
Every hanging valley carts a lid
toward the eye imprint
and its rock-
kernel.

Behind the templesplinters,
in the needfresh
woodwine,

(the place you come from,
it talks itself dark, southward),

dahlienfürchtig bei Gold,
auf immer heiterern
Stühlen.

BERGUNG allen
Abwässerglucksens
im Briefmarken-Unken-
ruf. Cor-
respondenz.

Euphorisierte
Zeitlupenchöre behirnter
Zukunftssaurier
heizen ein Selbstherz.

Dessen
Abstoß, ich wintre
zu dir über.

DAS GEDUNKELTE Splitterecho,
hirnstrom-
hin,

die Buhne über der Windung,
auf die es zu stehn kommt,

dahliascared near gold,
on always cheerier
chairs.

RESCUE of all
wastewater gurglings
in the poststamp-toad-
call. Cor-
respondence.

Euphorized
slowmotion choirs of cerebrized
future saurians
heat a selfheart.

Its
rejection, I winter
over to you.

THE DARKENED splinterecho,
brainstream-
ward,

the portcullis over the meander
on which it comes to stand,

soviel
Unverfenstertes dort,
sieh nur,

die Schütte
müßiger Andacht,
einen
Kolbenschlag von
den Gebetssilos weg,

einen und keinen.

DIE EWIGKEIT hält sich in Grenzen:
leicht, in ihren
gewaltigen Meß-Tentakeln,
bedachtsam,
rotiert die von Finger-
nägeln durchleuchtbare
Blutzucker-Erbse.

so much
unwindowed there,
just look,

the truss
of lazy fervor,
one
gunbutt blow from
the prayersilos,

one and not one.

ETERNITY stays within limits:
lightly, in its
powerful measure-tentacles,
deliberately,
the bloodsugar-pea, x-rayable
by fingernails,
rotates.

Zeitgehöft

Timestead

I

Wanderstaude, du fängst dir
eine der Reden,

die abgeschworene Aster
stößt hier hinzu,

wenn einer, der
die Gesänge zerschlug,
jetzt spräche zum Stab,
seine und aller
Blendung
bliebe aus.

Gehässige Monde
räkeln sich geifernd
hinter dem Nichts,

die sach-
kundige Hoffnung, die halbe,
knipst sich aus,

Blaulicht jetzt, Blaulicht,
in Tüten,

Elend, in harten
Trögen flambiert,

I

Nomadforb, you catch yourself
one of the speeches,

the foresworn aster
joins up,

should someone who
shattered the songs
speak to the rod now,
his and everyone's
blinding
wouldn't happen.

Spiteful moons
sprawl and slobber
behind Nothingness,

com-
petent hope, the half of it,
switches itself off,

bluelight now, bluetight,
in bags,

misery, flambéed
in hard troughs,

ein Wurfsteinspiel
rettet die Stirnen,

du rollst die Altäre
zeiteinwärts.

GOLD, das den nubischen
Handrücken fortsetzt – den Weg,
dann den Fußpfad zu dir, hinweg
über den Stein, den zugeschrägten,
aus Traumentzug-Zeiten,

zwei Sandschollen, umgeweht,
stehen mir bei,

sternverseucht legt sich ein Moor
um eine der Kiefern,

der Chor
der Platanenstrünke
buckelt sich ein zum Gebet
gegens Gebet,

aus gesiegeltem Floßholz
bau ich dir Namen, die pflockst du
fest, bei den Regenfeimen,

a throwstone-game
saves the foreheads,

you roll the altars
timeinward.

GOLD, that extends
the nubian back of a hand—the way,
then the footpath toward you, on
over the stone, the beveled one,
from dreamwithdrawal-times,

two sand clods, windblown,
stand with me,

starinfested a moor wraps itself
around one of the pines,

the choir
of plane-tree trunks
kowtows ready for the prayer
against prayer,

from sealed driftwood
I build names for you, which
you peg close to the rainschemes,

es werden die Kampfgrillen kommen,
aus meinem Bart,

vor den Denkkiemen steht schon
die Träne.

VON DER SINKENDEN WALSTIRN
les ich dich ab –
du erkennst mich,

der Himmel
stürzt sich
in die Harpune,

sechsbeinig
hockt unser Stern im Schaum,

langsam
hißt einer, der's sieht,
den Trosthappen: das
balzende Nichts.

DU LIEGST HINAUS
über dich,

über dich hinaus
liegt dein Schicksal,

the warcrickets shall come,
out of my beard,

in front of the thoughtgills already stands
the tear.

FROM THE SINKING WHALE FOREHEAD
I read you off—
you recognize me,

heaven
throws itself
on the harpoon,

sixlegged our star
hunkers down in the foam,

slowly
someone who sees it raises
the consolation morsel:
copulating Nothingness.

YOU OUTLIER
beyond yourself,

out beyond you
lies your fate,

weißäugig, einem Gesang
entronnen, tritt etwas zu ihm,
das hilft
beim Zungenentwurzeln,
auch mittags, draußen.

Das seidenverhangene Nirgend
widmet dem Strahl seine Dauer,

ich kann dich hier
sehn.

Eingehn dürfen bei euch, ausgehn –

Unter der Sandhaube steuert
dein unbelauscht schlafendes
Hirn
den unverwirkbaren, einen,
ozeanischen
Tag,

komm, ich hell auf,

komm, ich geb dich
mir und auch dir,
Überzüchtete,
Schwere.

white-eyed, escaped from
a dream, something joins it,
that helps
with the tongueuprooting,
even at noon, outside.

The silkbedecked Nowhere
devotes its duration to the beam,

I can see you
here.

To be received by you, and leave—

Under the sandhood steers
your unmonitered sleeping
brain
the unrealizable, single
oceanic
day,

come, I brighten,

come, I give you
to me and to you too,
overbred one,
heavy one.

Die Weinbergsmauer erstürmt
vom Ewigkeitsklirren,
die Reben
meutern,

miterklirrt
das Rückenmark, bei
Herzschwüle, im
wirklicheren Gehäus,

die fünf Körner verteilt
auf die vier Meere,

tauch ein.

Erst wenn ich dich
als Schatten berühre,
glaubst du mir meinen
Mund,

der klettert mit Spät-
sinnigem droben
in Zeithöfen
umher,

The vineyardwall assailed
by eternity jingles,
the vines
mutiny,

jingles too
the marrow brain, at
heartswelter, in
the realer housing,

the five grains distributed
over the four seas,

dive in.

Only when I touch
you as shadow
do you believe me my
mouth,

that one clambers
with late-
meanings up there
in the timehalos,

du stößt zur Heerschar
der Zweitverwerter unter
den Engeln,

Schweigewütiges
sternt.

IN DER FERNSTEN
Nebenbedeutung, am Fuß der gelähmten
Amen-Treppe:
die kahlgeplünderte
Phase Dasein,

nahebei, in der Gosse,
nudeln noch
Sprüche,

traumfaserverstärkt das Profil
der Schlafausscheidung,
an ihrer einen
herztätigen Schläfe
bildet sich Eis,

kein Buch schlägt sich auf,

das Übernichts hat sich
zu mir geschlagen,
es gibt seinen Kampf auf,
im Eis,

you happen upon the host
of secondusers among
the angels,

the mutefurious
stars.

IN THE REMOTEST
connotation, at the foot of the paralyzed
Amen-stairs:
the phase Being, plundered
bare,

nearby, in the gutter,
sayings still
noodle,

dreamfiberreinforced the profile
of the sleepexcretion,
at its single
heartactive temple
ice forms,

no book opens itself,

the Übernothing has
joined up with me,
it gives up its fight,
in the ice,

wir sind bereit,
das Tödlichste in uns zu tauschen,

der Dorn, der das Freizeichen gab,
steigt duch die Wiegen,

hinter der Stechuhr verschenkt sich
die wahnfeste Zeit.

EINGESCHOSSEN
in die Smaragdbahn,

Larvenschlupf, Sternschlupf, mit allen
Kielen
such ich dich,
Ungrund.

Alle die Schlafgestalten, kristallin,
die du annahmst
im Sprachschatten,

ihnen
führ ich mein Blut zu,

die Bildzeilen, sie
soll ich bergen

we are ready
to exchange the most deadly in us,

the thorn that gave the freesign
rises through the cradles,

behind the punch clock delusionsolid time
gives itself away.

INSERTED INTO
the emerald-trajectory,

larvaelag, starlag, with all
keels
I search for you,
unground.

All the sleepfigures, crystalline,
that you adopted
in the speechshadow,

them
I supply with my blood,

the imagelines, they
I should salvage

in den Schlitzvenen
meiner Erkenntnis –,

meine Trauer, ich seh's,
läuft zu dir über.

Zwei Sehwülste, zwei
Narbennähte,
auch hier, quer durchs
Gesicht,

ein Licht, deinen ersten
Bränden abgefragt, seit
langem draußen,
schlüpft ins
Erblickte.

VOR MEIN
wetterleuchtendes Knie
kommt die Hand zu stehn,
mit der du
dir übers Aug fuhrst,

ein Klirren
holt sich Gewißheit
im Kreis, den ich zog
um uns zwei,

in the slitveins
of my insight—,

my grief, I see now,
defects to you.

———————————————————————————

Two sightbulges, two
scarseams,
here too, straight across
the face,

a light, retrieved from
your first brands, a long
time outside,
slips into the
glimpsed.

———————————————————————————

BEFORE MY
sheet lightning knee
the hand comes to stand,
that you
passed over your eye,

a jingling
gathers certainty
in the circle I drew
around us two,

manchmal freilich
stirbt der Himmel
unsern Scherben
voraus.

DU WIRFST MIR Ertrinkendem
Gold nach:
vielleicht läßt ein Fisch
sich bestechen.

Gib mir, Tod,
meinen Stolz.

Das Flüsterhaus,
schalttags geöffnet,

auf Jute
weitergegeben, flächen-
tief,

es bürgert
den Enge-Laut ein,

für die Lallstufe
sorgen
die Lippen-
pflöcke,

sometimes, of course,
heaven dies
in advance of our
shards.

YOU THROW GOLD after me,
drowning:
perhaps a fish
can be bribed.

Give me, death,
my pride.

The whisperhouse,
open on leapday,

handed on
on jute, surface-
deep,

it naturalizes
the fricatives,

the lallation-stage
is taken care of
by the lip-
pegs,

– rastet das
Andere ein,
zeitig? –,

dieses, ja dieses
Gletschergeschrei
deiner Hände,

die Toten-Seilschaft
trägt mit an den Firnen,

der umgepolte
Mond
verwirft dich, zweite
Erde,

am Resthimmel, sterbestolz, das
Sterngedränge
nimmt die Hürde.

KLEINE NACHT: wenn du
mich hinnimmst, hinnimmst,
hinauf,
drei Leidzoll überm
Boden:

alle die Sterbemäntel aus Sand,
alle die Helfenichtse,

—does the
other snap in,
on time?—

this, yes this
glacierscreaming
of your hands,

the network of the dead
helps to carry the firnice,

the moon,
poles reversed,
rejects you, second
earth,

at the restheaven, deathproud, the
starthrong
takes the hurdle.

LITTLE NIGHT: when you
take me in, take me in,
take me up,
three woe-inches above
the ground:

all the sand-made dyingcoats,
all the helpnots

alles, was da noch
lacht
mit der Zunge –

***

AN DIE HALTLOSIGKEITEN
sich schmiegen:

es schnippen
zwei Finger im Abgrund, in den
Sudelheften
rauscht Welt auf, es kommt
auf dich an.

***

ICH ALBERE mit meiner Nacht,
wir kapern
alles,
was sich hier losriß,

lad du mir auch deine
Finsternis auf
die halben, fahrenden
Augen,

auch sie soll es hören,
von überallher,
das unwiderlegbare Echo
jeder Verschattung.

everything, that still
laughs
with the tongue—

TO HUDDLE AGAINST
the instabilities:

two fingers
snap in the abyss, in the
rough books
world roars up, it is
up to you.

I FOOL AROUND with my night,
we hijack
all
that broke loose here,

you, load your
darkness too on
half my driving
eyes,

it too shall hear it,
from everywhere,
the irrefutable echo
of every opacity.

DEIN UHRENGESICHT,
von Blaufeuern über-
lagert,
verschenkt seine Ziffern,

meine
Herkunft
hielt Umschau, sie geht
in dich ein, die mit-
vereinten
Kristalle
flennen.

ICH LOTSE DICH hinter die Welt,
da bist du bei dir, unbeirrbar,
heiter
vermessen die Stare den Tod,
das Schilf winkt dem Stein ab, du hast
alles
für heut abend.

MEINE
dir zugewinkelte Seele
hört dich
gewittern,

YOUR CLOCKFACE, over-
layered with
bluefires,
gives away its numbers,

my
provenance
looked around, it goes
into you, the co-
joined
crystals
bawl.

I PILOT YOU behind the world,
there you are at home, unflinching,
cheerfully
the starlings survey death,
the canebreak dismisses the stone, you have
all
you need for tonight.

MY
soul, youward creasebent,
hears you
a-thundering,

in deiner Halsgrube lernt
mein Stern, wie man wegsackt
und wahr wird,

ich fingre ihn wieder heraus –
komm, besprich dich mit ihm,
noch heute.

EIN STERN
lauscht einem Licht,
eine Stunde verstößt
eine Stunde,

herzschwer
rollt Azur
über dich hin,

dein blutiger
Speichel
beglückt
ein besessenes Staubkorn,

ein Mutterstummel
führt ein Frühgesicht
durch einen Schmerz,

sein Gott
schreitet mähend die Bilderfront ab,

in your neck hollows my
star learns how one sags away
and becomes true,

I finger it forth again—
come, confer with it,
this very day.

A STAR
listens to a light,
an hour repudiates
an hour,

heartheavy
azure rolls
over you,

your bloody
saliva
delights
an obsessed dustmote,

a motherstump
leads an earlyface
through a pain,

its god,
mowing, paces off the imagefront,

auf den Graten
der obersten
Wiege.

KLEINES WURZELGETRÄUM, das mich hier hält,
blutunterwaschen,
keinem mehr sichtbar,
Todesbesitz,

wölb du eine Stirn vor,
daß eine Rede gehe, von Erde,
von Inbrunst, von
Äugigem, auch
hier, wo du mich abliest vom Blindblatt,
auch
hier,
wo du mich so genau
widerrufst.

II

MANDELNDE, die du nur halbsprachst,
doch durchzittert vom Keim her,
dich
ließ ich warten,
dich.

on the ridges
of the upper
cradle.

LITTLE ROOTDREAMINGS that keep me here,
bloodwashedout,
no longer visible for anyone,
death's possession,

you, camber a forehead
that a speech may go, of earth,
of fervor, of
eyenesses, here
too, where you read me off the blinddial,
here
too,
where you revoke me
so thoroughly.

II

ALMONDING YOU, who only halfspoke,
yet was trembled from the seed on up,
you
I let wait,
you.

Und war
noch nicht
entäugt,
noch unverdornt im Gestirn
des Lieds, das beginnt:
Hachnissini.

ES STAND
der Feigensplitter auf deiner Lippe,

es stand
Jerusalem um uns,

es stand
der Hellkiefernduft
überm Dänenschiff, dem wir dankten,

ich stand
in dir.

DIE GLUT
zählt uns zusammen
im Eselsschrei vor
Absaloms Grab, auch hier,

Gethsemane, drüben,
das umgangene, wen
überhäufts?

And was
not yet
uneyed,
as yet unthorned in the song's
constellation, the song that begins:
Hachnisini.

IT STOOD
on your lip: the figsplinter

it stood
around us: Jerusalem

it stood
above the Daneship:
the bright pinescent, we thanked it,

I stood
in you.

THE SWELTER
adds us up
in the ass's bray before
Absalom's tomb, here too,

Gethsemane, over there,
bypassed, whom
does it bury?

Am nächsten der Tore tut sich nichts auf,

über dich, Offene, trag ich dich zu mir.

WIR, DIE WIE DER STRANDHAFER WAHREN,
in N'we Awiwim,

der ungeküßte
Stein einer Klage
rauscht auf,
vor Erfüllung,

er befühlt unsre Münder,
er wechselt
über zu uns,

eingetan ist uns
sein Weiß,

wir geben uns weiter:
an dich und an mich,

die Nacht, sieh dich vor, die sand-
befehligte,
nimmt es genau
mit uns zwein.

At the nearest gate nothing opens,

above you, open one, I carry you toward me.

WE WHO LIKE THE SEA OATS GUARD,
in Neve Avivim,

the unkissed
stone of a complaint
swells up,
before fulfillment,

it palpates our mouths,
it crosses
over to us,

alloyed to us
in its Whiteness,

we hand ourselves on:
to you and to me,

night, be careful, the sand-
commanded
is strict
with us two.

EIN RING, ZUM BOGENSPANNEN,
nachgeschickt einem Wortschwarm,
der wegstürzt hinter die Welt,
mit den Staren,

Pfeilige, wenn du mir zuschwirrst,
weiß ich, woher,

vergeß ich, woher.

―――――――――――――――――――

DAS LEUCHTEN, ja jenes, das
Abu Tor
auf uns zureiten sah, als wir
ineinander verwaisten, vor Leben,
nicht nur von den Handwurzeln her –:

eine Goldboje, aus
Tempeltiefen,
maß die Gefahr aus, die uns
still unterlag.

―――――――――――――――――――

DU GLEISSENDE
Tochtergeschwulst
einer Blendung im All,

A RING, FOR BOWDRAWING,
loosed after the wordswarm
that founders behind the world,
with the starlings,

arrowy one, when you whir toward me,
I know from where,

I forget from where.

THE RADIANCE, yes, the one that
Abu Tor
saw riding toward us, when we
orphaned into each other, for life,
not only up from the wrists —:

a goldbuoy, from
temple-depths,
surveyed the danger that
slyly underlay us.

YOU, NITID
daughtertumor
of a cosmic glare,

aufgegriffen
von überhimmlischen Suchtrupps,
verschoben
ins sehende, gott-
entratene
Sternhaufen-Blau,

du wildenzt
vor unsern
hungrigen, unverrückbaren
Poren
als Mitsonne, zwischen
zwei Hellschüssen
Abgrund.

KOMM, leg die Welt aus mit dir,
komm, laß mich euch zuschütten mit
allem Meinen,

Eins mit dir bin ich,
uns zu erbeuten,

auch jetzt.

EINEN STIEFELVOLL Hirn
in den Regen gestellt:

seized
by supracelestial search troops
shunted
into the seeing, god-
waiving
starheap Blue,

you turn gamy
before our
hungry, immovable
pores,
a co-sun, twixt
two brightshots
abyss.

COME, lay out the world with yourself,
come, let me fill you all up with
all that's mine,

one with you I am,
to capture us,

even now.

A BOOTFUL of brain
set out in the rain:

es wird ein Gehn sein, ein großes,
weit über die Grenzen,
die sie uns ziehn.

DIE POSAUNENSTELLE
tief im glühenden
Leertext,
in Fackelhöhe,
im Zeitloch:

hör dich ein
mit dem Mund.

DIE POLE
sind in uns,
unübersteigbar
im Wachen,
wir schlafen hinüber, vors Tor
des Erbarmens,

ich verliere dich an dich, das
ist mein Schneetrost,

sag, daß Jerusalem i s t,

there will be a going, a great one,
far across the borders
they draw for us.

———————

THE TRUMPET'S PART
deep in the glowing
Empty-text,
at torch's level,
in the timehole:

listen your way in
with the mouth.

———————

THE POLES
are in us,
insurmountable
while awake,
we sleep across, to the Gate
of Mercy,

I lose you to you, that
is my snowcomfort,

say that Jerusalem *is*,

sags, als wäre ich dieses
dein Weiß,
als wärst du
meins,

als könnten wir ohne uns wir sein,

ich blättre dich auf, für immer,

du betest, du bettest
uns frei.

DER KÖNIGSWEG hinter der Scheintür,

das vom Gegen-
Zeichen umtodete
Löwenzeichen davor,

das Gestirn, kieloben,
umsumpft,

du, mit der
die Wunde auslotenden
Wimper.

---

say it, as if I was this
your Whiteness
as if you were
mine,

as if without us we could be we,

I leaf you open, forever,

you pray, you lay
us free.

THE KINGSWAY behind the pretend-door,

before it, deathed
in by the counter-
sign, the lionsign,

the constellation, keel up,
mired in,

you, with the
wound-fathoming
eyelash.

Es KOMMT auch ein Sinn
die engere Schneise daher,

den erbricht
das tödlichste unsrer
stehenden Male.

———————————————

Ich TRINK WEIN aus zwei Gläsern
und zackere an
der Königszäsur
wie Jener
am Pindar,

Gott gibt die Stimmgabel ab
als einer der kleinen
Gerechten,

aus der Lostrommel fällt
unser Deut.

———————————————

Es WIRD etwas sein, später,
das füllt sich mit dir
und hebt sich
an einen Mund

Aus dem zerscherbten
Wahn

THERE ALSO comes a meaning
down the narrower cut,

it is breached
by the deadliest of our
standing marks.

I DRINK WINE from two glasses
and harrow
the king's caesura
like that other
does Pindar,

God turns in the tuning fork
as one of the small
just ones,

from the lottery drum falls
our doit.

SOMETHING SHALL BE, later,
that fills itself with you
and lifts itself
to a mouth

Out of shattered
madness

steh ich auf
und seh meiner Hand zu,
wie sie den einen
einzigen
Kreis zieht

DAS NICHTS, um unsrer
Namen willen
– sie sammeln uns ein –,
siegelt,

das Ende glaubt uns
den Anfang,

vor den uns
umschweigenden
Meistern,
im Ungeschiednen, bezeugt sich
die klamme
Helle.

IM GLOCKIGEN jappen
die gläubig-ungläubigen
Seelen,

I raise myself
and watch my hand
as it draws the one
single
circle

NOTHINGNESS, for the sake
of our names
—they gather us in—
seals,

the end believes us
the beginning,

before the
masters en-
silencing us,
in the undifferentiated, attesting
itself: the clammy
brightness.

IN THE BELLSHAPE the
believing-unbelieving
souls gasp,

Sternunfug
setzt sich fort, auch mit meiner
im Wüstensinn von dir
umhügelten Hand,

wir sind
längst da.

WIE ICH den Ringschatten trage,
trägst du den Ring,

etwas, das Schweres gewohnt ist,
verhebt sich
an uns,
unendlich
Entimmernde du.

DAS FREMDE
hat uns im Netz,
die Vergänglichkeit greift
ratlos duch uns hindurch,

zähl meinen Puls, auch ihn,
in dich hinein,

dann kommen wir auf,
gegen dich, gegen mich,

star-nonsense
propagates itself, even with my
hand, in desert-sense en-
duned by you,

we got here
long ago.

As I carry the ringshadow
you carry the ring,

something, used to heaviness,
strains itself
lifting us,
infinite
de-ternalizing you.

Strangeness
has netted us,
transience reaches
perplexedly through us,

take my pulse, it too,
into yourself,

then we shall prevail
against you, against me,

etwas kleidet uns ein,
in Taghaut, in Nachthaut,
fürs Spiel mit dem obersten, fall-
süchtigen Ernst.

UMLICHTET die Keime,
die ich in dir
erschwamm,

freigerudert
die Namen – sie
befahren die Engen,

ein Segensspruch, vorn,
ballt sich
zur wetterfühligen
Faust.

III

FORTGESALBT, draußen, im Stein-
weizen,
von singenden
Händen,

something enclothes us
in dayskin, in nightskin,
for the game with the highest, epi-
leptic seriousness.

ILLUMINATED, the seeds
which I in you
won swimming,

rowed free,
the names—they
sail the straits,

a blessing, up front,
compacts into
a weathersensing
fist.

III

SALVED AWAY, outside, in the stone-
crop,
by singing
hands,

die halbe Skabiose,
sparsam,
vorm Trommelfellriß,

unterm linken
Fuß
ein Fenster – der
Erde?

ORTSWECHSEL bei den Substanzen:
geh du zu dir, schließ dich an,
bei verschollenem
Erdlicht,

ich höre, wir waren
ein Himmelsgewächs,
das bleibt zu beweisen, von
obenher, an
unsern Wurzeln entlang,

zwei Sonnen gibts, hörst du,
zwei,
nicht eine –
ja und?

---

half the scabious,
thrifty,
before the eardrum rupture,

under the left
foot
a window—of
earth?

PLACE CHANGE by the substances:
you go to yourself, join up,
by missing
earthlight,

I hear, we were
a heavensgrowth,
that remains to be shown, from
above, along
our roots,

there's two suns, you hear,
two,
not one—
so what?

DIE WELT, Welt,
in allen Fürzen gerecht,

ich, ich,
bei dir, dir, Kahl-
geschorne.

WAS BITTERT
herein?

Die großen Alleinigkeiten
verzwergen
im Hörrinden-Hymnus,

selig
tuscheln die Daumenschrauben in
heiterer
Streckfolterhöhe,

die entscheidenden
Pausen
erhalten
Zufuhr,

in der Zählkammer,
rebellisch,
beten die Ringe
den Rest an.

THE WORLD, world,
just in all its farts,

I, I
with you, you, shaved
bald.

WHAT BITTERS
herein?

The great alonenesses
dwarfing
in the auditory cortex-hymn,

blessedly
the thumbscrews whisper in
sanguine
rack-torture-height,

the determining
pauses
are granted
access,

in the counting chamber,
rebellious,
the rings worship
the rest.

DIE GESENKTEN
Götterdaumen, ich hole, im Borken-
hemd,
die untersten Baumläufer ein, bald ist
heute, für immer, die
Markierungen, das
Strahlengezücht,
kommen
über die Antimaterie
getanzt, zu dir,
in die Kometen-
Schonung.

KROKUS, vom gastlichen
Tisch aus gesehn:
zeichenfühliges
kleines Exil
einer gemeinsamen
Wahrheit,
du brauchst
jeden Halm.

REBLEUTE graben
die dunkelstündige Uhr um,
Tiefe um Tiefe,

du liest,

THE LOWERED
godthumbs, in bark-
shirt I haul in the
lowest treecreepers, soon it will be
today, forever, the
markings, the
radiationbrood,
come a-
dancing across the antimatter,
toward you,
into the comet-
conservatory.

CROCUS, from the hospitable
table seen:
sign-sensing
little exile
of a shared
truth,
you need
each stalk.

VINEGROWERS dig up dig
under the darkhoured watch,
depth for depth,

you read,

es fordert
der Unsichtbare den Wind
in die Schranken,

du liest,

die Offenen tragen
den Stein hinterm Aug,
der erkennt dich,
am Sabbath.

the invisible
one commands the wind
to stay in bounds,

you read,

the Open Ones carry
the stone behind the eye,
it recognizes you,
on a Sabbath.

Commentary

Besides their obvious function of trying to provide some minimal yet specific information concerning difficulties both in the original poems and in the translations, these commentaries want to point out the kind of complexities an in-depth reading, hermeneutical or other, will have to contend with. Obviously, what is proposed here are only a few examples that should not be mistaken for an annotated translation of any completeness. These minimalia function more as a map of our ignorance than as a showcase of our knowledges regarding Celan's late poems. They are gleaned from the vast array of Celan scholarship available and a detailed system of references would be too cumbersome and diminish readability too much. The core sources for the information in these commentaries come from Barbara Wiedemann's *Paul Celan, Die Gedichte: Kommentierte Gesamtausgabe in einem Band*; from the two available scholarly editions (the so-called Bonner and Tübinger editions); from Jean-Pierre Lefebvre's French annotated editions of *Breathturn* and *Snowpart*; from the two volumes of annotated correspondence between Paul Celan and his wife, Gisèle Celan-Lestrange; as well as from various books and essays by Bertrand Badiou, Otto Pöggeler, Jean Bollack, and others. See also the bibliographies at the end of this book.

But a warning is also necessary in that however many links we can establish to an hors-texte (and there are such loci, *pace* Jacques Derrida), to this or that place or time or book, we should always remember Celan's own warning to Ilana Shmueli, who notes in her book after thinking of a specific biblical reference for a line in the poem "The trumpet's part" (p. 439): "But I note it down here with some hesitation and immediately remember that Celan often warned me about citations (especially biblical citations): 'please write without citations,' he said, 'let only your own words speak.' I shouldn't allow anything tendentious, didactic, I should remain 'open' for my own reading and experiencing. The last two short lines ('listen your way in / with the mouth') command you to be absolutely attentive to the text, the 'Empty-text,' that carries the glowing enigma inside itself" (IS, p. 42).

And yet, a lifetime of reading and writing poetry has also taught me that to read a poem is always at least a double movement: the systole of absolute attentiveness brought to bear on the text, and the diastole of letting your mind move from every word in the text out into the world of both books and experience.

Unless otherwise indicated, all translations are mine.

ATEMWENDE | BREATHTURN

The eighty poems in this volume were composed between September 1963 and September 1965 and are organized into six near-chronological cycles. The first cycle is made up of the twenty-two poems of *Atemkristall* (see below), cycle 2 of seventeen poems written between January 22 and August 2, 1964, and cycle 3 of sixteen poems (eleven of which were written between August 9 and December 15, 1964, with four—"Wenn du im Bett," "Von der Orchis her," "Die Gauklertrommel," and "In Prag"—written in September and October 1963 and moved as a block into this cycle). Cycle 4 gathers eighteen poems written between December 19, 1964, and May 23, 1965, while cycle 5 consists of seven poems dated June 7 to August 18, 1965. The final cycle 6 consists of a single poem. The poem "Coagula," placed in the fourth cycle after "Solve," had originally been part of a project conceived during the writing of *Die Niemandsrose* in 1962 called "Paris Elegy," but was moved to its place in *Atemwende* after the writing of "Solve" on February 2, 1965.

Concerning *Atemwende*, Celan wrote to his wife, Gisèle Celan-Lestrange, on March 8, 1967: "Yesterday and the day before I have been working on the manuscript of Atemwende. It is truly the most dense work I have written so far, also the most encompassing. At a number of turns in the text I have, I must admit, felt pride.—I finally divided the manuscript into cycles—it needed to be aerated—of unequal lengths, but 'in sich geschlossen' (self-contained) as they say in German. At the end, separated by an empty page, single poem and cycle simultaneously, the 'EINMAL' (ONCE)" (PC/GCL, #479).

The title was first used by Celan as a word/concept in the 1960 Meridian speech, where he wrote: "Poetry: that can mean an Atemwende, a breathturn. Who knows, perhaps poetry travels this route—also the route of art—for the sake of such a breathturn?" Speaking of Georg Büchner's character Lucile, he says: "Twice, with Lucile's 'Long live the king,' and when the sky opened as an abyss beneath Lenz, the Atemwende, the breathturn seemed to happen." In the notes he took for this speech he had written at one point: "I had survived some things,—but survival hopefully isn't 'everything'—, I had a bad conscience; I was searching for—maybe I can call it that?—a my breathturn." At the same time it should be noted that for a while Celan had several titles in mind, most, if not all, based on two words, breath (*Atem*) and/or delusion (*Wahn*), the latter pointing to the bouts of psychic instability, often accompanied by sojourns in psychiatric clinics, that Celan suffered from 1962 onward, triggered no doubt by the psychic load of the Goll affair. Among the rejected titles were: Wahndock | Delusiondock; Wahnspur | Delusionspoor; Atemkristall | Breathcrystal; Atemgänge | Breathpassages or -errands; also Atem, Aufruhr | Breath, Uproar (riot, tumult, insurrection, ferment); and Atemzeile | Breathline or -row.

The poems that make up the first cycle of *Atemwende* were published under the title *Atemkristall* with eight etchings by Gisèle Celan-Lestrange in a bibliophile edition from Brunidor, Paris, 1965. (The word *Atemkristall* appears in one of the poems of that cycle, "Weggebeizt" | "Eroded.") This represents a first major collaborative realization where reflecting on the art of etching and lithographic reproduction becomes important for Celan's poetic art, as he acknowledges in a letter to his wife of March 29, 1965: "In your etchings I recognize my poems: they go through them and are there still." And on May 20, 1965, from the clinic at Le Vésinet, the day before his release: "And we will pick up our work again. I have seen your etchings being born next to my poems, being born of those very poems, and you know well that 'Atemkristall / breathcrystal,' which has reopened the path of poetry for me, was born from your etchings."

I

"Du darfst" | *"You may"*
October 16, 1963. The next four poems were also written on that day. This cycle of *Atemwende* opens and closes with one of Celan's most powerful images:

snow. (See also Hans-Michael Speier's essay on the posthumous volume *Schneepart* in *Celan-Jahrbuch* 1, and the commentaries for that volume.) "Schnee" | "snow, "and the associated ice- and glacier-cosmos, marble Atemwende. See, for example, the well-known and much-commented lines (p. 24):

> Tiefimschnee,
>
> > Iefimnee,
>
> > > I – i – e.

The image of snow, in this poem only a few words away from an evocation of summer, always rhymes with winter and death. It is, as Lefebvre writes, "the meteor of 20 january, of the Wannsee conference, of Auschwitz, of the crossing of the mountain by Lenz. Each time the word appears, that historical and semantic horizon is deployed" (RDS, p. 192).

In his essay "Erfahrenes Sprechen – Leseversuch an Celan-Entwürfen," in *Argumentum e Silentio*, Rolf Bücher indicates that in the first manuscript version the second section (lines 3 through 6) of the poem reads: "ich komme mit sieben / Blättern vom Sieben- / stamm." (I come with seven / leaves from the seven- / trunk.) After analyzing the Jewish/kabbalistic component of the early version, including the relation of the seven-armed candelabra, the menorah, to the world tree, Bücher writes: "The poem should still be understood entirely with an eye to this image's genealogical heritage, in the sense of the original image of the 'seven-trunk'" (where *Stamm* means both tree trunk and tribe). Bücher goes on to suggest that a straightforward reading of the early version "would lead to a very abstract sense of 'heritage,' which must also be seen, in its narrowest context, as a very concrete Judaicism," concluding that it is specifically "this abstractness that is caught in the published version of the poem, and transposed into the image of a concrete life experience."

I disagree with Bücher's suggestion that the poem should be "understood entirely" from this perspective (especially since Celan did edit out the specific reference to Jewish religion and mythology) and prefer to read it both with a more personal and a wider view. Take the image of the mulberry tree: as personal reference we know that Celan planted three of these trees in the garden of the family's summer home in Moisville, life symbols for each of the three members of the family. Besides its associations with silk, the mulberry tree is richly represented in various mythologies; as Lefebvre suggests, for example, "in China it is the tree of the Levant, in Greek mythology it is the meeting place for Pyramus and Thisbe. The walking tree may evoke Orpheus" (RDS, pp. 192–93).

"Von Ungeträumtem" | *"By the undreamt"*
October 16, 1963. The earliest version of this poem begins: "Traumgeätzt, / wirft das durchwanderte Brotland den Berg auf." (Dream-etched, / the wandered-through breadland casts up the mountain.) A handwritten emendation inserts *schlaflos*, which then requires in the following version of the poem the logical change from *traumgeätzt* into its opposite, *von Ungeträumten geätzt*. Bürger's comment on this is worth quoting in extenso: "This will to paradox, which corresponds with the often observed paradoxes of Celan's work, here shows itself most clearly as determining and putting into motion the poetic fixing-process. Only insofar as a logical paradox seems to be cleared up, namely the contradiction between sleeplessness and dream-reality, does an extremely effective pictorial paradox arise—in the reality and effectiveness of an absence, the 'undreamt.' In this paradox, the 'undreamt' is yet again tendered in the poem as dream-reality, and enters into a new contradiction with "sleeplessly" in the second line."

geätzt | etched: Evoked here is the process of using strong acid or mordant (from French *mordre*, "to bite") to cut into the unprotected parts of a metal surface (usually copper, zinc, or steel) to create a design in intaglio in the metal. This was the core process GCL used in her art. See introduction notes for *Atemwende*, and this cycle, *Atemkristall*, above.

"In die Rillen" | *"Into the furrows"*
October 16, 1963.
Himmelsmünze: In the first edition, as in my 1969 translation of this volume, the word was given as *Himmelssäure* (heavensacid), which turned out to be a typo.

"In den Flüssen" | *"In the rivers"*
October 16, 1963. The north is for Celan associated with ice and snow, and thus landscapes of death and desolation. Useful here may be to remember that

the ur-mythologies the Nazi system misused were such Nordic settings and heroes, as Friedrich Nietzsche postulated, for example, in the opening paragraph of his *Antichrist*, worth quoting here in full (in H. L. Mencken's translation):

> Let us look each other in the face. We are Hyperboreans—we know well enough how remote our place is. "Neither by land nor by water will you find the road to the Hyperboreans": even Pindar, in his day, knew that much about us. Beyond the North, beyond the ice, beyond death—our life, our happiness . . . We have discovered that happiness; we know the way; we got our knowledge of it from thousands of years in the labyrinth. Who else has found it?—The man of today?—"I don't know either the way out or the way in; I am whatever doesn't know either the way out or the way in"—so sighs the man of today . . . This is the sort of modernity that made us ill,— we sickened on lazy peace, cowardly compromise, the whole virtuous dirtiness of the modern Yea and Nay. This tolerance and largeur of the heart that "forgives" everything because it "understands" everything is a sirocco to us. Rather live amid the ice than among modern virtues and other such south-winds! . . . We were brave enough; we spared neither ourselves nor others; but we were a long time finding out where to direct our courage. We grew dismal; they called us fatalists. Our fate—it was the fulness, the tension, the storing up of powers. We thirsted for the lightnings and great deeds; we kept as far as possible from the happiness of the weakling, from "resignation" . . . There was thunder in our air; nature, as we embodied it, became overcast—for we had not yet found the way. The formula of our happiness: a Yea, a Nay, a straight line, a goal.

Lefebvre also points to Henri Michaux's poem "Icebergs" and its hyperborean landscapes; the second stanza reads: "Icebergs, icebergs, cathedrals without religion of the eternal winter, wrapped in the glacial icecap of planet Earth."

beschwerst | weight: Besides the meaning "to weigh (down) with," the German *beschweren* also resonates with the meanings of *sich beschweren*, "to complain," and one can hear *beschwören* as "invoke," "conjure," "beseech."

"Vor dein spätes Gesicht" | *"Before your late face"*
Exact date of composition unknown.

"Die Schwermutsschnellen hindurch" | *"Down melancholy's rapids"*
October 17, 1963. On a list with corrections for the proofs, Celan noted: "re: melancholy's rapids: . . . / there the forty and four / (check the date in the original)" (TA, *Atemwende*, p. 16). Celan's forty-fourth birthday was November 23, 1964. Barbara Wiedemann (BW, p. 720) notes that, computing from Celan's birth year, the number forty gives 1960, the year Celan received the Büchner Prize and gave the Meridian speech. This is, however, also the year in which the Goll affair reached its paroxysm. Calculating backward from the date of composition of the poem, the number four gives October 17, 1959, the day on which Celan read the, to him, very painful review of *Sprachgitter* by Günter Blöcker.

vierzig | forty: Also connotes a range of biblical meanings; it is a number often used by God to represent a period of testing or judgment, thus the forty years the Israelites spent in the wilderness, the forty days of rain in the days of the flood, the forty-day periods of fasting, testing, and communing with God faced by Moses (who was forty when God called on him) and Jesus, etc.

Lebensbäume | lifetrees: The first draft of the poem had *Lebensstämme*, where *stämme*, the plural of *Stamm*, can refer to a tree trunk and/or to a tribe, that is, a family line. See also the later poem "Zwanzig für immer" | "Twenty forever" (p. 22).

"Die Zahlen" | *"The numbers"*
October 18, 1963. First notes toward the poem on a page of the French daily *Le Monde* dated October 18, 1963 (which means the paper came out the previous afternoon) and on an envelope postmarked October 16, 1965. The following poem was also written that day. Lefebvre suggests "a relation between the title and the fact that this is the seventh poem of the cycle. Celan showed an interest in numbers that at times bordered on superstition, and that often linked to the interpretations of the esoteric tradition. But here it is mainly a matter of the numbers' association with the images in language in terms of quantity (number of words in a text, or in a verse) and as order of the elements of an alphabet or discourse. The numbers' alliance [my 'in league'] with the

images is thus also the combination of a kind of abstract rigor with the changing fate of images in poetry (Verhängnis)" (RDS, p. 197).

"Wege im Schatten-Gebräch" | *"Paths in the shadow-break"*
October 18, 1963.

Gebräch | break: *Gebräch* is a hunting term and refers to the ground uprooted by wild boars. Unable to find the exact corresponding term, I have preferred to translate—albeit by an overly abstract word—the core term of the German word, which is the verb *brechen*, "to break." Lynch and Jakowsky have tried to keep the hunting image alive, and give the line as "PATHS in the boar-tusked shadowland," which sounds not only contrived, though vaguely Celanian, but also introduces two terms, "boar" and "land," that are not in Celan's text. By translating *wühlen* in the next stanza as "root up," I hope that some sense of the hunting/animal terminology is brought back in. See also Celan's early poem "In der Gestalt eines Ebers" | "In the shape of a boar" (*Von Schwelle zu Schwelle*).

Georg-Michael Schulz provides a fascinating analysis of this poem in an essay in the *Celan-Jahrbuch* 2 ("'Sterblichkeitsbeflissen.' Zu Paul Celans Gedicht 'Wege im Schatten-Gebräch,'" pp. 29–36). According to him, the poem is based on a very specific iconic image: "a figure one can find in Jewish cemeteries on a number of grave stones . . . a figure of two hands in the gesture of blessing." He goes on to quote a description of how the hands have to be held during the blessing ritual which lies at the origin of the grave inscription. It is this mudralike figure that creates the "four-finger-furrow": "the finger thus, with pinkie touching ring-finger, and the likewise linked middle and index fingers propped [*sic*], these (for their part) by both thumbs, so that five interstices ensue—two each opening up above; the middle ones, between the thumbs down below."

"Weißgrau" | *"Whitegray"*
October 25, 1963.

Strandhafer | sea oats: A psammophylic (sand-loving) species of grass in the Poaceae family, *Leymus arenarius*, is commonly known as sea lyme grass, or simply lyme grass. It could also be of the genus *Uniola*, that is, the species *U. Paniculata*, which we call sea oats. Both are strong grasses that consolidate seaside sand dunes, thus reducing land erosion. I prefer the literal translation "sea oats" here to "lyme grass," for being closer to the original. See also the poems "Vom Anblick der Amseln" | "From beholding the blackbirds" and "Wir, die wie der Strandhafer Wahren" | "We who like the sea oats guard" (pp. 94 and 432) and their respective commentaries (pp. 497 and 619).

ein Ohr, abgetrennt | an ear, severed: Reference to Van Gogh. See also the poem "Mächte, Gewalten" | "Principalities, powers" (p. 204).

Ein Aug, in Streifen geschnitten | An eye, cut in strips: Brings to mind a core image in Buñuel's film *Un chien andalou*.

"Mit erdwärts gesungenen Masten" | *"With masts sung earthward"*
October 26, 1963.

"Schläfenzange" | *"Templeclamps"*
November 8, 1963. Celan's firstborn son, François, had died exactly ten years and one month before this date, a death due to a mismanaged forceps delivery. This is the center poem of the first cycle.

Schläfenzange | Templeclamps: The usual German term for forceps is *Geburtszange* (birth tongs), but Celan's neologism is immediately obvious.

"Beim Hagelkorn" | *"Next to the hailstone"*
November 8, 1963. Same day as poem above.

den harten / Novembersternen | the hard / November stars . . . Schütze | archer: Celan was born on November 23, under the sign of Sagittarius, the archer.

"Stehen" | *"To stand"*
November 11, 1963. Armistice Day in France, the celebration of the end of World War I. Lefebvre (RDS, p. 203) links this poem to Celan's translations of Shakespeare's sonnets 79, 81, and 106. Exactly three years earlier, on November 11, 1960, an article by Rainer Kabel in *Die Welt* had made public in great detail Claire Goll's accusations of plagiarism against Celan and for the first time spoke of Goll's claims that the "Todesfuge" was essentially Goll. In the limited *Atemkristall* edition, the poem has a special position in that it is the only poem flanked on both sides by an etching by GCL (BW, p. 722).

Stehen | To stand: For the importance of this stance for Celan, see my introduction to PCS (p. 6); see also the earlier poem from *Die Niemandsrose*, "Eine Gauner- und Ganovenweise," which ends with the lines: "But, / but it rises up [*bäumt sich*], the tree. It, / it too / stands against / the plague." Further information can be found in the poems and commentaries on poems using the concept of the upright station, such as "Für Eric" | "For Eric" (pp. 362 and 594), "Wirk nicht voraus" | "Do not work ahead" (pp. 316 and 575), and "Es stand" | "It stood" (pp. 430 and 617).

für dich / allein | for you / alone: Both Wiedemann and Lefebvre link these lines to a quote, often cited by Celan during the Goll affair years, by Rabbi Hillel from the German edition by Reinhold Meyer, which says: "Wenn ich nicht für mich bin, wer ist dann für mich?" (If I am not for myself, who will be for me?) The Talmudic text continues: "And when I am for myself, what am 'I'? And if not now, when?"

"Dein vom Wachen" | *"Your dream"*

November 25, 1963. This twelve-line poem coincides with the twelfth anniversary of Paul Celan and Gisèle Celan-Lestrange's first meeting in November 1951. This and the following poem have been analyzed in detail in relation to Celan's use of dream language by Böschenstein-Schäfer ("Traum und Sprache in der Dichtung Paul Celans," pp. 223–38), who suggest that Celan, like many survivors of terrorist regimes, and despite his attraction to Surrealism, is wary of dreams and afraid of invasion or betrayal of/by that most private area, the unconscious. He has two ways of defending himself against this:

> Of these the first is the concentration on awakening, the second, the replacement of the structures of dream speech in the poetic. In the place of the dream image the poet thematizes the attempt to produce, through the recollection of the dream, contact with the unconscious. "Shaft," "gorge" and "suction pipe" are all variants of the vertical, which especially in the volumes *Breathturn*, *Threadsuns*, and *Lightduress* characterize the way dream elements enter into consciousness.

In these poems one could also hear a Lacanian theme: the unconscious/the dream is/as language. It is more than likely that during the sixties in Paris Celan was aware of, and probably read, Lacan.

Horn | horn: A very rich multisemic image invoking the shofar, traditionally the horn of a ram, used in Jewish religious ceremonies where shofar blowing, often mentioned in the biblical texts, is incorporated into services on Rosh Hashanah and Yom Kippur. Another image arising here, via the "helically carved spoor," is that of the torsions of the ivory unicorn, while a further turn could connect it to the "Gate of Horn," which according to Homer leads to the true dreams. *The Odyssey* 19, 562–69, in Charles Stein's 2008 translation (p. 474), says: "Guest-stranger / dreams are difficult to make sense of / and not all are fulfilled for men, / for there are two gates for fleeting dreams to pass through: one is fashioned of horn and one of ivory. / Dreams that come through the gate of sawn ivory deceive us, / bearing words that will not be fulfilled. / Dreams that come through polished horn / bring truth to pass / when some mortal sees them."

"Mit den Verfolgten" | *"With the persecuted"*
November 27, 1963. The following poem was also written on that day.

Das Morgen-Lot | the morning-plumb: Another complex paranomastic construction that creates insurmountable difficulties for the translator. This and many similar constructions are based on common German expressions—in this case *Morgenrot* (dawn redness)—that do not carry over into the translation, but that in the German poem the new word forces one to also read/hear. In this specific case the translation also loses a further connotation, that of the biblical figure Lot who was led by the angels from the condemned city at dawn—"And when the morning arose, then the angels hastened Lot, saying: 'Arise, take thy wife, and thy two daughters that are here; lest thou be swept away in the iniquity of the city'" (Gen. 19:15; Jewish Publication Society Bible). A *Lot* is, further, the plumb or lead instrument with which to measure water depth. One could be tempted to link this sailor's instrument to the marine imagery of the ferryman's pole in the previous poem.

"Fadensonnen" | *"Threadsuns"*
November 27, 1963. A poem much discussed and analyzed in the critical Celan literature. Hartmut Steinecke, for example, has written a sharp-tongued essay comparing the various analyses it has been subjected to.

Fadensonnen | Threadsuns: The title of this poem will provide the title of the next volume. We do not know if Celan was familiar with the measuring instrument (used to calculate the exact moment of noon) known as a *Faden-Sonnenzeiger* or *Filargnomon*, in French *méridienne filaire*. In the first draft of the poem, the word was hyphenated as *Faden-Sonnen*. Celan may also have had in mind a word he underlined in his reading of Jean Paul's *Die unsichtbare Loge*, namely, *Fadensommer*, something close to our Indian summer.

Lichtton | light-tone: "Light-tone" and "light-pitch" are literal translations of *Lichtton*, if one considers the word as a Celanian composite. The German word is, however, also a technical term in filmography, where it refers to the process of "sound-on-film" in which sound is inscribed as variations of light values on film.

"Im Schlangenwagen" | *"In the serpentcoach"*
December 16, 1963. Hanukkah was celebrated that year from December 11 to 18.

Schlangenwagen | serpentcoach: Grammatically the word can mean a serpentlike type of conveyance, or describe the content of the coach. Böschenstein-Schäfer (p. 234) suggests the following reading: "The image of the serpentcoach: in this are knotted the image of Medea of Kolchis, fleeing in despair in a chariot drawn by dragons, and of the muse's chariot, even as Pindar or Empedocles hoped to mount it." Lefebvre thinks of it as an "Orphic visit to the mother, deported from Czernowitz to the Michailovka camp (crossing the Bug river, the train snaked along all the way to death)" (RDS, p. 207). In the Orphic tradition, it is also remembered that Eurydice dies of a snakebite. In his volume of Georg Trakl's poems, Celan had written "strange. cf. Todesfuge" next to a line from the poem "Psalm" that reads: "In his grave the white magician plays with this serpents."

weißen Zypresse | white cypress: Celan owned a copy of the pre-Socratic fragments that contain the following Orphic text, consisting of directions on how to enter Hades, the English translation of which reads: "You will find a spring on the left of the halls of Hades, and beside it a white cypress growing. Do not even go near this spring. And you will find another, from the Lake of Memory, flowing forth with cold water. In front of it are guards. You must say, 'I am the child of Gê (Earth) and of starry Ouranos (Heaven); this you yourselves also know. And they themselves will give you to drink from the divine spring, and then thereafter you shall reign with the other heroes" (Kathleen Freeman, *Ancilla to the Pre-Socratic Philosphers: A Complete Translation of the Fragments in Diels, Fragmente der Vorsokratiker* [Cambridge, Mass.: Harvard University Press, 1983], p. 5).

"Harnischstriemen" | *"Slickensides"*
December 18, 1963. A fascinating poem by which to gauge various readings/interpretations. For one such reading, see Klaus Manger, "Paul Celans poetische Geographie" (*Psalm und Hawdalah: Zum Werk Paul Celans.* Bern/Frankfurt am Main/New York/Paris: Peter Lang, 1987). Hans-Georg Gadamer's reading of the same poem goes wrong, as James K. Lyon has shown, because he misunderstood the vocabulary. Thus: "Harnischstriemen" | "Slickensides" and the next two words, "Faltenachsen" | "fold-axes" and "Durchstich- / punkte" | "rechanneling- / points," are geological terms, the first of which refers to striae, that is, striations on rock surfaces that are visible where monolithic blocks have scraped against each other during large-scale volcanic upheavals. I prefer to use another geological term, "slickensides," a more interesting English word, which in geology is defined as fine parallel scratches or grooves on a fault surface that have been produced by the movement of the rocks on either side of the fault.

Faltenachsen | fold-axes: Refers to the direction of the thrust when the earth's strata are folded by volcanic activity to form rises and depressions.

Durchstich- / punkte | rechanneling- / points: In geology the term refers to a technical term in flood control for cutting through sharp curves in a meandering river, that is, a means of altering the landscape by rechanneling the river. But—see James K. Lyon's "Paul Celan's Language of Stone"—another meaning is also possible: "[It] can also refer to the points left in a chart or map which is copied by means of pinpoints."

An beiden Polen | On both poles: For a discussion of Celan's use of "poles," see E. Hünnecke's essay "Hoffnung auf ein menschliches Heute und Morgen" (*Celan-Jahrbuch* 1, pp. 149–50). In the posthumous volume *Zeitgehöft*, in the poem "Das Flüsterhaus" | "The whisperhouse," the poles return. Compare page 418 and the commentary on that poem (p. 614).

Kluftrose | cleftrose: The rose/flower as image/metaphor is present throughout Celan's work, most insistently so in the volume *Die Niemandsrose*.

It becomes rarer in the later volumes and appears only three times (twice as a composite and once as the flower name) from *Breathturn* onward. The present composite, *Kluftrose*, is most likely derived from *Windrose*, or compass rose, or maybe also plays on the geological term "joint rosette" (see Pajari Räsänen, "Counter-figures: An Essay on Anti-metaphoric Resistance," Ph.D. diss., Department of Comparative Literature, University of Helsinki, 2007, p. 213).

"Wortaufschüttung" | *"Wordaccretion"*
December 24, 1963. On the previous day, December 23, which was also his eleventh wedding anniversary, Celan completed the typescript of his Shakespeare translations that would be broadcast on Norddeutscher Rundfunk for Shakespeare's four hundredth birthday on April 23, 1964, and published as *William Shakespeare: Einundzwanzig Sonnette* by Insel Verlag in 1967.

Wortaufschüttung | Wordaccretion: The German *Aufschüttung* comes again from the vocabulary of geology, where it designates accretion or aggradation, where an elevation is created by successive deposits. Celan underlined the three words of the opening two lines in Siegmund Günther's *Physische Geographie*: "In earlier geological eras the process of underwater volcanic accretion [*unterseeischer Vulkanaufschüttung*] was not rare." The qualifier "word" here points the poem toward a poetological statement. Other reading traces (underlinings) appear in similar scientific sources.

Nachbild | replica: See Ernst Bloch, vol. 1, p. 743 of the German edition of *Das Prinzip Hoffnung* | *The Principle of Hope* (Frankfurt am Main: Suhrkamp Verlag, 1954).

Königs- / geburten | kings- / births: Note the date of the poem's composition—Christmas Eve. See also the translation of Shakespeare's sonnet 60: "Nativity, once in the main light, / crawls to maturity, wherewith being crown'd, / Crooked eclipses 'gainst his glory fight . . ." In Celan's translation: "Geburt, ins volle Licht gerückt, sie kraucht | zur Reife hin; und so, gekrönt, umglänzt noch eben . . ." (translated the previous month).

"(Ich kenne dich" | *"(I know you"*
January 9, 1964. This poem, written for his wife, has had many commentators. For one of the most complete analyses, see James K. Lyon's 1987 essay "Ganz und gar nicht hermetisch." Lefebvre suggests that "this rhymed quatrain

could resemble a parody of Rilke, or of Goethe (The Divan) or another great lyric poet. The parentheses (which are not present in the *Atemkristall* volume) underline its deliberate isolation in the volume—as well as the specificity of the you—, but also draw attention to the very term Klammer (parenthesis), remanent in Celan. This framing and the classical form isolate and iconize the poem (making it a sort of pietà). 'To know,' here, in the lover's aparte, keeps its eroto-biblical sense: the loved woman thus melts into the mother of the pietà, with the mother of the poet transperced by pain" (RDS, p. 210).

"Weggebeizt" | *"Eroded"*

December 30, 1963. The last poem of 1963, this is also the last poem of the *Atemkristall* cycle, returning to the first poem's snow imagery. Here, however, the snow is not proffered, no "you" is invited to partake of the snow: the snow has frozen into classical glacier features, terms found and underlined in Siegmund Günther's *Physische Geographie*: *Büsserschnee*, "penitent's snow," *Gletschertisch*, "glacier table," *Gletscherstube*, "glacier parlor," *vom Winde weggebeizt*, "eroded by the wind," *Auswirblung oder Evorsion*, "evorsion/ed," *Wabeneis*, "honeycomb-ice."

Weggebeizt | Eroded: Besides the geological reference, the word *wegbeizen* also refers to the vocabulary of art, where acid is used to create patterns on metal. GCL used such techniques in her etchings.

Mein- / gedicht | perjury- / poem: Celan's neologism "Mein- / gedicht" is based analogically on the German word *Meineid*, "a false oath," "perjury," while the other meanings of *mein* of course vibrate along: "mine" and *ge- mein*, common in both senses as communal and cheap, maybe even *Meinung*, "meaning."

II

"Vom großen" | *"By the great"*

January 22, 1964. First published in the *Festschrift Auf gespaltenen Pfaden* (ed. Manfred Schlösser, Darmstadt, 1964) for the ninetieth birthday of Margarete Susman (1872–1966). Susman was a poet, dramatist, and essayist (on Kafka, Jean Paul, Adalbert Stifter, Gustav Landauer, and Rosa Luxemburg, among others, all thinkers important to Celan, and on modern poetry and Jewish questions). Celan, who had met her in 1963 in Zurich, had read her 1946 book, *Das Buch Hiob und das Schicksal des jüdischen Volkes* (The Book of Job and the Fate of the Jewish People), the first book on the Shoah, as well as her work on Spinoza.

sechs- / kantige | six- / edged: Wiedemann locates a reading trace in Franz Lotze's *Geologie* (Berlin: Walter de Gruyter, 1955): "As the minute components are blown away in the arid regions, there come into existence . . . stone deserts with wind-blown sand on rocks and boulders (triple-edges [Dreikanter]; such like also under other climatic conditions as on sandy shores)" (BW, p. 727). See also the poem "Einkanter" (p. 376). The six-edged stone also links to the star of David (see also note on Esther below).

Findling | erratic: In German the word *Findling* has two distinct meanings: (1) as a variant of *Findelkind* it means a foundling (child); (2) as a geological term it translates as "glacial erratic" and refers to a large piece of rock, or a boulder, that has been carried by ice for some distance and has then come to rest where the ice has melted.

Esther: The biblical Esther was an orphan who, married to the non-Jewish King Ahasuerus, managed to thwart a plot to kill all the Jews. Here the name also honors Margarete Susman, making her "into a figure of the resistance: Esther, consonant with *Stern* (star), *stehen* (to stand). The name itself, Ishtar, of Babylonian origin, seems to be connected to the Persian *stareh*: 'star'; Esther is the Babylonian name of Hadassa, which in Hebrew also means 'star.' The tyrant Ahasuerus, to whom Esther had been married by force, is identified with Hitler in the Jewish community" (Lefebvre, RDS, p. 214).

"Singbarer Rest" | "Singable remnant"

January 29, 1964. Also published in the Susman Festschrift, and thus also readable as a conversation with her and her work, the poem is a poetological statement speaking of those remains that can be sung, which are a human figure—possibly the ghost shape of the exterminated—that yet manages to break through at a place associated with death—the snowplace—and witness, even if with "disenfranchised lip," announcing that "something happens, still."

"Flutender" | *"Flowing"*
January 30, 1969.

"Zwanzig für immer" | *"Twenty forever"*
End-of-year 1962 into 1963; finished February 5, 1964. Early note in *Die Niemandsrose* folder: "Zwanzig Schlüsselburgblumen und / zwanzig Gesänge dazu." (Twenty key-castle-flowers and / twenty songs too.)

Schlüsselburg-Blumen | Schlüsselburg-primroses: A complex pun combining the name Schlüsselburg (an infamous Russian prison castle in Petrokrepost, a town on an island of the river Neva, where during the days of the czar many revolutionaries were imprisoned and/or executed) and *Schlüsselblumen* (primroses or cowslips), a traditional symbol of spring. *Schlüssel* means "key," and *Burg*, "castle." The town's coat of arms included a golden key. The Russian revolutionary and writer Wera Figner (1852–1942), who was imprisoned there for twenty years, writes in her autobiography, *Nacht über Russland* (Night over Russia) (Berlin, 1928): "20 years in casemates. When the clock of life stopped." (quoted by Wiedemann in BW, p. 728). Renate Böschenstein-Schäfer suggests that the number twenty may point to the twenty-one members of the Narodnaya Volya movement who were imprisoned in Petrokrepost in 1884 and nearly all died.

"Keine Sandkunst mehr" | *"No sandart anymore"*
February 10, 1964. The single draft shows that Celan made no emendations or changes to this poem, except for a pencil mark indicating a larger break between the last two lines.

Sandkunst | sandart: Badiou has pointed to reading traces in Eis, elaborated on in Barbara Wiedemann's commentary (BW, p. 728): "'Geomancy or sandart (in Arabic, ilm al-raml "Sand science"') is an ancient method of exploring the future' and 'most German sandbooks of the 14th to 16th centuries cannot be ascribed to a specific author' (pp. 7 and 8)." She goes on: "Further on the process, which elsewhere is also called the 'sandscience of the sixteen masters' (p. 12), is explained: Through quadruple marking of a random number of points in the sand or by throwing the dice one of sixteen fixed figures is determined via fixed rules. The soothsaying text contains sixteen answers to sixteen fixed questions concerning the future directed to the 'judges,' who have Hebrew names (p. 9). The sandbook may only be used where no noise may disturb the operation (p. 8). The procedure spread throughout Europe through the agency of Jews, among others (p. 8)."

"Helligkeitshunger" | *"Brightnesshunger"*
February 15, 1964. The following poem was also written on that day.

"Als uns das Weiße anfiel" | *"When whiteness assailed us"*
February 15, 1964. Celan had written a poem on December 15, 1962, that started with the lines "als aus dem Spendekrug mehr / kam als Wasser" | "when from the libation-ewer more | than water came," taken up here again. Here, that poem (note that Celan's play on the homophonic words *mehr*, "more," and *Meer*, "sea," is lost in translation):

When from the libation-ewer more
than water came. When
pus came after the more.
And more than pus. When
the sea also
had come, then

a breath braided a face that was
sharp as the newly
born keel, standing upward, travelready, into
the other sea—the one
with the splinter and signs
and the signsplinters.

Don't say there was
no lid
above the pair of eyes in
that face.
　　　　There were flightlids, lashed, the gazes
had their tent.

Opferglocke | sacrificebell: In all drafts, except the final print proof, the word is given as *Opferlocke* (Sacrifice-[hair]lock). We cannot be sure if Celan missed the typo or let it consciously stand as a meaningful "error," in the way Robert Duncan was wont to speak—and make use—of such occurrences.

"Hohles Lebensgehöft" | *"Hollow lifehomestead"*
February 20, 1964.

Lebensgehöft | lifehomestead: The German noun *Gehöft* translates into our "farmstead," which *Merriam-Webster* defines as "the buildings and adjacent service areas of a farm; *broadly*: a farm with its buildings," or "homestead," defined as the home and adjoining land occupied by a family. Celan will make use of the word—and even more so of its core seme, *Hof* (farm, space, courtyard, etc.)—on a number of occasions. *Gehöft* most visibly enters into the composition of the title of his last (posthumous volume) *Zeitgehöft*, which I translated as "Timestead." These terms, as well as *Zeithof* (timehalo), also interest Celan because of the use to which they are put by the philosopher Edmund Husserl. For more details on this, see the commentary for the poem "Schwimmhäute" | "Webbing" (p. 566).

Schlafkorn | sleepcorn: Celan came across this term for a soporific grain in Jean Paul's *Hesperus*. In the same sentence Jean Paul uses the word *weggebeizt*, "eroded," which becomes the title of another Celan poem (see p. 18).

"Über drei" | *"Over three"*
February 26, 1964. Eve of Purim.

Braunalgenblut | brownalgae-blood: Reading traces indicated by Wiedemann (BW, p. 730) in Roland Brinkman's *Abriß der Geologie* (p. 84): "On the oceanfloor the seaweeds belonging to the brown algae take root, as do the geologically important chalk-algae, that are composed of the lime-producing forms of the blue, red, and green algae."

Brust- / warzensteine | breast- / nipplestones: Celan combines two words: the word *Brustwarze* refers to the nipple or teat of the breast. A *Warzenstein*, according to the Grimms' *Deutsches Wörterbuch*, is "ein versteinerter seeigel oder theil davon, mit erhöhungen an den stellen, wo stacheln gestanden haben" (a petrified sea urchin or a part thereof, with tubercles where the spines stood). Celan may have come across the latter term in Jean Paul's *Das Kampaner Thal*.

"Am weißen Gebetriemen" | *"On the white philactery"*
March 5, 1964.

Gebetriemen | phylactery: Literally translated, *Gebetriemen* means "prayer-belt"; the term is, however, a specific object in Judaism (called "phylactery" in English), where it refers to either of two small leather boxes, each containing strips of parchment inscribed with quotations from the Hebrew scriptures. One is strapped to the forehead, the other to the left arm by observant Jewish men during morning worship, except on Sabbath and holidays.

A second, archaic meaning of "philactery" is "amulet, reminder." Although the technical, Greek-derived term "phylactery" may seem odd or to even overdetermine the German compound, the context here clearly points to the Jewish cult object, something an English neologism such as "prayer belt" would not.

"Erblinde" | *"Go blind"*
March 13, 1964.

"Engholztag" | *"Latewoodday"*
March 15, 1964.

Engholztag | Latewoodday: *Engholz*, literally "narrow wood," is rarer than its synonym *Spätholz*, literally "late wood." The words come from botany and describe the yearly growth of trees: thus the inner portion of a tree's growth ring, formed early in the growing season, when growth is comparatively rapid (hence the wood is less dense), is known as "early wood" or "spring wood" or "late-spring wood," *Frühholz* in German. *Engholz* refers to the outer portion and is "late wood" (or "summer wood") and is denser, as *eng* (narrow, tight, dense) indicates.

Tierblütige | Animal-bloodsoming: *Blütig* is a neologism that mixes *blutig* (bloody, bleeding, etc.) with *blühen, blüte*, etc.—that is, the word convolutes around flower/flowering/blossom. The translator's neologism "bloodsoming" tries, however clumsily, to render this double load.

"Heute" | *"Today"*

April 6, 1964, Moisville (for place, see commentary for "Du darfst" / "You may," p. 461).

Nacktpflanzenreigen | naked-plants-dance: *Nacktpflanze* is a botanical term (present in Celan's Brockhaus dictionary of geology) for a kind of plant also called a psilophite, which literally means "naked plant." These are simple dichotomously branched plants that first appeared during the Late Silurian, are now limited to two extant genera, lack true leaves and roots, and include the oldest known land plants with vascular tissue.

Halb- und Viertel-verbündete | Half- and quarter-allies: A number of references in this poem could point to Celan thinking about the Goll affair, during which people he thought were allies seemed often not to back him as much as he expected. Another possible reference to this could be the term "owl-pebble" above, which Lefebvre tentatively links to "the publishing house Ullstein (which had an owl as its emblem), expropriated by the Nazi regime and bought back by Axel Springer in the sixties" (RDS, p. 225).

Reichtümer an / verloren-vergällter / Sprache | Riches of / lost-soured / language: See certain formulation's in Celan's Bremen speech: "Only one thing remained reachable, close, and secure amid all the losses: language. Yes, language. In spite of everything, it remained secure against loss. But it had to go through its own lack of answers, through terrifying silences, through the thousand darknesses of murderous speech. It went through. It gave me no words for what was happening, but went through it. Went through and would resurface, 'enriched' by it all" (PCCP, p. 34).

"Mittags" | *"Midday"*

April 30, 1964.

zwei Tage in Rom | two days in Rome: Celan traveled in Italy, first Rome, then Milan, from April 16 to April 21. From Rome, he visited Cerveteri, the largest extant Etruscan necropolis. Compare also the poem "Die Ewigkeit" | "Eternity" from the volume *Fadensonnen* | *Threadsuns* (p. 176).

"Unter die Haut" | *"Sown under"*

June 3, 1964.

"Das Stundenglas" | *"The hourglass"*
June 4, 1964, Moisville. Compare two earlier versions in the letters to his wife (PC/GCL, #184).

Päonienschatten | paeony shadow: The flower is named after Paeon—the name means "she who heals"—a student of Asclepius, the Greek god of medicine and healing. It was traditionally used in medicine to treat epilepsy, convulsions, and nervous troubles (RDS, p. 227). In German it is also called a *Pfingstrose*, or "Pentecost rose."

wo du versandend verhoffst | where you, mired, test the wind: This last line poses difficulties for the translation. *Versandend* has the sense of being progressively mired in sand, to "silt up"; *Verhoffst*, repeating the *ver-* particle in a typical Celanian way, seems at first semantically to reduplicate the meaning of *versandend*, suggesting the progressive loss of hope. But the verb *verhoffen*—in which one could hear *hoffen*, "to hope"—is, in fact, a technical hunting term usually used in reference to deer and meaning "to stand quietly and scent the wind." This double meaning of loss of hope and yet of a still active listening to the world in literal translation loses the repetition (sameness in difference) and ambiguity of the German particle *ver-*. In previous versions, given the negative connotation of "bogged down" (now changed to "mired"), I tried to translate the active, hunting sense of "verhoffst" with "scent" (as in "to scent danger"), but now prefer to go with "test the wind"—longer but more accurate. It is also how I translated the "verhoffen" that Celan uses in the Meridian speech, where it occurs in the following sentence, which also uses a double "ver-," though with a difference: "The poem tarries [*verweilt*] or tests the wind [*verhofft*]—a word related to the creaturely—through such thoughts . . . Nobody can tell how long the breath pause—the testing [*das Verhoffen*] and the thought—will last" (MFV, p. 8).

"Hafen | *"Harbor"*
June 24–25, 1964—Moisville, August 2, 1964. First notes (nautical vocabulary) toward the poem date to a stay in Hamburg for two readings on June 24 and 25 (TA, *Atemwende*, p. 82) and were possibly made on the occasion of a tour of the harbor, suggests Wiedemann (BW, p. 732).

Mutter Clausen | Mother Clausen: *Mutter Paulsen* in one of the early drafts, though no bar with either name can be verified as actually existing in Hamburg at that time. Mutter Paulsen is a figure in Theodor Storm's *Pole Poppenspäler*.

zeitgrünen Uhrturm | timegreen clocktower: The word "clocktower" occurs in Celan's Hamburg notes and refers to a clocktower on the jetties that besides the time also indicates the water level; its copper roof was discolored by verdigris (BW, p. 733).

ein Wahndock, / schwimmend, | a delusion-dock, / swimming: The notes also have the word *Schwimmdocks* (floating dock), on which the neologism is based.

die / Buchstaben der / Großkräne einen / Unnamen schreiben | the / letters of the / tower cranes write / an unname: Wiedemann, informed by Jürgen Köchel, indicates that the goliath cranes (*Portalkräne* in the notes) in the Hamburg harbor "consisted of an H-shaped structure topped by an A-shaped crane; the initials 'AH' Celan could possibly have read as 'Adolf Hitler,' certainly an 'unname' for him" (BW, p. 733).

Laufkatze Leben: An untranslatable compound in which Celan obviously wants the reader to hear *Katze* (cat) and *Lauf* (run) as descriptive of *Leben*, but the word *Laufkatze* is clearly, given the poem's harbor geography, the technical apparatus called in English a "trolley" or "trolley hoist." So far I have been unable to find an English equivalent that would render this meaning-complex in a satisfactory manner. Paratactic juxtaposition of both meanings seems the only way, combined with the female pronoun "she" rather than the expected "it."

Ziehbrunnenwinde | draw well winch: An old reading trace locates the word *Ziehbrunnen* in Celan's copy of the translation of James Joyce's *Ulysses*, and in several poem fragments from that time.

eulenspiegelt | owlglasses: The play on *spiegeln*, "to mirror," "to reflect," and on the name Till Eulenspiegel, the Saxon *Narr* (fool), clear in German, does not translate well. The name has been translated as "Owlglass" in English versions of the tales and this seems to be here the best—or least deleterious—way of proceeding.

It may be noteworthy that Osip Mandelstam had been falsely accused of unethical translation practices close to plagiarism (as had Celan—see the Goll affair) in a 1928 scandal that came to be known as the Eulenspiegel affair, as it concerned the translation of the Belgian novelist Charles de Coster's novel of that title.

III

"Schwarz" | *"Black"*
August 3–9, 1964. First notes closely connect to the next two poems.

Kronland | crownland: Celan's homeland, the Bukovina, today part of Ukraine, was a (partly autonomous) crownland of the Habsburg Austro-Hungarian Empire.

"Hammerköpfiges" | *"Anvilheadedness"*
August 3–15, 1964. Lefebvre makes an interesting comment—valid for English as well as for French—concerning the translation of two terms in this poem, the neutral word *Hämmerköpfiges* and *Silbriges*, which, he writes, are "adjectives made into substantives that designate an apparent substantiality (that the proposed translation unhappily reduces into nouns—and thus into metaphors, which is not the status of the original terms)" (RDS, p. 92).

Hammerköpfiges | Anvilheadedness: The first drafts add the word *Wolken*, indicating the meteorological origin of the word, as "anvil clouds." But the vocabulary quickly moves to horse-connected imagery, so that the first image of a possible "hammer-headed" horse cannot be excluded, thus:

Zeltgang | palfrey pace: The ability of certain horses (palfreys—the word comes from the German for horse, *Pferd*) to advance in a smooth, ambling gait rather than at a trot.

kentaurisch / gebäumt | centaurishly / rearing: The "palfrey" here becomes the centaur, half horse, half man, usually shown holding a bow and arrow, as archer, which is Celan's astrological sign.

"Landschaft" | *"Landscape"*
August 3–16, 1964. Started in Moisville, where Celan noted on the back of the leaf on whose other side he sketched out the poem "Schwarz" | "Black": "in dieser / Stunde der nuschelnden / Urnenwesen / lebten wir königlich

nach / den erfüllten Gesetzen der Liebe" (in this / hour of the mumbling / urnbeings / we lived like kings according to / the fulfilled laws of love); the first actual draft has "Garotten- / Spanisch / von Rauchmund zu Rauchmund" (Garotte- / Spanish / from smokemouth to smokemouth), while the final version has simple "Gespräche" | "conversations" (TA *Atemwende*, p. 92). Lefebvre suggests that of this Spanish horizon there remains only "the half-shell (Jakobsmuschel | pilgrim's scallop) of the pilgrims of St. James' Way (the pilgrimage route to the Cathedral of Santiago de Compostalla in Galicia, Spain) and the possible allusion to an execution. The Spanish state used the garrote to execute its condemned until 1975. But Muschel also calls up, via Mauscheln, the Jewish speech of the exiled, of the wandering pilgrim Jew (just as the urn and the smoke connote the crematory ovens)" (RDS, pp. 231–32).

Wiedemann (BW, p. 734) adds the following information: "During a visit by Celan's friends Jean and Mayotte Bollack in the summer of 1964 to Moisville, Peter Szondi's letter to the editor (6/25/1964) against Hans Egon Holthusen's review of *Die Niemandsrose* in the FAZ of 5/2/1964 was at the center of the conversation: Holthusen had repeated his thesis, already stated in 1954, that phrases like 'The mills of death' were just made up and had no relation to the real. Afterward, Celan was hosted by the Bollacks in their house in the Périgord region of France." That visit possibly inscribed in the "Tollhäusler-Trüffel" | "bedlamite's truffle," as the Périgord is famous for its truffles.

Klinkerspiel | clinker game: *Klinker* is a word of Dutch origin, usually connected to a kind of brick that is partially vitrified, thus very hard and making a clinking noise when hit, used in the construction of buildings. In north Germany *Klinkers* is the name given to small, hard clay marbles used in playing marbles.

"Die Gauklertrommel" | *"The jugglerdrum"*
October 12, 1963. Written on the same day as the poem "In Prague." This sequence of poems was composed prior to the one of the first cycle, *Atemkristall*, and, inserted here, disrupts the chronological continuity of the volume.

Odysseus, mein Affe | Ulysses, my monkey: Possibly an allusion to the East German poet Erich Arendt (1903–1984), who had dedicated his poem "Prager Judenfriedhof" ("Jewish Cemetery in Prague") to Celan, a poem that contained very Celanian elements (imitations, "apings," of Celan's poetics were fairly common in the early sixties). Arendt had also asked Celan to help him find a West German publisher for a manuscript of poems (*Ägäis*) that he had sent him, poems that made use of the Ulysses theme. Wiedemann further notes that one of the quarters of Prague is called Troy (BW, p. 734).

rue de Longchamp: Celan's Paris address at that time, where Arendt had dined with the Celans in late fall 1959.

"Wenn du im Bett" | *"When you lie"*
September 8, 1963. A Sunday. A poem with clear erotic undertones. The crane (a male bird in German) is a bird Celan associates with Odessa and Russian poetry, such as that of Sergei Yesenin (who has lines such as these: "And the cranes, sad as they flying by, / No longer regret anyone . . . Alone, I stand on the empty plain, / While wind carries the cranes far away"). Lefebvre (RDS, p. 234) also points to "Schiller's ballad 'Die Kraniche des Ibykus,' and to Georg Heym's story 'Der Kranich.' The directest reference is, however, to Klebnikov's poem 'The Crane,' which also plays on the verbal kinship between the animal and the steel contraption."

Further to the Russian connection, one could also think of Mandelstam's Pindaric ode "The Horseshoe Finder," specifically with reference to recurrent images of time and coins.

"Hinterm kohlegezinkten" | *"Behind coalmarked"*
September 1963.

"In Prag" | *"In Prague"*
October 12, 1963. A much-commented-on poem. Prague, where Celan never went, evokes for him Bohemia, Kafka, Rabbi Loew, and a whole range of connected historical and mythological themes. He thus writes in a letter to Franz Wurm of April 29, 1968 (PC/FW, pp. 142–43): "You know well that, because of a three-year residence in Bohemia by my mother also . . . I am somewhat bohemianized [angeböhmt].—also, cf. 'In Prague,' from one (and another and another) side, and recently I read her that the motto of Bohemia is 'La Bohème vaincra'—how is that in fact, Czech or Latin?"

The critic Bernd Witte argues that this poem, and the one preceding it, commemorate a meeting with Celan's friend and former lover, the poet Ingeborg Bachmann, and include references to Bachmann's poem "Prag Jänner 64," whose lines "Unter den berstenden Blöcken / meines, auch meines Flusses / kam das befreite Wasser hervor" (Under the bursting blocks / of my, yes even my river / the freed water appeared) are echoed in the previous poem's lines: "there the rods dipped royally before our eye, / water came, water." Lefebvre, on the other hand, does not endorse the Bachmann connection. Witte goes on to read the poem as a metapoem, or statement of poetics (which is true of many Celan poems). Witte: "So baut 'der halbe Tod,' der Tod-im-Text, sich ins 'Wohin,' auf den offenen Ausgang des Gedichtes zu" (Thus "half death," death-in-the-text, builds itself into the "whereto," toward the open exit/conclusion of the poem). According to Otto Pöggeler's more hermeneutical reading (SPUR, p. 366), the *wir* concerns essentially "die Begegnung des Dichters mit seinem Du" (the encounter of the poet with his You).

einer der Wieviel- / unddreißig | one of thirty- / and-how-many: Possibly the number of steps that lead to the Hradčany castle's entrance, but possibly also a reference to the legend of the thirty-six Just Ones. Pöggeler asks: "Are the stairs those of the Hradshin, and are those holy figures meant that stand on the Karlsbrücke, something like a thirty-figure group? One should rather think of the thirty-six just men, who vouch their own lives to help the persecuted, who perhaps outweigh the extermination machinery of evil in the scales of time, to which in any case they don't leave the last word" (SPUR, p. 354). According to Jewish tradition, as formulated by the Talmudic sage Abaye (a rabbi who lived in Babylonia, and died in 339), who gets to the number thirty-six by using gematria: "There are never less than 36 just men in the world who greet the Shekhinah [God's worldly presence] every day, for it is written [in the book of Isaiah 30:18], "Blessed are all who wait for Him" [*ashrei kol h.okhei lo*], and [the word] *lo* ["for Him," spelled Lamed-Vav] is numerically equal to 36." (Cited by Philologos in "The Thirty-Six Who Save the World," *Forward*, May 30, 2008, available at www.forward.com/articles/13406/the-thirty-six -who-save-the-world [accessed May 30, 2014].)

Gershom Scholem, the great scholar of Jewish mysticism, in a short essay published in in 1962 under the title "The Tradition of the Thirty-Six Hidden

Just Men," speculates that the number thirty-six "originates in ancient astrology, where the 360 degrees of the heavenly circle are divided into thirty-six units of ten, the so-called 'deans' ['decans,' in astrological parlance]. A dean-divinity ruled over each segment of the thus divided circle of the zodiac, holding sway over ten days of the year . . . [In Egyptian Hellenistic sources] the deans were regarded also as watchmen and custodians of the universe, and it is quite conceivable that [in Hellenistic astrology] the number thirty-six, which Abaye read into Scripture, no longer represented these cosmological powers or forces but rather human figures."

Hradschin | Hradčany: The great castle in Prague, said to be the biggest castle in the world and housing the St. Vitus Cathedral and a number of noble historical palaces.

Goldmacher-Nein | goldmaker's No: A reference to the Alchimistengasse, situated close to the Hradčany in Prague, and the street on which Kafka lived when he wrote the short stories gathered in the *Landarzterzählungen*.

Knochen-Hebräisch, / zu Sperma zermahlen | bone-Hebrew, / ground to sperm: Compare in the volume *Mohn und Gedächtnis* the poem "Spät und tief" with the line: "Ihr mahlt in den Mühlen des Todes das weiße Mehl der Verheißung." (In the mills of death you grind the white flower of Promise.) See also the poem "Aus Engelsmaterie" | "Out of angel-matter" from the volume *Threadsuns* (p. 192).

"Von der Orchis her" | *"Starting from the orchis"*
September 11, 1963.

Orchis | orchis: The other German name, *Knabenkraut* (boy's weed), and the etymology of the Greek word, ὄρχις, "orchis," also "testicle," due no doubt to the testicle-shaped paired root, link this flower from the orchid family to matters of childhood, manhood, and reproduction. See also the poem "Todtnauberg" (p. 254). There is, further, an interesting rhyme with Colchis on the Black Sea (Lefebvre, RDS, p. 238).

Zwölfnacht | twelfth-night: A festival marking the coming of Epiphany in some Christian churches. According to the *Oxford English Dictionary*, it is "the evening of the fifth of January, preceding Twelfth Day, the eve of the Epiphany, formerly the last day of the Christmas festivities and observed as a time of merrymaking"; it also describes the period of the twelve nights that separate Christmas from Epiphany, in German also known as *Rauhnächte* (raw/rough nights).

"Halbzerfressener" | *"Halfgnawed"*
August 4, 1964.

"Aus Fäusten" | *"From fists"*
October 1, 1964. During this period, Celan took a leave of absence from his teaching and spent time in psychiatric hospitals. It is possible that the first stanza alludes to electroshock treatments he received at that time. The final stanza's complexly convoluted syntax is not reproducible in English. The first version of my translation read:

> The from you also star-
> eyed loafer melancholy
> hears of it.

A second version tried to clarify the English while still keeping what I have elsewhere called the "corkscrew motion" of the syntax in Celan's sentence:

> The—because of you also star-
> eyed—vagabond Melancholy
> learns of it.

Defeated, I decided for once to alter the syntax in English and reconstruct the stanza.

"Schwirrhölzer" | *"Bullroarers"*
October 3, 1964.
    Schwirrhölzer | Bullroarers: An ethnological term referring to a cult object used in Africa and Australia. The German word lets the reader also hear the two basic words that make up the compound, namely "wood" and "whirring." I have tried to retain some of that whirr/whizz sound by translating the indeterminate *fahren* as "whizz." There are reading traces in Celan's copy of Leo Frobenius's *Kulturgeschichte Afrikas*.

"Abends" | *"Evening"*

November 8, 1964. Hamburg. Celan stayed in that city in early November 1964 for a radio recording at the Norddeutscher Rundfunk. The poem is drafted on paper bearing the logo of the Hotel Alster-Hof. On November 8 he saw Bertolt Brecht and Kurt Weill's opera *Rise and Fall of the City of Mahagonny*.

unendlicher Schuhriemen | endless shoelace: In the margin of an essay by Hugo Bergmann ("Die Heiligung des Namens [Kiddusch haschem]," in *Vom Judentum: Ein Sammelbuch*, edited by Verein jüdischer Hochschüler Bar Kochba [Prague] [Leipzig: Kurt Wolff Verlag, 1913], p. 43), Celan wrote, "Reread 2/20/65. What a confirmation!" next to the sentence asking that in a time of persecution the Jew be serious about the "sanctifiction of the Name," and that he should "refuse to knot the shoelace in the manner of the heathens."

"Bei den zusammengetretenen" | *"At the assembled"*

November 17–25, 1964. On November 17 Celan returned from his trip to Germany, after a stop in Cologne to visit with Heinrich Böll. Wiedemann reports that "in Cologne he remembered his first visit there in 1954, when he saw the plague-cross in the Saint Mary church in the Capitol: 'destroyed romanesque church, one of which, I thought about it again yesterday, with a so-called "plague-cross," arms V-shaped' (PC/GCL, #191). Celan links the concept of the plague-cross to the plague outbreak in Cologne in 1349, which was followed by a pogrom in which the whole Jewish community of the city was wiped out" (BW, p. 737).

Ölzelt | oiltent: Lefebvre reads this as referring probably to the "tabernacle where the chrism, the consecrated oil was kept" (RDS, p. 241).

"Das aufwärtsstehende Land" | *"The upward-standing country"*
December 3, 1964.

Steinschlucht | steep ravine: The first draft had *Wortschlucht*, "word-ravine."

"Das umhergestoßene" | *"The pushed-around"*
December 9–10, 1964.

"Aschenglorie" | "Ashglory"

December 15, 1964.

Pontisches Einstmal | Pontic erstwhile: In 1947 Celan spent his summer holidays in Mangalia on the Black Sea—*Pontus Euxinus* in Latin—with his friends Petre Solomon and Nina Cassian. Mangalia, a resort much frequented by artists, was partly peopled by Tatars.

The Black Sea is also the place where Ovid was exiled and wrote his *Tristia* and Pontic epistles, and where Osip Mandelstam spent much time. In his letter to Petre Solomon of November 23, 1967, Celan says of this poem: "C'est quelquechose comme l'anamnèse de Mangalia." (It is something like the anamnesis of Mangalia.) (PC/PS, p. 238)

ertrunkenen Ruderblatt | drowned rudder blade: Wiedemann (BW, p. 738) connects this with the death by drowning (a possible suicide) of Celan's friend Lia Fingerhut (with whom he had also been in Mangalia) in the Mediterranean off Israel, of which he learned on November 2, 1961, and about which he wrote to Petre Solomon on November 23, 1967: "I'm thinking of our excursion into the Carpathians more than 20 years ago, Lia, Lia, drowned, drowned" (PC/PS, p. 238). Lefebvre suggests that Celan may also have been thinking of the actress Corinna Marcovici, with whom Celan had a relationship at that time (RDS, p. 243).

Niemand / zeugt für den / Zeugen | No one / bears witness for the / witness: For an analysis of this statement and the translation problems it poses, see my essay "Paul Celan's Counterword: Who Witnesses for the Witness?" (*Justifying the Margins*, pp. 79–86). See also Jacques Derrida's essay "Poetics and Politics of Witnessing" (*Sovereignties in Question*, pp. 65–96).

IV

"Das Geschriebene" | "The written"

December 19, 1964.

Tümmler | dolphins: The German word for "dolphin" is more descriptive of movement: *sich tummeln* means "to splash about in the water" and can be said of children as much as of dolphins. (Celan marked the word in his etymological dictionary.)

wo nur? | where only?: The first draft had *in Dortmund* replaced in the final version by the question (TA, *Atemwende*, pp. 122–23).

"Cello-Einsatz" | "Cello-entry"

December 24, 1964.

Cello-Einsatz | Cello-entry: Gisela Dischner informed Wiedemann (вw, p. 739) of a connection to the solo cello entry in the Adagio ma non troppo section of Antonín Dvořák's Cello Concerto op. 104.

Schwarz / -blütige | black / -biled: *Schwarzblütig* (blackblooded) is a common term describing someone melancholic. As the Greek word μελαγχολία (melancholia) literally means "black bile," I've elected to stay with that word.

"Frihed" | "Frihed"

December 25, 1964.

Frihed: The Danish word meaning "freedom." In early November 1964 Celan had visited the Frihedsmuseet (Freedom Museum) in Copenhagen with its exhibits of the Danish resistance against the Nazi occupation, including documentation of acts of sabotage and of the efforts to save the Jewish population.

Steinboote | stone boats: The Danes transported many Jews to safety in Sweden in fishing and leisure boats in October 1943, an act remembered in a stone monument in Jerusalem. See also "Es stand" | "It stood" and the commentary to that poem (pp. 430 and 617).

Orlog-Wort | man-of-war-word: *Orlog* is an old German word meaning "war," which has survived in the Scandinavian countries in the vocabulary of the navy; there is thus an Orlogsmuseet, a museum of the Royal Danish Navy, in Copenhagen. Celan seems to have known the word from his readings in Hans Henny Jahnn's 1949 novel *Das Holzschiff*, where the expression *Orlogschiff* is underlined.

ich singe – // was sing ich? | I sing— // what do I sing?: In the draft versions Celan had written: "ich sang // El Canto, El Canto / de Riego" (I sang // El Canto, El Canto / de Riego), which refers to the revolutionary patriotic hymn of the Spanish republic.

mit den roten, den weißen | with the red, with the white: red and white are the national colors of Denmark.

"Den verkieselten Spruch" | *"The silicified saying"*
December 27, 1964, Paris.

verkieselten | silicified: A term from petrology describing the process in which organic matter becomes saturated with silica. A common source of silica is volcanic material. Celan had the term via his book on geology by Roland Brinkman.

schießen / . . . an | crystallize: The German verb *anschießen* (though also having a range of meanings connected to shooting, and thus to speed and noise) here refers to the process of crystal formation in crystallography. Lefebvre refers the reader to Celan's earlier poem "Engführung" | "Stretto" (PCS, p. 67) in the volume *Sprachgitter* | *Speechgrille*, adding: "The points and the edges of the crystal are in a way structured by a network of punctuations" (RDS, p. 247).

"Wo?" | *"Where?"*
December 30, 1964, Paris.

Lockermassen | friable matter: A geological term Celan located in his geology books. I use "matter" rather than "mass," as the compound "friable mass" in English is used specifically in medicine to describe tumorlike formations.

"Königswut" | *"King's rage"*
February 1, 1965, Paris.

"Solve" | *"Solve"*
February 20, 1965. On the same day "Coagula" was finished. It is useful to read the diptych "Solve" and "Coagula" as programmatic of the poetics of late Celan: a dissolving and a reorganization of both reality and language. See also next note. In Celan's notebook under the date of May 24, 1964, he reports a visit to "Waterloo-Plein / 41: Spinoza's birthhouse: no longer there" and a draft for a poem "To the memory of Leo Shestov." The first draft of the poem "Solve" also has the place indication "Amsterdam, Waterloo-Plein," edited out of the second draft, while the geographic indication "rheinaufwärts . . . rheinabwärts" (referring to the river Rhine) will also be reduced to the final "stromaufwärts, strom- / abwärts" | "upstream, down- / stream." That draft

also included the phrase "Denkerbildnis aus Wolfenbüttel" (Thinker's portrait from Wolfenbüttel), which refers to a portrait of Spinoza, of which Celan owned a copy (TA, *Atemwende*, p. 136). See also the poem "Pau, Später" | "Pau, Later" (p. 126).

Solve: Part of the classical alchemical formula "Solve et Coagula." There are reading traces in Hugo von Hoffmanthal's *Andreas oder die Vereinigten*: "True poetry is the arcanum that united us with life, that separates us from life. The separation—through separating we start to live—we separate, so then death too remains bearable, only the composite is gruesome (a fine, pure hour of death like Stillings's)—but joining is just as essential as separating—the aura catena of Homer—'Separabis terram ab igne, subtile ab spisso, suaviter magna cum ingenio | thou shalt separate earth from fire, the subtle from the dense, smoothly and with great skill' and—solve et coagula. the universal binding agent: gluten; the universal seperating agent: alkahest." Otto Pöggeler also points to a further phrase in Andreas: "Das 'Ergon,' sagt die Fama, 'ist die Heiligung des inneren Menschen, die Goldmacherkunst ist das Parergon'—solve et coagula" (The "Ergon," says the Fama, "is the sanctification of the inner man, the art of making gold is the parergon"—solve et coagula) (SPUR, p. 306). Celan's use is more poetological, as this action of dissolving and (re)joining closely approximates the process to which his work subjects language. Wiedemann also points us to a note by Celan dated November 1, 1966, "concerning a phrase by [Margarete] Susman in connection with a remark by Rosa Luxemburg: 'To be good is the main thing. To be good simply and humbly, that dissolves and joins everything and is better than all intelligence and self-righteousness' (From *Geheimnis der Freiheit*, p. 274)" (BW, p. 741).

Gift- / pfalzen | Poison- /Palatinates: An easy misreading here would let one hear *Giftpflanze* (poisonous plant) rather than *Giftpfalze* (poison-palatinate), which would also make sense in the alchemical mode of the poem. Interestingly enough, *Gift* here could further be understood in an older meaning, still current in Goethe's time, where, besides the meaning of poison, it also had the meaning that the English word "gift" has today, that of something given, offered, a present.

"Coagula" | *"Coagula"*

February 18, 1962–February 20, 1965. First notes date to the time of *Die Nie-mandsrose*. The title completes the alchemical theme of "solve et coagula." There are also possible references to the esoteric Christian mysticism of the Rosy Cross, though the "Rosa" here is usually read as referring to Rosa Luxemburg through the "Romanian buffaloes," which Celan mentions in a letter to Petre Solomon of November 23, 1967 (PC/PS, p. 238): "The Romanian buffaloes seen by Rosa Luxemburg through the bars of her prison window converge with the three words of Kafka's 'Country Doctor'—and with that name—Rosa. I coagulate, I try to make coagulation happen." In relation to Rosa Luxemburg, compare the poem "Du liegst" | "You lie" (p. 322) from "Schneepart" | "Snowpart" and the relevant commentary (p. 578). A further reference enriching the word "Rosa" leads to a friend and lover from Czernowitz and Bukarest named Rosa Leibovici who died of tuberculosis in the early sixties; Israel Chalfen reports that "Celan, who received the news of her death in Paris, was said to have been deeply distressed" (Chalfen, p. 187).

Compare also the poem "In Prag" | "In Prague" (p. 52) for alchemical themes. On the image of the rose in Celan's poems, see also M. Winkler's 1972 essay "On Paul Celan's Rose Images" (*Neophilologus* 56 (1):72–78).

"Schädeldenken" | *"Skullthinking"*

February 4, 1965.

"Osterqualm" | *"Eastersmoke"*

March 1–4, 1965. Easter fell on April 18; Passover fell April 17–23. Passover in the Jewish tradition symbolizes the release from slavery and the gift of freedom, the journey from Egypt to the Land of Israel. The core of the holiday is the Seder ceremony, during which the story of the Exodus is told as it is written in the Haggadah.

This is the most reworked poem of *Breathturn*, with at least five extant drafts. There is also a further addition marked "Tuesday 4 May 1965," not used in the final version, replacing the final stanza and separated from the rest of the poem by a dotted line, that reads: "But / everything cheers up: / Our son, you and I, / we live, grow, work / free" (not included in the *Atemwende* volumes of either the BA or the TA; information Badiou to Wiedemann, BW, p. 742).

Osterqualm | Eastersmoke: The German *Qualm*—in comparison to the word *Rauch*—refers to a thicker smoke, but the English alternatives to "smoke" (fumes, exhaust, effluvium, pollution, etc.) are not accurate enough here. *Qualm* can also, for example, be the thick smoke from a pipe smoker.

"Kaimauer-Rast" | *"Quaywall-rest"*
March 11, 1965, Paris.

"Erhört" | *"Answered"*
March 25, 1965, Paris.
Erhört | Answered: meant here in the sense of "granted."

"Schaufäden, Sinnfäden" | *"Sight threads, sense threads"*
April 19, 1965, Paris. Passover was celebrated that year from April 17 to April 23.

Schaufäden | Sight threads: *Schaufäden* translates the Hebrew word *zizit* (tzitzit), literally "tassel," the fringes or tassels on the corners of the tallith. Literally the word refers to threads (*Faden*) meant to be shown, thus seen (*schauen*) and not hidden. These literal meanings seem, to me at least, to outweigh the purely ritual cult item, especially given the parallel construction with *Sinnfäden*, meaning- or sense-threads, which would lose its meaning if the initial word was not constructed according to its concrete morphology.

Zehn Blindenstäbe | Ten blindstaffs: the number refers probably to the minyan, the quorum of ten Jewish males over the age of thirteen that have to be present for a public religious service. *Blindenstäbe*, or *Blindenstab* in the singular, though clearly a blind man's staff, calls up the word *Buchstab*, that is, letter, thus linking to writing and poetry.

"Ein Dröhnen" | *"A roar"*
April 6, 1965. Wiedemann (BW, p. 745) mentions that the German paper *Die Welt* reported that day, under the title "Witnesses from Nineteen Countries Spoke Out," that the evidential hearing of the Frankfurt Auschwitz trial ended on that day. She further links the word *Dröhnen*, "roar," to an article in the FAZ of November 14, 1964, describing a witness's evidence: "He (Wilhelm Boger) opened them (the canisters of Zyklon B) and handed them on. Other

SS-men threw them into the open windows, from which came a roar, as if there were many people below the earth."

die Wahrheit selbst | truth itself: Wiedemann further quotes Leo Shestov (p. 409 of *Auf Hiobs Waage*, a book Celan had read) quoting Pascal: "Ce n'est point ici le pays de la vérité: elle erre inconnue parmi les hommes" (Here is not the country of truth: she wanders, unknown, among mankind) (BW, p. 744).

"Irrennäpfe" | *"Lunatic-bowls"*
May 9–23, 1965, Le Vésinet. Celan was hospitalized from May 8 to May 21 in the private psychiatric hospital in Le Vésinet (Seine-et-Oise, Haute Yvelines).

"Lichtenbergs zwölf" | *"Lichtenberg's twelve"*
May 9–10, 1965, Le Vésinet. The poem links to Celan's reading of Georg Christoph Lichtenberg's letters to his brother Friedrich August of October 4, 1790, and September 9, 1791, in which Lichtenberg asks for a "beautiful tablecloth with napkins" from his mother's estate, and then offers thanks for it (TA, *Atemwende*, p. 156). Lichtenberg (1742–1799) was a scientist and satirical writer, today best remembered for what he called his *Sudelbücher*, or scrapbooks, published posthumously.

Planetengruß | planet-greeting: Goethe has the phrase "Gruß der Planeten" in the first poem, titled "Dämon," of the cycle *Urworte*. See also the note on the following poem.

in der totzuschweigenden Zeichen- / Zone | in the to-be-silenced-to-death sign- / zone: Wiedemann points out reading traces (underlinings) in the introduction by Wilhelm Grenzman to Lichtenberg's collected works: "He was in the habit of taking everything as a sign, drawing a premonition from everything, and turning plain daily objects into oracles. Every crawling movement by an insect furnished him with answers concerning his fate; if his candle went out, he would take that as an unfavorable omen and would change far-reaching plans . . . 'I don't believe in these things, yet it is pleasant for me, when they don't turn out bad'" (BW, pp. 744–45).

kein Himmel . . . Blauspecht | no heaven . . . nuthatch: This stanza, standing between dashes, functions as an interjection, at the end of which *sein* is repeated and the sentence completed. But this interjection allows for the possibility of reading the first *Sein* not as the possessive pronoun it first was—or at least seems to be—and becomes again later ("sein . . . weißer Komet") but as the verbal noun *Sein*, "Being." Although the stanza looks like a citation, no source has been found so far.

weißer Komet | white comet: In his scrapbooks, Lichtenberg used the code name "white comet" when speaking of his mistress Maria Dorothea Stechard.

das Rotverlorene | the redlorn: Grenzmann mentions that Lichtenberg had the reputation of being distracted, thus "always in danger of losing the thread [den roten faden | the red thread] of his thought."

"Give the Word" | *"Give the Word"*
May 13–14, 1965, Le Vésinet. Celan gave his wife a manuscript of the poem on May 15.

Give the word: See Shakespeare, *King Lear*, act 4, scene 6: "Lear: Give the word. / Edgar: Sweet Marjoram. / Lear: Pass." In his edition, Celan also underlined the following: "Lear: Nature's above art in that respect. There's your press money. That fellow handles his bow like a crow-keeper: draw me a clothier's yard. Look, look! a mouse. Peace, peace! Bring up the brown bills. O! well flown, bird; I' the clout i' the clout: hewgh!" (followed by the title phrase) (PC/GCL, vol. 1, #236).

Ins Hirn gehaun | Cut to the brains: *King Lear*, act 4, scene 6: "Lear: No rescue? What! a prisoner? I am even / The natural fool of fortune, Use me well: / You shall have ransom. Let me have surgeons: I am cut to th' brains."

Sipheten und Probyllen | Siphets and probyls: See Goethe's poem "Dämon," opening the cycle *Urworte*: "Wie an dem Tag, der dich der Welt verliehen, / Die Sonne stand zum Gruß der Planeten, / Bist alsobald und fort und fort gediehen / Nach dem Gesetz, wonach du angetreten. / So mußt du sein, dir kannst du nicht entfliehen, / So sagten schon Sibyllen, so Propheten; / Und keine Zeit und keine Macht zerstückelt / Geprägte Form, die lebend sich entwickelt." (As on that day that lent you to the world, / The sun stood for the greeting of the planets, / Right away you started to prosper and prosper / According to the law you represented. / Thus you have to be, you can't escape yourself, / This already said by the sibyls and the prophets; / And no time nor any power will dismember / Shaped form which, alive, keeps unfolding.)

Aussatz | lepra: The translation is literal, and thus has to miss the word-particle *satz* in *Aussatz*, which by itself means "sentence," "phrase."

"Vom Anblick der Amseln" | *"From beholding the blackbirds"*
May 20, 1965, 10:00 p.m.–May 21, 1965, Le Vésinet. A first draft was sketched out in Celan's Shakespeare edition. On May 21, Celan leaves the clinic, and this is the last poem composed there. He wrote to Gisèle that afternoon: "A blackbird is walking across the lawn, the weather is fine, the sun is out, calmness comes over me—I write to you" (PC/GCL, #242).

Amseln | blackbirds: He wrote in French to his wife, using the word *merle*, though the German word *Amsel* calls up immediately the family name Antschel, as well as Kafka's name bird, the jackdaw. See the commentaries to the poems "Anredsam" | "Addressable" and "Frankfurt, September" (pp. 567 and 502).

V

"Große, glühende Wölbung" | *"Great, glowing vault"*
June 7, 1965, Paris.

Widders | ram: The German word connotes "wider," "against," and *Widerstand*, "resistance" (the manuscript version includes the struck words ~~was widersteht?~~ | ~~what resists~~). The image of the ram's horn also links to the shofar, with the ram itself being the iconic sacrificial animal.

"Schieferäugige" | *"Slate-eyed one"*
July 10, 1965, Paris.

"Schlickende" | *"Oozy"*
July 11, 1965, Paris.

Riesensporangien | giant sporangia: A sporangium is an enclosure in which spores are formed. All plants, fungi, mosses, algae, and many other lineages form sporangia at some point in their life cycle.

"Du, das" | *"You, the"*
July 15, 1965, Moisville.

"Der mit Himmeln geheizte" | *"The with heavens heated"*
July 17, 1965, Moisville.
Die Wer da?-Rufe | The Who's there?-calls: Celan was using Baudissin's German translation of Shakespeare, in which Lear's "Who's there?" is given as "Wer da?" See also the citizens' call at the end of Büchner's *Danton's Death* of "He, wer da?" | "Hey, who's there?" immediately preceding Lucile's "Long live the king," the phrase Celan called a counterword (BW, p. 748).

"Dunstbänder-, Spruchbänder-Aufstand" | *"Vaporband-, banderole-uprising"*
August 3–5, 1965, Paris. A much-reworked poem that first appeared in the *Neue Zürcher Zeitung* on December 3, 1966. On August 4, Celan sent a version to Gisèle in a letter stating: "Moved by your question, at the Fontaine de jade, while meditating on Chinese mushrooms and bamboo sprouts—there was some chicken too [these last five words in English] and then, at my table—where nothing grows, I wrote the poem I'm including. As you can well see, it is insurrectional and glacial at the same time. Banderole uprising, redder than red, under the—astonished?—eyes of the seals. Insurrection of other things too, geological, scriptural ones, matters of the heart.—But no commentaries! Poetry first (France, Germany etc. later)!" (PC/GCL, #253, notes in vol. 2). Reading traces for some of the vocabulary ("Dunstband" | "vaporband," "-poller" | "-bollard," and "vertäuen" | "moor") in Arno Schmidt's novel *Gelehrtenrepublic* | *The Egghead Republic*, which also contains descriptions of brain transplants by Soviet scientists in a utopian island republic.
In a letter to Gisèle of August 21, 1965 (PC/GCL, #267), Celan tells of watching the Eisenstein film *October*:

"So, all alone, I saw Petersburg, the workers, the sailors of the Aurora. It was very moving, at times reminding one of the 'Potemkin,' bringing to mind the thoughts and dreams of my childhood, my thoughts of today and of always, poetry-always-true-always-faithful, I saw my placards, many of them, those that, not very long ago I evoked in the poem I sent you—

"Vaporband-, banderole-uprising"—I saw the October Revolution, its men, its flags, I saw hope always en route, the brother of poetry, I saw . . .

Then, at a certain moment, at the moment when the insurgents occupy the Winter Palace, it began to desert poetry and to become Cinema, motion-picture shots, tendentious and overdone, the intertexts became propaganda—all that was History and its Personages had anyway been, from the very beginning, what was the least convincing, the role of the Left Social-Revolutionaries was completely expunged—, so then the heart loosened, searched for its silences (won, lost, won again), wrapped them around itself and led me outside, alone, as I had come in, running the gauntlet between young cinephile gents and young girls "mit tupierter Frisur," with too much makeup, in pants, sort of leftist sixteenth arrondissement, erratic and flabby.—But there were some, no doubt, who knew, taking, here too, responsibility for the terrible eclipses.

> Long live the sailors of Kronstadt!
> Long live the Revolution! Long live Love!
> Long live Petersburg! Long live Paris!
> Long live Poetry!

"Ruh aus in deinen Wunden" | *"Rest in your wounds"*
August 17–18, 1965, Paris. In the letter to Gisèle in which he sent her the poem (PC/GCL, #264), Celan writes: "It works pretty well, it seems to me, maybe not opaque enough, not 'there' enough. Though at the end it picks up—picks itself up." Many drafts showing much reworking.

VI

"Einmal" | *"Once"*
September 1965. Except for the longer, multisectioned poems "Stimmen" and "Engführung" in *Sprachgitter*, only the "Todesfuge" and this final poem of *Atemwende* | *Breathturn* are given a complete cycle of their own. Celan wrote to Gisèle (PC/GCL, #479): "At the end, preceded by a white page, all alone and simultaneously cycle, the 'EINMAL.'"

ichten | I'ed: Several interpretations—per direct indication by the poet—point to the verb *ichten* (in the Grimms' *Wörterbuch*, an important helper of Celan's compositional process), used here in the preterit and defined as "'ich' sagen, eine frage mit ich beantworten" (to say "I," to answer a question with I). The extraction of *ichten* from the preceding word "vernichtet" | "annihilated" is not as obvious in the English "I'ed"—though maybe the two *i*'s of "annihilated" do point to this origin.

FADENSONNEN | THREADSUNS

Published in March 1968, this, Celan's largest single volume, gathers 105 poems written between September 5, 1965 (some, therefore, contemporaneous with the last ones of *Breathturn*) and June 8, 1967. During the same, obviously very fertile period, he composed the cycle *Eingedunkelt* | *Tenebrae'd* (p. 222), which, like all the poems written between November 1965 and the beginning of June 1966 in the psychiatric clinics in Suresnes and Paris, were not included in this volume. Thus, from the final poems of the second cycle through the following three cycles, the poems were all written in 1967 in a creative rush that produced close to a poem a day—and organized chronologically in the volume.

Surprisingly, *Threadsuns* may well be the least commented on and most critically neglected volume of Celan's oeuvre. As the preceding volume, *Breathturn*, initiated the change toward the late work, it rightfully attracted much attention ab initio, given its hinge position in the oeuvre and its programmatic title linking it directly to the most important statement on poetics Celan had published, the speech/essay *The Meridian*. Noting that the book received few reviews, Kai Fischer writes: "This refusal is astounding in view of the fact that this volume is not only the gateway into the late work but also introduces and performs a new way of saying that will be characteristic for the following volumes" (CHB, p. 99). Indeed, many of the reviewers expressed the belief that Celan's work had now moved into a hermetic code that made it inaccessible, or into, as the anonymous reviewer of *The Times Literary Supplement* called it, "an esoteric Geheimsprache whose associations are known to the poet alone." Given that the title of this volume goes back to a poem in *Breathturn*, some such turning back is comprehensible, but not the lazy use by critics of an off-the-cuff remark Celan made to Esther Cameron, reported as suggesting that she not busy herself too much with this volume, as it was something *randgängerich*—a difficult word to translate that suggests someone or something walking on the edge, the boundary, a marginal or fringe event, clearly something with an edge, something liminal. On the other hand, we have Celan's own words in a letter to Nelly Sachs, stating that he "found it infinitely difficult to let go of the previous book—*Threadsuns*—but no doubt you own it." Kai Fischer proposes that in terms of *Threadsuns*, this last quote, whatever may have been meant by *randgängerich*, "opens the way to a different reading. Without wanting to efface the ambivalence of the first quote, one can recognize in Celan's statement a higher estimation, that made it 'infinitely difficult to let go' of *Threadsuns*" (CH, p. 99).

Another way of explaining the dearth of attention *Threadsuns* received is by taking into consideration the fact that it appeared just one year after *Breathturn* (which received marked attention, even if an attention already afflicted by puzzlement about a perceived "hermeticism" that would greet all the late books) rather than the four or five years usually separating Celan's volumes. Moreover, 1968 saw a plethora of other Celan books come out, including a number of volumes of translations (William Shakespeare, Giuseppe Ungaretti, Jules Supervielle, and André du Bouchet); a complete cycle of poems, *Eingedunkelt | Tenebrae'd*, published in a book gathering such "abandoned works" (see p. 543); and, most important in terms of negative impact on the visibility of *Threadsuns*, a volume of selected poems. These *Ausgewählte Gedichte*, offering poems from all the early volumes up to and including *Breathturn*, plus the two essays on poetics, edited by Paul Celan himself, were published in the popular Suhrkamp paperback series. The book was an immediate success and for many readers has remained the best introduction to the oeuvre—so much so that when in 1998 the French publisher Gallimard decided to include a Selected Paul Celan in the prestigious Poésie/Gallimard paperback series, they used that very same volume, translated and presented by Jean-Pierre Lefebvre.

I

"Augenblicke" | *"Eye-glances"*
September 19, 1965, Paris. The volume opens with a compound noun containing that most loaded of Celan's words: *Auge*, "eye."

Augenblicke | Eye-glances: The normal English translation would be "moments," or, if one wanted to insist on the spatial sense of the word rather than on the temporal, "glances." Although the German compound is in common usage, I have preferred to create an English neologism, "eye-glances," in order to retain the seed-image of the eye.

steh | stand: See the various notes on Celan's insistence on this upright stance, for example, "Es stand" | "It stood" (p. 617) and "Wirk nicht voraus" | "Do not work ahead" (p. 575). See also my introduction to PCS (p. 6).

"Frankfurt, September" | *"Frankfurt, September"*
September 5–6, 1965, Frankfurt am Main. The title points to the time of the Frankfurter Buchmesse, the great annual book fair visited by Celan, and the poem makes use of images from the fair. Celan spent ten days in Frankfurt at that time, working with his cotranslator Kurt Leonard on the volume of translations of poems by Henri Michaux that would be published the following year by S. Fischer Verlag, his last book for that publisher, as he would move to Suhrkamp Verlag. Wiedemann writes that, according to Klaus Reichert (who worked at Suhrkamp and Insel Verlag, and in front of whose house the poem was conceived), Celan saw this poem as his final reckoning with S. Fischer Verlag (BW, p. 751). Celan wrote to Gisèle (PC/GCL, #273): "I am doing fine. This morning, in fact, I am in a little poetic trance, a kind of effervescence: I've written a little poem I'll copy out for you tonight or tomorrow, and that I'll comment for you." (He never wrote the proposed commentary.)

Blinde, licht- / bärtige | Blind, light- / bearded: Compare the expression "Lichtbart / der Patriarchen" | "lightbeard of / the patriarchs" in the poem "Tübingen, Jänner" from *Die Niemandsrose* (PCS, p. 79) with the adjectival form *luftalgenbärtig* in the poem "Die Eine" | "The one" (p. 170). Notice that the (by this time rare) title of the poem is grammatically constructed on the model of the earlier title "Tübingen, Jänner."

Stellwand | partition: The movable wall or partition with a portrait of

Freud that the publisher S. Fischer had set up at the book fair the previous year, but which had been saved and which Celan had seen.

Maikäfertraum | cockchaferdream: Compare Celan's use of the old *Maikäferlied* in the poem "In der Luft" from *Die Niemandsrose*. Given the Kafka quote that follows here, the *Käfer* also calls to mind that author's beetle. Another possible reading could point to the scarabaeus symbolizing resurrection in Egyptian mythology (SPUR, p. 289). Compare also the poem "Was näht" | "What sews" from *Snowpart* (p. 326), which contains the line "ein Käfer erkennt dich" | "a chafer recognizes you." There is also a link with Freud's analysis of a dream involving cockchafers (given as "May beetles" in the English translation) (Freud, *Interpretation of Dreams*, #203, p. 324).

Zum letzen- / mal Psycho- / logie | For the last / time psycho- / logy: Citation from Kafka's ninety-third entry in the posthumous collection *Betrachtungen über Sünde, Leid, Hoffnung und den wahren Weg* (Kafka, *Hochzeitsvorbereitungen*, #204, p. 30). Celan had already used the phrase in a withheld letter to Kurt Hirschfeld from January 8, 1961, in connection with the Goll affair: "'For the last time, psychology!' What is essential, I believe, is not the representation of the motivations and inducements, but the unmasking of the malice (and of its allies)" (BW, p. 752).

Simili- / Dohle | imitation / jackdaw: In Czech the word *kavka* means *Dohle*, "jackdaw." Compare the following comment on the expression "Simili- / Dohle": "As Kafka's name means 'jackdaw,' the Kafka family had the image of the jackdaw on its letterhead; at the Frankfurt Book Fair with its tax-deductible work-related conversations, it is, however, an 'imitation jackdaw' that breakfasts" (SPUR, p. 290). See also Kafka's story "A Hunger Artist": "He was happiest, however, when morning came and a lavish breakfast was brought for them at his own expense, on which they hurled themselves with the appetite of healthy men after a hard night's work without sleep. True, there were still people who wanted to see in this breakfast an unfair means of influencing the observers, but that was going too far, and if they were asked whether they wanted to undertake the observers' night shift for its own sake, without the breakfast, they excused themselves. But nonetheless they stood by their suspicions." (Translation by Ian Johnston; http://records.viu.ca/~johnstoi /kafka/hungerartist.htm.)

Celan's closeness to Kafka has been well documented. An odd coincidence, which certainly did not escape Celan, has to do with their names. Kafka wrote in his diary: "Ich heiße hebraïsch Amschel" (In Hebrew my name is Amschel)—close to the word *Amsel*, "blackbird," and to Celan's own original name, Ançel or Antschel.

Der Kehlkopfverschlußlaut / singt | The glottal stop / sings: See the Kafka story "Josephine the Singer, or the Mouse Folk," which Kafka wrote as he himself was losing his voice in the final stages of laryngeal turberculosis, in German *Kehlkopftuberkulose*. As Pöggeler notes: "In the final stage of Kafka's tuberculosis, his larynx closed up—he wasn't allowed to even speak anymore, and literally starved to death . . . Does the glottal stop of the larynx (that k—j as in 'Kehlkoph' and 'Kafka') make for a song—Songs beyond mankind?" (SPUR, p. 290). In the earliest draft of the poem, Celan had inserted between the two title words the Hebrew letter ע (ayin), a guttural sound, as is the glottal stop (TA, *Fadensonnen*, p. 6).

"Gezinkt der Zufall" | "Chance, marked"
September 24–26, 1965, Paris, Rosh Hashanah.

Lügen | lies . . . Meineid schwören | perjure themselves: Probable rumination on the Goll affair.

"Wer / herrscht?" | "Who / rules?"
September 24–October 4, 1965, Paris.

Springkraut | touch-me-not: The plant *Impatiens noli-tangere*, in German *Großes Springkraut* or *Rühr-mich-nicht-an*, the only representative of the order Impatiens that originates in central Europe, is known in English as touch-me-not balsam, yellow balsam, jewelweed, or wild balsam.

Gauklergösch | juggler jaws: Celan had considered this word (as *Gaukler-Gösch*) as a possible title for the volume *Lightduress*. The term *Gösch* was noted several times by Celan in his German edition of James Joyce's *Ulysses*: "weiß die Pfoten, rot deine Gösch / dein Balg ist auch ganz lieblich" | "White thy fambles, red thy gan / And thy quarrons dainty is." This is the second stanza of the canting song, "The Rogue's Delight in Praise of His Strolling Mort," which Richard Head includes in his book *The Canting Academy* (London, 1673, pp. 19–20); in translation: "White thy hands, red thy mouth, / And thy body dainty is" (http://en.wikibooks.org/wiki/Annotations_to_James _Joyce's_Ulysses/Proteus/047).

"Die Spur eines Bisses" | *"The trace of a bite"*
October 5, 1965.

"In der ewigen Teufe" | *"In the eternal depth"*
October 10, 1965, Paris.
    ewigen Teufe | eternal depth: In the *Brockhaus-Taschenbuch der Geologie* (p. 174): "Keine Faltung geht bis in the 'ewige Teufe'" (No convolution reaches into "the eternal depth").
    brennst ein Gebet ab | blow up a prayer: *Abbrennen* (literally, "to burn off") in mining parlance refers to setting off an explosion (TA, *Fadensonnen*, p. 14).

"Sichtbar" | *"Visible"*
October 14, 1965.
    Hirnstamm | brainstem: The brainstem (or brain stem) is the posterior stemlike part of the base of the brain that is connected to the spinal cord. The brain stem controls the flow of messages between the brain and the rest of the body, including the corticospinal tract (motor), the posterior column-medial lemniscus pathway (fine touch, vibration sensation, and proprioception), and the spinothalamic tract (pain, temperature, itch, and crude touch). It also controls basic body functions, such as breathing, swallowing, heart rate, and blood pressure, and is pivotal in maintaining consciousness and regulating the sleep cycle. The brain stem consists of the midbrain (mesencephalon), the pons (part of metencephalon), and the medulla oblongata (myelencephalon), the base of the brain, which is formed by the enlarged top of the spinal cord. The medulla oblongata directly controls breathing, blood flow, heart rate, eating, and other essential functions (adapted from MedicineNet.com and other sources). In an article on the risks of psychopharmacopoeia, extant in Celan's estate, the following sentence occurs: "In contrast to sleeping pills like Luminal the new medications act directly on the brainstem."

"Umweg- / Karten" | *"Detour- / maps"*

October 15, 1965, Paris.

folie à deux: Literally, "a madness shared by two," a psychiatric syndrome in which symptoms of a delusional belief are transmitted from one individual to another; now more often referred to in the medical literature as "shared psychotic disorder" or "induced delusional disorder." By this time, Paul Celan's psychological problems had come to a crisis, and he and Gisèle, their relationship having become deeply conflictual, begin speaking of a separation, necessary according to Gisèle, though Celan refuses to entertain the idea. The concept of a "folie à deux" is his reaction to this looming separation.

"Sackleinen-Gugel" | *"Sackcloth-mold"*

October 17, 1965, Paris.

-fibrille | -fibril: A fibril is a fine fiber, such as a nerve fiber or neurofibril, that is about ten nanometers in diameter.

"Spasmen" | *"Spasms"*

October 18, 1965, Paris.

Knochenstabritzung | bone-rod-incisions: In Behn, *Kultur der Urzeit* (Berlin: Walter de Gruyter, 1950), there is a reading trace mentioning the natural arts of the Old Stone Age, including "Eskimo incisions on reindeer bones" (BW, p. 755).

Grandelkranz | eyetooth-circlet: *Grandel* is given as "upper eyetooth" (Langenscheid's *Encyclopaedic Muret-Sanders*) and as "large canine tooth in the upper jaw of a deer" (Harrap's *Standard Dictionary*). The Grimms give it the meaning *härchen*, "little hair," and link it to *Granne*, meaning "stacheliges, steifes Haar, vorzüglich vom Barthaar, nicht aber vom Haupthaar; älterer Sprache zugehörig" (prickly, stiff hair, rather from beard hair than from head hair; belonging to an older language). Wiedemann indicates that the word can be used both for the hair and for the tooth (BW, p. 755).

"Deine Augen im Arm" | *"Your eyes in the arm"*

October 20–21, 1965.

Herzschatten | heartshadow: See the similar word formation in "Osterqualm" | "Eastersmoke" (p. 78), where the poem speaks of a *Herzschattenseil*, a "heartshadowcord."

"Hendaye" | *"Hendaye"*
October 22, 1965, Hendaye/Saint-Jean-de-Luz. Celan's psychological crisis has deepened, and on October 21 he starts an impromptu journey through France that will last until October 29. "In seven days Celan performs a sort of tour de France: Paris, Saint-Jean-de-Luz, Ascain, Hendaye, Pau, Tarbes, Toulouse, Montpellier, Avignon, L'Isle-sur-la-Sorgue, Valence, Lyon, Paris. He sends a postcard to his son from nearly each stopping place . . . During this errancy he writes or drafts seven poems that will make up one part of the first cycle of *Threadsuns* and sends two of them to his wife ['The ounce of truth' and 'In the noises,' p. 128]." He wrote from the border town Hendaye to his son Eric: "Same day, a bit further on, in Hendaye. I came here over the road along the steep coastal cliffs—it lies at a distance of 14 kilometers from St-Jean-de-Luz" (PC/GCL, #287).

Hendaye: An early draft title for the poem was "Garotten-Grenze" | "Garrote-Border," the method of execution used in Franco's Spain. On October 23, 1940, exactly twenty-five years earlier, Hitler and Franco had a meeting in this town.

"Pau, Nachts" | *"Pau, by Night"*
October 23, 1965, Pau. Celan was born on a twenty-third of November and married on a twenty-third of December; he attributed a talismanic meaning to this day in the month, calling those days in November and December *grands anniversaires* (great birthdays/anniversaries) and the twenty-thirds of the other months *petits anniversaires* (small birthdays/anniversaries). As he points out in the letter to Gisèle written that day from Pau: "Again, a happy anniversary! In two months it will be out great anniversary—may we have many more like them, in midst our strengths, <u>all</u> our re-found strengths, raising Eric!" (PC/GCL, #287).

Heinrich / dem Vierten | Henry / the Fourth: Henry IV of France (1553–1610), king of Navarre, then king of France, was born in a room in the castle in Pau, in which a tortoise shell that supposedly served as his cradle is exhibited. Henry IV was murdered by the Catholic fanatic François Ravaillac.

Unsterblichkeitsziffer | immortality cypher / Schildkrötenadel | tortoise-nobility / eleatisch | eleatically: Zeno of Elea (ca. 490 B.C.E.–ca. 430 B.C.E.), a member of the Eleatic school founded by Parmenides, was famous for his paradox of the tortoise and Achilles, which suggests that motion is impossible as it plays on the concept of infinity.

"Pau, Später" | *"Pau, Later"*
October 23, 1965, Pau–October 30, 1965, Paris.

Albigenserschatten | Albigenses-shadow: Catharism was a Christian religious movement that flourished during the twelfth and thirteenth centuries in the Languedoc region of southern France. Seen as heretics by the Catholic church, the Cathars were reviled by the pope, who called for their suppression, which eventually led to twenty years of war against the Cathars and their allies in Languedoc, the so-called Albigensian Crusade (the castle town of Albi being a central stronghold)—a true extermination campaign in which a vast number of men, women, and children were killed.

Waterloo-Plein: See the commentary on the poem "Solve" | "Solve," page 491. For a more detailed comment on this poem, see Janz, *Vom Engagement absoluter Poesie*, #114, p. 185.

Baruch: Baruch Spinoza (1632–1677), a major Jewish-Dutch philosopher who, accused of being a heretical thinker, had been excluded from his religious community.

die / kantige | the / angular . . . [to end of poem]: Spinoza made his living as a lens grinder.

"Der Hengst" | *"The stallion"*
October 23, 1965, Pau/Tarbes. Early versions were titled "In the Pyrenees."

"Die Unze Wahrheit" | *"The ounce of truth"*
October 25, Montpellier–October 26, 1965, on train from Montpellier to Avignon. That latter town had also been the first stage of his honeymoon trip in December 1952. The first draft of the poem read: "The ounce of truth / behind delusion / shoved my enemies / into boiling nothingness."

das kämpfend in Herz- / höhe | in struggle to heart- / level: Jean Starobinski had written to Celan in a letter dated March 29, 1965: "My father was a Jew according to *the law of the heart* (and not the rite); you belong to that same community, and I feel more strongly attached to it today" (editor's emphasis).

Celan had thanked Starobinski exactly for those words, repeating the expression "the law of the heart" (PC/GCL, 2:261 and 209).

Sohn, siegt | son, wins: In his notebook, next to the version of October 25, Celan had added: "You win, Eric, with me / and your mother" (PC/GCL, 2:261).

"In den Geräuschen" | *"In the noises"*
October 26, 1965, Valence.

"Lyon, Les Archers" | *"Lyon, Les Archers"*
October 29–30, 1965, Paris. The poem arises from a note Celan took on October 25 in Lyon: "Café Les Archers, the girl reading the Stranger." The reference is to Albert Camus' novel *L'Étranger* | *The Stranger* (TA, *Fadensonnen*, p. 39).

Archers | Archers: Celan's astrological sign was Sagittarius.

"Die Köpfe" | *"The heads"*
November 12, 1965, Paris.

"Wo bin ich" | *"Where am I"*
November 17, 1965, Paris.

"Die längst Entdeckten" | *"The long discovered"*
November 21, 1965, Paris–February 8, 1967. On November 21, 1965, Celan undertook a trip to Switzerland and also wrote the following poem, not included in *Threadsuns* (BW, p. 485):

BELEAGUERED

The delusion-runs: say,
that they are delusion-runs,
of the murder-
mouths and -writings and -signs,
say, that they are composed [erdichtet]
by you.

Of the rain don't say:
he rains.

Say: it
rains.

Say
Don't say
Say
Don't say
Say
Don't say it

Treppe / zum Hafen | staircase / to the harbor . . . Odessitka | Odessitka:
The final word of the poem is the Russian name for a female inhabitant of
Odessa, and the final stanzas of the poem recall the scene in Sergei Eisenstein's
Battleship Potemkin (1925) when czarist troops goose-step down the seemingly
endless flight of stairs known as the "Odessa steps," mowing down men,
women, and children. Celan had a lifelong interest in the Russian Revolution,
revolutionary politics in general, and Eisenstein's work, but always with a crit-
ical mind for both the politics and the art. In a letter to Gisèle of August 21,
1965, he writes after watching Eisenstein's *October* at the Cinémathèque (PCS,
#267):

> So, all alone, I saw Petersburg, the workers, the sailors of the Aurora. It
> was very moving, at times reminding one of the "Potemkin," bringing to
> mind the thoughts and dreams of my childhood, my thoughts of today
> and of always, poetry-always-true-always-faithful, I saw my placards, many
> of them, those that, not very long ago, I evoked in the poem I sent you—
> Vaporband-, banderole-uprising," I saw the October Revolution, its men,
> its flags, I saw hope always en route, the brother of poetry, I saw . . .
>
> Then, at a certain moment, at the moment when the insurgents occupy
> the Winter Palace, it began to desert poetry and to become Cinema,
> motion-picture shots, tendentious and overdone, the intertexts became
> propaganda—all that was History and its Personages had anyway been,
> from the very beginning, what was the least convincing, the role of the Left
> Social-Revolutionaries was completely expunged—, so then the heart loos-
> ened, searched for its silences (won, lost, won again), wrapped them around
> itself and led me outside, alone, as I had come in, running the gauntlet be-

tween young cinephile gents and young girls "mit tupierter Frisur," with too much makeup, in pants, sort of leftist sixteenth arrondissement, erratic and flabby.—But there were some, no doubt, who knew, taking, here too, responsibility for the terrible eclipses.

> Long live the sailors of Kronstadt!
> Long live the Revolution! Long live Love!
> Long live Petersburg! Long live Paris!
> Long live Poetry!"

"All deine Siegel erbrochen? Nie." | "All your seals broken open? Never." Composed on the train from Montpellier to Avignon on October 26 and completed on November 23, 1965 (his forty-fifth birthday) in Switzerland.

verzedere | cedarize: A Celanian neologism, of which Ulrich Konietzny says: "The verb 'verzedern' can only be deduced connotatively maybe with the meaning that something like cedar wood should be worked through. One can also read it as an allusion to the habitual burning of strongly aromatic cedar wood in Israel" (Konietzny, 1988, p. 108). I do, however, always hear the particle *ver-* in Celan as indicating a deviation from a direction or aim into something that is wrong, or into the opposite of what was intended, and as the destructive motion in words like *verreißen*, "to pull to pieces," etc. There are of course some positive meanings to this particle, as in *verknüpfen*, "to tie together," *verdichten*, "to tighten," etc. There are close to three hundred occurrences of the particle *ver-* in Celan's work, many of them in neologic constructions, such as *verzedere*, and many of these with somewhat negative connotations.

honig- / ferne, die milch- / nahe | honey- / distant, milk- / close: Compare Exod. 3:8: "And I am come down to deliver them out of the hand of the Egyptians, and to bring them up out of that land unto a good land and a large, unto a land flowing with milk and honey; unto the place of the Canaanites, and the Hittites, and the Amorites, and the Perizzites, and the Hivites, and the Jebusites."

Elektronen-Idioten | electron- / idiot . . . Datteln | dates: The double meaning of the English word "dates," as *Datteln*, the fruit, and as *Daten*, dates and even data, the latter suggested by the "Elektronen-Idioten" of the previous line, according to at least one commentator, was an intended pun by Celan (Oelmann, *Deutsche poetologische Lyrik nach 1945*, p. 394f; quoted by Konietzny).

menetekelnde / Affen | portentous / apes: Compare Dan. 5:24–27: "Then was the part of the hand sent from him; and this writing was written. / And this is the writing that was written, MENE, MENE, TEKEL, UP-HARSIN. / This is the interpretation of the thing: MENE; God hath numbered thy kingdom, and finished it. / TEKEL; Thou art weighed in the balances, and art found wanting." Rembrandt's painting *Belshazzar's Feast* shows the moment when the divine hand writes on the wall the Hebrew phrase that only Daniel can decipher. Celan had seen this painting in the National Gallery in London.

II

"Schlafbrocken" | *"Sleepmorsels"*
June 13, 1966, Paris. The first poem Celan wrote after his release from Sainte-Anne, the psychiatric clinic in Paris where he concluded a six-month internment after his attempt to kill Gisèle on November 24, 1965, an internment that took him first to the Garches, then Suresnes, and finally the Paris psychiatric clinics (see Introduction, p. xxxviii). The first draft has the dedication "for Gisèle." A first printing by Brunidor, Vaduz (Liechtenstein), included an etching by Gisèle.

"Die Wahrheit" | *"Truth"*
July 29, 1966, Paris.

"Aus den nahen" | *"Out of the near"*
August 1–4, 1966, Moisville.

"Ausgeschlüpfte" | *"Hatched"*
August 8, 1966, Paris.

Gebetmäntel | prayercoats: The German word connotes the tallith, or prayer shawl, which is, however, traditionally white. Compare the poem "Schaufäden, Sinnfäden" | "Sight threads, sense threads" (p. 86).

Brandkraut | lampwick: Plant of the *Phlomis* family, possibly here *Phlomis lychnitis*, which has astringent qualities; its leaves have been used to make wicks for oil lamps.

"Ewigkeiten" | *"Eternities"*

August 9, 1966. Celan has at least six poems with the word "eternity" or its plural in the title or opening line: "Ewigkeiten" | "Eternities" (p. 140), "Die Ewigkeiten tingeln" | "The eternities honkytonk" (p. 162), "Die Ewigkeit" | "Eternity" (p. 176), "Die Ewigkeiten" | "The eternities" (p. 272), "Huriges Sonst" | "Whorish else" (p. 326), and "Die Ewigkeit" | "Eternity" (p. 398).

"Der puppige Steinbrech" | *"The perty saxifrage"*

August 20, 1966, Moisville. The next poem was also written on that day, and the following one begun.

Steinbrech | saxifrage: The German name Steinbrech literally means "stone breaker," as does its Late Latin root, *saxifrage*; from Latin, feminine of *saxifragus*, "breaking rocks," from *saxum*, "rock," and *frangere*, "to break" (*Merriam-Webster*). Traditionally thought to indicate its ancient medicinal use for treatment of urinary calculi, i.e., kidney stones.

"Die zwischenein-" | *"The between-whiles"*

August 20, 1966, Moisville.

Gletschermilch | glacier milk: Waters of a glacial stream in which particles of light-colored silt are suspended.

"Der geglückte" | *"The successful"*

Begun August 16, 1966, in London; finished August 20, 1966, in Moisville.

Paulownia: A tree Celan liked and links both to his homeland, the Bukovina, and to his name, Paul, though it also appears in darker circumstances in the poem "La Contrescarpe" (in *Die Niemandsrose*). As this poem will be referred to several times in the commentaries but is not included in this volume, I will insert it here in its entirety:

LA CONTRESCARPE

Break out the breathcoin
from the air around you and the tree:
so
much

is required from him
whom hope carts up and down
the hearthumpway—so
much

at the turning,
where he meets the breadarrow
that drunk the wine of his night, the wine
of the misery-, the kings-
vigil.

Didn't the hands come along, the awake
ones, didn't happiness, deeply
embedded in her chalice-eye, come?
Didn't the human-toned, lidded
Marchpipe come along, that gave light,
back then, widely?

Did the carrier pigeon sheer off, was its ring
to be deciphered? (All those
clouds around it—they were readable.) Did the
flock suffer it? And understand
and take off while it stayed away?

Roof shingle slipway,—on pigeon-
keel what swims is laid. Through the bulkheads
the message bleeds, time-barred things
go overboard:

Via Kraków
you came, at the Anhalter
railway station
a smoke flowed toward your glance,
it already belonged to tomorrow. Under
paulownias
you saw the knives stand, again,

made sharp by distance. There was
dancing. (Quatorze
juillets. Et plus de neufs autres.)
Overdwarf, monkeyverse, slantmouth
mimed lived experience. The lord,
wrapped in a banner, joined
the swarm. He snapped
himself
a little souvenir. The self-
timer, that was
you.

O this dis-
friending. Yet again,
there, where you have to go, the one
exact
crystal.

"Auf überregneter Fährte" | *"On the rained-over spoor"*
August 23, 1966, Moisville.

"Weißgeräusche" | *"Whitesounds"*
September 5–October 10, 1966. A poem commissioned for a Festschrift for
Hans Mayer; the first draft has the initials H.M. as title.

Flaschenpost | bottle post: Wiedemann (BW, p. 762) locates the idea of the
poem as a letter in a bottle or a bottle post in an improvised contribution by
Hans Mayer on a poem by Goethe at an October 1957 meeting, where Celan
and Mayer first met. Mayer couldn't locate the source of his quote after Celan
asked for it on several occasions, but in a letter to the literary scholar Joachim
Seng, he says: "In remembrance of conversations with Adorno on his favorite
theme of 'literature as an esoteric bottle post.'" Wiedemann further suggests
that with this poem Celan is thanking Mayer for having sparked the idea for-
mulated in 1958 in his Bremen Prize speech: "A poem, being an instance of
language, hence essentially dialogue, may be a letter in a bottle thrown out to

sea with the—surely not always strong—hope that it may somehow wash up somewhere, perhaps on a shoreline of the heart. In that way, too, poems are en route: they are headed toward" (PCCP, p. 35).

"Die teuflischen" | *"The devilish"*
September 1, 1966, Moisville.

"Die Dunkel-Impflinge" | *"The dark vaccination candidates"*
September 6, 1966, Paris.

"Die zweite" | *"The second"*
September 27–October 5, 1966, Paris.

"Das ausgeschachtete Herz" | *"The excavated heart"*
October 7, 1966. The following poems also started on this day.

"Die fleißigen" | *"The industrious"*
October 7–9, 1966.

Synkope | syncope: A rich word in both languages that can refer to (1) in medicine, loss of consciousness, or (2) in linguistics, the loss of one or more sounds from the interior of a word, especially the loss of an unstressed vowel, or (3) in music, a musical effect caused by a syncope, missed beat, or off-the-beat stress.

Halljahr | jubilee: Compare Lev. 25:10–13: "And ye shall hallow the fiftieth year, and proclaim liberty throughout the land unto all the inhabitants thereof; it shall be a jubilee unto you; and ye shall return every man unto his possession, and ye shall return every man unto his family. / A jubilee shall that fiftieth year be unto you; ye shall not sow, neither reap that which groweth of itself in it, nor gather the grapes in it of the undressed vines. / For it is a jubilee; it shall be holy unto you; ye shall eat the increase thereof out of the field. / In this year of jubilee ye shall return every man unto his possession." Compare also the poem "Und Kraft und Schmerz" | "And strength and pain" (p. 380).

der barock ummantelte, / spracheschluckende Duschraum | the baroquely cloaked, / language-swallowing showerroom: In the extermination camps, the gas chambers were camouflaged as shower rooms.

Stehzelle | standing-cell: Wiedemann points to two occurrences of this word in newspaper articles in Celan's possession, the first describing a visit by legal experts to such a cell in Auschwitz in December 1964, recorded in *Die Welt* of January 13, 1965, as is the following quote from the same article: "Under no circumstances could one speak here of a disparagement of the victims. In the standing cells of Bloc 11 in Auschwitz many detainees starved to death" (BW, p. 763).

"Die kollidierenden" | *"The colliding"*
October 11, 1966, Paris–October 14, 1966, Cologne. From October 11 to October 18, 1966, Celan was in Germany for poetry readings. A draft of the poem was found on an October 12 concert program from Cologne, which Celan sent to his friend Ruth Kraft.

"Eingehimmelt" | *"In-heavened"*
October 24, 1966, Paris. Celan dated the poem with his full address, "78 rue de Longchamp, XIVth," a rare event.

Lidschlagreflexe | eyeblinkreflexes: An involuntary reaction, the corneal reflex is the blink that occurs upon irritation of the eye. It is mediated through the trigeminal nerve (cranial nerve); its aim is to protect the eyes from foreign bodies. The absence of corneal reflex may indicate damage to the brain stem (adapted from MedicineNet.com and other sources). The corneal reflex is also very noticeable during the dream-heavy period of REM (rapid eye movement) sleep. Celan had encountered the term in his reading of Reichel/Bleichert, *Leitfaden der Physiologie des Menschen*.

"Wenn ich nicht weiß, nicht weiß" | *"When I don't know, don't know"*
December 23, 1966, Paris. Celan's fourteenth wedding anniversary. On December 27, 1966, he wrote to Gisèle: "I wrote a hard, difficult to translate poem, with among other lines, this one: 'The Jewess Pallas Athena'—" (PC/GCL, #469).

Wenn ich nicht weiß, nicht weiß | When I don't know, don't know: Compare the opening line/stanza of Hölderlin's hymn fragment "Heimath" (Home): "Und niemand weiß" (and no one knows). Otto Pöggeler also points out that "in the ode 'Rousseau' one finds the line 'and no one / knows how to show the modest way' ['und niemand / weiß den bescheidenen Weg zu weisen']. The second stanza of the elegy 'Brot und Wein' says concerning the 'wonderful' goodwill of the heavenly ones: 'and no one / knows from whence and what befalls one from it' ['und niemand / Weiß von wannen und was einem geschiehet von ihr']" (SPUR, p. 270).

Aschrej | Ashrei: *Ashrei* (Hebrew אשרי) is a word meaning "happy," "praiseworthy," or "fortunate" as in Deut. 33:29: "Happy art thou, O Israel." The Ashrei is a prayer that is recited at least three times daily in Jewish prayers, twice during Shacharit and once during Mincha. It is composed primarily of Psalm 145 in its entirety, with a verse each from Psalms 84 and 144 added to the beginning and a verse from Psalm 115 added to the end. The first two verses that are added both start with the Hebrew word *ashrei*, hence the prayer's name. In Luther's translation, the verse from Deuteronomy reads: "Wohl dir, Israel!" The other German word that most closely translates this word is *Heil*.

der Jüdin / Pallas / Athene | the / Jewess / Pallas / Athena's: Writes Barbara Hahn in her book of the same title:

> In Greek mythology, Pallas Athena with her double name wears a helmet upon her head and a shield across her breast. Ovaries, however, she does not have. She was neither born of a mother nor can become one. She is the daughter of her father, Zeus, from whose head she sprang, and which, in some traditions, split asunder, so that in thunder and lightning she could come into the world . . . Athena, this daughter without a mother, interrupts all female genealogies and founds no traditions. Pallas Athena, the warrior, the thinking woman, whose symbol is the owl, is a unique occurrence. A point without history, with no before and no after.
>
> The "Jewess" is something quite different. Since the end of the eighteenth century, an erotically charged word with a meaning that depends on exclusion. It signaled a danger for the German man and threatened a "corruption of German culture"; it stood for the foreign, the ominous, the other. Celan's poem shatters this context. Ovaries have no erotic connotation. Ovaries designate the fecundity of women, and women were targeted by the National Socialist genocide because they could be mothers. They

were sterilized—squirted in the ovaries—so that they could no longer hand on life. And they were murdered, so that never again would a Mother Rahel weep for her children.

The "Jewess Pallas Athena." This shocking phrase demolishes an anchor of National Socialist ideology: the supposed contradiction between "Semitic" and "Indo-European"—what German philology calls "Indo-Germanic." Beyond this opposition, something in common is asserted that encompasses both the culture of ancient Greece and the Jewish tradition. What appear to be entirely contrary meanings can suddenly be thought together, meanings that had been lost in the clichéd images of the "Jewess." Two traditions interweave, and to monotheistic Judaism is joined a culture that understood Wisdom, Knowledge, Art, and Memory as feminine nouns. Sophia and Mnemosyne, the Muses and Theoria. A culture in which feminine words and female figures bear memories just as Rahel, Esther, and Sulamith recall the Jewish people for Celan. (pp. 5–6)

karpatisches | Carpathian: The Carpathian Mountains are a range of mountains forming an arc roughly 1,500 kilometers (932 miles) long across central and eastern Europe, making them the second-longest mountain range in Europe, stretching in an arc from the Czech Republic in the northwest to Serbia in the south. Celan's homeland, the Bukovina, now part of Ukraine, was part of the Carpathian stretch. Wiedemann adds that the Bukovina "ceased to exist after the resettlement of its German and the extermination of its Jewish inhabitants" (BW, p. 765).

Allemande: A popular instrumental dance form of baroque music and an element of a suite. The French word means literally "German," interesting here for its linguistic triangulation between the German of the poem, the Hebrew word *ashrei*, and the French word for "German." Hahn (pp. 4–5) notes an interesting coincidence with that linguistic triangle and the triangle formed by the "I, You, and He" of the poem.

sich übergebende | vomiting: The German verb has two meanings, a literal sense of *über-geben*, "to hand or give over," and the figurative sense of "to vomit," just as in the poem "Es kommt" / "There also" (p. 442) Celan uses the expression *erbricht* ("breached"), where the German verb also has two meanings, one describing an infraction, a breach.

"Eingewohnt-entwohnt" | *"Acclimatized-disclimatized"*

December 31, 1966, Paris. Compare Franz Wurm's letter of December 15, 1966, mentioning the publication of French translations of poems by Celan in the *Nouvelle Revue Française*: "There lay the December issue . . . and your name was as acclimatized [*eingewohnt*] on it as is possible for someone who was forced to take a long time to acclimatize himself [*lange hat einwohnen müssen*]." Celan answered his friend in a letter of December 21, 1966: "'Acclimatized,' that's what you say. Maybe. Acclimatized-disclimatized, seems more like it to me" (PC/FW, letters #33 and #34).

-lötige | carat: The German *Lot* is an old measure expressing the purity of silver and equivalent to our "carat" (now used only for gold), before the use of the millesimal system.

"Riesiges" | *"Giant"*

January 1, 1967, Paris.

Quincunx | quincunx: This is the single occurrence of the word in Celan's oeuvre. Meaning literally "five-twelfths"—from the Latin *quinque*, "five," and *uncia*, "twelfth part"—a quincunx is an arrangement of five things in a square or rectangle, with one at each corner and one in the middle. Originally a Roman coin whose value was five-twelfths of an as, a quincunx is a standard pattern for planting an orchard. The English physician Sir Thomas Browne, in his philosophical discourse *The Garden of Cyrus* (1658), elaborates upon evidence of the quincunx pattern in art and nature and mystically as evidence of "the wisdom of God." Browne possessed several books by the German astronomer Johannes Kepler (1571–1630), including his *Ad vitellionem paralipomena* (1604), which is credited as first introducing the pattern to astronomy and astrology in modern times (adapted from *Merriam-Webster* and *OED*).

"Gewieherte Tumbagebete" | *"Neighed tombprayers"*

January 4, 1967, Paris. The poem draws on a FAZ article of January 4, 1967, reporting on the funeral for the Austrian writer Heimito von Doderer, someone early on much compromised by adherence to Nazi ideology. Celan owned his novel *Die Strudelhofstiege oder Melzer und die Tiefe der Jahre*, inscribed to him with the dedication: "For Paul Celan, cordially, Heimito von Doderer, Munich, December 1954." In a letter to Gisèle of January 4, 1967, he notes: "I have written a new poem, hard and harsh."

Tumbagebete | tombprayers: *Tumbagebete* are mentioned in the FAZ article, and the word had already been underlined by Celan in Heinrich Böll's *Haus ohne Hüter* (House without guardians) (BW, p. 766).

zerstrahlten | irradiated: Reading traces for this word in Celan's copy of Arno Schmidt's *The Egghead Republic*.

"Die Ewigkeiten tingeln" | *"The eternities honkytonk"*
January 18, 1967, Paris.

"Müllschlucker-Chöre" | *"Trashswallower-choirs"*
January 21, 1967.

Frieselfieber | Miliary fever: Wiedemann links this term to Mozart, who is said to have suffered toward the end of his life from a "fever accompanied by 'Frieseln'" (BW, p. 766), that is, miliary fever—"miliary" referring to the appearance of millet-sized bumps on the skin.

Dezember | December: Mozart died on December 5, 1791.

III

"Entteufelter Nu" | *"Dedeviled instant"*
February 28, 1967. On January 30 Celan attempted suicide by stabbing himself with a letter opener, barely missing his heart. His wife saved him in extremis. Transported to Boucicaut hospital in the fifteenth arrondissement, he was immediately operated on, as the stab had punctured his left lung and gravely damaged it. On February 13 he was interned in the Sainte-Anne psychiatric clinic, in the care of Professor Delay, and though allowed outings starting at the end of April, he was confined to Sainte-Anne's until October 17. More than half of the poems in *Fadensonnen* | *Threadsuns* (starting with this, the third cycle), as well as a large part of *Lichtzwang* | *Lightduress* (the first four cycles and parts of the fifth), were composed during this stay.

Bocklemünd: The name of neighborhood of Cologne, which includes a large Jewish cemetery visited by Celan on October 9 or 19 while traveling in Germany to pay homage to his childhood friend Marcel Pohne, who died in an accident in December 1964.

"Hüllen" | *"Shells"*

March 1, 1967. The following poem was written on the same day.

Jeden Pfeil, den du losschickst | Each arrow you loose: The "you" here is the poet himself, using, as he often does, a reference to his astrological sign—Sagittarius, the archer.

"Die Liebe" | *"Love"*

March 1, 1967. The preceding poem was written on the same day.

zwangsjackenschön | straitjacket-pretty: When Celan had attempted to kill Gisèle in November 1965, he had been taken to the psychiatric hospital bundled in a straitjacket. Compare the poem "Schlafbrocken" | "Sleepmorsels" (p. 136).

Kranichpaar | pair of cranes . . . da er durchs Nichts fährt | drives through the void: Wiedemann (BW, p. 768) points to Bertolt Brecht's poem "Die Liebenden" | "The Lovers," from *The Rise and Fall of the City of Mahagonny*. Jenny says in the second act: "Sieh jene Kraniche im großen Bogen!" | "Look at those cranes sweeping wide!" . . . "So mag der Wind sie ins Nicht entführen / wenn sie nur nicht vergehen und sich bleiben." | "So it matters not, if the wind should lead them off into the void, / as long as they don't perish and they have each other" (translation by Guy Stern). See also the "pair of cranes" in the poem "Herzschall-Fibeln" | "Heartsound-fibulas" (p. 274) and the crane in "Wenn du im Bett" | "When you lie" (p. 48).

"Du warst" | *"You were"*

March 10, 1967. On that day Celan received a letter from Gisèle that said: "I can no longer endure Paris, or this apartment with the telephones, and all that drama we are living through. I will not be able to come on Sunday, I am leaving tomorrow evening before I have a complete nervous breakdown, which wouldn't help anyone—" The underlining is in Celan's hand, who added in the left margin "Thursday!" (PC/GCL, #480).

"Zur Rechten" | *"To the right"*

March 16, 1967. On this day Celan sent a letter (PC/GCL, #483) to his wife to wish her well on her impending fortieth birthday.

Zur Rechten—wer? | To the right—who?: In the original volume this poem stood on the right side of the page with the previous poem, "Du warst" | "You were," on the left side.

Tödin | Shedeath: This female form of the word *Tod,* "death," occurs only once in German literature, according to the Grimms' dictionary, namely, in a text by Abraham a Sancta Clara, where it is used as a local dialectical expression connoting *nächtliche Wehklage,* "nightly lament." One should, however, remember that in French the word death"—*la mort*—is feminine.

außer- / himmlische Ort | outer- / heavenly place: Celan had first written "am hyper-uranischen Ort" | "At the hyper-uranian place," a reference to Plato's *Phaedrus,* line 247C, which speaks of a *tópon hyperouránion,* "the place beyond heaven—none of our earthly poets has ever sung or ever will sing its praises enough!" Plato's Greek word—*hyperouranos*—describes his realm of the pure forms, that is, Platonic ideas.

"Die abgewrackten Tabus" | *"The dismantled taboos"*

March 18, 1967.

Die abgewrackten Tabus | The dismantled taboos: Reading traces in Peter Chotjewitz's review of Konrad Bayer's *Der sechste Sinn* (*Literatur und Kritik* 12 [March 1967]: 122–26) (LPC): "The writer in this situation for himself and as a dismantled [circled by Celan] institution just good enough to give proof of his own uselessness" (p. 122). And: "But each attack on and each victory, no matter how small, over a taboo is only an illusionary attack and an illusionary victory. The public success of books supposedly freed of taboos [circled by Celan] is only the expression of a widespread tendency for social ersatz-satisfaction" (p. 123).

Grenzgängerei | bordercrisscrossing: See Chotjewitz: "This attempt by a novel to be simultaneously an essay about the novel in the sense in which Heinrich Vornweg once described literary border-crossing [*Grenzgängerei*] [circled by Celan] as literary activity become autonomous, proposes a multitude of enigmas." The word is used today mainly to describe workers crossing borders in the morning to work in one country and returning to their own country in the evening, that is, border crosser, border worker, cross-border commuter.

"Wutpilger-Streifzüge" | *"Rage-pilgrim raids"*
March 20, 1967.

"Stille" | *"Silence"*
March 30, 1967.

"Die Eine" | *"The one"*
March 31–April 1, 1967. A first draft of the poem was jotted down in Edmond Jabès's *Le Livre des Questions* III | *The Book of Questions* III.
　　eigen- / sternige / Nacht. // Aschendurchfadmet | self- / starred / night. // Threathed through by ashes: In the first draft, Celan had "von / Fäden durchwoben" | "by / threads woven through." Compare also reading traces in Jabès: "C'est un homme de vérité, disait de Reb Massé, Reb Eloun; il marche sur des tapis de cendres" (He is a man of truth, Reb Eloun said of Reb Massé; he walks on carpets of ashes) (Celan's underlines; p. 40), and "Il a dit: Le mal est quelquefois l'habit du bien. Et il pensait: L'étoile est l'orne-ment et le bouton de l'ample manteau des nuits." (He said: evil is sometimes the garment of the good. And he thought: The star is the adornment and the button of night's ample mantle.") (marginal mark on p. 46; BW, p. 770).

"Bei Glüh- und Mühwein" | *"Over mulled and toiled wine"*
April 4, 1967. On this day, after several weeks without news, Celan received a letter from Gisèle informing him that she had returned to Paris, a letter he immediately answered, reaffirming, against Gisèle's doubt, his conviction that "there had to be a future, for us three, one way or another" (PC/GCL, #485).
　　Bei Glüh- und Mühwein | Over mulled and toiled wine: Compare the poem from *Die Niemandsrose* "Bei Wein und Verlorenheit" | "Over Wine and Lostness").
　　Hohlzahn | hollow tooth: The German word *Hohlzahn* literally means "hollow tooth." I have been unable to trace the word in a maritime context, as sail, mast, or anchor would suggest. The word is also a botanical term referring to the plant hemp nettle (*Galeopsis tetrahit*).

"Schief" | *"Aslant"*
April 5–6, 1967.

Hörklappe | hearing-flap: The first draft had *Hörkappe*, in the context of a reading trace and citation from Freud's *The Ego and the Id*: "Schief, wie uns allen, / sitzt dir die Hörkappe auf // Freud XIII, D. 252." The reference pertains to the following quote: "One can add that the ego wears a 'hearing-cap,' but on one side only, as attested by the anatomy of the brain. You could say that the cap sits crooked (awry, aslant)." The form "Hörklappe" | "hearing-flap" may have been a typo that Celan then sanctioned (TA, *Fadensonnen*, p. 118).

Schläfenfirn | temple-firn: Compare a similar neological word formation in the term "Schläfenzange" | "templeclamps" in the poem of the same name (p. 10).

"Die herzschriftgekrümelte" | *"The heartscriptcrumbled"*
April 8, 1967. This is the first poem written after the conversation with his wife on April 6 in which Gisèle expressed her wish to live separately from then on. Celan also wrote the next poem on that day, and started the following one (BW, p. 771).

"Unverwahrt" | *"Unkept"*
April 8, 1967. The first draft was written on the torn-out title page of a paperback edition of Thomas Mann's *Der Zauberberg* | *The Magic Mountain* (TA, *Fadensonnen*, p. 122). Other notes for the poem can be found in Celan's copy of Thomas Bernhard's novel *Verstörung* (meaning something like "devastation," "deterioration," "blight," though it was translated as *Gargoyles*).

"Das unbedingte Geläut" | *"The unconditional chiming"*
April 8–11, 1967.

"Die Ewigkeit" | *"Eternity"*
April 11, 1967. Draft provided with place of composition: C.P.D. (Clinique Professeur Delay). The same day he wrote the next poem and started the following one.

Die Ewigkeit | Eternity: Compare several poems with the same or similar titles throughout the oeuvre.

Cerveteri: An Italian city, at center of the Etruscan culture, that Celan had visited during a stay in Rome for a reading at the Goethe-Institut in April 1964. As this poem was written so shortly after his wife's announced intention to live separately, he may also have had in mind the letter she had sent him on January 19, 1965, from Rome, after a visit to the Etruscan museum in the Villa Giulia (BW, p. 772). In that letter she had written: "An hour . . . among the vases, the statuettes, the jewelry, the magnificent sarcophagi remarkably well presented. I remember before all a very beautiful <u>Sarcofagi degli sposi</u>, deeply moving in its serenity, charm, love, which made me pray to be with you for all eternity, and to know that it can be thus is a marvelous help. To have seen these two lovers, serene and united, calm and so tender in death has made me believe that we two also, with our difficult life, but beyond all full of love, will maybe eventually have the right to share the fate of these two Etruscan lovers, that I saw on January 19, 1965, in the Villa Giulia in Rome while thinking of you" (PC/GCL, #198).

Asphodelen | asphodels: A flower famously connected with the dead and the underworld. Homer, in chapters 11 and 24 of *The Odyssey*, describes it as covering the great meadow (ἀσφόδελος λειμών), the haunt of the dead. It was planted on graves, and is often connected with Persephone, who appears crowned with a garland of asphodels. See also, for example, the use made of this flower by William Carlos Williams's 1953 poem "Asphodel, That Greeny Flower" (*The Collected Poems of William Carlos Williams*, ed. Christopher MacGowan [New York: New Directions, 1991], p. 2:310).

"Spät" | *"Late"*
April 11, 1967.

"Die Sämlinge" | *"The seedlings"*
April 11–12, 1967.
   causa secunda: In scholastic philosophy and theology, if God was given as the *causa prima*, the first cause of creation, then what was created, the world, beings, mankind included, were the *causa secunda*, or second cause.

"Die Hügelzeilen entlang" | *"Along the hill lines"*
April 13, 1967.
   Hügelzeilen | hill lines: Reading trace in the final chapter of Thomas

Mann's *Magic Mountain*, which Celan was reading then, as a note in a letter of April 10 to Gisèle makes clear: "After lunch, diverse readings, among them two chapters of the Zauberberg which I adored at eighteen: 'Snow' and 'Walpurgis Night' (the latter containing the dialogue between Hans Castorp and Clawdia Chauchat mainly in French). Well, I found it insipid, not at all 'cool,' as Eric would say, not for him, but, alas, neither any longer for us. Alas? No, there's need for less regrets. But harshnesses (self-made), but rock faces emerging from the depths, but spirit that's rigorously anti-bourgeois" (PC/GCL, #489). Fernand Cambon, a student at the École Normale Supérieure in those years, remembers Celan's dislike for Mann. When he told Celan that he was reading *The Magic Mountain*, Celan pulled a face and said sarcastically: "Oh, Thomas Mann—he's a pasticheur!" (PC/GCL, 2:353–54).

"Komm" | "Come"
April 21, 1967.
Komm | Come: Compare the poem "Komm" | "Come" from the volume *Zeitgehöft | Timestead* (p. 436).

Nervenzellen | nerve cells . . . multipolar | multipolar . . . Rauten- / gruben | rhomboid / fossas: Reading traces in Celan's copy of Adolf Faller's book on human anatomy, *Der Körper des Menschen: Einführung in Bau und Funktion* (1966).

"Entschlackt" | "Deslagged"
April 21, 1967.
Wenn wir jetzt Messer wären, / blankgezogen wie damals | If we were knives now, / unsheathed like back then: Compare the poem "La Contrescarpe" from *Die Niemandsrose*, speaking to Celan's first arrival via Kraków and Berlin in Paris, specifically the lines:

. . . Under
paulownias
you saw the knives stand, again,
made sharp by distance.

(Compare pp. 513–515)

"Seelenblind" | "Soulblind"

April 22, 1967.

Seelenblind | Soulblind: reading traces in Reichel/Bleichert: "If this [temporal lobe] is also destroyed, the the capacity to learn is irremediably lost. After injuries to areas 18 and 19, man loses the ability to differentiate between and recognize visually perceived objects ('soulblindness'; optical agnosia)" (p. 142).

hinter den Aschen, / im heilig-sinnlosen Wort | behind the ashes, / in the holy-meaningless word: Above a draft of the poem, Celan had written the third line of Osip Mandelstam's poem "In Petersburg" in Russian, which says literally "the blessed, senseless word," though Celan here says "heilig-sinnlos" | "holy-meaningless," whereas in his Mandelstam translation volume he will write: "jenes selige, deutunglose Wort" (that blessed meaningless / uninterpretable / word) (TA, *Fadensonnen*, p. 138).

Hirnmantel | cerebral mantle: Anatomically, the pallium (Latin for "cloak," "mantle")—the layers of gray and white matter that cover the upper surface of the cerebral cortex in vertebrates.

Sehpurpur | visual purple: Rhodopsin, a biological pigment in photoreceptor cells of the retina that is responsible for the first events in the perception of light. See also reading trace in Faller: "Vitamin A is responsible for the normal development of the visual purple in the cornea of the eye" (p. 243).

"Anrainerin" | "Borderess"

April 23, 1967. Eve of Passover.

"Möwenküken" | "Gullchicks"

April 24, 1967. Passover begins; it lasts until May 1. The first two stanzas of this poem are based on the following passage in Adolf Portman's *Das Problem der Urbilder in biologischer Sicht* (Zurich: Rhein-Verlag, 1950), p. 420:

> As example we may use the trigger for the begging response of newly hatched herring gull chicks, as studied by von Tinbergen. They direct their begging to a red spot on the yellow lower beak of the parent bird . . . This is not, however, a special effect of the red stimulus color: a black spot works

even better, as decoy heads show, and a blue-and-white spot is also quite effective. A beak without a spot, however, provides nearly no stimulus. Experiments show further that the red spot placed somewhere else, anywhere on the head, for example, is a very minor stimulant; only the typical disposition on the lower beak triggers optimal begging responses. The structure the chick needs for its behavior is thus not a randomly located stimulus color, but a "stimulus gestalt," a configuration. This has to be hereditarily predetermined in an ordered fashion in the chick's nervous system.

IV

"Irisch" | "Irish"
April 26, 1967. This and the following poem are the first poems Celan wrote after he was granted permission to temporarily leave the hospital.

"Die Stricke" | "The ropes"
April 26, 1967.

"Tau" | "Dew"
April 27, 1967.
    der Herr brach das Brot | the Lord broke the bread: Compare 1 Cor. 11:23–24: "For I have received of the Lord that which also I delivered unto you, That the Lord Jesus the same night in which he was betrayed took bread: / And when he had given thanks, he broke it . . ."

"Üppige Durchsage" | "Lavish message"
April 29, 1967. Compare reading traces in Albert Vigoleis Thelen, Die Insel des zweiten Gesichts: "The second Pilar, a Stußhure [brain-dead whore?] in an odor of 'lenigster' [?] sanctity" and "Theodosius regarded the priest who stood in such an odor of sanctity, so highly" (my translation). This is a seven-hundred-plus-page novel published in 1953, which Celan much admired and called a "genuine work of art." It was recently translated by Donald O. White and published as The Island of Second Sight by Overlook Press in 2013.

"Ausgerollt" | *"This day"*
April 30, 1967.

"Ölig" | *"Oily"*
April 30, 1967.

lidlos| lidless: Celan wrote this adjective in the margins of Gershom Scholem's *On the Mystical Shape of the Godhead* next to the sentence: "His (that is, God's) eyes have no lids, as the guardian of Israel neither sleeps nor slumbers" (p. 42 in German edition; read by Celan on April 25, 1967) (BW, p. 778).

"Ihr mit dem" | *"You with the"*
May 1, 1967. On the same day he wrote the next poem and started the following one. The first two show reading traces from Scholem's *On the Mystical Shape of the Godhead*: "All of the prophets gazed into a dark mirror, but Moses our teacher gazed into a clear glass" (p. 258). Compare St. Paul, 1 Cor. 13:12: "For now we see through a glass darkly . . ."

Joachim Schulze analyzes the whole of this poem as an example of Celan's Jewish mysticism and, in relation to the compound *Leuchtspiegelfläche*, he cites the following extract from Scholem's *Major Trends in Jewish Mysticism* (p. 155):

> When, however, [in the process of meditation] you pass beyond the control of your thinking, another exercise becomes necessary which consists in drawing thought gradually forth—during contemplation—from its source until through sheer force that stage is reached where you do not speak nor can you speak. And if sufficient strength remains to force oneself even further and draw it out still farther, then that which is within will manifest itself without, and through the power of sheer imagination will take on the form of a polished mirror. And this is "the flame of the circling sword," the rear revolving and becoming the fore. Whereupon one sees that his inmost being is something outside himself.

In "Mystische Motive in Paul Celans Gedichten," Schulze comments on this citation as follows: "The 'polished mirror,' 'the flame of the circling sword,' seems to me to be most exactly equivalent to Celan's 'Leuchtspiegelfläche zuinnerst' | 'light-mirror-surface innermost.'" He then associates the expression "Boten-Selbst" | "messenger-self" in the next stanza of the poem with another extract from Scholem's book dealing with the medieval kabbalist Abraham Abulafia's directions for meditating on the letters of the Hebrew alphabet. The extract he quotes is the following: "Then turn all thy true thought to imagine the Name and His exalted angels in thy heart as if they were human beings sitting or standing about thee. And feel thyself like an envoy whom the king and his ministers are to send on a mission, and he is waiting to hear something about his mission from their lips, be it from the king himself, be it from his servants."

Dreivokal | trivowel: Semitic languages such as Hebrew, Arabic, and Syriac are characterized by morphemic verb and noun structures based on the roots of three consonants (triconsonantal root) to which various affixes (prefixes, suffixes, and infixes), which can be vowels or other non-root consonants, are attached to create a word or inflect its meanings. Celan here turns this into a "triple vowel" root; it is interesting to note that in his late work he makes great use of all such affixes to transform basic single or composite German words, treating the syllables of his language as if they were linguistic structures like the Semitic triliterals.

"Aus Engelsmaterie" | "Out of angel-matter"

May 1–2, 1967. During the first week of May, Celan was reading Gershom Scholem's *On the Mystical Shape of the Godhead*. This poem too can be read as a mystical commentary, the erotic component being assimilated to the *unio mystica*, and the "Schwester" to the Shekinah (compare "Nah, im Aortenbogen" | "Near, in the aortic arch," and commentary for same, pp. 200 and 534). The "Kanäle" | "channels" and the "Wurzelkrone" | "rootcrown" do indeed refer to notions of kabbalistic origin. Pöggeler also points to Jewish mysticism in relation to this poem when he writes: "According to ancient teachings, the emanations of the divine ur-ground are made of an especially sublime matter, the same as the matter angels are made of, here the Enlivening-Just [der Belebend-Gerechte] living, according to the Zohar, with the Shekhinah, sleeping it toward [zuschläft] mankind and thus also the poet" (SPUR, p. 355).

der Belebend-Gerechte | the Enlivening-Just: Reading trace in Scholem: "The last triad consists of Netsaḥ (endurance), Hod (splendor and majesty), and Yesod (the foundation) or Tsaddik (the Righteous One). This completes the picture of the creative forces, enabling them to operate together through the living force of God, by which everything finds its place and is maintained. As the living force by excellence, it is likewise the force of procreation, represented through symbols of male sexuality" (pp. 42–43).

noch zu zersamenden Knochen | still-to-be-dissemened bones: Compare "In Prag" | "In Prague" (p. 52) and its lines: "Knochen-Hebraïsch, / zu Sperma zermahlen" | "bone-Hebrew, / ground to sperm."

vom Osten gestreut | strewn from the East: Compare Isa. 43:5: "Fear not: for I am with thee: I will bring thy seed from the east, and gather thee from the west."

"Die freigeblasene Leuchtsaat" | *"The free-blown lightcrop"*
May 1–2, 1967.

Leuchtsaat | lightcrop: Compare Scholem: "The Zohar likewise discusses the 'sowing of light' by the righteous in its explication of Psalm 97:11, 'Light is sown for the Righteous One'" (*Major Trends in Jewish Mysticism*, p. 113).

"Kleide die Worthöhlen aus" | *"Line the wordcaves"*
May 2, 1967. Much of the anatomical vocabulary can be traced back to Celan's reading of Faller's book on anatomy, especially the terminology for the heart: "Vorhöfe, Kammern, Klappen" | "courtyards, chambers, drop doors," which refer to the heart's two atria, the four chambers, and the valves. Given the underlying architectonic images Celan creates by a literal use of those terms as they structure the poem, I have decided on a literal translation of the terms, rather than a strictly anatomical one. For a close reading of the poetics proposed by this poem, see Introduction (p. xlvii). See also footnote 13 of Werner Hamacher's essay "The Second of Inversion: Movements of a Figure Through Celan's Poetry" for a fascinating reading of this poem. A rather daring translation of the poem's third and fourth line gives:

> . . . infur and ecspelt,
>   adsense and absense,

though the clearly intended sound-puns of "infur" (infer) and "absense" (absence) seem to me to go beyond what the original states.

"Die Hochwelt" | *"The highworld"*
May 3, 1967.

"Die brabbelnden" | *"The muttering"*
May 5–12, 1967.

". . . auch keinerlei" | *". . . though no kind of"*
May 7, 1967. On one of the early drafts, Celan has jotted down a nearly illegible note that reads "Freud repetition compulsion," which points to the core reference, namely *Beyond the Pleasure Principle* (TA, *Fadensonnen*, p. 171), specifically the following marginally marked (and partially underlined) sentences: "If we take into account observations such as these, based upon behavior in the transference and upon the life-histories of men and women, we shall find courage to assume that there really does exist in the mind a compulsion to repeat which overrides the pleasure principle" (Bantam Books, 1967, pp. 45–46). "They arise, rather, in obedience to the compulsion to repeat, though it is true that in analysis that compulsion is supported by the wish (which is encouraged by 'suggestion') to conjure up what has been forgotten and repressed" (p. 61). "The manifestations of a compulsion to repeat (which we have described as occurring in the early activities of infantile mental life as well as among the events of psycho-analytic treatment) exhibit to a high degree an instinctual character and, when they act in opposition to the pleasure principle, give the appearance of some 'daemonic' force at work" (p. 65). "The opposition between the ego or death instincts and the sexual or life instincts would then cease to hold and the compulsion to repeat would no longer possess the importance we have ascribed to it" (p. 79).

otterhaft | otterlike: The German word *Otter* can refer to two distinct animals: (1) to the acquatic carnivorous mammal of the genus *Lutra*, called "otter" in English; (2) to the viper, from Middle High German *nater*, *Schlange*, *Natter*. The latter word gave us the English "adder." Depending on one's choice, different interpretations—or at least colorations of interpretation—are possible. In this context I prefer the aquatic image of swarming otters.

Grau-in-Grau | grisaille: A pun on the opposition between *graue Substanz* and *weiße Substanz*, the gray and the white brain matter; the part of the brain richest in nerve cells has a grayer coloring. See also Freud, *Beyond the Pleasure*

Principle, p. 48: "We have merely adopted the views on localization held by cerebral anatomy, which locates the 'seat' of consciousness in the cerebral cortex—the outermost, enveloping layer of the central organ."

Camaïeu | monochrome: Means both a cameo (in jewelry) and a monochrome (in art: painting in a single line).

"Nah, im Aortenbogen" | *"Near, in the aortic arch"*
May 10, 1967. Draft on inside cover of Celan's book on anatomy by Adolf Faller (TA, *Fadensonnen*, p. 173), where much of the anatomical vocabulary can be found (BW, p. 782).

Hellblut | light-blood: Faller: "Blood saturated with oxygen, appears light red" (p. 1,370).

Mutter Rahel | Mother Rachel: Compare Gen. 29 and 30, 23 ff, 35, 16 ff: "And God remembered Rachel, and God hearkened to her, and opened her womb. / And she conceived, and bore a son; and said, God hath taken away my reproach: / And she called his name Joseph; and said, The LORD shall add to me another son . . .

And they journeyed from Bethel; and there was but a little way to come to Ephrath: and Rachel travailed, and she had hard labour. / And it came to pass, when she was in hard labour, that the midwife said unto her, Fear not; thou shalt have this son also. / And it came to pass, as her soul was in departing, (for she died) that she called his name Benoni: but his father called him Benjamin. / And Rachel died, and was buried on the way to Ephrath, which is Bethlehem."

Compare also Scholem (Celan's underlines): "However, we should also mention some other personifications that were subsequently combined with the image of the Shekhinah, like Sophia/Wisdom, which has appeared repeatedly since the famous image of Jeremiah (chap. 31) of Rachel weeping for her children as they go off into exile; or the personification of Zion as a maternal figure, in contrast with the phrase 'daughter of Zion' that alone appears in Scripture" (*On the Mystical Shape of the Godhead*, p. 145).

weint nicht mehr | weeps no more: Jer. 31: "Thus saith the LORD; A voice was heard in Ramah, lamentation, and bitter weeping; Rahel weeping for her children refused to be comforted for her children, because they were not."
Reading trace in Scholem: "This presence may be manifested in a supernat-

ural glow of light, known as the radiance (ziv) of the Shekhinah" (p. 147). Celan noted in the lower margin of his Scholem three lines from a Jewish lullaby by Moyshe-Leyb Halpern, the Yiddish-language modernist poet (1886–1932): "Wet di mame Rochl wejnen / Wet Meschiech nit mer kenen / Doss gewejn aribertrogn" (When Mother Rachel weeps, the Messiah will no longer be able / to carry over [bear] the weeping).

Ziw / Ziv: The light, in Hebrew, *Ziv*, is also a reference to the mystical light of the Shekinah. "Shekinah" is a word derived from the Hebrew verb שכן, meaning literally to settle, inhabit, or dwell. In the kabbalistic tradition, based on readings of the Talmud, the Shekinah represents the feminine attributes of the presence of God (Shekinah being a feminine word in Hebrew). Scholem writes in his essay "Zur Entwicklungsgeschichte der kabbalistischen Konzeption der Schechinah" (quoted by Schulze, "Mystische Motive," p. 490): "God's dwelling, his Shekinah in the most literal sense, means . . . his visible or hidden presence in a given place. This presence can manifest itself as an otherworldly light shimmer—just such a light (Ziv) of the Shekinah is often mentioned."

In this tradition, the Shekinah becomes not only the queen, daughter, and bride of God but also the mother of everyone in Israel. See also Jerry Glenn: "Rachel, the first among the women upon whom the house of Israel is built, is said to have risen from her grave during a dark period of Jewish history and begged God to save her 'children,' the Jewish people. God was moved and promised her that Israel would be restored" (Glenn, *Paul Celan*, p. 153).

It would seem that Celan himself had a mystical light experience in the company of Nelly Sachs, first in Zurich and then in Paris. The following letters make reference to and would seem to corroborate this experience (PC/NS, #105 and #108):

December 8, 1967
My dear Nelly,
it was so good to hold your letter in my hands and to be reminded by you yourself of that light that shone over the water in Zurich and then in Paris. Once, in a poem, a name for it even came to me through hebrew.
And with my warmest congratulations upon your birthday!
Your Paul

Paris, March 22, 1968

My dear Nelly,

thank you for your lines, for the reminder of that light.

Yes, that light. You will find it named in my next book of poetry, which is to appear in autumn—called by a Hebrew name.

Warmest!

Paul.

"Wirf das Sonnenjahr" | *"Throw the solar year"*

May 11, 1967.

Sonnenjahr | solar year: Compare Freud: "According to the large conception of Wilhelm Fließ (1906), all the phenomena of life exhibited by organisms—and also, no doubt, their death—are linked with the completion of fixed periods, which express the dependence of two kinds of living substance (one male and the other female) upon the solar year" (pp. 80–81).

Pantoffeltierchen | slipper animalcule: The more common translation of *Pantoffeltierchen* would be "paramecia," but I prefer to use the more cumbersome but more descriptive "slipper animalcule"—for the perceived sarcasm associated with the reemergence of the zoon after passage through the *Heimat*, as being associated with wearing *gemütliche* slippers. Compare Freud: "An American biologist, Qoodruff, experimenting with a ciliate infusorian, the 'slipper-animalcule,' which reproduces by fission into two individuals, persisted until the 3029th generation (at which point he broke off the experiment), isolating one of the part-products on each occasion and placing it in fresh water" (p. 84).

bewimpert | ciliated: The adjective here qualifying "Pantoffeltierchen" | "slipper animalcule" needs to be translated as "ciliated," which, however, hides the rhyme on "Wimper" / "eyelash" that runs through all of Celan's work.

"Weil du den Notscherben fandst" | *"Because you found the woe-shard"*

May 12, 1969.

"Es ist gekommen die Zeit" | *"It has come the time"*

May 13, 1969. The next poem was also written on that day.

Es ist gekommen die Zeit | It has come the time: Compare Jer. 50:27 and

31: "Slay all her bullocks; let them go down to the slaughter: woe unto them! for their day is come, the time of their visitation." And: "Behold, I am against thee, O thou most proud, saith the Lord GOD of hosts: for thy day is come, the time that I will visit thee."

Also, Rev. 11:18: "And the nations were angry, and thy wrath is come, and the time of the dead, that they should be judged," and other places in the Bible (BW, p. 784).

Hirnsichel | brainsickle: In anatomy, falx cerebri, also called cerebral falx, named because of its sicklelike form, is a strong, arched fold of dura mater descending vertically in the longitudinal fissure between the cerebral hemispheres. I am translating the German word literally so as to keep the sickle image, which Celan foregrounds, to create his double image of brain shape and sickle moon.

"Lippen, Schwellgewebe" | *"Lips, erectile-tissue"*
May 13, 1967.

Lippen, Schwellgewebe | Lips, erectile-tissue: Reading traces in Faller: "External female sexual organs: They are formed by the two large lips (labia majora), two cutaneous folds stuffed with fatty tissue, and the small lips (labia minora), that are well provided with nerves and contain erectile tissue" (BW, p. 784).

Kommissur | commissure: Faller: "At the front commissure of the small lips lies the clitoris, a small, single organ made of erectile tissue, richly provided with nerve endings" (BW, p. 784).

Otto Pöggeler, in his essay "'Schwarzmaut': Bildende Kunst in der Lyrik Paul Celans," sees the word *Kommissur* as referring to the anatomy of the brain only (p. 287). But there is also a rhyme on the French word *commissure (des lèvres)*, playing back to the first word in the poem, which can hold both kinds of lips, facial and sexual. Etymologically the word comes from the Latin *commissura*, "connection"; in English the word also has both denotations; see *The American Heritage Dictionary*, p. 381: "2.a. A tract of nerve fibers passing from one side to the other of the spinal cord or brain. b. The angle or corner of such structures as the lips, eyelids, or cardiac valves."

Thus the word itself, whose etymology points toward "a place at which

2 things are joined, a seam, a juncture" (ibid.), presents a joining of at least three familiar Celan motives: brain anatomy (deep structure of human mind), surface anatomy (the lips, and here sexual union), and a buried reference to that most abiding of Celan's images, the eye.

Schwarzmaut | Blacktoll: *Maut*, obsolete for *Zoll*, "toll," as in road toll. The word *Schwarzmaut*, constructed after the model of *Schwarzhandel* (black market), thus corresponds to a forbidden, illegal toll or tax. Celan will use the word as the title of a limited edition of an artist's book with eighteen poems and etchings by Gisèle Celan-Lestrange (see the introductory note to *Lightduress*, pp. 547–50).

Leuchtkäfer | glowworms: In French *vers luisants*, where *vers* means both "worm" and "verse"—as in a poem.

v

"Mächte, Gewalten" | *"Principalities, powers"*
May 13, 1967.

Mächte, Gewalten | Principalities, powers: A New Testament, often Pauline expression. Compare Eph. 6:12: "For we wrestle not against flesh and blood, but against principalities, against powers, against the rulers of the darkness of this world, against spiritual wickedness in high places"; Col. 2:15: "And having spoiled principalities and powers, he made a shew of them openly, triumphing over them in it." The expression refers to satanic and demonic forces able to take over social or political institutions as well as individual humans.

Vincents verschenktes / Ohr | Vincent's offered / ear: When Van Gogh in an act of insanity cut off his ear, he offered it to a prostitute by the name of Rachel, whom he asked to take good care of it (report in the *Forum Républicain* newspaper of December 30, 1888) (BW, pp. 784–85).

"Tagbewurf" | *"Daybombardment"*
May 15, 1967. The two following poems were composed on the same day.

"Redewände" | *"Speechwalls"*
May 15, 1967.

"Verwaist" | *"Orphaned"*

May 15, 1967. This poem is clearly a reworking of a classical kabbalistic theme. The next day Celan finished his reading of Gershom Scholem's *On the Kabbalah and Its Symbolism* (BW, p. 785).

die vier Ellen Erde | the four ells of earth: In his essay on the golem (an important figure in Celan's volume *Die Niemandsrose*), Scholem writes the following: "We come across the story that God and Earth concluded a formal contract concerning the creation of Adam . . . God demands Adam for a thousand years as a loan from Earth, and gives her a formal receipt for 'four ells of earth,' which is witnessed by the Archangels Michael and Gabriel and lies to this day in the archives of Metatron, the heavenly scribe" (*On the Kabbalah*, p. 165).

Hebe | share: *Hebe* literally means "leaven." But compare Scholem: "Just as according to the Torah a portion of dough is removed from the rest to serve as the priest's share, so is Adam the best share that is taken from the dough of the earth" (*On the Kabbalah*, p. 160).

"Beider" | *"Of both"*

May 16, 1967.

beider Todesblatt über der Blöße | of both: the deathleaf over their nakedness: Scholem: "The leaves of the Tree of Death, with which Adam veils his nakedness, are the central symbol of true magical knowledge" (*On the Kabbalah*, p. 175; Celan's underlines).

"Fortgewälzter" | *"Rolled-away"*

May 20, 1967.

"Als Farben" | *"As colors"*

May 21, 1967.

"Die Rauchschwalbe" | *"The chimney swallow"*

May 24, 1967. Celan had started teaching again on the previous day, though returning to the clinic in the evening. He sent this poem to Gisèle on May 25, with beneath it the following line: "The times are hard. May Israel last and live!" (PC/GCL, p. 508).

The complex intertwined imagery here is difficult to sort out. (1) Barbara

Wiedemann links the shark to the biblical big fish that spat out Jonah. (2) Though we have no information about Celan's sources, she connects the Inca figure to the Spaniard Garcilaso de la Vega (1539–1616), a relative of the poet with the same name, who was the illegitimate son of a conquistador and an Inca noblewoman (thus his surname) and wrote a critical narrative on the conquest of the Inca territories (*Commentarios Reales de los Incas*) that was eventually banned and not republished in the Americas until 1918. (3) There is a reading trace for the term *Landnahme* in Hans Krahe's *Germanische Sprachwissenschaft I: Einleitung und Lautlehre* (Berlin, 1948), p. 25: "Because of political disagreements many Norwegian noblemen had felt forced to leave their homeland. They emigrated to Iceland, which they settled during the so-called landnāma-tīd 'Landnahmezeit' | 'conquest-time' (about 872–930)" (BW, p. 787).

"Weiß" | *"White"*
May 25, 1967.

"Unbedeckte" | *"Bare one"*
May 25–June 2, 1967.

"Der Schweigestoß" | *"The silence-butt"*
May 27, 1967. The next poem was also written on that day.

"Haut Mal" | *"Haut Mal"*
May 27, 1967. It is impossible to translate this title, as it can be read both as a German and a French title: In German "Haut Mal" could be a variation on *Mutter-Mal*, a birthmark, or mole, where *Haut* means "skin." Thus "skin-mark," "skin-blemish." But the title could more obviously be read in French as "Haut Mal," literally "High Evil/Sickness," and could be a citation of the title of one of Michel Leiris's books of poems. It would seem that Leiris's title plays against/with the more idiomatic term "grand mal," which refers to the strong form of epilepsy. Barbara Wiedemann also reports that Celan kept a magazine page with a part translation of a Boris Pasternak poem by Pierre Pascal with the title "Haut Mal" in his Italian edition of Pasternak's poetry (BW, p. 788).

Concerning the medical images of the poem, Wiedemann locates most of these in Hippocrates's essays (*Fünf auserlesene Schriften* [Zurich: Fischer Bücherei, 1955]), although the presence of the book in Celan's library is not attested.

"Das taubeneigroße Gewächs" | *"The pigeon-egg-size growth"*
May 28, 1967. According to some sources, the philosopher Leibniz is said to have had a growth the size of a pigeon egg on his neck. Thus the "Denkspiel" | "thoughtgame" most likely refers to Leibniz's idea of a mathesis universalis.

"Angewintertes" | *"Bewintered"*
May 30, 1967.

"Draußen" | *"Outside"*
June 3, 1967. The following poem was written on the same day.

"Wer gab die Runde aus?" | *"Who stood the round?"*
June 3, 1967.

"Heddergemüt" | *"Dysposition"*
June 4, 1967. The following poem was written on the same day.

"Kein Name" | *"No name"*
June 4, 1967.

"Denk Dir" | *"Imagine"*
June 7–13, 1967. The Six-Day War between Israel and its Arab neighbors lasted from June 5 to June 10. Much of Celan's thinking and feeling during that week can be seen in the three letters to Franz Wurm of June 8, 12, and 13 (PC/FW, #47, #49, #50), as well as in his letter to Gisèle of June 6 (PC/GCL, #514), in which he tells her that "at noon there was a mimeo sheet in my mail slot [at the École Normale Superieure] that says: 'That / Israel may live / Everyone to the / Concorde / Tuesday 6 June at 7 p.m.' I called Jean, whom I'll meet up with there at a quarter to seven behind Palais-Bourbon to take part in the demonstration (which, I believe, is organized by young people). /

Israel will win and will live." In a later letter (PC/GCL, #531) he calls this poem "an important poem," which the position of the poem as the final one in the volume tends to bear out.

Moorsoldat | moorsoldier: From "Die Moorsoldaten," title of a song (usually translated as "The Peat Bog Soldiers") written by prisoners in Nazi moorland labor camps of Börgermoor, which held about one thousand socialist, anarchist, and communist internees. The words were written by Johann Esser (a miner) and Wolfgang Langhoff (an actor); the music was composed by Rudi Goguel and was later adapted by Hans Eisler and Ernst Busch. In his often cited memoir, *Es war ein langer Weg* (Düsseldorf: Mahn- und Gedenkstätte, 2007 [first published in 1947 by Komet-Verlag]), Goguel described the first performance: "The sixteen singers, mostly members of the Solinger workers choir, marched in holding spades over the shoulders of their green police uniforms (our prison uniforms at the time). I led the march, in blue overalls, with the handle of a broken spade for a conductor's baton. We sang, and by the end of the second verse nearly all of the thousands of prisoners present gave voice to the chorus. With each verse, the chorus became more powerful and, by the end, the SS—who had turned up with their officers—were also singing, apparently because they too thought themselves 'peat bog soldiers.'"

Massada | Masada: ancient fortification on a isolated rock plateau on the eastern edge of the Judean desert overlooking the Dead Sea. The siege of Masada by troops of the Roman Empire toward the end of the First Jewish–Roman War ended in the mass suicide of the 960 Jewish rebels and their families holed up there, in 73 C.E.

vom Unbestattbaren her | from what cannot be buried: In the first three drafts the final line read: "vom Allverwandelnden her." | "from the all-transforming." In his letter to Franz Wurm of June 13, Celan explains the change: "You see it exactly, you hear it accurately, for example, the Allverwandelnden: this word from Hölderlin's Empedocles puts me in that state, which you know well, which ever more tautly toward the poem—every possible poem—tensing toward—and then, out of gratitude, returned in the text. Except that this gratitude, that is witnessed here, wanes in the face of the sudden, stronger call: now it says—rightly so, I believe—: vom Unbestattbaren her | from what cannot be buried" (PC/FW, #50).

The eleven poems that make up this cycle, all written during the time of the composition of *Threadsuns*, and originally conceived as part of that volume, were composed between March 17 and April 19, 1966, thus falling chronologically between the first and second cycles of *Threadsuns*. During that period Celan was hospitalized in Paris in the psychiatric clinic Sainte-Anne. He chose these eleven from a folder of twenty-six poems, but here, rejecting the chronological arrangement he used for the late volumes, he organized the cycle on different principles. Wiedemann suggests that the selection "seems to have consciously avoided thematic overlaps." In January 1968, Celan sent the cycle with the added title *Eingedunkelt* to Siegfried Unseld, the publisher of Suhrkamp Verlag, who had asked for a contribution to an anthology to be called *Aus aufgegebenen Werken* (From Abandoned Works).

The title, *Eingedunkelt*, refers not only to one of the poems in the cycle, but also to a 1966 etching by Gisèle Celan-Lestrange, named by Paul Celan, as was their habit, *Enténébrée—Eingedunkelt*.

The more obvious translation of the title would be "Endarkened," which was my first choice. But despite the fact that Celan's version of Ungaretti's expression *nella tenebra* uses *umdunkelt*, which is closer to *eingedunkelt*, I decided on "tenebrae'd," which of course recalls the earlier poem titled "Tenebrae" (in *Sprachgitter*) and the title in French he gave GCL's engraving (most likely his own back translation—or simultaneous creation—of the German title).

"Bedenkenlos" | *"Unscrupulously"*
April 3–8, 1966. Written during Passover week (April 5–11). Wiedemann (BW, p. 792) points to reading traces in Joseph Conrad's *Secret Agent* (read on April 6) for lines 5–7, namely the sentences (given here in the original English, though Celan read a German translation): "His own skin had sizzled under the red-hot brand, he murmured softly," and "Stevie knew very well that hot iron applied to one's skin hurt very much."

"Nach dem Lichtverzicht" | *"After the lightwaiver"*
March 29–31, 1966. Wiedemann (BW, p. 792) points to reading traces in Thomas Wolfe for lines 4 and 5, quoting the lines "Der Frühling hat keine Sprache außer den Schrei, grausamer aber als April ist die Natter der Zeit" ("Spring has no language but a cry; but crueler than April is the asp of time") from *Of Time and the River*.

"Deutlich" | *"Explicit"*
March 29, 1966. Further Thomas Wolfe reading traces pointed out by Wiedemann (BW, p. 793) of lines Celan marked in the margins of his copy: "The flower of love is living in the wilderness, and the elm-root threads the bones of buried lovers. / The dead tongue withers." "Beglänztes" (line 7), Wiedemann further suggests, could also link to Wolfe's line "Later, when they left his rooms and went out on the street, the sensuous quickening of life, the vital excitement and anticipation which Starwick was somehow able to convey," where in German *Beglänzung* is used to translate both "the sensuous quickening of life" and "the vital excitement." "Ulmwurzel-Haft," via the German translation of Wolfe's "elm-root," can also be a pun on his workplace, the École Normale Supérieure, situated on the "rue d'Ulm."

"Vom Hochseil" | "Forced off"

April 7–19, 1966. Wiedemann points to two reading traces in Conrad: (1) "The Chief Inspector, driven down to the ground by unfair artifices, had elected to walk the path of unreserved openness," which in German contains the image of "vom Hochseil auf den Boden gezwungen," not there in the original; (2) "His pasty moon face drooped under the weight of melancholy assent," again closer in the German translation of "pasty" as *Käse-weißes* face. Wiedemann also cites Theodor Adorno for the expression *unbotmäßigen* from the following sentence (marginally annotated by Celan) in the essay "Zeitlose Mode," which was translated into English as: "The Element of Excess, of Insubordination in Jazz, Which Can Still Be Felt in Europe, Is Entirely Missing Today in America."

"Über die Köpfe" | "Heaved far over"

March 28, 1966. Wiedemann (p. 794) points to reading traces in Homer's *Odyssey* (which Celan read on March 27) for the expression "hinweggewuchtet" (line 2). The English version of this section in Charles Stein's translation reads: "Then he put in place / an enormous heavy door-stone, having easily lifted it. / Twenty-two four-wheeled wagons / would not have been able to budge it from the ground, / such was the giant stone he put in the doorway," where "not able to budge" in the German reads "nicht . . . wegwuchten können."

"Wirfst du" | "Do you throw"

March 27–28, 1966. More Homer traces. The "anchor stone" comes from lines 200–201 of *The Odyssey*, in Stein's translation: "so there'd be no need for moorings, / no need to throw anchor stones or secure stern cables."

"Angefochtener Stein" | "Contested stone"

March 17, 1966. Celan offered this poem as present to his wife for her thirty-ninth birthday (PC/GCL, #373).

"Eingedunkelt" | "Tenebrae'd"

March 8–18, 1966. See discussion of translation of title above.

The word "Schlüsselgewalt" (line 2) most likely goes back to Leo Shestov, a major figure for Celan, who read his "Le Pouvoir des Clefs" (which comments on Jesus's words to Saint Peter concerning the keys to heaven) in 1959 and again in 1967. Shestov, born Yehuda Leyb Schwarzmann to a Jewish family in Kiev in 1866, was a Ukrainian/Russian philosopher who emigrated to France in 1921, fleeing from the aftermath of the October Revolution. He lived in Paris until his death on November 19, 1938.

"Füll die Ödnis" | "Shovel the void"
March 31, 1966. Wiedemann (BW, p. 795) points to another Wolfe line for "Äugensäcke" | "eyebags," which I was unable to locate in the original. The German translation, underlined by Celan, gives: "Die Mutter war eine kleine, volle Frau mit einem weißen, kloßigen Gesicht und Augensäcken."

"Einbruch" | "Irruption"
March 31, 1966. The two opening lines show reading traces (BW, p. 795) from Homer: "Dort stand es (das Trojanische Pferd) nun. Sie aber sprachen viel Ungeschiedenes, während sie um es saßen." In Charles Stein's translation: "So it stood there while the people discussed it / in long, inconclusive debate, / standing about it." "Ungeschieden" feels much stronger than "inconclusive," no matter how accurate the latter is, as I hear a near-biblical tone in the German, the undifferentiated before the beginning, that is, before the Word separates the undifferentiated, as Genesis has it—while in the Celanian universe, the opposite happens: the unseparated breaks into one's language.

Nachtglast | nightshimmer: Wolfe: "Und dieser letzte rote Nachglast [*sic*] des Tags lag auf diesen Leuten" and "der rote Nachglast der untergegangenen Sonne." I am unable to locate the original phrase.

Sperrzauber | counterspell: Wolfe: "Inständig-augenblicklich, und wie erlöst von einem Sperrzauber, der ihn jahrelang ans Fremdferne gebannt hatte, und mit einem unerträglichen Gefühl von Schmerz und Verlust erinnerte er sich seines Zuhause, seiner Heimat und der verlorenen Welt seiner Kindheit" ("And suddenly, out of this dream of time in which he lived, he would awaken, and instantly, like a man freed from the spell of an enchantment which has held him captive for many years in some strange land, he would remember home with an intolerable sense of pain and loss, the lost world of his childhood").

Flutgang unterwaschen | floodflow washed out: Underlined in Wolfe: "Du aber bist gegangen: unsre Leben sind zerstört und zerbrochen in der Nacht, unsre Leben sind <u>unterwaschen vom Flutgang</u> des Stromes" ("But you are gone; our lives are ruined and broken in the night, our lives are mined below us by the river, our lives are whirled away into the sea and darkness and we are lost unless you come to give us life again").

"Mit uns" | "With us"
April 9, 1966. Werner Hamacher (WHH, p. 195, n. 44) points to motives from Rilke's Fifth Duino Elegy, which in turn picks up motives from Picasso's *Saltimbanques*, depicting a family of traveling acrobats. (It is interesting to note that Celan's son Eric would become a professional acrobat, though a sedentary one), and suggests that Rilke's "Und kaum dort, / aufrecht, da und gezeigt: des Dastehns / großer Anfangsbuchstab" ("And just arrived, / upright, there and pointed out—Destiny's / first letter," translated by Leonore Hildebrandt and Tony Brinkley) "dynamically becomes the 'rebellious / grief.'" He argues that "Celan's 'Leerstellen-Lyrik' [blankspace / gap / poetry] has learned more from Rilke's than from any other German-language poetry."

Gram | grief: See also the occurrences of *Gram* in the title of the uncollected poem "Niemals, stehender Gram" (Never, standing grief), and in the uncollected poem that starts: "Diese / freie, / grambeschleunigte / Faust (sie / bahnt sich den Weg):" | "This / free / griefquickened / fist (it / clears its way):"

LICHTZWANG | LIGHTDURESS

The poems in *Lichtzwang | Lightduress* were written between June and December 1967, gathered by Paul Celan in the chronological order of their composition, and organized into six cycles. The book itself appeared in July 1970, roughly three months after the poet's suicide, thus constituting the first posthumous volume of his work, yet being simultaneously the last book Celan himself saw through publication. Nineteen sixty-seven was a very difficult year for Celan. On January 30, he tried to kill himself with a knife (or a letter opener) that missed his heart by an inch. His wife had him transported to the Boucicaut hospital, where he was operated on immediately. From mid-February until mid-October he was interned at the Sainte-Anne psychiatric hospital, though from late April on he was allowed out for work and travel. In April he and Gisèle Celan-Lestrange, after long and difficult discussions initiated by his wife, concluded that a separation was necessary, and Celan reluctantly started looking for an apartment in Paris. Throughout these difficult months, he was, however, able to concentrate on his work, and during this period of internment he composed more than half of the poems that make up *Threadsuns*, as well as a major part of *Lightduress*—the first four cycles and a few poems of the fifth cycle. In March he sent the final manuscript of *Breathturn* to his publisher; in April he started teaching again at the École Normale Supérieure; in early June he took part in a pro-Israel march and wrote several poems concerned with Israel and the Six-Day War; from June to August he translated a book of poems by Jules Supervielle. Between June 9 and July 17, he composed a cycle of fourteen poems first published with engravings by Gisèle Celan-Lestrange under the title *Schwarzmaut* in March 1969, in a limited edition of eighty-five copies by Brunidor, Paris, which became the opening cycle of *Lightduress*. Between July 22 and August 2, he traveled in Germany, where on July 24 he gave a reading at the University of Freiburg im Breisgau attended by more than one thousand people, among them the philosopher Martin Heidegger. The next day the poet visited Heidegger in the philosopher's Todtnauberg "Hütte" in the Black Forest—an unsatisfactory meeting for Celan, who had great expectations for it, as his inscription in the guest book shows: "Into the Hütte-book, while gazing on the well-star, with a hope for a word to come in the heart / July 25, 1967 / Paul Celan." (See the poem "Todtnauberg" on p. 254, written on August 1 in Frankfurt am Main as response to the meeting.) From August 12 to August 23, Celan was in London, visiting with his aunt Berta Antschel, and in September he spent two weeks in Switzerland, mainly with his old friend Franz Wurm in Tegna in the Tessin. On the latter's counsel, once returned to Paris later that month, Celan met with the neurophysiologist Moshé Feldenkrais (1904–1984) in the hope of finding an alternative treatment to the antidepressants he had been undergoing for his anxiety attacks. October saw the publication of his translations of twenty-one Shakespeare sonnets in book form, and of the first reviews of *Breathturn* on the occasion of the Frankfurt Book Fair—a book from which he would give a private reading at the house of his publisher, Siegfried Unseld, in Frankfurt am Main on October 12. Five days later he was definitively released from Sainte-Anne hospital after eight months of therapeutic supervision, first as an inpatient and then as outpatient, and on November 20 he moved into a small studio apartment on rue Tournefort in the fifth arrondissement, where he would live until late 1969. Later that month he again traveled to Germany to record a reading of poems from *Breathturn* for German television. His reading during that year, established via diaries and letters, included a wide range of authors, among them Adorno, Thomas Bernhard, Leo Shestov, his prefacer Benjamin Fondane, Adolf Faller on anatomy, Sigmund Freud, Edmond Jabès, Bartolomé de Las Casas, Claude Lévi-Strauss, Thomas Mann, Shakespeare, John Millington Synge, and Osip Mandelstam. All the poems that make up *Lightduress* were composed by December 15, as the finished manuscript was referred to (though still under the early title *Schwarzmaut*) in a testamentary note Celan wrote that day.

Lightduress is a continuation of the poetic investigations began by Celan after what he himself called *die Wende*, "the turn"—a term inscribed in the title of the first volume that represents the mature expression of these poetics, *Atemwende | Breathturn*. After *Threadsuns*, *Lightduress* thus constitutes the third volume (and the last book-length manuscript Celan himself was able to give as finished work to his publisher for publication) in the poet's ongoing investigation of a new poetics.

Title: Compare the last two lines of the poem "Wir lagen" | "We already lay" in the first cycle. The title can be seen as programmatic if we take the poem in which the word first appeared into consideration. The German poet and critic Horst Bienek, meditating on how to read late Celan, and focusing on this very word, wrote: "Once we've found the basis of the poem, it stands rather clearly in front of us: the maquisard, the resistance fighter, maybe wounded, whom one wanted to bring into the safety of darkness, the darkness of his very body—but 'lightduress' ruled, maybe daylight, or the moon, or the enemy's searchlight? Or is it the truth of the poem, performing a feat: timelessly it arrives, full of secrets, apocryphal: and then it opens up, in one word, with one word: and maybe that one word is 'Lichtzwang' | 'lightduress,' simultaneously the demand to open up the darkness of his poems with light: Lightduress, that is the name of the last volume of poems Paul Celan handed to his publisher a few weeks before his suicide."

I

"Hörreste, Sehreste" | *"Soundscraps, visionscraps"*
April 1–June 9, 1967. Compare the earlier poem "Anabasis" (*Gedichte in zwei Bänden*, p. 1:256), in which Celan speaks of "Sichtbares, Hörbares," something "visible, hearable." Also (BW, p. 798) Celan's reading in April of Sigmund Freud's *Das Ich und das Es* | *The Ego and the Id*: "Die Wortreste stammen wesentlich von akustischen Wahrnehmungen ab . . . Es darf uns nicht beifallen, etwa der Vereinfachung zuliebe, die Bedeutung der optischen Erinnerungsreste—von den Dingen—zu vergessen, oder zu verleugnen, daß ein Bewußtwerden der Denkvorgänge durch Rückkehr zu den visuellen Resten möglich ist und bei vielen Personen bevorzugt scheint." ("Verbal residues are derived primarily from auditory perceptions . . . We must not be led away, in the interests of simplification perhaps, into forgetting the importance of optical memory-residues—those of *things* [as opposed to *words*]—or to deny that it is possible for thought-processes to become conscious through a reversion to visual residues, and that in many people this seems to be a favourite method.") (*Das Ich und das Es*, p. 248; *The Ego and the Id*, p. 23)

"Ihn ritt die Nacht" | *"Night rode him"*
June 9–11, 1967.

"Muschelhaufen" | *"Musselheap"*
June 14, 1967. Celan draws from a range of readings for this poem, among others on Friedrich Behn's *Kultur der Unzeit*, the encyclopedic *Fischer Weltgeschichte*, and the geological dictionary *Brockhaus-Taschenbuch der Geologie*.
Allverwandelnde | all-transforming: Following his friend Franz Wurm's advice, Celan had replaced this word borrowed from Hölderlin's *Death of*

Empedokles in the poem "Denk Dir" with *Unbestattbaren*, but was able to let his friend know that he had managed to find a place for the word (BW, p. 800).

"Mit der Aschenkelle geschöpft" | *"Scooped with the ashladle"*
June 15, 1967. The first three lines seem to bring up extermination camp matters: the ashes from the crematorium were used to make soap.

Tränentrumm | tearbrink: The word *trumm*, as singular of *Trümmer*, "ruins," refers to a piece of something, or the end bit. The English cognate "thrum" is today used only in knitting—a fringe or warp, a wisp of unspun fleece—and in music.

unpaariger . . . Lunge | unpaired . . . lung: Trying to commit suicide, Celan had stabbed himself with a knife or letter opener, and, missing the heart, he had perforated his left lung. One of the working titles of the collection had been *Fahnenlunge* (Flaglung).

"Mit Mikrolithen" | *"Larded with microliths"*
June 16, 1967. The *Fischer Weltgeschichte* offers reading traces; microliths as arrow- and spearheads; "rockart" referring to prehistoric art.

"In die Nacht gegangen" | *"Gone into the night"*
June 20, 1967. "The word *stern-/durchlässig* suggests a ritual requirement concerning the roof of the tabernacle which has to be definitely a covering of some sort, usually greenery, but transparent enough to admit the light of stars," according to Elizabeth Petuchowski ("Bilingual and Multilingual *Wortspiele*," p. 644). The commentator has just been discussing the poem "Hüttenfenster" (*Gedichte in zwei Bänden*, pp. 1:76–77) in reference to the Jewish Feast of Tabernacles (Sukkoth).

"Wir lagen" | *"We already lay"*
June 24, 1967.
Macchia | underbrush: The Italian word for thick underbrush calls up the French equivalent, *le maquis*, which was used to name the secret organized resistance to the Nazi occupiers during World War II, *les maquisards*, who took refuge in the maquis.

In accordance with her attempt to draw Jewish and Hebrew themes from Celan's work, Petuchowski suggests the following link—somewhat far-fetched as far as my understanding of the word goes: "*Lichtzwang* may well refer to the requirement of the roof of the ritual hut and some of its figurative implications. The symbolism surrounding the festival and the tabernacle is rich" (p. 644).

"Tretminen" | *"Contact mines"*
June 27–28, 1967.

"Wer schlug sich zu dir?" | *"Who sided with you?"*
July 1, 1967.

The image of the lark, here as "lark-shaped / stone," reappears in another poem of *Lichtzwang* as "larkshadow," in the poem "Für den Lerchenschatten" | "For the larkshadow." These are the two only appearances in Celan's oeuvre of that bird, so favored by the Romantic poets.

"Abglanzbeladen" | *"Reflection-laden"*
July 5, 1967. Bertrand Badiou pointed out a reading trace in Freud's *Interpretation of Dreams*, in connection with the "Three Fates" dream: "I acquiesced in the belief which I was later to hear expressed in the words: '*Du bist der Natur einen Tod schuldig*'" (Freud, *The Interpretation of Dreams*, p. 296). This "You owe nature a death" is evidently the transformation of the Shakespearean line (*Henry IV*, act 5, scene 1) "Thou owest God a death." An interesting trace, which to me confirms a sense of Celan's agnosticism. Wiedemann (BW, p. 802) also notes that in Celan's interlinear French translation of this poem, he very carefully "avoids a determination of the 'you' as either male or female: 'La mort / dont tu m'es resté(e) redevable.'"

"Freigegeben" | *"Cleared"*
July 8, 1967. Much of the vocabulary of this poem comes via Celan's reading of Lincoln Lee, *Fluggäste, Flieger und Maschinen. Wie man heute geflogen wird* (Frankfurt am Main/Hamburg, 1967) (LPC), the German translation of

Three-dimensioned Darkness: The World of the Airline Pilot in the Jet Age (Boston, 1963).

Corona | fermata: Compare Celan's early poem titled "Corona" (BW, p. 39). Wiedemann (BW, p. 803) also notes the leaf with the French translation of the poem, where Celan explains "Corona" according to the Italian word, via a drawing of a fermata (musical pause, hold) above a quaver. This made me decide to change the translation from "corona" to "fermata."

"Bakensammler" | *"Beaconcollector"*
July 8, 1967.

On two previous occasions Celan had used the word *Meister* (besides his most well-known use of the word in the "Todesfuge"): it first occurred in *Mohn und Gedächtnis* (*Gedichte in zwei Bänden*, p. 1:76), where he writes "denk, daß ich war, was ich bin: ein Meister der Kerker und Türme." It reoccurs in *Atemwende* (*Gedichte in zwei Bänden*, p. 2:39), where he writes "Keine Sandkunst mehr, kein Sandbuch, keine Meister." Here the context seems to point to a sense of the poet as a master of the signal tower. One could also note that this tower, which serves communication with the outside world, is, in a way, the opposite of the traditional poetic "ivory tower"—though association with Hölderlin's tower and the poet as silenced by madness are never far away in Celan. The specialized vocabulary also carries traces from aeronautics via Lincoln Lee (see previous commentary), from a novel on the German Imperial Navy, and (BW, p. 804) from Arno Schmidt's *Gelehrtenrepublik* | *The Egghead Republic*, in which Celan has marked the line: "Aber jetzt vorsichtshalber das Signal zurechtmachen; zum Anpeilen; die Bake" (p. 27), as well as, on the same page, the note: "die Bake = festes Seezeichen | (frz.: balise)"

"Aus Verlornem" | *"A you"*
July 17, 1967.

"Was uns" | *"What threw"*
July 17, 1967–c. February 13 1969.

II

"Einmal" | *"Once"*
July 18, 1967.

"Beilschwärme" | *"Hatchetswarms"*
July, 20, 1967. Reading traces (BW, p. 804) via *Fischer Weltgeschichte* and Behn's *Kultur der Urzeit.*

"Vorgewußt" | *"Precognition"*
July 21, 1967.

"Bei Brancusi, zu Zweit" | *"Two at Brancusi's"*
August 4, 1967. The poem remembers a visit by Paul Celan and Gisèle Celan-Lestrange (the "two" of the title) to the sculptor Constantin Brancusi's studio on February 24, 1954. In a letter of August 8, 1967, he tells Gisèle that he has "made, for a Romanian poet whose name you know, Ion Caraion, who is putting together a book on Brancusi, the little poem I am sending along" (PC/GCL, #540). Celan had already met Brancusi once, back in 1951, when he and some ten other French and German writers and artists went to visit him. Celan had met the Surrealist poet Ion Caraion back in 1946; a year later Caraion would print Celan's first published poems in German in the Bucharest magazine *Agora.*

"Wo ich" | *"Where I"*
August 5, 1967.

"Seit langem" | *"Long ago"*
June 9, 1967.

"Todtnauberg" | *"Todtnauberg"*
August 1, 1967, Frankfurt am Main. Probably the single most discussed poem of this volume, it is the record of Celan's visit to the philosopher Martin Heidegger at the latter's *Hütte* in the village of Todtnauberg in the Black Forest on July 25, 1967, the day after the poet gave a poetry reading at the University

of Freiburg in the presence of the philosopher. The poem was composed on August 1 in Frankfurt. In a letter of August 2 (PC/GCL, #536), written immediately upon his return to Paris, Celan tells his wife: "The reading in Freiburg was a major, an exceptional success: 1200 people listened to me with bated breath for an hour, then, after much applause, they listened to me for another fifteen minutes . . . Heidegger had approached me—The day after my reading I went with Mr. Neumann, Elmar's friend, to Heidegger's little hut [the Hütte] in the Black Forest. In the car, a serious dialogue ensued, I spoke with explicit words. Mr. Neumann, who witnessed the exchange, told me afterward that for him this conversation had an epochal character. I hope Heidegger will take up his pen and write a few pages in response, also to forewarn, given the increase of Nazism." Heidegger didn't, was proud of the poem Celan sent him, misreading it as an homage, as his student, Hans Georg Gadamer did, in turn, when he came to write about it.

"Translation at the Mountain of Death," a close reading of the poem in the act of translating it into English, was included in my 2009 book of essays, *Justifying the Margins*. Here, a shortened version of that analysis:

> The poem itself is a single sentence, divided into eight stanzas . . . essentially composed of parataxically juxtaposed nouns and noun-clauses commenting on those nouns, separated by commas until a single period brings the poem to a close. It gives the feeling of something cut-up . . . , foreshortening itself: . . . the remainder, the residue, of an aborted or impossible narration . . .
>
> The poem's opening line, Celan's account of the surrounding botany he espies upon arriving, is, however, full of hope and healing: Arnica is a bright-yellow flower, whose mountain variety, *A. montana*, is used to prepare a tincture helpful for healing sprains and bruises. Eyebright—*Augentrost*—is a small white and purplish flower of the old world, whose very name indicates its healing faculties: it is used to bring succor to failing or ailing eyesight . . . Notice also the two bright *A*'s that begin the words: the English translation, as well as the various French ones, lose the second *A*, though, by a happy coincidence, the English plant-name, "Eyebright," rather accurately translates the German one.
>
> The next two lines indicate that the traveler . . . takes a draft of water

from a well . . . , [which is] described as having a *Sternwürfel*, literally a star-dice, on top. This was indeed the case: old photos of Heidegger's *Hütte* show this wooden cube with a painted or carved star-motto on it, which seems to have been a piece of local folk-art . . . *Würfel*, though indeed a cube, is primarily a dice—here the whole complex of Celan's relation to Mallarmé and his "Coup de dé" comes into play . . . The topos is . . . even more complexified by the star on it: think of the six sides of the dice, which no matter how often you throw it, cannot come up with the number seven, Mallarmé's famous "constellation," Celan's *Siebenstern*, that is, the Pleiades (the seven sisters of Atlas transformed into stars, of which only six are visible to the naked eye) and much more. The star on the dice rimes with the yellow arnica, giving the five-pointed Jewish star: the Jewish poet at the door of the politically suspect philosopher, etc. . . .

Then, the briefest stanza, three words distributed over two lines: "in der / Hütte" ["in the / cabin," or "in the / hut"]. I have preferred to retain the German word *Hütte* here, because in a Heideggerian context . . . the word is heavily and symbolically loaded: . . . the *Hütte* itself, which Heidegger had built in 1922, was not only his holiday house in the mountains, but also his essential work and thinking place and, maybe more importantly, the refuge he went to in times of trouble. It was from there that he went down to Freiburg to take up the job as rector in 1933 and militate for what can be at best described as his own idiosyncratic version of a Hitlerian Germany. It is there that he took refuge during the denazification years . . . It was also there that in 1933 Heidegger ran Nazi indoctrination sessions.

Not any hut or cabin or mountain refuge, then . . . The tight stanza "in der / Hütte" translates the gingerly steps, the hesitations that must have befallen Celan as he enters the *Hütte* as Heidegger's guest. And then the longest—10-line—stanza, about the lines written into the guest-book. Before Celan's actual entry, a further hesitation: Who else recorded his name in the book before him? What to write in a book that probably carries the names of those Nazis that took part in the 1933 indoctrination sessions?

. . . In the poem . . . Celan transforms [his] actual inscription only slightly. He adds two important words: *heute* and *eines Denkenden. Heute,* "today," indicates the burning necessity of the need for a word to come now, in this situation, in postwar Germany. The *Denkender*, the one who thinks, is clearly Heidegger, and is as close as Celan comes to naming the philosopher himself in the poem . . .

The German syntax of this stanza makes, as Pöggeler has pointed out, for an ambiguity: the phrase *im Herzen*, "in the heart," can mean either "a hope in the [visitor's] heart for a thinker's word" or "a hope for a word in the heart of a thinker [the visited thinker's]." The first meaning is rather banal, associating hope with its traditional topos, the heart. The second possibility—the word in the heart—makes for a much more complex philosophical argument—one that Pöggeler discusses at some length, bringing in Augustin, Meister Eckhart, Heraklitus, Laotse (whom Heidegger translated in the *Hütte* at one point), as well as Pindar. Celan's poetics, and the rhythm of his lines, rather clearly point to this reading . . .

The rest of the poem consists of 5 short stanzas—only one of which has three lines—and takes us immediately outside again: The two men go for a walk on the moor in the mountains behind the *Hütte*. Celan again uses botany to set the scene: "Orchis und Orchis, einzeln" | "Orchis and orchis, singly." Whereas in the first line arnica and eyebright, two different flowers, are simply juxtaposed, both part of the same scene, here the same flower, the orchids, standing for the two men, are separated by the word *und* and, as if that was not enough to show their separateness, the last word of the line insists on it: *einzeln*, "singly"/"single." In German the plant is also known as *Knabenkraut*, "boy's weed," for its testicle-shaped roots (which, as Pöggeler notes, links it to a number of other Celan concepts and words, such as the *Mandelhode*, the almond-testicle, and the other Orchis poem which talks of the *Fünfgebirg Kindheit*, the five-mountain childhood . . .).

. . . The bright, hopeful *A*'s of the first line have been replaced by the darker *O*'s—have we come from alpha to omega? . . . [The men] walk on "halb- / beschrittenen Knüppel- / pfade" | "half- / trod log- / trails," literally on "paths made of wood"—the German *Holzwege*, which refers to a path in a forest, but also, in common parlance, to a dead-end, to a mistaken route, and is, of course, the title of a well-known book by Heidegger. Celan is too subtle to use Heidegger's word, and his "log-trails" complexify the image further, as *Knüppel*—the German word means both "logs" and "rods"—are also used as weapons to beat people, prisoners, etc.

"Half-trod" only: . . . The walk is interrupted, the walkers return to the car, Celan is driven back. In the car there is talk, *Krudes*, not a common word in German, "something crude" passes between Celan and another passenger, and the poet calls upon the third person present, "he who drives us, the mensch," as a witness to this exchange ("he also hears it"). Clearly the *Krudes* cannot be the "word in the heart" Celan expected from the visit . . .

[The word that caused me the most problems, however,] is *Waldwasen*, which is not a common word, and thus something that should make us aware that the poet intends something specific . . . At first glance one could conceivably think that the poet has simply chosen an erudite or "poetic" word instead of the more obvious and thus banal *Waldwiesen*—forest meadows, forest meadows, literally, or [the translator Robert R.] Sullivan's "glades." Or that *Waldwasen* was picked because it echoed, darkly [following on the *O*'s of "orchis"], via the two *a*'s following on the two *w*'s, the poem's initial *A*-vowel rhyme of "Arnika, Augentrost."

[But on closer inspection] the choice is much more deeply and complexly motivated than by mere *Tonmalerei*, "sound-painting." A *Wase*, according to Grimm's *Dictionary of the German Language*, is, first of all, a piece of sod together with the plants that grow in it . . . Celan is not talking of some grassy surface, a pleasant meadow, but has in mind something that goes deeper and incorporates the network of underground roots. His thought is, as usual, directed below the surface. Further, in North Germany, the term *Wasen* is used essentially as a homonym for *Torf*, "turf," "peat"—a word, and substance, that . . . plays a role in other Celan poems (something that can be used for making a fire and something that preserves matter, for example, the Danish peat bogs of prehistoric fame). From being a nicely romantic glade, the *Waldwase* has already become something slightly *unheimlich*, "uncanny"—to use one of Heidegger's favorite terms.

. . . Grimm further glosses *Wasen* as "the piece of land on which the knacker or *Wasenmeister* (the 'Master of the *Wasen*') guts and buries the dead livestock, also known in South Germany and on the Rhine as *Schindanger*—'the knacker's yard,'" which one could nearly translate as the "killing fields."

. . . Walking singly over the *Wasen*, Celan cannot but be close to that realm he is most familiar with: the realm of the dead. The walk is over a cemetery . . . the all-pervasive topos of Celan's work. This is made even clearer by the next word, *uneingeebnet*, "unevened," thus hilly, giving the image of grassy graves, over which the two walk on *Knüppelpfaden*—paths made out of logs, pieces of wood; we have seen above that these pieces of wood, at least under the German form of *Knüppel*, remind us of deadly weapons . . .

As I was reading Grimm on *Wase*, and found the *Schindanger*, I thought I had gotten to the bottom . . . Then my eye fell on yet another *Wase*, a word current in North Germany, and used to describe a bundle of dead wood, the etymology of which Grimm leads back through French *faisceau* to Latin *fasces*, the curator's bundle of rods, which became the symbol of, and gave the word for, "fascism."

. . . I have not found a word in English that would be truly "accurate" to [the polysemic richness of] the German *Waldwasen*, though "sward," the word I am using at this point in the infinite project of revising, refining, reworking these translations (the same word is used by Michael Hamburger), which my dictionary glosses as "land covered with grassy turf; a lawn or meadow . . . from OE *sweard*, *swearth*, skin of the body, rind of bacon, etc." comes close and does have that *a*. But then again it does not include the difference, that essential difference Celan's *a* makes in the movement of its substitution for the *ie* of *Wiesen*. What in the original poem is truly a *mise-en-abîme* becomes in the English translation only a "poetic" word, albeit solid and useful enough per se, as its etymology, via the connotations of the "skin" root, creates a membrane that could possibly be porous enough to lead the reader through and into the dark underground Celan points to— without, however, creating that chain of meanings leading to the "fasces" connotation of *Wasen*.

Further reading: The most compelling hermeneutical approach to the poem can be be found in the "Todtnauberg" section of Otto Pöggeler's book *Spur des Wortes* (1986). Useful also is Philippe Lacoue-Labarthe's *Poetry as Experience* (1999) and James K. Lyon's monograph *Paul Celan and Martin Heidegger: An Unresolved Conversation, 1951–1970* (2006), especially pp. 173–91.

"Sink" | "Sink"
August 10, 1967.

"Jetzt" | "Now"
August 10, 1967.

"Einem Bruder in Asien" | "To a Brother in Asia"
August 11, 1967. The first version had "Eiter-Geschütze," "pus-cannons," when Celan showed the poem to Peter Szondi. The latter questioned the word "pus," and Celan took his advice and removed it in the final version. The poem coincides with a period of marked intensification of America's war in Vietnam via bombing raids, napalm attacks, and further troop landings.

"Angerempelt" | "Jostled"
August 10, 1967.

"Wie du" | "How you"
August 15, 1967. In August 1967 Celan spent ten days in London, visiting with his aunt Berta (his father's sister). On August 15 he wrote to GCL: "This past night I dreamed—literally: <u>dreamed</u>—a little poem, I woke up instantly and was able to write it down: such a thing has only happened very rarely to me" (PC/GCL, #544).

"Highgate" | "Highgate"
August 17, 1967, London. Highgate is a section of north London with a cemetery of the same name where Karl Marx is buried. The toponym had already been noted by Celan when working on *Die Niemandsrose* in 1962 (BW, p. 809).

"Blitzgeschreckt" | "By lightning scared"
August 23, 1967. Celan had seen Théodore Géricault's painting *Cheval effrayé par la foudre | A Horse Frightened by Lightning* in the National Gallery in London and owned a postcard reproduction of it.

Trittstein | stepstone: may refer to a fall from horseback Géricault took, which, combined with his tuberculosis, led to his early death (BW, p. 810).

"Wurfscheibe" | *"Discus"*
August 24, 1967, Paris.

"Klopf" | *"Knock"*
August 25, 1967.

"Die entsprungenen" | *"The escaped"*
August 27, 1967.

"In den Dunkelschlägen" | *"In the darkclearings"*
August 27, 1967.

Dunkelschlägen: Plural of *Dunkelschlag*, in German defined as "Samen-, Besamungsschlag, in der Forstwirtschaft die erste Lichtung . . . eines alten Bestandes zum Zwecke der Verjüngung," that is, a first clearing in a forest, leaving enough trees standing for the crowns to still touch and give protection to seedlings. My translation creates a pun on light and dark that is not there in the original.

"Streubesitz" | *"Scattered property"*
August 29, 1967.

Klage- / vögte | grievance- / reeves: Wiedemann (BW, p. 811) proposes to link this term to the *Klage-Fürsten* of the Tenth Duino Elegy, where Rilke writes: "And she leads him gently through the wide landscape of Lament, / shows him the columns of temples, the ruins / of castles, from which the lords of Lament / ruled the land, wisely" (as translated by A. S. Kline).

"Der von den unbeschriebenen" | *"The letter read from"*
August 30, 1967. Reading traces (BW, p. 811) of an annotation in Rudolf Bilz, *Die unbewältigte Vergangen-heit des Menschengeschlechts*: "when a delirium tremens patient reads a letter from a completely white page" (my translation).

"Schneid die Gebetshand" | *"Cut the prayerhand"*
August 30, 1969. Reading traces in Bilz: "I do not address the prayerhand, especially the physiognomic change that has occurred."

Barbara Klose, in "'Souvenirs entomologiques': Celans Begegnung mit Jean-Henri Fabre," has shown that this poem, as well as ten further poems in the next section of *Lichtzwang*, show traces of Celan's reading of French entomologist Jean-Henri Fabre's selected writings in German, edited by Adolf Portmann.

"Was es an Sternen bedarf" | "What's required as stars"
September 2, 1967.

"Ich kann dich noch sehen" | "I can still see you"
September 2, 1967, Paris.

"Lauter" | "Nothing but"
September 3, 1967, Paris.

"Im Leeren" | "In the void"
September 5, 1967, Paris.

"Die lehmigen Opfergüsse" | "The loamy sacrifice downpours"
September 2, 1967, Paris.

"Das Wildherz" | "The wildheart"
September 8, 1967, Camedo, in the Domodossola–Locarno train.

vom halbblinden Stich | by the halfblind stab: A reference to Celan's recent suicide attempt, when he stabbed himself with a knife (or a letter opener, depending on the source), barely missing the heart but puncturing his left lung.

This and the next poem were written on a trip to Switzerland (September 7–22, 1967), where Celan would spend a few days with his friend Franz Wurm, after a long forced residence in the Paris hospital. These two, as well as the previous poem ("The loamy sacrifice downpours"), are connected with the poems that Celan gathered under the title *Eingedunkelt | Tenebrae'd* (p. 222). Compare, for example, "Einbruch" | "Irruption" for "unterwaschen" / "washed out" (p. 232) and, in *Zeitgehöft | Timestead*, "Kleines Wurzelgeträum" | "Little rootdreamings" for "blutunterwaschen" | "bloodwashed-out" (pp. 232 and 428), as well as the poem "Unterhöhlt" | "Hollowed out" (from the poems around *Eingedunkelt* not collected here):

HOLLOWED OUT
by flooding pain,
soulbitter,

amidst the wordbondaged
steepstood, free.

The oscillations that
once more
report
to us.

IV

"Die Ewigkeiten" | *"The eternities"*
September 20, 1967, Zurich. Compare the poem "Die Ewigkeiten tingeln" | "The eternities honkytonk" (p. 162).

"Herzschall-Fibeln" | *"Heartsound-fibulas"*
September 23, 1967, Jardin du Luxembourg, Paris.
   dem Fangbein der Mantis | the mantis's trapleg: reading traces of Fabre's "Souvenirs entomologiques."

"Aneinander" | *"Grown weary"*
September 25, 1967, Paris.

"Ein Extra-Schlag Nacht" | *"An extra dollop of night"*
September 26, 1967, Hotel Raspail (where the next poem was written as well), just before Celan's meeting with the physicist and neurophysiologist Moshé Feldenkrais, a friend of Franz Wurm's, from whom Celan expected to receive

an alternative treatment to the heavy antidepressant pharmacopeia of his Parisian doctors.

Reading traces (BW, p. 815) cite a note on an early draft that mentions *Extra-Schlag Suppe* (an extra ladle/scoop/dollop of soup) from a *Spiegel* magazine article on Stalin's eldest son as wounded prisoner of war of the Germans in 1941: "In the officer's prisoner of war camp Hammelburg, Dzhugashvili carved . . . cigarette holders and exchanged them with the guards for tobacco, bread and an extra scoop of soup."

"Hinter frostgebänderten Käfern" | *"Behind froststreaked beetles"*
September 26, 1967, Hotel Raspail, Paris.

"Die Irin" | *"The Irishwoman"*
September 27, 1967.

"Die mir hinterlassne" | *"The left-to-me"*
September 28, 1967, Paris.

"Verworfene" | *"Repudiated"*
September 30, 1967, Paris.

kunkelbeinige | distaff-legged: Reading traces (BW, p. 815) in Fabre, who uses the image of the spindle when describing the "murderous machinery" of the praying mantis's forelegs. (The only available English translation—*Fabre's Book of Insects, Retold from Alexander Teixeira de Mattos' Translation of Fabre's "Souvenirs entomologiques" by Mrs. Rodolph Stawell* [New York: Dodd, Mead, 1921]—has omitted this image.)

Gegenblut- / Sinn | counterblood / sense: Reading traces in Rudolf Bilz (Celan's underlines): "Bei primitiven Völkerschaften gibt es ein Winken im Gegenzeiger- und ein Winken im Uhrzeigersinne. Im Uhrzeigersinne winken bedeutet: 'Komm!' 'Her zu mir!'" (Among the primitive peoples there exists a counterclockwise and a clockwise. To nod clockwise means: "Come!" "To me!") (BW, p. 815).

"Fertigungshalle" | *"Productionhangar"*

October 1, 1967, Paris–June 23, 1969. In a July 4, 1970, letter to his publisher, Siegfried Unseld, cited by Wiedemann, Celan expands on his sense that he is not writing abstract or hermetic poetry, saying, "My poems have not become more hermetic or more geometric; they are not cyphers, they are language; they do not move further away from the everyday, they stand, in their very wording—take for example 'Productionhangar'—in the today" (BW, p. 816).

Indeed, as Barbara Wiedemann shows, a range of this poem's technical vocabulary comes directly from an article in the previous weekend edition of the FAZ, "Stress am Fließband" (Stress on the assembly line) by K. L. Ulrich, relating a walk through a car assembly plant with the company physician.

"In der Blasenkammer" | *"In the vesicle chamber"*

October 3 1967, Paris.

Blasenkammer | vesicle chamber: A terminus technicus from nuclear physics; its literal referent is the "bubble chamber," where atoms are ionized. But the association with breath via "das Entatmete"—and Celan's constant linking of breath and speech—suggest strongly the image of the lung's alveoli. According to James K. Lyon, it is, however, a Celanian construct based on the geological term *Blasenräume*, "the geological term for the spaces formed in basalt and other igneous rock through intense heat" (Lyon, "Paul Celan's Language of Stone," p. 306). Given the volcanological vocabulary of the second stanza ("crater," "porphyry") I tend to agree with that reading and rather than translating the word as "bubble chamber," I have used the neologism "vesicle chamber."

"Magnetische Bläue" | *"Magnetic blue"*

October 3, 1967, Paris.

"Vorflut" | *"Outfall"*

October 4, 1967, Paris.

"Die Mantis" | *"The mantis"*

October 7, 1967, Paris.

im Nacken | in the nape: In the English edition of Fabre's book, we find this: "The Mantis attacks the Locust first at the back of the neck, to destroy its power of movement. This enables her to kill and eat an insect as big as herself, or even bigger." And later on the following: "She even makes a habit of devouring her mate, whom she seizes by the neck and then swallows by little mouthfuls, leaving only the wings." Wiedemann points to further such killing/devouring references in the edition Celan read.

"Kein Halbholz" | "No halfwood"
October 7, 1967, Paris.

Wiedemann (BW, p. 818) points to Fabre's description of climbing Mont Ventoux in Provence (not in the English version), for the provenance of the terms "halfwood," "peakslopes," "thyme," and "bordersnow."

"Schwimmhäute" | "Webbing"
October 3, 1967, Paris.

Zeithof | timehalo: Celan encountered the term *Zeithof* in his readings of Edmund Husserl, where he underlined and marginally marked it with a double stroke in section 14 of *Leçons pour une phénoménologie de la conscience intime du temps* (Paris: Presses Universitaires de France, 1964) (LPC); compare Husserl, *Zur Phänomenologie des inneren Zeitbewußtseins*; and pp. 35–36 in the English translation (*The Phenomenology of Internal Time-Consciousness*, ed. Martin Heidegger, trans. James S. Churchill [Bloomington: Indiana University Press, 1964]), which is cited here:

> Let us consider a case of secondary memory: We recall, say, a memory we recently heard at a concert. It is obvious in this case that the whole memory-phenomenon has exactly the same constitution, mutatis mutandis, as the perception of the memory. Like the perception it has a privileged point: to the now-point of the perception corresponds a now point of the memory. We run through the memory in phantasy; we hear, "as it were" ["gleichsam"], first the initial tone, then the second tone, and so on. At any particular time there is always a tone (or tone-phrase) in the now-point. The preceding tones, however, are not erased from consciousness. Primary memory of the tones that, as it were, I have just heard and expectation (protention) of the tones that are yet to come fuse with the apprehension of the tone that is now appearing and that, as it were, I am now hearing. The now-

point once again has for consciousness a temporal fringe which is produced in a continuity of memorial apprehension; [Der Jetzpunkt hat für das Bewußtsein wieder einen Zeithof, der sich in einer Kontinuität von Erinnerungsauffassungen vollzieht,] and the total memory of the melody consists in a continuum of such continua of temporal fringes and, correlatively, in a continuum of apprehension-continua of the kind described. [und die gesamte Erinnerung der Melodie besteht in einem Kontinuum von solchen Zeithofkontinuen, bzw. von Auffassungskontinuen der beschriebenen Art.]

Jean Greisch reads this poem as "something like a variation on the Husserlian image of the comet's tail of protensions and retentions, marking the temporal slipstream of the living present and allowing it to shift toward the past. With this difference, however, that the incessant surge of the living present sustains a rather disquieting deformation: the 'source-point' of the present becomes a pool of stagnant waters, the luminous head of the present has an obverse, maybe the grayness of the impossible to forget non-sense." He suggests that "to orient oneself in as 'floating' a temporality maybe one does indeed need words that are webbed" (in C-J, pp. 167–83).

Celan uses the term twice more, next in the poem "Mapesbury Road" in *Snowpart* (p. 348), and a variant (*Zeitgehöft*) becomes the title of his last posthumous volume (p. 400). In *Breathturn* we find the composite term *Lebensgehöft* in the poem titled "Hohles Lebensgehöft" | "Hollow lifehomestead" (p. 28). I have chosen to translate *Zeithof* as "timehalo"—though other possibilities, such as "timeyard," "timecourt," even "timepatio," came to mind at one time or another—and *Zeitgehöft* as "timestead" (with *Lebensgehöft* logically becoming "lifestead").

"Anredsam" | *"Addressable"*
October 8, 1967, Paris.
Amsel | blackbird: In the German word for the blackbird, *Amsel*, which occurs a number of times in Celan's work, it is difficult not to hear a rhyme on Celan's original name, Antschel. See also the poem "Frankfurt, September" (p. 110), which in German points out the sound-rhyme between Celan's original name and Kafka's Hebrew name, Amschel, while the name Kafka also refers to a black bird, the jackdaw.

V

"Oranienstraße 1 " | *"Oranienstraße 1 "*
October 11, 1967, Frankfurt am Main, where Celan gave a reading from the just published *Breathturn* in the context of the annual book fair.

Title: the address of a bed-and-breakfast and restaurant, then called Römerkrug, in Frankfurt.

Ossietzkys | Ossietzky's: Carl von Ossietzky (October 3, 1889–May 4, 1938) was a German pacifist and the recipient of the 1935 Nobel Peace Prize (which Hitler prohibited him from accepting) for his work in exposing clandestine German rearmament. He was convicted of high treason and espionage in 1931 after publishing details of Germany's alleged violation of the Treaty of Versailles by rebuilding an air force, the predecessor of the Luftwaffe, and training pilots in the Soviet Union. Ossietzky was convicted and sentenced to eighteen months in prison, being released at the end of 1932 in the Christmas amnesty. On February 28, 1933, after the Reichstag fire, he was arrested and held in Spandau prison. In May 1936 he was sent to the Westend hospital in Berlin-Charlottenburg because of his tuberculosis, but under Gestapo surveillance. He died in the Nordend hospital in Berlin-Pankow, still in police custody, on May 4, 1938, of tuberculosis and from the aftereffects of the abuse he suffered in the concentration camps. He was supposedly so weak that he couldn't raise up a teacup without help.

durchstünde | endure: Wiedemann (BW, p. 819) points to the motto of the Oranien-Nassau family (Nassaustraße runs parallel to Oranienstraße), which is "Je maintiendrai" (I will hold steadfast), and its importance for Celan in the post–Goll affair days. See PC/GCL correspondence, letters 154, 198, 272, and 445. See also cover illustration of this book.

"Brunnenartig" | *"Well-like"*
October 19, 1967, Paris. Sukkoth, the Feast of Booths, Tabernacles, or Huts (see the penultimate line). There is a page of handwritten notes by Celan concerning this poem and reproduced in TA (*Lichtzwang*, p. 132), indicating readings in an unidentified book on early Italian/Etruscan burial customs. Wiedemann (BW, pp. 819–20) points also to Behn and the *Fischer Weltge-*

schichte for further elucidation of terms from the note, such as *Brunnengräber*, "welldigger," *Sargkammer*, "coffin chamber," *Hockerstellung*, "crouching position," *Urnenfelder*, "urnfields," etc.

"Mit Traumantrieb" | *"With dreampropulsion"*
October 20, 1967, Paris. The vocabulary of this poem—written on October 20, 1967—draws on an article in the FAZ of that same day concerning the Soviet *Venus 4* probe and the U.S. *Mariner 5* spacecraft; the latter flew by Venus on October 19 at an altitude of 2,480 miles and was able to shed new light on the hot, cloud-covered planet and on conditions in interplanetary space.

"Für den Lerchenschatten" | *"For the larkshadow"*
October 22, 1967, Paris.

"Der durchschnittene" | *"The cut-through"*
October 23, 1967, Paris.

"Fahlstimmig" | *"Wan-voiced"*
October 25, 1967, Paris. Wiedemann (BW, p. 821) points to an article in the FAZ of that day titled "Klimaanalyse durch Eisbohrung" (Climate analysis through ice drilling).

"Schalltotes Schwestergehäus" | *"Sounddead sistershell"*
October 27, 1967, Paris.

"Wetterfühlige Hand" | *"Weathersensing hand"*
October 28, 1967, Paris.

"Im Zeitwinkel schwört" | *"In time's corner"*
October 28, 1967, Paris.

"Auch mich" | *"Me too"*
October 30, 1967, Paris.

"Die rückwärtsgesprochenen" | *"The backwardspoken"*
November 1, 1967, Paris.

"Allmählich clowngesichtig" | *"Gradually clownfaced"*
November 5, 1967, Paris.

"Sperrtonnensprache" | *"Roadblockbuoy language"*
November 6, 1967, Paris.

"Unter der Flut" | *"To fly under"*
November 11, 1967, Paris. Wiedemann (p. 822): A range of the vocabulary comes from an article in the FAZ of that day titled "50.000 Fragen an den Tod: Die erstaunlichen Methoden der Flugunfall-Untersuchung" (50,000 Questions for Death: The Wondrous Methods of Flight Accident Investigations) by Dieter Vogt.

VI

"Wahngänger-Augen" | *"Delusionstalker eyes"*
November 14, 1967, Paris.

"Sperriges Morgen" | *"Unwieldy morrow"*
November 14, 1967, Paris. Wiedemann (BW, p. 823) suggests this poem draws on an article in the FAZ of that day titled "Serielles Farbenspiel" (Serial play of color) by Ulrich Schreiber on the premiere of Bruno Maderna's Second Oboe Concerto in Cologne. She points to the three terms *pastos, durchquäckt,* and *Schallbecher,* citing the following sentence from the review: "Durch solchen um ein vom Schlagzeug begleitetes Streicher-Notturno gruppierten Wechsel wird eine Ausweitung des musikalischen Farbenspiels erreicht, dadurch verstärkt, daß zwei verschiedene Schalltrichter der Musette einen pastosen und einen an das Sopransaxophon de Jazz erinnernden quäkenden Klang geben. Schallbecher, Instrument und Farbe wechseln, die Faktur ist streng seriell, der Charakter kantabel." (Through such a change, grouped around a string-notturno accompanied by drums, a widening of the musical play of color is achieved, and strengthened because two different bells of the piccolo oboe give one a pastose and one a squawking sound that recalls the soprano saxophone in jazz. Pavilion, instrument and color change, the facture is strictly serial, the character cantabile.)

You can hear the piece (which Celan probably did not do) here: www
.youtube.com/watch?v=Hko41IJ29xQ.

Two examples of translation problems: (1) the title word *Morgen* means
both "morning" and "tomorrow," more or less translatable via the more (too?)
recherché/poetical "morrow," which carries the older sense of "morning"; (2)
a problem relating to gender-specific pronouns. The construction "bei ihr, der
Erd- / achse" insists on *ihr*, the feminine pronoun, putting it in relation with
the "male" image of the first line of that stanza: "den beschleunigten Herz-
schritt." In this case I choose to use the feminine pronoun in English too.

"Merkblätter-Schmerz" | *"Notepaper-pain"*
November 18, 1967, Paris. Composed on the same day as "Sperriges Mor-
gen" | "Unwieldy morrow"; see commentary above.

"Streu Ocker" | *"Strew ocher"*
November 20, 1967, Paris. On the day he wrote this (and the next) poem,
Celan moved into a one-bedroom apartment on the rue Tournefort, a move
that completed the separation from his family.

    Title: Compare mark in margins of the *Fischer Weltgeschichte*: "Very often
the dead were sprinkled with red ocher, or pulverized red ocher was strewn
into the graves" (original, p. 63).

"Schwanengefahr" | *"Swandanger"*
November 20, 1967, Paris. Written on the same day as the preceding poem.
Wiedemann (BW, p. 825) notes that the exhibition *Russian Art from the Scythi-
ans to Today* had opened at the Grand Palais in Paris, and that in a letter to his
wife from November 18, 1967, Celan mentioned his intention to take his son
Eric to visit the exhibition (PC/GCL, #580). Two days later he sent the poem
to his friend Franz Wurm in a letter, writing: "Well, that's what happens
to someone who expels a clawed Yakut-Pushkin from himself, on the way to
the twice-redeeming-demonic Siberian Chebeldei, Chebeldei—" (PC/FW,
#115).

    Jakuten- | Yakut-: A seminomadic people in present-day Russia, divided
into two basic groups based on geography and economics. Yakuts in the north
are historically seminomadic hunters, fishermen, and reindeer breeders, while

southern Yakuts engage in animal husbandry, focusing on horses and cattle. Their language belongs to the northern branch of the Turkic family of languages.

Jakuten- / Puschkin | Yakut- / Pushkin: Wiedemann points to the following lines from Alexander Pushkin's 1836 poem "Exegi Monumentum": "I shall be noised abroad through all great Russia, / Her innumerable tongues shall speak my name: / The tongue of the Slavs' proud grandson, the Finn, and now / The wild Tungus and Kalmyk, the steppes' friend." (Translation by D. M. Thomas [New York: Viking Press, 1982])

Chebeldei: According to Micha F. Lindemans in the *Encyclopedia Mythica*, Chebeldei are "the inhabitants of the underworld in Siberian myth. They are composed mainly of iron and are black in color and are not particularly friendly towards human beings."

"Schaltjahrhunderte" | *"Leapcenturies"*

November 14, 1967, Paris. Celan's forty-seventh birthday. Written at his workplace, the École Normale Supérieure. Celan wrote to Petre Solomon (PC/PS, #237): "It is still the 23rd, nine in the evening, I'm still in rue d'Ulm, in my office, I have just written a poem that ends with these words: / Kaltstart, trotz allem / mit Hämoglobin [cold start, despite all / with hemoglobin]." A range of the poem's cybernetic vocabulary—"stocked in honeycomb-troughs / bits / on chips, . . . archived . . . reading stations"—comes via the article "Datenspeicher für eine Billion Bits" (Data Storage for One Billion Bits), extracts of which Celan wrote down in his notebooks (BA, vol. 9.2, p. 239; BW, p. 826).

Schaltjahrhunderte | Leapcenturies: The year of Celan's birth, 1920, was a leap year.

das Menoragedicht aus Berlin | the menorah-poem from Berlin: According to Bertrand Badiou, the young poet Sabeth Sadei-Uhlmann sent Celan a letter on November 17 that included the typescript of a poem titled "Menora," in the shape of a seven-armed candelabrum; the words of the poem do not come into Celan's. On December 25 she thanked him for having read "Schaltjahrhunderte" to her (TA, *Lichtzwang*, p. 171).

Kammlinien unter Beschuß / crestlines under fire: in several drafts annotated with "~~Dak To~~." Dak To was a U.S. Army base in South Vietnam. *Der Spiegel* of November 20, 1967, printed a photo with the caption "Burning U.S. Base Dak To: In the bitterest phase of the war so far, the first dead general" (TA, *Lichtzwang*, p. 171).

Hämoglobin | hemoglobin: Reading traces in Reichel/Bleichert: "In the erythrozytes, oxygen is bound to the red blood coloring, the hemoglobin. Hemoglobin is a proteid, whose effective group, the hemo [Häm], is a protoporphyrin with a 2-valence Fe-atom in the molecule" (p. 247).

"Quellpunkte" | *"Sourcepoints"*
November 25, 1967, Paris–Cologne train.

"Treckschutenzeit" | *"Trekscowtime"*
December 3, 1967, Paris, rue de Longchamp. The last two poems of *Lichtzwang* | *Lightduress* were written on the same day. Both draw on a sermon by the great German theologian and mystic Meister Eckhart, a source cited by Celan himself, specifically sermon 14 in the edition of Eckhart's sermons as edited by Joseph Quint.

Treckschutenzeit | Trekscowtime: Wiedemann cites Badiou, pointing to unidentified reading notes by Celan from August 11, 1957: "(Zugschiff) – bateau tiré pas des chevaux ou par des hommes" ([barge]—ship pulled by horses or by men) (BW, p. 827).

der Enthöhte, geinnigt | the diselevated one, interiorized: Wiedemann points to Joseph Quint's commentary (on p. 237 of his edition) on sermon number fourteen: "Eckhart came upon the idea that God should not be elevated through me abasing myself, but that God should be elevated and man should be elevated simultaneously by taking God from outside and from above into himself, 'interiorizing' him, as it were, so that man will grasp the godly not as something foreign on the outside, but as his own, inside himself" (BW, p. 827).

Gottes / quitt | quits with / God: Wiedemann points to a handwritten note by Celan that quotes a motto by Meister Eckhardt that the German-Jewish politician Gustav Landauer (1870–1919), one of the leading theorists on anarchism in Germany and an avowed pacifist (also known for his study and translations of Shakespeare's works into German), used as epigraph to his book *Skepsis und Mystik: Versuche im Anschluß an Mauthners Sprachkritik* (Berlin, 1903): "That is why I beg God to make me quits with God, for unessential [*unwesenthaftes*] Being [*Wesen*] is above God and above differentiation [*Unterschiedenheit*]; there I myself was, that's where I wanted myself to be and recognized myself making this human, and that's why I am cause of myself according to my Being, that is eternal, and according to my Being, that is itself. And that's why I am born and can, following the mode of my birth, which is eternal, never die" (BW, pp. 827–28).

"Du sei wie du" | *"You be like you"*
December 3, 1967, Paris, rue d'Ulm.

Stant up Jherosalem inde / erheyff dich . . . inde wirt / erluchtet: Middle High German version of Isa. 60:1 literally translates as: "Stand up, Jerusalem, and raise yourself, and become illuminated." King James version: "Arise, shine; for thy light is come."

wer das Band zerschnitt | he who cut the band: Eckhart's sermon 14 quotes Ps. 2:2 and 3: "The kings of the earth set themselves, and the rulers take counsel together, against the Lord, and against his anointed, saying, / Let us break their bands asunder, and cast away their cords from us" (King James version).

Gehugnis | gehugnis: From the Middle High German word *Hugnis*, for *Erinnerung*, "memory" (memory, recollection, remembrance). Used by Meister Eckhart, transformed into "Gehugnis" by Celan.

Finster-Lisene | dark pilaster strip: Wiedemann finds a reading trace in Hans Weigert's *Stilkunde*: "The first means of articulation is as with the capital-shield [*Kapitellschild*] the splitting of the plane into layers. This is done with a pattern of round arch friezes on pilaster strips [*Pilastern ohne Kapitell*]" (p. 85f) (BW, p. 828).

kumi / ori: The Hebrew words that open Isa. 60:1: "Arise, shine." There is another "biblical" interpretation of these words, proposed by Celan's last lover, Ilana Shmueli, who was interviewed a short time before her death in 2011 (as reported by Mako Martin in *Die Welt* of January 31, 2013): "But how loud Ilana Shmueli's laughter in her old age home in Jerusalem when she spoke about her renewed early love for Paul Celan: 'May the German literature specialists chew on this—I know what Paul Celan meant when he wrote, *Kumi, ori*, raise yourself, stand up, shine. It was in praise of a part of his own anatomy, which woke up again on the occasion of a visit here in Jerusalem."

"Wirk nicht voraus" | *"Do not work ahead"*
December 6, 1967, Paris, rue d'Ulm.

steh / herein | stand / inward: Note the importance of "standing" for Celan, as already suggested in the poem "Eine Gauner- und Ganovenweise." See also my introduction to *Paul Celan: Selections* (p. 6).

feinfügig | fine-fugued: A classical Celanian neologism, the word is not found as such in German, but echoes immediately with *feinfühlig* (sensitive), so, as Hans-Georg Gadamer also noted (*Argumentum e Silentio*, p. 65), the word recalls *gefügig* (amenable, supple) and *feingefügt* (neatly assembled, leading to *Feingefüge*, microstructure). The root constituent, *fügig*, the Grimms' *Wörterbuch* gives as "adj. passend, geschickt, aptus, idoneus" (apt, deft, with finesse), never occurs by itself. Listening very hard, one could even hear the word *Fuge* (fugue) and the fine contrapuntal mode of construction. Thus my "fine-fugued," though I'm aware I may be overplaying my hand in this case.

SCHNEEPART | SNOWPART

The poems in this, the first posthumous volume, were composed between December 16, 1967, and October 18, 1968, and are, according to their author in a letter to Ilana Shmueli from January 24, 1970, "probably the strongest and boldest" he wrote. The German poet Helmut Heißenbüttel, sharing this evaluation, writes: "Whatever irritation and disorientation these poems may express, they show an unerring ability of expression [Unbeirrbarkeit an der Fähigkeit dieses Ausdrückenkönnens]. They show the mastery and control Celan has over his materials, maybe better than any of the earlier volumes."

The manuscript as such, containing seventy poems, constitutes a selection from among the poems written during this period, and was put together by Celan, who prepared a clean, handwritten copy for his wife on September 22,

1969 (which was then used for the 1971 Suhrkamp edition). Still, this is the first volume he was no longer able to hand in to his publisher in absolutely finished form. There are therefore questions concerning the final manuscript: one of the poems is crossed out (though rather tentatively, one could suggest) and accompanied by question marks; there are also differences between the table of contents and the manuscript's organization into cycles. It is not certain whether the fifth, final cycle would have been part of the final manuscript had Celan prepared it for the publisher. In a letter to GCL (#611) from August 23, 1968, Celan suggests that he has recently written new poems (that would be those in cycle 5) for which "I had found the compact diction I had wished for. It will be a new book."

The short year encompassing the composition of the poems was also the first one in some time that Celan spent teaching uninterruptedly at the École Normale Superieure. It is also the first full year that he lived apart from his wife and son in a small apartment on the rue Tournefort close by his place of work. This is, of course, also the year marked by the uprising in Czechoslovakia and of the student uprising in Paris (and beyond) of May 1968—all events that Celan was profoundly interested in and that enter his poems of this period.

Schneepart | *Snowpart*

The title of the collection is taken, as is often the case, from one of the poems, the last one of the first cycle (see p. 334). On an early surviving draft page, Celan had written down a number of further title possibilities, all crossed out except for *Schneepart*. The discarded ones were *Sehstamm*, "visionstem," *Leseast*, "reading branch," and *Leuchtstäbe*, "lightrods," also all taken from poems in this volume.

The title element "part" comes from German *der Part*, a musical (or theatrical) term from the Latin *pars* that has the same meaning as its English cognate: "The music or score for a particular instrument, as in an orchestra," and "One of the melodic divisions or voices of a contrapuntal composition" (*American Heritage Dictionary*). I had first translated the word as "share," as "Snowshare" seemed to me a pregnant Celanian concept, but decided to use "part" when I saw the early draft of the poem (TA, *Schneepart*, p. 28) from which the title is taken and where the word is embedded grammatically in the sentence "Den Schneepart spielen" | "to play the snowpart," clearly, I believe, pointing toward the musical or theatrical meaning of "part."

I

"Ungewaschen, unbemalt" | *"Unwashed, unpainted"*
Written during the Paris–Berlin flight on December 16, 1967. The flight path led between Fulda and Eisenach over the Rhône, where potash was mined. This was Celan's first trip to Berlin since the railroad journey he had taken on Kristallnacht 1938 as a young student traveling from his hometown, Czernowitz, to Paris. The current trip was a major one for him, with readings planned at the Academy of the Arts and the Free University and for radio Sender Freies Berlin.

Kaue | pithead: The room, usually on top of a mine shaft, where miners washed up and dressed.

wo wir uns finden | where we find ourselves: Wiedemann points to the opening stanza of the well-known folk song "Abendslied im Sommer" (Evening Song in Summer) by Anton von Zuccalmaglio: "Kein schöner Land in dieser Zeit / als hier das unsre weit und breit / wo wir uns finden / wohl unter Linden / zur Abendzeit" ("No land more beautiful in this day / as ours here so wide and large / where we find ourselves / at ease under the Linden / at evening time") (BW, p. 832).

mit Narren-/beinen | on Fool's / legs: *Narrenbein* is also the term for what in English is called the "funny bone," that is, the ulnar nerve. For me, however, the image in the poem brings out the sense of the *Narren* as the "fool" more than something funny.

Sieben- / höhe | seven- / heighth: At one time Celan considered this term as a possible title for the volume *Lightduress*. It is also a place-name in the Black Forest. The French translator Jean-Pierre Lefebvre suggests as relevant here that the number seven is associated with mourning in Jewish culture, for example, sitting shivah (where shivah = the number seven) (PDN, p. 108). This further suggests a reading of the poem as a meditation on the death by extermination of the Jewish people, this time locating the mourning on the surface of the earth while the poet flies through the air, that is, this poem could be read as a mirror image of the "Todesfuge," where the dead are buried in the air. Celan's last passage through Berlin on the eve of Kristallnacht 1938 is likely to have been on his mind (compare the poem "La Contrescarpe," where he remembers that night: "Via Kraków / you came, at the Anhalter / railway station / a smoke flowed toward your glance, / it already belonged to tomorrow" [see p. 514]).

The manuscript has no final period after the last word.

"Du liegst" | *"You lie"*

December 22–23, 1967, Berlin. This poem narrates a walk Paul Celan took in Berlin (carefully documented by Peter Szondi) in company of the psychiatrist Walter Georgi that led to the banks of the rivers Havel and Spree and to Plötzensee, as well as to a Christmas market. During his stay Celan read the newly published book *Der Mord an Rosa Luxemburg and Karl Liebknecht: Dokumentation eines politischen Verbrechens*, edited by Elisabeth Hannover-Drück and Heinrich Hannover (Frankfurt am Main: Suhrkamp Verlag, 1967).

Fleischerhaken | butcher hooks: Plötzensee was the place where the conspirators of the July 1944 assassination attempt on Hitler were executed and hung on butcher hooks.

Äppelstaken / aus Schweden | apple stakes / from Sweden: In a first version sent to Peter Szondi on December 22–23, 1967, the word *Äppelspaken* is used rather than *Äppelstaken*, and was titled "Winter Poem" (PC/PS, #232). The reference is to Advent and Christmas decorations using apples and candles at a Swedish market stand.

er biegt um ein Eden | he turns around an Eden: Szondi had shown Celan the ex–Hotel Eden in the Budapester Straße, which had served as general quarters for the Cavalry Guard Division in 1919 and where the Spartakist leaders Rosa Luxemburg and Karl Liebknecht spent the last hours of their lives.

Der Mann ward zum Sieb, die Frau / mußte schwimmen, die Sau | The man became a sieve, the woman / had to swim, the sow: Compare the documentation gathered in the Hannovers' book: "I approached the table and asked if Dr. Liebknecht was, in fact, really dead, to which one of the comrades answered that Liebknecht had as many holes in him as a sieve" (p. 99). And: "About Luxemburg it was said: 'The old sow already swims'" (p. 129).

Landwehrkanal | Landwehr canal: an eleven-kilometer canal parallel to the Spree River and crossing much of Berlin. After Rosa Luxemburg was murdered on January 15, 1919, her body was dumped in the canal, where it was not found until June 1. Today a memorial marks the site.

Nichts / stockt | Nothing / stalls: Here Celan is most likely referencing a line (he marked marginally) in Büchner's *Danton's Death*, where Lucile says just before the execution of her husband: "The stream of life should stall if but one single drop is spilled. The earth should receive a wound from that blow. / Everything moves, the watches tick, the clocks advance, the people run, the water seeps and so on everything there up to there—no! it must not happen, no—I want to sit down on the ground and scream so that, scared, everything now stands still, everything stalls, nothing any longer moves" (act 4, scene 8 of *Dantons Tod*, in Georg Büchner, *Werke und Briefe*, eds. Karl Pörnbacher, Gerhard Schaub, Hans-Joachim Simm, and Edda Ziegler [Munich: Carl Hanser Verlag, 1980], p. 132).

"Lila Luft" | "Lilac air"
Another walk through Berlin with Walter Georgi and the literary scholar Marlies Janz, who describes the walk in her book *Vom Engagement absoluter Poesie*:

> On the night of 19 to 20 December, Celan, Walter Georgi and I drove along the Landwehr canal to the Anhalter railroad station . . . The reason for this drive had been the fact that Celan had earlier spoken of his journey through Berlin in 1938 . . . To the historical reminiscence of 1938, the year of the so-called "Kristallnacht," correspond in "Lilac air" the "yellow window-stains"—the yellow stain being an urform of the yellow star Jews were made to wear. On the large empty space in front of the Anhalter ruin we stomped through the snow . . . and when Walter Georgi spoke of the "three stars of Orion's belt," we searched the sky for that constellation. When we had found it, Celan suggested that "their name is, yes, they are called Jacob's staff, those three" (p. 235).

The title probably refers to a well-known song Celan may have heard in the "standing bar" of the penultimate line, namely Paul Lincke's 1904 hit

"Berliner Luft," lines of which could be (mis)heard as "lila Luft" (lilac air) in, for example, Lizzi Waldmüller's 1944 recording (BW, p. 833).

Trumm | ruin: In a letter to GCL (#595) Celan explains the word as being "the singular of Trümmer, ruins—moignon (stump), ruin."

Kokelstunde | flamehour: In the same letter (#595) Celan explains the *kokeln* as a Berlin expression meaning "playing with fire and light."

nichts / Interkurrierendes | nothing / intercurrent: Celan underlined this term in Rudolf Bilz (p. 140f). In English the term is found mainly in medical literature, where it is defined as occurring at the same time as and usually altering the course of another disease. In Bilz the German term was widened to refer to animal behavior patterns.

"Brunnengräber" | *"Welldigger"*

Written on Christmas Day 1967 in Berlin. The title word is a semantically ambiguous compound: it can mean "well-graves" (as I had translated it at first in 1997), linking back to several poems from *Lichtzwang* | *Lightduress* that use early Italian archeological funeral terminology (see the poem "Brunnenartig" | "Well-like" on page 288 and commentary on page 568). See also the poem "Es war Erde in ihnen" | "There was earth in them" in *Die Niemandsrose* (English version by Cid Corman in my PCS, p. 75). But it can also refer to the person who digs wells, in the singular or the plural. Given the addressee in the final lines of the poem, a young "digger- / well," that is, a personified well (with a "twelvemouth," I prefer to use "welldigger" in the title).

Bratsche | viola: The French translator uses the Italian term *viola da braccio*, which gets in the sound and etymology of the German word *Bratsche*. I have preferred to stay with the straight translation, as *viola*, as the use of the Italian term, though sound-informative, may (at least in English) indicate more preciosity than intended.

"Das angebrochene Jahr" | *"The breached year"*

Written on January 2, 1968, on Celan's return to Paris, and sent to GCL on January 8.

Wahnbrot | delusion bread: Lefevbre (PDN, p. 110) suggests that the word built on the model of *Wahnsinn* (madness, loss of meaning, from *Wahn* [delusion, vain hope] and *Sinn* [sense] "gives 'Brot / bread' the sense of sense").

"Unlesbarkeit" | *"Unreadability"*
January 5, 1968, Paris, rue d'Ulm.

Alles doppelt | Everything doubles: Reading trace in Joseph Joubert, *Pensées* (p. 69), where Celan has underlined "Souvenons-nous que tout est double" (Let us remember that everything is double) (PC/GCL, #597). In a letter to Franz Wurm, he similarly declared: "A poem just arose from, I noticed, simple words" (PC/FW, p. 125).

"Huriges Sonst" | *"Whorish else"*
January 7, 1968, Paris, place de la Contrescarpe.

"Was näht" | *"What sews"*
Written on January 10, 1968, at 8:00 p.m. and sent the same day to GCL with the note: "I just wrote a poem composed with rather simple words—I'm sending it to you. I hope that it will speak to you." As Lefevbre (PDN, p. 112) notes, this is (with "Ein Leseast " | "One reading branch" [p. 386]) the longest poem in the volumes, and that length "accentuates the threadlike character of the text, linked to the paradigm of sewing. The deliberate absence of a final period contributes to the thread-effect, the thread that links speech to that of which it speaks."

"Ich höre, die Axt hat geblüht" | *"I hear the axe has blossomed"*
The first line/title of the earliest versions gave as the date of composition "the twentieth January [*Jänner*] 1968," an essential date in Celan's cosmos, referred to in the Meridian speech, where (quoting Büchner) Lenz, "on 20th January walked through the mountains" (MFV, p. 7). It was also the date in 1942 when, at the Wannsee Conference, the "final solution"—that is, the extermination of the Jews—was planned and set in motion by the Nazis. A little further along in the Meridian speech (MFV, p. 8), Celan writes: "Perhaps one can say that each poem has its own '20th of January' inscribed in it? Perhaps what's new in the poems written today is exactly this: theirs is the clearest attempt to remain mindful of such dates?"

In that early version he had located the place where "the axe has blossomed" as Hungary, but when he sent that version to Franz Wurm, the latter suggested that this place-name of a state would narrow the poem too much, and Celan changed it to an "unnameable" place (PC/FW, #93).

"Mit der Stimme der Feldmaus" | *"With the voice of the fieldmouse"*
January 20, 1968, Paris, rue d'Ulm.

Possibly Celan had in mind Franz Kafka's last short story, "Josephine the Singer, or the Mouse Folk."

"In Echsen-" | *"In lizard-"*
January 20, 1968, Paris, rue d'Ulm. See the poem "Haut Mal," which also speaks of epilepsy (p. 212).

"Schneepart" | *"Snowpart"*
January 22, 1968, Paris, rue d'Ulm. The poem that gives its title to the volume. See notes on the title above (p. 576).

II

"Die nachzustotternde Welt" | *"The to-be-restuttered world"*
January 23, 1968, Paris. If the poem that gave its title to the whole volume closes the first cycle of the book, then the poem following it and opening the second cycle can be seen as programmatic—as Lefebvre argues cogently (PDN, p. 115). The work of the poem can be seen as a restuttering of the world, not mimetic reproduction, but a rearticulation, thus a re-creation. Lefebvre: "To re-say the world with re-made words, decomposed into syllables that bang against each other and have trouble gathering together, privileging hard onsets, to re-say a world that is a passage where one is only invited. Note the inscription of this program in a retrospective gaze anticipating on the totality of existence: the (unreadable) world in which I will have lived (written, and read)."

Also useful is this quote from *The Meridian* (MFV, pp. 124–25): "Büchner's last words on his deathbed, Lenz's words (Moscow) have not come down to us—it is the return into the just still voiced, as in Woyzeck—it is language as involution, the unfolding of meaning in the one, word-estranged syllable—: the it is the 'rootsyllable,' recognizable in the [death-rattled] stuttering, the [language as] what has returned into the germ—the meaning-carrier is the {mou} mortal mouth, whose lips won't round themselves. Muta cum liquida,—and vowel-buttressed, the rhyme-sound as self-sound."

See the related term "lallation-stage" in the poem "Das Flüsterhaus" |

"The whisperhouse" from *Zeitgehöft* | *Timestead* (p. 418), but before all, see
"Tübingen, Jänner" | "Tübingen, January" in *Die Niemandsrose* (PCS, pp. 79–
80), which speaks to Hölderlin (*Pallaksch* is an invented word Hölderlin used
during his madness):

Eyes con-
vinced to go blind.
Their—"a
riddle is pure
origin"—, their
remembrance of
swimming Hölderlin-towers, gull-
blown.

Visits of drowned carpenters by
these
diving words:

If,
if a man,
if a man was born, today, with
the lightbeard of
the patriarchs: he could,
speaking of these
days, he
could
but babble and babble.
always, always
agagain.

("Pallaksch. Pallaksch.")

"Du mit der Finsterzwille" | *"You with the darkness slingshot"*
January 23, 1968, Paris. The "Zwille" | "slingshot and stone" image could eas-
ily be associated with the biblical David. Lefebvre suggests (PDN, p. 116) that
it functions as an image for poetry (as do other projectile instruments such as
boomerangs and bows). Celan's astrological sign was Sagittarius, the archer.

"Eingejännert" | *"Enjanuaried"*
January 26, 1968, Paris. See the poem "Tübingen, Jänner" | "Tübingen, January" (p. 583), as well as the commentary for the poem "Ich höre, die Axt hat geblüht" | "I hear the axe has blossomed" (p. 581).

"Schludere" | *"Be sloppy"*
Night of January 29–30, 1968, Paris, rue Tournefort. Celan very carefully dated this poem to this specific night—that is, the anniversary of his suicide attempt the previous year.

"Stückgut" | *"Parceled goods"*
February 2, 1968, Paris.
    Stückgut | Parceled goods: Celan found and underlined in a German translation of Marguerite Duras's novel *Le Vice-Consul*: "Stückgut mit Büchern kommt aus Frankreich an ihre Adresse" (Parceled goods containing books arrives from France at your address). A note in Celan's hand reads: "Stückgut: Man [*sic*] und Holz, Stückgut und Vieh" (Parceled goods: man and wood, parceled goods and livestock).

"Von querab" | *"From abeam"*
February 2, 1968, Paris.

"Holzgesichtiger" | *"Woodfaced"*
February 6, 1968, Paris, rue d'Ulm. Wiedemann points out that the feuilleton page of the FAZ for that day reproduced a Swiss Shrovetide's mask made of wood with a large hanging mouth, illustrating an article on folk art by Gisela Brackert, and another one, "Collapse of the Ego," by Hans-Jürgen Heise, that compares the art of schizophrenics and the positions of contemporary poets (BW, p. 838).

"Largo" | *"Largo"*
February 9, 1968, Paris.
    Largo: A musical term for a very slow tempo or a musical piece or movement in such tempo.
    über- / sterbens- / groß | sur- / dying- / large: At the root of this Celan neologism one can hear the verb *überleben*, "to survive." He had first used the term two days earlier in a poem he didn't include in *Shneepart* | *Snowpart*:

In my shot-up knee
stood my father,

sur-
dying large he stood
there,

Michailowska and
the cherry orchard stood around him,
I knew it would
come to this, he said.

Michailowska is the the labor camp in Transnistria where Frederike and Leo Antschel, Celan's parents, died in 1942. "The cherry orchard" is, of course, Chekhov's.

die Zeit- / lose | fall / crocus: the colchicum flower, or crocus; for Celan, a complex association, as colchicum (in French the flower is called *colchique*) links to Colchis and the Black Sea, which links to both Celan's lost home country and to Mandelstam. Also, the literal translation of *Zeitlose* is "timeless"— obviously lost in translation here. This flower (and the "timeless" echo of its name) also links to Celan's mother, as is made clear in the poem "The syllable pain," which says: "fall / crocus in his sight, the mother- / flower" (PCS, p. 92).

Lidern | lids: In a first draft of the poem was the homophonic *Lieder*, or songs (TA-SP, p. 47). Cutting out the *e* changed the semantic meaning but not the sound.

Amselpaar | pair of blackbirds: The German bird name immediately calls up Celan's original family name, Antschel, which could, in fact, be a deformation of *Amsel*. In the first draft of the poem, the pair of birds were cranes; changing it to *Amsel* points to a deliberate decision to cite this name, referencing his parents.

"Zur Nachtordnung" | *"To nightorder"*
Written on February 19, 1968, and, the manuscript tells us, on the place de la Contrescarpe, site of several of Celan's poems, such "La Contrescarpe" (p. 513) and "Huriges Sonst" | "Whorish else" (p. 326).

Weißkies- / stotterer | whitepebble- / stutterer: See note above for "The to-be-restuttered world," as well as in the poem "Siberian" the lines: "with your / white pebble in the mouth" (PCS, p. 89).

"Mit den Sackgassen" | *"To speak with"*
Febraury 21, 1968, Paris.

"Etwas wie Nacht" | *"Something like night"*
March 8, 1968, Paris, place de la Contrescarpe.

III

"Warum dieses jähe Zuhause" | *"Why this sudden at-homeness"*
Written on March 26, 1968, less than a week after Celan had met with Gisèle for the first time in a year, Gisèle having taken the decision to live apart in April 1967 as Celan's psychic troubles posed a danger for her and their son Eric.

einer, der sich in dich stach | someone who stabbed himself into / you: In a letter to me, the poet and translator Peter Cockelbergh wrote: "It's strange, but I can feel why the 'you' is just right on the next line, but wonder what motivated you—is it because you changed that non-defining relative clause into a defining one? or the sound play (ich, dich, stach, stich > who, into, you + stabbed, bebreathes . . . which is more emphasized thus." I responded:

> The Celan line: well, I don't think I thought it totally through, that is, to start with the enjambment felt right as I was putting the words on paper, then, on second thought, it felt better even, because of the ambiguity the slight pause creates: he stabbed himself (as PC did with a *Brieföffner*, letter opener, missing his heart by a couple inches, in front of his wife) but he also tried to kill her at some point. And obviously unable to reproduce the tight/rhyming grammatical sequence of the German "einer, der sich in dich stach," very trochaic but ending with a spondee, which is differently— but with similar expectations, maybe, reproduced, I think, by the enjambment. Of course my main focus was on how to translate *beatmet* and I am happy you like the "bebreathes"—a bit wild, but then given the importance

of the word *Atem* in PC's world, and the various neologisms he creates with it, why not create one in English even if it isn't present in the original at that specific locus.

Geschlecht | sex: The German word has the double meaning of sexual organ and progeny, family, lineage. Though the first meaning prevails here, the second, wider concept needs to be heard. For a complex philosophical investigation of this term, see Jacques Derrida's essay *"Geschlecht*: Sexual Difference, Ontological Difference," in *A Derrida Reader: Between the Blinds*, edited by Peggy Kamuf (New York: Columbia University Press, 1991), p. 381.

"Warum aus dem Ungeschöpften" | *"Why, from the uncreated"*
March 31, 1968, Paris, rue d'Ulm. One of the sources of this poem is no doubt *Das Prinzip Hoffnung* | *The Principle of Hope* by Ernst Bloch (1885–1997), published in three volumes (1954 to 1959) and exploring the utopian impulses present in art, literature, religion, and other forms of cultural expression. Celan marked and underlined several sentences in the first volume: "Mercury, the essence of quicksilver, counted as the most essential metal constituent; made of water and earth it permits elasticity and fusibility. Because of these passive qualities, mercury was considered a female power, as such it stands closest to the 'materia prima'" (vol. 1, p. 749). "Like the 'materia prima' . . . Mercurius can be compared to the Virgin Mary, as the stone can be with the son" (vol. 1, p. 750f), and "The Virgin is Mercury, from here the Son is born, that is the stone" (Marsilio Ficinus quote, vol. 1, p. 151f).

ein Weisensteinchen | a philosopher's pebble: In the alchemical context of the poem, the German word suggests *Stein der Weisen* (see Bloch, p. 749), or the philosopher's stone, which is supposed to be able to turn metals into gold and was the central symbol of the mystical terminology of alchemy, symbolizing perfection at its finest, enlightenment, and heavenly bliss. Celan underlined Bloch's tracing of the word *Aufklärung*, "enlightenment," back to the vocabulary of alchemy (BPPC, p. 318). Efforts to discover the philosopher's stone were known as the Magnum Opus (Great Work).

Magnalia: Ernst Bloch, on p. 765, writes: "Das Haus Salomonis birgt weiter Flugzeuge, Dampfmaschinen, Wasserturbinen und noch andere 'magnalia naturae, Großtaten der Natur,' mit ihr und über sie hinaus" (The house of Solomon further holds airplanes, steam engines, water turbines and other "magnalia naturae, major deeds of nature"). The word usually refers to the greater works of God (*magnalia dei*); in the United States the word is familiar mainly from the title of Cotton Mather's *Magnalia Christi Americana*.

"Mapesbury Road" | "Mapesbury Road"

April 14–15, 1968, London. The title names a road in London that connects with Willesden Lane, where Celan stayed from April 3 to April 16 with his father's sister, Berta Antschel (1894–1981). In a letter from April 18 he wrote to Franz Wurm: "And then the darknesses from both 'farther' sides. But also walking and a walked-up poem, (Mapesbury Road: between the borough of Willesden and the borough of Hampstead, on an Easter—and Passover—Sunday, more accurately: on 14 April of this year" (PC/FW, #102). Those "darknesses" point to the assassination of Martin Luther King, Jr. (April 4, 1968) in Memphis, Tennessee, and the assassination attempt on Rudi Dutschke (April 11, 1968) in Berlin.

magnolienstündige | magnolia-houred: In a letter to Gisèle, Celan mentioned that the magnolia already blooming in London reminded him of his hometown of Czernowitz (PC/GCL, #138).

Zeithof | timehalo: See commentary on "Schwimmhäute" | "Webbing" (p. 566) and, below, on the title of the next volume, *Zeitgehöft* | *Timestead* (p. 610). In a letter to his friend Gisela Dischner of April 23, 1968, Celan writes: "By the way: the word timehalo you'll find in Husserl."

Steckschuß | lodged bullet: The German papers (for example, FAZ of April 13, 1968) reported that Dutschke had been hit by "a bullet that lodged in his brain, another hit his cheek and a third one his right torso." Celan confirmed to Dischner that the "Steckschuß" referred to Dutschke (letter of April 23, 1968).

"Der überkübelte Zuruf" | "The overloaded call"

April 17, 1968, Paris, rue d'Ulm.

die Barrikade | the barricade: Following the assassination attempt on Rudi Dutschke, student demonstrations became widespread and more forceful in Berlin, including the building of barricades.

"Hervorgedunkelt" | "Darkened forth"
April 22, 1968, Paris, rue d'Ulm. The title plays with and against that of the cycle of poems called *Eingedunkelt | Tenebrae'd* (p. 222)

Buche | beech tree: A marker of Celan's origins in the Bukovina (*Buchenland*, "land of the beeches"; thus also *Buchenwald*, "beech tree forest").

"Mit dir Docke" | "With you, ragdoll"
April 25–26, 1968, Paris, rue d'Ulm.

Docke | ragdoll: Celan had nine months earlier (July 1967) made a note concerning the word *Teichdocke*, which he had found in Jean Paul's *Kampaner Thal* (vols. 39–40, p. 40). The word refers to a skein or hank of yarn, and by extension (in southern Germany) to a doll made of yarn.

kungeln | to fiddle: Also *kunkeln*, from the noun *Kunkel*, which in south and west German dialect refers to the distaff in spinning. The verb (similar to another Celan word, *mauscheln*), according to Lefebvre (PDN, p. 125), means to talk and to make plans secretly in a lowered voice. Originally it meant to make a mess of a ball of threads, and then referred to doing bad work in the *Kunkelstube*, the room in which the spinning was done. By extension it came to refer to the flirting that went on in the spinning rooms between men and women. Maybe our "spinning a tale" links to this.

"Auch der Runige" | "The runic one too"
Composed on May 4 and 5, 1968, and finalized on May 14 with the dated note "das steht" (it holds up). On May 3 and 4, Celan had been reading several essays by Rudi Dutschke in *Rebellion der Studenten oder Die neue Opposition*, edited by Uwe Bergmann (Rowohlt Verlag, 1968), titled "The Contradictions of Advanced Capitalism, the Anti-authoritarian Students, and Their Relationship with the Third World" and "From Antisemitism to Anticommunism." In Germany, the student demonstrations had been mounting in intensity for two

years already (Benno Ohnesorg, a student, was shot dead by police at a demonstration in June 1967); in France, the "events of May 1968" started with a large student demonstration on May 3, and over the following two days a number of the arrested students got solid jail sentences.

The TA (*Schneepart*, p. 69) indicates that on one of the typescripts Celan made the following handwritten notes in the lower margin: "Night before last, place Contrescarpe, the young PC [French Communist party]-man who defended leftwing nationalsocialism" and: "Yesterday, the 13th, at the demonstration, the arms stretched 'ironically' in the Hitler salutation behind the ~~red and the~~ black flag-," and in the left margin: "also: next to the Trotsky portrait in the yard of the Sorbonne: CRS=SS (SS in runic script)."

der Runige | The runic one: In a letter to Franz Wurm, Celan points to both extreme right-wing and extreme left-wing anti-Semitism in French newspapers, and also points it out in Dutschke's essays (PC/FW, 146f). Celan also cites what became one of the best-known graffiti of May 1968 in France, "CRS=SS," with the SS usually spelled in runic writing, a formulation Celan disagreed with totally.

Greiftrupp | arrest-squad: Reading trace in Dutschke: "It should be mentioned that on April 6 the police engaged a large number of arrest-squads against the demonstrators for the first time. The arrest-squads had the task to go and arrest the active and leading students and workers within the mass of demonstrators and thus hinder the activity of the masses" (p. 79).

Mohrrübe | carrot: Reading trace (BW, p. 843) in Achim von Arnim, *Die Kronenwächter*: "But the woman didn't care for anything Anton undertook in the house, except when he sat down next to her at the window where she was scraping carrots, and spoke good words to her." *Mohrrübe* is the north German for the usual *Möhre* (carrot); here, Lefebvre suggests (PDN, p. 127) a possible reference to Karl Marx's nickname, "the Moor" (which would seem to point to Marx's "Moorish" Jewish origins). In the poem, *Mohr* is picked up by "Moorigen," and "Morgen," here probably in the sense of "tomorrow" rather than "morning," and thus bringing to mind the "tomorrows that sing" of communist revolutions. *Moorig* also recalls Celan's poem "Denk Dir" | "Imagine" and the "moorsoldier from Masada" (p. 220). *Der Morgen* is also a measure of land, and further points to the *Morgenland*, the Orient—with Lefebvre suggesting this may connect to the Mao-influenced students at Celan's school, the École Normale Supérieure.

Zündschwamm | tinder-sponge: Reading trace (BW, p. 843) in Arnim, *Die Kronenwächter*: "to wash and clean the marks of the nails and bind them with tinder-sponge" (vol. 1, p. 923).

Hirntransplantat | braintransplant: In a letter to Franz Wurm (PC/FW, #107) Celan writes: "Because earlier, dining contrescarpishly, and espying Karl Marx too on television and said to my table companion: 'Eventually we'll be able to transplant heads, but it's not sure that we'll know how to regrow the beards.'" Other traces (BW, p. 843) point to the poem "Dunstbänder-, Spruchbänder-Aufstand" | "Vaporband-, banderole-uprising" (p. 102) in connection with his reading of Arno Schmidt's *Gelehrtenrepublik* | *The Egghead Republic*, which describes brain transplants.

Wundstein | woundstone: A stone or mineral composite used for healing purposes.

"Deinem, auch deinem" | *"Your, even your"*
May 7, 1968, Paris.

fehldurchläuteten | falsenotes: See last sentence of Kafka's "Ein Landarzt": "Einmal dem Fehlläuten der Nachtglocke gefolgt—es ist niemals gutzumachen" (Once you respond to the nightbell's false alarm, there's no making it good ever again.) In Celan's notebooks from 1962, he already pointed to this Kafka sentence: "The nightbell's false alarm: that is not something falsely, erroneously heard, but belongs most profoundly to the quality of the nightbell itself. (It is not a matter of 'daybells'!) At least the 'right' cannot be differentiated from the false-notes—is thus the same."

Sechsstern | six-star: The star of David has six points.

Zeitunterheiligtes | time undersanctified: In Achim von Arnim's unfinished 1817 novel, *Die Tronenwächter*, which Celan read during May 1968, he makes a note of the word *unterheiligt* (double underline and exclamation point), when he marks a passage that criticizes the era's tendency to oversanctify everything: "This I say earnestly to our era, which likes to oversanctify its temporality with completed, eternal determination, with holy wars, eternal peace and apocalypses" (see PDN, pp. 128–29; BW, pp. 843–44).

"Mauerspruch" | *"Wallslogan"*

First called "Mauerspruch für Paris" ("Wallslogan for Paris"), it was written on May 26, 1968 (after what looks like two weeks without a poem). By now a general strike had succeeded the many student demonstrations and the great student and workers' march of May 13, followed by a range of spontaneous strikes throughout the country. On the twenty-sixth, the unions began negotiations with the Gaullist government. The previous day a regiment of paratroopers had arrived in Paris.

ein Engel, erneut | an angel, anew: reading traces marked in with margins in Walter Benjamin's essay on Karl Kraus: "Like a creature sprung from the child and the cannibal, his conqueror stands before him: not a new man—a monster, a new angel. Perhaps one of those who, according to the Talmud, are at each moment created anew in countless throngs, and who, once they have raised their voice before God, cease and pass into nothingness" (translation by Edmond Jephcott, in Walter Benjamin, *Selected Writings*, vol. 2, p. 457). Further traces in Benjamin's *On the Concept of History*:

> There is a painting by Klee called *Angelus Novus*. An angel is depicted there who looks as though he were about to distance himself from something which he is staring at. His eyes are opened wide, his mouth stands open and his wings are outstretched. The Angel of History must look just so. His face is turned towards the past. Where we see the appearance of a chain of events, he sees one single catastrophe, which unceasingly piles rubble on top of rubble and hurls it before his feet. He would like to pause for a moment so fair [*verweilen*: a reference to Goethe's *Faust*], to awaken the dead and to piece together what has been smashed. But a storm is blowing from Paradise, it has caught itself up in his wings and is so strong that the Angel can no longer close them. The storm drives him irresistibly into the future, to which his back is turned, while the rubble-heap before him grows sky-high. That which we call progress, is this storm. (Translation by Dennis Redmond)

denkenden Löwen | thinking lions: Celan had written to Franz Wurm on May 7: "Let me greet your and all our lions" (PC/FW, #108). This was a response to something Wurm had written in a letter of May 5, comparing the heraldic animals of his country (Bohemia) and of Germany: "That the double-tailed (and often tail-wagging) Lion seems more reasonable to me than the two-headed eagle, one of whose heads never knew what the other one's couldn't think anyway" (PC/FW, #145).

"Für Eric" | "For Eric"
May 31, 1968, Paris, rue Tournefort. The dedicatee is Celan's son Eric (b. 1955). Despite his separation from Gisèle at this point, Celan sees his son regularly. See also the poem with the same title farther on in the cycle, page 362.

pfeilende | arrowing: Possible reference to Celan's astrological sign, Sagittarius.

"Wer pflügt nichts um?" | "Who doesn't plough up something?"
May 31, 1968, Paris, rue Tournefort.

er kätnert | he roustabouts: A verb Celan builds on the noun *Kätner*, someone who lives in a *Kate*, or shack, a transient or migrant worker.

"Levkojen" | "Gillyflowers"
May 31, 1968, Paris, allée de l'Observatoire.

The German name for a flower native to the eastern Mediterranean seaboard comes from a mispronunciation of the first syllable of the Greek name (*leukos* = white), and in *Lev* one can hear the Russian version of Celan's father's first name, Leo, corresponding in Hebrew to the word "heart" (PDN, p. 132).

katzenbemündigt | cat-enfranchised: *Bemündigen* (rare) is the opposite of *entmündigen*, meaning "to disenfranchise, to incapacitate legally." What is lost in the translation is the word *mund* (mouth), here meaning "to give speech," "the permission to express oneself."

der / maltesische Jude | the / Maltese Jew: Compare Christopher Marlowe's 1591 play *The Famous Tragedy of the Rich Jew of Malta*. Lefebvre, via the original spelling of the title word with an *I*, "Iew," suggests that the word here links to Lew, Lev, Leo (PDN, p. 132).

"Du durchklafterst" | "You transfathom"
June 1–2, 1968, Paris, rue Tournefort/while traveling.

"Für Eric" | "For Eric"

June 2, 1968, Paris, rue Tournefort. See poem (and its commentary) with same title earlier in the cycle, pages 356 and 593.

Flüstertüte | megaphone: BA, vol. 10.2, p. 143, points to Robert Held's article "Revolutionary Spring" (FAZ, June 1–2, 1968) on the expulsion and readmittance of Daniel Cohn-Bendit, one of the leaders of the French student movement, who, though born in France, designated himself as German and Jewish. Held: "Cool, loud and clear his voice sounds through the megaphone [*Flüstertüte*]. The transistor-powered megaphone has become the tactical weapon." When Cohn-Bendit was expelled from France by the Gaullist government, the student movement created the slogan "We are all German Jews."

raupen | crawl: Celan found the word *raupen* in relation to the movement of tanks in Arno Schmidt's book *Leviathan*. In German it is a noun that means "caterpillar," which Schmidt turned into a verb evoking the movement of a caterpillar.

Seide | silk: Possible reference to the rich silk clothes of the bourgeois progovernment counterdemonstrators in the Right Bank quarters that included the rue de Longchamp, where Eric Celan lived.

wir stehen | we stand: See Celan's numerous references to the act of standing throughout the work, and, for example, the commentary on the poem "Wirk nicht voraus" | "Do not work ahead" (p. 575).

"Dein Blondschatten" | "Your blondshadow"

June 2, 1968, Paris, rue Tournefort.

Blondschatten | blondshadow: Compare Held's article: "Cohn-Bendit, blue eyes, slightly messy eyelashes, reddish blond hair, stubble beard, brandishes a few white pages."

The four terms *Trense, Schabracke, Hankenmal,* and *Levade* (snaffle, shabrack, haunchmark, and levade) used in the poem are horse-riding terms that Celan found in an article on horsemanship by Maria von Loesch, next to Held's article in the FAZ. Celan had already noted these words in the fifties when reading Friedrich Behn's *Kultur der Urzeit*.

Schwimm . . . Wasser | swim . . . water: The water images here seem to refer back to a Cohn-Bendit quote in Held's article: "When we say: the movement is carried by the workers movements in Paris, by the students, by the intellectuals, that means that each of these is interchangeable and that no one in France is indispensable. That's why my expulsion is like giving a thrashing to water."

"Die Abgründe streunen" | *"The abysses roam"*
Composed on June 6, 1968, with place of the composition given on the draft as the "Pont des Arts," the footbridge that links the Louvre on the Right Bank of the Seine to the Académie Française and the Institut de France on the Left Bank. Linked, probably, to Celan's reading of that day's FAZ.

Taubheitsgefühlen | feelings of numbness: FAZ article on thalidomide victims: "One morning she woke up and found her left foot numb, a few days later the right one . . . The operation was a success, she started gaining weight again, but the feelings of numbness remained."

Lockstoffe | baits: possibly via article in FAZ on how rabbits mark their territories and a short piece titled "Sexuallockstoffe bei den Trichinen" (Pheromones among trichinellas).

"Dein Mähnen-Echo" | *"Your mane-echo"*
June 13, 1968, Paris, rue d'Ulm.
beleu- / mundet | be- / famed: Celanesque construction of the intransitive verbal expression (*gut/schlecht*) *beleumundet sein* (to be in [good/bad] repute).

IV

"Das Im-Ohrgerät" | *"The in-ear-device"*
Written on a reading trip to Germany in Freiburg im Breisgau on June 25, 1968. That week's *Spiegel* magazine published an article on industrial espionage with a photo of a hearing aid completely insertable into the ear. The article quoted the following line: "Do not trust anyone—not even yourself," as the motto of a successful antispying system (BW, p. 848).

"Der halbzerfressene" | *"The halfgnawed"*
Written June 30, 1968, at the Kieler Förde, a small inlet through which the harbor town Kiel has access to the Baltic Sea.

"Ein Blatt" | *"A leaf"*

July 1968, Freiburg, Frankfurt am Main, Kiel. Celan's response to Bertolt Brecht's poem "An die Nachgeborenen," the second stanza of which asks:

> What kind of times are these when
> To talk about trees is nearly a crime,
> Because it avoids speaking of all that's evil!

"Playtime" | *"Playtime"*

July 16, 1968, Paris, rue Tournefort. Allusion to *Playtime*, a 1967 film by Jacques Tati, in which American tourists visit a futuristic Paris, and in which many scenes are shot through windows and mirrors.

Lines 2–5: Wiedemann (BW, p. 849) suggests a possible connection to Shakespeare's *Hamlet*, act 1, scene 2, where Horatio recalls the ghostly apparition: "a figure like your father . . . Thrice he walked / by their oppress'd and fear-surprised eyes, / Within his truncheon's length; while they, distill'd / Almost to jelly with the act of fear, / stand dumb and speak not to him. This to me / in dreadful secrecy impart they did."

du stehst | you stand: See the importance of this stance as detailed in other commentaries, for example, pages 617–18.

vergleichnisten | parabelized: Celanian neologism incorporating *vergleichen* (to compare) and *Gleichnis* (parable or allegory).

"Aus der Vergängnis" | *"Out of future-past fate"*

July 18, 1968, Paris, rue Tournefort.

Vergängnis | future-past fate: A neologism that combines *Vergangen*, "passed," and *Vergangenheit*, "the past," with *Verhängnis*, "fate," "fatality," "doom"—that is, the past and the future. (Trying to find an English neologism, I came up with "pasture," which does not work. Nor does "transience," which I had used in an earlier version, have the complexity the temporal load that Celan's term carries.)

das ins Ohr Geträufelte | what's poured in the ear: *Hamlet*, act 1, scene 5: "Upon my secure hour thy uncle stole, / With juice of cursed hebona in a vial, / And in the porches of my ears did pour / The leperous distilment."

mündigt | emancipates: Verbalized form of *mündig*, "of age," "adult emancipated," but also carries sound rhymes that link the work to *münden*, "to flow into," as a river, thus the fjords of the next stanza, and *Mund*, "mouth," as the mouth of a river or a human mouth that speaks or says.

nüchtern Erzähltes / träumt | what's recounted on an empty stomach / dreams: See Walter Benjamin, the opening sentence of the chapter "Breakfast Room" in *One-Way Street*: "A popular tradition warns against recounting dreams the next morning on an empty stomach" (*Selected Writings*, vol. 1, p. 444).

"*Offene Glottis*" | "*Open glottis*"

Composed on July 19, 1968, one of ten poems written that day. For all of those poems, as for the one above, Celan's reading of Walter Benjamin is important. The first draft sheet has Benjamin quotes, and Benjamin quoting Freud, on it. This poem can be read as a poetological statement or, as Lefebvre puts it, "a brief manifesto of Celan's philosophy of language . . . [using] the linguistic terminology of the 50s and 60s, strongly influenced by [Ferdinand de] Saussure and [Emile] Benveniste."

Offene Glottis, Luftstrom | Open glottis, airstream: Reading trace in Reichel/Bleichert: "The narrowing (of the by quiet breathing open) glottis to a slit rests on the collaboration of the muscles of the larynx, that bring the arytenoid cartilage closer together . . . and tauten the vocal cords" (p. 215).

Formanten | formant: Any of several bands of frequency that determine the phonetic quality of a vowel. The spectral peaks of the sound spectrum | P(f) |' of the voice (Gunnar Fant). It also refers to the acoustic resonance of the human vocal tract, often measured as an amplitude peak of the frequency spectrum of a sound (*New Oxford American Dictionary*).

Mitlautstöße | consonant-thrusts: In *Mitlaut* one probably hears the *mit*, "with," and *laut*, "sound/ing," better than in "consonant," though of course our Latinate term has the "con" (with) and "sonare" (to sound), so it has the same two meaning syllables. Reading trace in Reichel/Bleichert, page 215: "The very variable character of the consonants rests without exception on a typical form of the supraglottic air passages in mouth and nose, through which the air is blown spasmodically or more continuously."

Reizschutz | protection shield: A term from Freud's *Beyond the Pleasure Principle*, where Celan underlined it, usually translated as "protection against stimulation (or stimuli)."

As Rainer Nägele, whose term "protection shield" I am using, writes: "Like his name, Freud's vocabulary gives us no license to translate the poems into psychoanalytic theory. Yet we cannot discard the signals set by this vocabulary. We have to take the poem on its own terms, which includes the recognition that its 'own terms' are not entirely its own. We have to recognize the poem as a translation, not a translation of Freud's text, but a translation like Freud's text" (*Reading After Freud*, p. 157).

"Aus dem Moorboden" | *"From the moorfloor"*
This poem of July 17, despite its shortness, has given rise to a wide range of commentaries. Core to it is Celan's reading of Walter Benjamin, and specifically the latter's Kafka essay (wbsw, vol. 2, pp. 794–818). The most essential secondary literature on it is Werner Hamacher's essay "Häm," unhappily not yet translated into English.

Ohnebild | sans-image: At the surface level this neologism can be read as that which is without an image, in a poetics that, according to Lefebvre (PDN, p. 141), "puts metaphor and parable on trial . . . but also as the image 'without,' 'sans,' the anti-image that takes on nothingness."

Häm | hemo: See commentary on "Schaltjahrhunderte" | "Leapcenturies" (p. 572). This links *Häm* to "hemo(globin)," though there are many more ways of reading the word, or part word. What elsewhere I have referred to as the "polysemy without mask" of Celan's text, can be seen in this term, which, beyond "hemoglobin" can be linked to *heim(at)*, "home(land)"; *hem*, the Hebrew third (male) person plural pronoun; the English "aim" (picked up in *Ziel*, "aim," two lines farther down); the first syllable of *Hemmung*, "interruption," "stopping," as in a stutter ("hemming and hawing"), etc. See also, possibly, Celan's use of the word *Gram* in "Mit uns" | "With us," the final poem of the series *Tenebrae'd*, written two years earlier (p. 232).

im Flintenlauf | in the gun barrel: The poem's first draft has "in der Pfanne" | "in the pan" instead, which is also readable as a gun term, the flash or priming pan. Another reading sees a play on Benjamin's word *Finte*, meaning a feint.

Dorfluft | Village air: Compare Benjamin: "Kafka's America ends with the rustic ceremonies of Oklahoma. 'In Kafka,' said Soma Morgenstern, 'there is the air of a village, as with all great founders of religion'" (WBSW, vol 2., p. 805).

rue Tournefort: The street on which Celan was living at this time, named after the botanist Joseph Pitton de Tournefort (1656–1704). The French name can also be read as the verb *tourner*, "to turn," and the adjective *fort*, "strong." In a letter to Franz Wurm of November 22, 1967, Celan had punned on his new address, wondering if it meant something "qui tourne (et tournera) fort?" (that is [and will be a] strong turn [away]). Such a "strong turn" can also be seen poetologically as the *Wendung*, or *Wende*, named in *Atemwende | Breathturn*.

"Hochmoor" | "Highmoor"
July 20, 1968, Paris, rue Tournefort. In his Brockhaus geology manual, Celan underlined several terms descriptive of moor and swamp geology, such as *uhrglasförmige aufgewölbte Oberfläche, Lagg, Schwingmoor oder Wassenkissen, vertorft*, and *Vertorfung*. In Kurd von Bülow's *Moorkunde*, he underlined *Schwingrasen* (pp. 77 and 84). Compare also the previous poem and the ongoing Benjamin readings.

Ritter | knights: Meant here is the knight butterfly (*Lebadea martha*).

sonnentausüchtig | sundewaddicted: *Sonnentau*, literally "sundew," is the name of a carniverous plant (*Drosera rossolis*) that grows on moors, owing its name to the dewlike drops of mucus that form on its leaves and in which insects get trapped.

Lagg | lagg: Is the swamp at the edge of rain moors, in which water collects. From the usually convexly shaped center of the hochmoor (compare "watch-glass-shaped") water flows through narrow grooves down the often steep wall to the foot of the edge wall, where it collects and meets here at the border of the moor floor and the mineral floor with the water from the surroundings.

Sabbatkerzen | Sabbath candles: The poem was written on July 20, 1968, which was a Sabbath; Lefebvre suggests that the word is also another name for a variety of reeds, *Typhia latifolia* (bulrush, cattail).

"Erzflitter" | *"Oreglitter"*

July 20, 1968, Paris, rue Tournefort.

Angiospermen | angiosperms: The class of flowering and seed-producing plants. Etymologically, "angiosperm" means a plant that produces seeds within an enclosure.

Karstwannen | karst depression: A karst is a geological formation shaped by the dissolution of a layer or layers of soluble bedrock, such as limestone or dolomite. As the result of subterranean drainage, there may be very limited surface water with no rivers or lakes. Many karst regions display distinctive surface features, with cenotes, sinkholes, or dolines being the most common.

"Einkanter" | *"Einkanter"*

July 20, 1968, Paris, rue Tournefort. The title refers to a stone with a single sharp edge worn by wind-driven sand (compare *Dreikanter*, "ventifact"). Celan found the term in his Brockhaus.

Rembrandt: in 1967 and again in 1968, on his visits to London, Celan saw Rembrandt's painting *A Man Seated Reading at a Table in a Lofty Room* in the National Gallery (mentioned in his letter to Franz Wurm of April 18, 1968 [PC/FW, #102]).

Bartlocke | beardlock: Traditional Jewish *payot*. Rembrandt painted a number of portraits of Jews in traditional dress as well as illustrations of the Bible.

sechzehnte Psalm | sixteenth psalm: In the King James version, this psalm, named "A Goodly Heritage," opens: "Preserve me, O God: / for in thee do I put my trust. / O my soul, thou hast said unto the LORD, Thou art my Lord: / my goodness extendeth not to thee; / but to the saints that are in the earth, / and to the excellent, in whom is all my delight." But see above all verse 8: "I have set the LORD always before me: / because he is at my right hand, I shall not be moved." In the poem "24 rue Tournefort" (not included in any volume, but see BW, p. 525, and Nomadics blog: www.pierrejoris.com /blog/?p=9851), Celan cites the core term of Psalm 16, *Shiviti*, translated in the King James version as "set before me."

24 RUE TOURNEFORT

You and your
kitchensink German—yes, sink-,
yes, before—ossuaries.

Say: Löwig. Say: Shiviti

The black cloth
they lowered before you,
when your breath
swelled scarward,

brothers too, you stones,
image the word shut behind
side glances.

"Mit Rebmessern" | *"With pruning hooks"*
July 21, 1968, Paris, rue Tournefort. A poem with a nearly exclusive nautical vocabulary, in which Lefebvre sees "an existential, biographico-poetological poem, through the figure of the sailor on great world circumnavigating sail ships, crossing or following the meridians, armed with a pruning knife with curved blade in the shape of a large lunar crescent—used here like a sailor's knife or shackle opener. A number of the terms used were underlined by Celan in books read at different times: Siegmund Günther's *Physische Geographie* for 'Kalmenzone' | 'calmzone' (p. 63), Joseph Conrad's *Lord Jim* for 'die Spaken' (handspike, capstan bar), and Conrad's *An Outcast of the Islands* for 'das Beiboot' | 'the dinghy'" (PDN, p. 145).

Gebetshub | prayer's tidal range: Neologism based on *Tidenhub* (tidal amplitude or range).

Lößpuppen | *Loessdolls*
July 21, 1968, Paris, rue Tournefort. The title refers to geological formations that in Celan's Brockhaus *Taschenbuch der Geologie* are called *Lößkindel* or *Lößpuppen* (loess-children or loess-dolls). Loess is an aeolian sediment formed by the accumulation of wind-blown silt.

V

"Stahlschüssiger Sehstein" | *"Steeluginous visionstone"*
July 24, 1968, Paris, rue Tournefort.

Stahlschüssiger | Steeluginous: Reading traces in the Brockhaus *Taschenbuch der Geologie*, where Celan underlined *eisenschüssige*, meaning "ferrous" or "ferruginous," and used it to create the neologism "steeluginous."

Palmfarne | palm ferns: Also from the Brockhaus. Cycads, of the biological division *Cicadophyta*, are gymnosperm seed plants typically characterized by a stout and woody trunk with a crown of large, hard, and stiff evergreen leaves.

Castrup: Could refer to Copenhagen airport, Kastrup (given some of the other images in the poem); could also refer to a town in the Ruhr region of Germany, called Castrop(-Rauxel), though that would mean a spelling error by Celan, which Wiedemann suggests could be willed, in that Celan may have consciously wanted an interior rhyme with *Vortrupp* (BW, p. 855). Near Castrop there are marl pits in which fossil remains have been found.

Vortrupp | vanguard troop: Word underlined by Celan in his copy of the German translation of Joyce's *Ulysses* (vol. 2, p. 101). I have not been able to verify original word.

Flughaut | flightskin: The term occurs in Brockhaus, and refers to the alar membranes of the pterosaurians, the first vertebrates to fly (technically, like bats today) during the Jurassic period. The word was already underlined by Celan in Jean Paul, though there it was associated with butterflies.

"Und Kraft und Schmerz" | *"And strength and pain"*
July 27, 1968, Paris, rue Tournefort. In the last draft the poem is diagonally struck out, with a question mark in the top right-hand corner. In her collected volume, Wiedemann has restored the poem, using its penultimate, uncrossed-out version, though restoring a line Celan had crossed out in that one: "your typhus, Tanja."

Hall-Schalt- / Jahre | jubilee-leap- / years: 1968 was a leap year; *Hall* also means "sound." For *Halljahr*, see "Die fleißigen" | "The industrious" (p. 152), with the lines: "The not-to-be-deciphered / jubilee."

Tanja: Tanja Adler (Sternberg, by marriage) was a friend of Celan's from university days in Czernowitz who emigrated to the Soviet Union, where she married, and then returned to Czernowitz. Celan had gotten back in touch with her in 1962. He had dedicated the 1941 poem "Gemurmel der Toten" ("Mutterings of the Dead") to her.

"Miterhoben" | "Raised together"
July 28, 1968, Paris, rue Tournefort.

seine Aura | his aura: Leads back to Celan's reading of Walter Benjamin during the summer of 1968. Compare "On Some Motifs in Baudelaire," specifically: "If we think of the associations which, at home in the *mémoire involontaire*, seek to cluster around an object of perception, and if we call those associations the aura of that object, then the aura attaching to the object of a perception corresponds precisely to the experience [*Erfahrung*] which, in the case of an object of use, inscribes itself as long practice" (WBSW, vol. 4, p. 337). Lefebvre notes that "aura" is not without relationship to the "halo" (*Hof*) of Husserlian phenomenology of the consciousness of time or to the Baudelairian "correspondences."

On the same day Celan wrote an uncollected poem that also uses the word "aura":

YOU MICHAELA,
and as you talk-
stammer, there:

You, aura,
and big-lipped like you,
Be-yidst, res-
ponded, Jewess,

you, knowing-unknowing,
at the point of indifference
of the reflexion
the bitter-planet spoke
overprecise.

Quentchen | quantum: Originally from Latin, *quintus*, "fifth," has come to mean "a tiny part," easily, nearly homophonically, rendered in English as "quantum," though that loses the older connection of the German term to alchemical lore. (Also a measure, as in: "For the sake of experiment I took for several days four *quentschen* [that is, two drams] of good Cinchona twice a day.")

"Steinschlag" | *"Falling rocks"*
August 10, 1968, Paris.

heimstehen in seine | home-standing into: Lefebvre notes regarding the grammatical form of the German that "the accusative, as often in Celan, signals the dynamic force and the historicity of what in all appearance stands immobile and fixed (you could call this a syntactic oxymoron)" (PDN, p. 149).

ausschreitende | striding: See also title/opening line of the next poem.

"Ich schreite" | *"I stride across"*
Written probably on August 16, 1968, though reworked in November of that year while Celan was hospitalized in Épinay-sur-Orge for psychiatric treatment. At that point he added the end line "Eric, live strong and large," cut out of the final manuscript version.

kalben | calf: The verb covers two domains, (1) biological: a cow giving birth to a calf, and (2) geological: the sudden breaking away of a mass of ice from a glacier, giving birth to icebergs.

irgendein Toter | a, any, dead one: Possible reference to François, the dead son, as the whole poem seems to be a bitter attack on his estranged wife, Gisèle.

"Leuchtstäbe" | *"Lightrods"*
Composed on August 21, 1968, the night Warsaw Pact troops occupied Czechoslovakia, putting an end to the so-called Prague Spring.

Leuchtstäbe | lightrods: This term was for a while considered as a possible title for this (and for the next) volume of poems. The German *stab* (rod) has also the connotation of "letter," as in *Buchstab*. It also suggests neon tubes and could possibly be connected to an article in the FAZ of that day on blindness (see next poem).

grätschen | straddle: To spread the legs wide laterally, as when hopping over an aggressive defense in soccer.

Klöten | ballocks: Reading trace in Celan's German translation of Joyce's *Ulysses*, where he circled: "ZOE: (Turns) Ask my ballocks that I haven't got"

(p. 667), and an earlier mark for: "ZOE: How's the nuts? BLOOM: Offside. Curiously they are on the right" (p. 599 of the 1966 Bodley Head edition). The German translation uses the word *Klöten* on both occasion.

ZK: *Zentralkomitee*, literally, "Central Committee." I prefer to leave the German *ZK*, especially as it ghosts its infamous reverse, *KZ* (*Konzentrationslager*, "concentration camp").

Evidenz | evidence: In May 1968, Celan had noted: "There is no evidence anymore | Margarete Susman, über Kafka, | p. 360." (Bertrand Badiou pointed this out.) Celan is referring to a 1929 essay by Susman, "Das Hiob-Problem by Franz Kafka," reprinted in 1954 under the title "Früheste Deutung Franz Kafkas," in her *Gestalten und Kreise* (Stuttgart/Konstanz/Zurich: Diana Verlag, 1954), p. 355. The longer sentence, quoted by Wiedemann, is: "The last link to a world that is shared, ordered according to ideas: memory, is torn— there is no evidence anymore; that is, the illumination of things is no longer proof of their Being in truth; there is only presence: irrefutable, overpowering presence" (BW, p. 858).

"Ein Leseast" | *"One reading branch"*
A range of the vocabulary and information of this poem of August 21–22, 1968, comes from several articles from the Nature and Science section of the FAZ of August 21, 1968, such as N. Wyss's "Noch keine brauchbaren Seehilfen für Blinde" (No useful visual aids yet for blind people), Beatrice Flad-Schnorrenberg's "Wo sitzt die Intelligenz der Vögel?" (Where is the seat of birds' intelligence?), and the article "Basaltisches Mondgestein" (Basalt moon rocks) signed R. (BW, pp. 858–59; PDN, pp. 151–53). At some point *Leseast* was considered as possible title for the volume as a whole.

Leseast | reading branch . . . Stirnhaut | forehead skin: N. Wyss mentions inconclusive experiments toward a transistorized device that would send photoelectric impulses to the brain through electrodes implanted above the eyes, in the skin of the forehead, via the ophtalmic branch (*Ast*) of the trigeminal nerve.

Lichtquelle | light source: N. Wyss: "The device was tried out on a largish number of blind people; of light sources it transmits a blurred, uncolored image."

Wirtsgewebe | host-tissue: Another FAZ article, "Immunological Mimicry," signed "R.F.," says: "In a sort of immunological mimicry the worms protect themselves against their hosts' immunological defense reactions through the incorporation of host tissue."

Rückstreu-Sonden | backscatter-probes: *Surveyor 5* (launched September 8, 1967; landed on the moon September 11, 1967) carried a miniature chemical analysis lab with an alpha particle backscatter device used to determine that the lunar surface soil consisted of basaltic rock.

Hornhautüber- / zogner | Cornea-covered: Reading traces in another FAZ article of that day: "Hornhautprothesen" (Cornea prostheses), stating that such prostheses so much improved the vision of seven blind adults that they could care for themselves again.

The sixth stanza contains allusions to Celan's suicide attempt of the previous year, when he tried to stab himself, missing the heart but seriously wounding his lung. The postcard seems to refer (BW, p. 859) to a New Year's postcard he had received from František Fabian from Radio Pilsen, and further to a newspaper article Celan read that mentioned the silencing of the radio station that had backed Alexander Dubček even as the Soviets crushed the Prague Spring.

"Zerr dir" | *"Tear your"*
August 23, 1968

pack deinen Schuh rein | pack your shoe into: Possible reference to Ingeborg Bachmann's poem "Die gestundete Zeit": "Sie dich nicht um. / Schnür deinen Schuh." (Don't look back. / Lace up your shoe.) (In *Werke*, edited by Christine Koschel, Inge von Weidenbaum, and Clemens Münster [Munich/ Zurich: Piper Verlag, 1978], 1:37.)

Rauschelbeeräugige | mezery-eyed: *Rauschelbeere* does not exist, though *Rauschbeere* does and corresponds to *Vaccinium uliginosum* (our bog bilberry or northern bilberry) and/or to *Daphne mezereum*, which produces a red, very toxic berry, at home in the subalpine vegetation zone of Germany and Austria.

"Kalk-Krokus" | *"Chalk-crocus"*
August 24, 1968.

In July 1969 Celan sent this poem to Franz Wurm in Prague—thus by the Vltava River; in German, the Moldau—and, citing the end of Kafka's story "An Imperial Message," writes: "You may show both, 'when evening comes,' to the city of Prague and your friends there—if your index finger agrees" (PC/FW, #162).

Delle Dasein | Dasein Dent: Celan has the note "Delle = flache Vertiefung; Beule" in Weigert (plus underlinings): "die zügigen Faltenbahnen, dellen und wellen sich wie natürlicher Stoff" (the fast fold plications, dent and wave like natural matter).

"Es sind schon" | *"The cables are"*
August 24, 1968. On that date FAZ carried an article on "Futurism in city building," speaking of the "Entlastungsstadt Perlach für München," that is, Perlach as "decongestion town" for Munich.

"In den Einstiegluken" | *"In the access hatches"*
August 26, 1968. Underlying this poem are *Der Spiegel* (#35/1968) and that day's FAZ reporting on events in Czechoslovakia.

In den Einstiegluken | In the access hatches . . . Spürgeräte | detectors: The *Spiegel* story relates how young men would climb up on the Russian tanks and drop political tracts in Russian rather than Molotov cocktails into the access hatches. The article also mentions how the Russians tried to use detectors to locate the Czech radio stations that were set up in a number of towns and cities after the Russian invasion and were constantly moved to escape being detected.

Krähe | crow: A bird related to the jackdaw, that is, Kafka's name in Czech, and to the blackbird, *Amsel* in German, close to Celan's original name, Antschel.

halbmast | halfmast: The main article in *Der Spiegel* (p. 24) reports that "in Znaim the inhabitants flew the flags at half-mast or replaced them with a black one."

"Und jetzt" | *"And now"*
August 27, 1968. The poem braids events in Czechoslovakia and a reference to Walter Benjamin's "Origin of German Tragic Drama," in the expression "gesamtbarock" | "all-baroque."

Lametta | tinsel: The German word refers to the shiny decorations on Christmas trees and here designates ironically the decorations on high military officers' uniforms. The stanza, Lefebvre suggests (PDN, p. 156), refers to the "pseudo-accords signed under duress by the Communist parties (Dubček among them) and the militaro-political dignitaries."

Kommissur | commissure: See my comments pp. 537–38.

"Schnellfeuer-Perihel" | *"Rapidfire-perihelion"*
August 27, 1968. Second poem of the day. The title draws on the *Spiegel* article of August 27, 1968, "The Conjurors of Empty Fists," which says: "On Thursday morning, after a night filled with light flares and the rataplan of rapid fire guns . . ." (p. 22).

Perihel | perihelion: From Greek *peri* (near) and *helios* (sun); the point in the orbit of a planet where it is nearest to the sun.

-Pawlatschen | -pawlatschen: From the Czech word *pavlač*, it refers to the makeshift stages put up by street singers in Vienna. As a reference to popular (street) theater it may (Lefebvre suggests) connect to Celan's reference to Benjamin's "baroque" in the previous poem.

"Wir Übertieften" | *"We the overdeepened"*
August 28, 1968. Vocabulary shows traces of Celan's Brockhaus geological dictionary.

Übertieften | overdeepened: Brockhaus gives the noun *Übertiefung*, describing glacial erosion and deepening of the bedrock of glaciers that can reach several hundred yards under the tongue of larger glaciers, less so on Firnfeld glaciers and small glacier spots. The second poem of the volume *Die Niemandsrose* is titled "Das Wort vom Zur-Tiefe-Gehn," which Joachim Neugroschel translated as "The word of going-to-the-depth." That poem was a present for Gisèle Celan-Lestrange, and the image links to a Georg Heym poem they had read together in the early fifties; the first stanza of the Heym poem says: "Your eyelashes, the long ones, / of your eyes, the dark water, / let me dive into it, / let me go into the depth" ("Laß mich zur Tiefe gehn") (BW, p. 673).

Augenabdruck | eye imprint . . . Steinkern | rock- / kernel: Brockhaus: "But when the solid particles are dissolved and carried away, so that a hollow chamber is created inside the rock, its interior surface will at times show a faithful, though negative outer form of the erstwhile organism, the imprint.—If after the removal of the soft parts the interior of embedded mussel or snail shells is filled up, that creates a rock kernel" (BW, p. 865).

"Hinter Schläfensplittern" | *"Behind the templesplinters"*
Written August 31, 1968, in the Jardin des Plantes, not far from Celan's home in the rue Tournefort, the street named after a botanist who had been for a time in the garden's employ. The Jardin des Plantes is well-known in German literature, because Rilke wrote some of his best-known poems there—"The Panther," subtitled "In the Jardin des Plantes," among others. See also Franz Wurm's poem "An Ecksteinen, in Pflanzenbüchern," dedicated to Paul Celan, of August 13, 1968, included in his letter of August 24, and Celan's response on August 27 (PC/FW, pp. 164–66).

der Ort, wo du herkommst | the place you come from: Franz Wurm hailed from Prague.

"Bergung" | *"Rescue"*
September 2, 1968. First poem of the day on which he also wrote "Mandelnde" | "Almonding you," which opens the second cycle of *Timestead* (p. 428). That days's FAZ has an article titled "8.222 Tote geborgen" (8,222 dead rescued), in relation to the earthquake in Iran.

Cor- / respondenz | cor- / respondence ... Sebstherz | selfheart ... Abstoß | rejection: See article in the same FAZ on four heart-transplant operations in South Africa and the phenomenon of transplant rejection.

"Das gedunkelte" | *"The darkened"*
September 5, 1968, in his office on rue d'Ulm.

Buhne | portcullis: Reading trace in Albert Vigoleis Thelen, *Die Insel des zweiten Gesichts*. Celan had marked the passage that reads: "while you lie supine and despondent on the truss of a youth wasted wandering" (p. 258).

Kolbenschlag | gunbutt blow: The previous day's FAZ had an article on the musical program for early 1969 in West Berlin, *From Ulysses to Rosa Luxemburg*, in which Rosa Luxemburg, who had been assassinated by blows from a gun butt, was to be the central figure.

"Die Ewigkeit" | *"Eternity"*
October 18, 1968, in his office in rue d'Ulm. See several other poems in Celan's oeuvre with the same or similar titles.

ZEITGEHÖFT | TIMESTEAD

Celan wrote the fifty poems that make up this, the final posthumous volume, between September 2, 1968, and February 25, 1970. It was published by Suhrkamp Verlag in 1976 without indication of who edited the volume. None of the poems had been published or okayed for publication by Celan himself. The book is put together from three sheafs of poems that contain typed versions of the poems, though at times with handwritten corrections or additions (BW, p. 865). The title of the volume was that of the first cycle. The second cycle gathers the poems Celan wrote in the context of his October 1969 Israel trip organized by Czernowitz friends (David Seidman, professor of French language and literature at Tel Aviv University, and Celan's last lover, Ilana Shmueli). The Jerusalem stay lasted only seventeen days, as Celan broke off the journey suddenly and returned to Paris. The final short cycle is made up of the last seven poems written by Celan between February and mid-April 1970.

Title: See note for *Zeithof* and Edmund Husserl citations above, pages 566–67. James K. Lyon sees another possible origin for the word *Zeitgehöft*, as an echo from the Rilke poem "Ausgesetzt auf den Bergen des Herzens," which contains the lines: "die letzte Ortschaft der Worte . . . / noch ein letztes / Gehöft von Gefühl" | "the last place of the words . . . / one last farmstead of feeling" (Colin, *Argumentum e Silencio*, p. 203).

I

"Wanderstaude, du fängst dir" | *"Nomadforb, you catch yourself"*
February 25, 1969–January 21, 1970. Celan joined his own French interlinear translation when he sent a handwritten version of the poem to his wife on February 15, 1969, probably via his son Eric (PC/GCL, #639).
Wanderstaude | Nomadforb: According to the Jewish calendar, on this day (seventh of Adar) Moses's birth and death days were remembered. Wiedemann connects the poem to this feast, recalling that Moses "had received a wonder-making rod from God that served him as mark of recognition and as instru-

ment for the feats he was to accomplish." (Exod. 4:2–4 reads: "and the LORD said unto him, What is that in thine hand? And he said, A rod. / And he said, Cast it on the ground. And he cast it on the ground, and it became a serpent; and Moses fled from before it. / And the LORD said unto Moses, Put forth thine hand, and take it by the tail. And he put forth his hand, and caught it, and it became a rod in his hand.") Sieghild Bogumil-Notz suggests that with this first image of *Zeitgehöft* | *Timestead* (as with most images in this, his last book), Celan "refers to and negates earlier images and statements," in this case the word *Wandergestalt* (BW, p. 34) from the 1946 poem "Dunkles Aug im September" | "Dark eye in September," as well as the whole theme of wandering, which appears at least sixteen times via variations on the word *wandern* in the oeuvre.

Next to the draft of the poem there are, however, also the following notes by Celan: "Pindar: singer of sewed verses: Rhapsode," and below that: "Rhapsode: singer to the rod [*Sänger zum Stabe*]."

Blendung | blinding: The German word can mean both "to make blind" and "to dazzle." Bernhard Böschenstein sees in the rod and the blinding an Oedipal scene/seen "évoqué et révoqué en même temps" (evoked and revoked simultaneously). He goes on to say: "This blind man of today sees what what needs to be seen thanks to his state for which he is himself responsible. His rod is also that of the rhapsode, but his song, because it is broken, brings the clarity that only Apollo had been able to bring to Oedipus. The labor of the poet today consists in making himself blind in order to make himself a seer [*voyant*]" (C-J, pp. 151–52).

"Gehässige Monde" | "Spiteful moons"

March 21, 1969, Paris. Celan joined his own French interlinear translation when he sent a handwritten version of the poem to his wife, probably via his son Eric (PC/GCL, #642), which moved GCL to create a watercolor by the same title (illustration XII in PC/GCL-French, vol. 2).

"Gold" | "Gold"

April 12, 1969, Paris/Dampierre-en-Burly, where Celan spent weekends at that time in the house of his friends Edmond and Rita Lutrand.

Platanenstrünke | plane-tree trunks: With the chestnut tree, one of Celan's talismanic trees; see PC/GCL, #27, n. 2.

"Von der sinkenden Walstirn" | *"From the sinking whale forehead"*
May 5, 1969, Paris.

"Du liegst hinaus" | *"You outlier"*
May 9, 1969, Paris, rue d'Ulm.

"Das seidenverhangene Nirgend" | *"The silkbedecked Nowhere"*
June 4, 1969, Paris, rue d'Ulm.

"Die Weinbergsmauer erstürmt" | *"The vineyardwall assailed"*
June 9, 1969, Paris, rue d'Ulm.

"Erst wenn ich dich" | *"Only when I touch"*
June 25, 1969, Paris, rue d'Ulm.
Spät- / sinnigem | late- / meanings: Constructed from the German word *Spürsinn* (flair, instinct, ability, nose [for a dog]).
Zeithöfen | timehalos: See pp. 566–67.

"In der fernsten" | *"In the remotest"*
July 18–19, 1969, Paris, rue d'Ulm.
traumfaserverstärkt | dreamfiberreinforced: See the article "Die Garderobe der Raumfahrer" (The wardrobe of the astronauts) in the FAZ of that day, which speaks of a *glasfaserverstärkten*, "fiberglass-reinforced," protection layer for the helmets.
Freizeichen | freesign: Celan had thought at some point of using this word as overall title of the volume.

"Eingeschossen" | *"Inserted into"*
July 19, 1969, Paris, rue d'Ulm. Celan sent this poem and "Chalk-crocus" (p. 388) to Franz Wurm in Prague (PC/FW, #162) in his letter referring to the moon landing of July 20, comparing it to his own "landing" in his new apartment on avenue Émile Zola: "I migrated [*übersiedelte*] drop by drop, braindrop by braindrop, one of these days I will indeed land in the new apartment and start the prospecting [*zu schürfen beginnen*]." The poem draws for some of its images on an article on the return flight of the command module, which was *eingeschossen*, "inserted," into the orbit of the command spacecraft.

Ungrund | unground: an older German word for the more usual *Abgrund*, "abyss." Here it may play on the opposition of cosmic space (where the moon landing takes place) and the ground, with a rhyme on his well-known image from the Meridian speech, where Lenz wants to walk on his head so as to have the abyss beneath him. Another possible direction to explore is the term *Ungrund* in the mystical teachings of Jacob Boehme, as explicated by Nicolas Berdiaev in his "Etude I. The Teaching About the Ungrund and Freedom": "The mysterious teaching of Boehme about the Ungrund, about the abyss, without foundation, dark and irrational, prior to being, is an attempt to provide and [*sic*] answer to the basic question of all questions, the question concerning the origin of the world and of the arising of evil. The whole teaching of Boehme about the Ungrund is so interwoven with the teaching concerning freedom, that it is impossible to separate them, for this is all part and parcel of the same teaching. And I am inclined to interpret the Ungrund, as a primordial meonic freedom, indeterminate even by God" (www.berdyaev.com /berdiaev/berd_lib/1930_349.html#q).

If this mystical direction is correct, then the "Smaragdbahn" | "emerald-trajectory" of the second line could refer back to the Tabula Smaragdina, the Emerald Tablet, a core mystical and alchemical treatise supposedly composed and handed down by the mythical Hermes Trismegistus, and now believed to date back to the sixth to eighth century C.E. Celan, we know, had an abiding interest in alchemy.

"Alle die Schlafgestalten, kristallin" | *"All the sleepfigures, crystalline"*
July 23, 1969, Paris, place de la Contrescarpe.

"Zwei Sehwülste, zwei" | *"Two sightbulges, two"*
July 30, 1969, Paris, rue d'Ulm.
Narbennähte | scarseams: as *Narbennaht*, "scarseam," considered at one point as possible title for the volume *Lightduress*.

"Vor mein" | *"Before my"*
August 3, 1969, Paris, rue d'Ulm.
kommt die Hand zu stehn | the hand comes to stand ... im Kreis, den ich zog | in the circle I drew: Wiedemann (BW, p. 869) points to Celan's unpub-

lished translations of Romanian poet Nina Cassian's poem "Jocul vu lumina," which says: "I draw a yellow circle / on the white sheet, / and the sun comes and sits on your hands" (Jürgen Lehmann and Christine Ivanović, eds., *Stationen* [Heidelberg, 1997], p. 156).

"Du wirfst mir" | *"You throw gold"*
August 4, 1969, Paris, rue Tournefort. On this day Celan took off his wedding ring and sealed it in a dated envelope (BW, p. 869).

"Das Flüsterhaus" | *"The whisperhouse"*
August 29, 1969, written in Alpnachstad on Lake Lucerne in Switzerland, where Celan holidayed from August 16 to August 31.
 den Enge-Laut ein, // für die Lallstufe | fricatives, // the lallation-stage: Nonidentified reading note in the notebook that also holds early drafts and fragments of the poem: "die vorsprachliche Lallstufe / Verschluß- und Enge-laute" (the prelanguage lallation-stage / plosives and fricatives).

"Kleine Nacht" | *"Little night"*
September 5, 1969, Paris, rue Tournefort.

"An die Haltlosigkeiten" | *"To huddle against"*
September 6, 1969, Paris, avenue Émile Zola. The first poem written there, probably on a visit to the new apartment, where he would start living, however, only on November 6, 1969. See the poem "Du gleißende" | "You, nitid," p. 434, and the commentary on that poem, p. 620.
 Sudelheften | rough books: A first draft of the poem was jotted down in a *Sudelheft* (a rough book), from *sudeln* (to make a mess), *Sudelei* (a mess, slovenly work). Georg Christoph Lichtenberg used to call his notebooks *Sudelbücher*.

"Ich albere" | *"I fool around"*
September 12, 1969. Written in Dampierre-en-Burly on the eve of Rosh Hashanah. Marked as the first poem of that day, a day on which he also wrote the two following poems. For location, see commentary for "Gold," page 611.

"Dein Uhrengesicht" | *"Your clockface"*
September 12, 1969. Written in Dampierre-en-Burly on the eve of Rosh Hashanah.

"Ich lotse dich" | *"I pilot you"*
September 12, 1969. Written in Dampierre-en-Burly on the eve of Rosh Hashanah.

"Meine" | *"My"*
September 13, 1969. Written in Dampierre-en-Burly. First day of Rosh Hashanah.

"Ein Stern" | *"A star"*
September 17, 1969, Paris, rue d'Ulm. First poem of that day. On top of the first draft of the poem, Celan wrote: "Mon judaïsme: ce que je / reconnais encore dans / les débris de mon existence" (My Judaism: what I still recognize among the wreckage of my existence) (BA, vol. 14, p. 271).

"Kleines Wurzelgeträum" | *"Little rootdreamings"*
September 17, 1969, Paris, rue d'Ulm. Marked as second poem of that day.

II. (JERUSALEM CYCLE)

"Mandelnde" | *"Almonding you"*
September 2, 1968, Paris, rue Tournefort. Written on the same day as "Bergung" | "Rescue" (p. 396), it is the only poem in the volume that is earlier than all the other poems, which are arranged chronologically as written, between February 1969 and April 1970. Given the core image of the poem, the almond, Celan's decision to use it as the opening poem of a cycle that gathers all the poems he wrote in relation to his visit to Israel, and more specifically, Jerusalem, is obvious. In this volume see also "almondeye" in "Sight threads, sense threads," page 86, and "the almond-testicle" in "Me too," page 298.

Mandelnde | almonding: A core image of Celan's work, reaching back to the 1944 poem "Nähe der Gräber" with the stanza: "And doesn't the God with the flowering rod / climb up the hill, climb down the hill." Maybe the most explicit working of the theme is the poem "Count the almonds," here in Jerome Rothenberg's translation (PCS, p. 49):

Count the almonds,
count what was bitter and kept you awake,
count me in with them:

I searched for your eye which broke open and nobody saw you,

I spun that mysterious thread,

down which the dew that you dreamed

slithered into a pitcher,

kept from harm by a word found in nobody's heart.

There you first came into a name that was yours,

sure of foot you advanced on yourself,

the clappers swung free in your silence's belltower,

the one who had heard it laid into you,

the one who was dead laid a hand on you too,

and threefold you moved through the evening.

Make me bitter.

Count me in with the almonds.

The Old Testament has a range of references worth quoting (here, in the *Jewish Publication Society Bible*):

Num. 17:20: "And it shall come to pass, that the man whom I shall choose, his rod shall bud; and I will make to cease from Me the murmurings of the children of Israel, which they murmur against you"; 17:23: "And it came to pass on the morrow, that Moses went into the tent of the testimony; and, behold, the rod of Aaron for the house of Levi was budded, and put forth buds, and bloomed blossoms, and bore ripe almonds."

Jer. 1:11–12: "Moreover the word of the LORD came unto me, saying: 'Jeremiah, what seest thou?' And I said: 'I see a rod of an almond-tree.'"

Eccles. 12:5: "Also when they shall be afraid of that which is high, and terrors shall be in the way; and the almond-tree shall blossom, and the grasshopper shall drag itself along, and the caperberry shall fail; because man goeth to his long home, and the mourners go about the streets."

Celan always spelled the name of his poet "brother" Osip Mandelstam with a double final *m*—as if to insist on the meaning *stamm* (tribe, family, descendance) in the context of the almond, thus emphasizing the Jewish descendance of that poet, of the poet.

The almond is also the bitter fruit, and that bitterness is chemically linked to cyanhydric acid, in turn connected to Zyklon B, the gas used in the death chambers of the Nazi extermination camps.

Hachnissini | *Hachnisini*: Opening word of Chaim Nachman Bialik's poem "Hachnisini Tachat Knafech" (Shelter me under your wing), first published in 1905. Bialik (1873–1934), who wrote in Hebrew and Yiddish, is recognized as one of the fathers of modern Hebrew literature. Born in Russia into a traditional Jewish household, he received a traditional Jewish religious education but also explored European literature. He was later to translate work by a range of major European authors (Schiller, Shakespeare, Cervantes, Heine, and others) into Hebrew. He lived for many years in Odessa, a city important in Celan's universe, linking to his own youth, and to Osip Mandelstam.

Hachnisini means literally "take me in," "take me under your wing," "shelter me," and here, as the last word before the Jerusalem cycle, the poet's quest for hospitality is clear. Ilana Shmueli remembers an occasion in Jerusalem: "Often [Celan] would look for new words in Hebrew or tried to remember old ones, together we recited the little poem by Chaim Nachman, "Hachnisini," that he still knew by heart, though he no longer understood it completely. I had to translate it word for word for him. Then he would research the roots of the Hebrew words, that fascinated him again and again" (IS, p. 26).

"Es stand" | *"It stood"*

October 17, 1969, Paris, rue d'Ulm. On October 20 he sent this poem and "Almonding you" to Shmueli.

Es stand | It stood: the concept of standing upright, already noted in "Wirk nicht voraus" | "Do not work ahead" (pp. 316 and 575). See also my introduction to PCS (p. 6).

In her memoir, *Sag, daß Jerusalem ist*, Ilana Shmueli writes (IS, p. 33):

"And now our feet stand in your gates, Jerusalem"; "It stands" and "I stood"—*Stehen*: a meaningful word that demanded its place in all of his poems, in his letters and in our conversations. It meant: to stand forcefully, to stand against, to stand into something, to stand for oneself or to stand with and for someone else. And it also meant: "geschrieben stehn | to stand written." I stood in You "written" as in a book, in the You—in Jerusalem . . .

"on your lip: the figsplitter // it stood," soft and hard, real, a "splinter," that can also wound, despite the sweetness. Jerusalem stood, and above us stood the bright scent of pines, and I stood in you: I have arrived, the wish, the query "Hasnisini" has been fulfilled.

Dänenschiff | Daneship: On the morning of October 9, 1969, Shmueli and Celan visited the momument of the Daneship on Kikar Denya (Denmark Square), erected in remembrance of the many Danes who, in October 1943, had helped as many as seven thousand Jews to safety in Sweden in their fishing and leisure boats. See also the poem "Frihed" (p. 68).

"Die Glut" | *"The swelter"*
October 21, 1969, Paris, rue d'Ulm.

Shmueli (IS, p. 34) explains that the Jerusalem visit happened on a very hot day—October 9, 1969—on which the sweltering *Khamsin*, or desert wind, blew.

Absaloms Grab | Absalom's tomb: "Absalom's Tomb is the most impressive and complete of the ancient tombs of wealthy Jewish families that lived in Jerusalem in Second Temple times . . . A popular Jewish tradition associates the monument with Absalom, King David's rebellious son, of whom the Bible says: 'Now Absalom in his life-time had taken and reared up for himself the pillar, which is in the king's dale; for he said: "I have no son to keep my name in remembrance"; and he called the pillar after his own name; and it is called Absalom's monument unto this day' (2 Samuel 18:18). The identification is, of course, erroneous, for the monument was built about one thousand years after the time of Absalom. Nevertheless, it was customary in Jerusalem . . . for whoever passed by the monument to throw a stone at it, as if to proclaim the fate of a rebellious son." (Jerusalem Archaeological Park website, www.arch park.org.il/article.asp?id=117)

Shmueli writes (IS, p. 25): "Walked slowly down along the Jewish cemetery, past the Mary Magdalene church with its onion domes, the Garden of Gethsemane, which we did not enter—down to 'Absalom's tomb,'—Noon swelter—donkeys and mules braying."

Absalom was the disobedient son of King David, who after his rebellion died ignominiously while fleeing—so that now the father had to lament the son's death. Writes Otto Pöggeler: "When Celan makes connections to this story, we may remember the father-son conflict that was renewed in the Western world in the late 60s, but also that Celan—married to a Christian—according to strict Jewish belief did not have a son. Celan's 'Mal' [mark, (tomb)stone, mausoleum, etc.] his poetic oeuvre, is, like the ass's bray, a protest against the swelter and burden of this world, and yet this scream unites the poet with his You, the Shekina" (STEIN, p. 69).

"Wir, die wie der Strandhafer Wahren" | *"We who like the sea oats guard"*
October 31, 1969, Dampierre-en-Burly.

Strandhafer | sea oats: See "Weißgrau" | "Whitegray" (p. 8).

N'we Awiwim | Neve Avivim: A residential neighborhood of Tel Aviv, located in the northwestern part of the city, by the sea; Celan stayed there at the house of friends.

der ungeküßte / Stein einer Klage | the unkissed / stone of a complaint: On October 9, 1969, Celan had very briefly visited the Wailing Wall, which pious Jews traditionally kiss. Shmueli remembers him saying "no excavations, please" (IS, p. 25).

"Ein Ring, zum Bogenspannen" / *"A ring, for bowdrawing"*
November 2, 1969, Dampierre-en-Burly.

"Das Leuchten" | *"The radiance"*
November 7, 1969. Café le Royal, boulevard de Port-Royal, Paris. He sent this poem the same day to Shmueli and in the accompanying letter speaks of his fears: "The news of last night, Nasser's speech, which said war against Israel was the Arabs' only way, —I know, all of you in Israel, or at least very many of you, bear that with equanimity, and something of this equanimity has communciated itself, you know that, to me as well; but you must know . . . that my thinking of Israel is also a deep worry about Israel" (PC/IS, p. 21).

Abu Tor: (literally "Father of the Bull") a mixed Jewish and Arab neighborhood in eastern Jerusalem, south of the Old City and with the Valley of Hinnom to its north. During the Ayyubid period, this area was assigned to an officer in Saladin's army called Sheikh Ahmed et Toreh (Sheikh Ahmed of the bull) or Abu Tor (the man with the bull, or the father of the bull), as he was said to have accompanied Saladin riding on a bull.

Shmueli noted: "Bethlehem in the afternoon (October 9, 1969), past the Mar Elias monastery, Rachel's tomb, the Church of the Nativity. On the way back to Jerusalem: the light—Abu Tor, the view toward the Valley of Hinnom (Moloch's altars)—the light" (IS, p. 25).

Goldboje | goldbuoy: The golden dome of the Omar mosque can be seen in the distance from Abu Tor. Celan wrote to Shmueli on November 26, 1969: "I unfurl Jerusalem. I see the paths we walked down and up, not all, but some of them. Who was leading us, who and what? / The golden buoy must rise up so that the danger is defeated" (PC/IS, p. 46). And already in his letter of November 10, 1969: "Have no fear, love: I will never turn away from you, I remain turned toward you, always. The golden buoy knows it—it too" (PC/IS, p. 25).

"Du gleißende" | *"You, nitid"*
Night of November 7–8, 1969, Paris, at 6, avenue Émile Zola, Paris. On November 6, Celan had finally, after many problems, moved into what would be his last dwelling, a three-room apartment in the fifteenth arrondissement, a mere five-minute walk from the Pont Mirabeau, from which he would jump most probably on the night of April 19–20, 1970.

wildenzt | turn gamy: Wiedemann points to reading traces in the Thelen book (see also commentary to "Das gedunkelte" | "The darkened," p. 609), which Celan had read in the fifties and which uses the verbal noun *Wildenzen*, and his note in his copy of *L'univers de la parole* by Rolland Renéville, where he annotated the phrase *La délicate gloire des choses faisandées* (The delicate glory of gamy things) with "Se faisander—den Wildgeruch annehmen (haben)/wildenzen, alt werden" (to take on [to have] the smell of game/to taste gamey, to become old) (BW, p. 873).

"Komm" | *"Come"*
November 8, 1969, Paris, rue d'Ulm. A poem of the same title appeared in the volume *Threadsuns*; see page 180.

"Einen Stiefelvoll" | *"A bootful"*
November 9, 1969, Paris, avenue Emile Zola.

"Die Posaunenstelle" | *"The trumpet's part"*
November 16, 1969, Paris, avenue Emile Zola.

As Wiedemann reminds us (BW, p. 874), "trumpet sounds are often connected to destruction in the Bible, as in the fall of the walls of Jericho (Josh. 20) and the trumpet blowing angels of John's Revelation (Rev. 8:2 and 8:13). There and elsewhere they are also the audible signs for the terrifying presence of God in connection with fiery apparitions, see, for example, the story of God's apparition on Mount Sinai: 'And it came to pass on the third day, when it was morning, that there were thunders and lightnings and a thick cloud upon the mount, and the voice of a horn exceeding loud; and all the people that were in the camp trembled' (Ex. 19:16)." Bernhard Böschenstein comments (C-J, pp. 152–53): "In opposition to the title *Schneepart* [Snowpart], and in opposition to the 'snowcomfort' of the next poem, the trumpet's part situates itself in the context of a cosmic conflagration recalling that triggered by the six angels of the apocalypse blowing on the trumpet so as to destroy earth and its inhabitants. The 'timehole' signals the destruction of that which is subjected to time, it suspends the text to the benefit of an empty text that evokes, with the annulment of time, the hearing of a second text, linked to the liberating sound of the seventh angel . . . The torch sent by the angel of the apocalypse burns a hole into time and opens access to a different temporality. There is an end of the world and a new birth."

"Die Pole" | *"The poles"*
November 21, 1969, Paris, avenue Émile Zola. An early version of the poem (BA, vol. 14, p. 321) has the title "Mit Brief und Bild" (With letter and picture) and starts: "Hang the lionsign / before this pretend-door." The title will be lost and the opening lines changed to become material for the following poem, "The kingsway."

Tor / des Erbarmens | Gate / of Mercy: Bernhard Böschenstein comments (C-J, pp. 154–55):

The poles exist in the relationship between two partners as well as in each one of them. This polarity can only be crossed when the state of wakefulness gives way to the sleep state, which implies a forgetting of the self. In that state, death engenders consolation and mystical love crosses the "gate of mercy" that is closed in the state of wakefulness, but only provisionally, a Scheintür [a pretend-door] as long as the Messiah has not come. It is the same golden gate, located next to Gethsemane, near Absalom's tomb, that appears in another poem . . .

There is thus simultaneously the awareness of a closure and the experience of a crossing. The latter presupposes the double forgetting of the self and brings the double recovery: by losing themselves mutually in their partners, the I and the you find themselves again via a detour summed up in the line "I lose you to you" ("ich verliere dich an dich"). This detour that crosses the poles is nothing else than the path described by *The Meridian.* Loss and recovery are linked to the crossing of the poles, to the "breathturns": "something circular that returns to itself across both poles [*Meridian*, p. 12]."

Schneetrost | snowcomfort: "Consolation" would have been the more literal translation, but it does not sound right and also leans too much toward a Christian sense. It is a complex, paradoxical term, as in Celan's work snow is always linked to death, the winter landscape in which his parents perished. But see also the poem in *Breathturn* (p. 2): "YOU MAY confidently / serve me snow." Or the poem "Schneebett" | "Snowbed" in *Sprachgitter*, with the lines: "The snowbed beneath us both, the snowbed. / Crystal by crystal, / timedeep grilled in, we fall, / we fall and lie and fall."

"Der Königsweg" | "The kingsway"
November 23, 1969, Paris, avenue Émile Zola. Celan's forty-ninth birthday, the last he was to celebrate; on that day he sent this poem to Shmueli. See also "Königswut" | "King's rage," page 74, and "the king's caesura" in "Ich trink Wein" | "I drink wine," page 442.

Scheintür | pretend-door: See previous commentary.

Gegen- / Zeichen | counter- / sign: Wiedemann (BW, p. 875) points to Celan's note in the back of his copy of Claude Lévi-Strauss's *La pensée sauvage* (*The Savage Mind*): "Note for Fadensonnen [Threadsuns]: / countersign / in the countersign." The reference is to a marked paragraph on page 14 of the French edition (page 8 of the English edition), itself a citation of an article on reptile lore by F. G. Speck, that reads: "The whole class of reptiles . . . affords no economic benefit to these Indians; they do not eat the flesh of any snakes or batrachians, nor do they make use of other parts except in a very few cases where they serve in the preparation of charms against sickness or sorcery." Celan has noted in the margin: "snakeskin as countermagick."

Löwenzeichen | lionsign: Jerusalem's Lions' Gate is located in the Old City walls and is one of seven open gates. Shmueli (IS, pp. 44–45): "The words come again from the gates of Jerusalem, but what speaks now is the feeling of powerlessness that is burdening his days. The King's way lies behind the 'pretend-door.' No king, no path, no gate of Mercy for him. The 'constellation,' his direction-giving sign, lies keel up and mired in: the lion is deathed about by the countersign."

"Es kommt" | *"There also"*
November 29, 1969, Paris, avenue Émile Zola.

die engere Schneise | the narrower cut: See the poem "Das Stundenglas" | "The hourglass" (p. 38) in *Breathurn*, which speaks of thinking coming down the "Pfingst- / schneise" | "the Pentecost-lane."

erbricht | breached: The German verb has two meanings, one describing an infraction, a breach, the other referring to the act of vomiting, of expelling like vomit, the word thus subsuming in a very Celanian manner two simultaneous movements in opposite directions. Bernhard Böschenstein (C-J, p. 157) suggests that one can give an erotic reading to this poem, as to the previous one, linking it to the sexual symbolism of the Kabbalah, reading the last line thus:

stehenden Male | standing marks: "This stela, erected, phallic can merge with the column that in the Kabbalah represents the just one, the Zaddik. He is in the void, in him flows the vital flux. Through him, everything concentrates around the root of things." Böschenstein refers the reader to Gershom Scholem's *On the Mystical Shape of the Godhead*.

"Ich trink Wein" | *"I drink wine"*
November 29, 1969, Paris, avenue Émile Zola.

zackere | harrow: In Wilhelm Michel's biography *Das Leben Friedrich Hölderlins* (Frankfurt am Main: Insel Verlag, 1967; first published 1940 by Carl

Schünemann), in a letter by Hofrat Gerner, state employee and amateur poet, Celan triply marked the following sentence: "Hölderlin, der immer halbver-rückt ist, zackert auch am Pindar" (Hölderlin, who is always half-crazed, also harrows Pindar [BW, p. 875]). In a letter of November 30, 1969, to Shmueli, Celan writes: "'The other one': Hölderlin is meant here, about whom, when he was translating Pindar, a mean-spirited person wrote that he was 'harrow-ing through' [probably: making a mess of (tinkering with, P.J.)] Pindar—" He then points Shmueli to the poem "Tübingen, Jänner" from the volume *Die Niemandsrose* (PC/IS, p. 49).

Celan himself (as Bertrand Badiou pointed out to Barbara Wiedemann) uses the word in a notebook, writing: "Harrowing Mandelstam, again."

Königszäsur | king's caesura: Hölderlin writes in his *Anmerkungen zum Ödipus* (Annotations to Oedipus): "For the tragic transport is actually empty, and the least restrained.—Thereby, in the rhythmic sequence of the represen-tations wherein the transport presents itself, there becomes necessary what in poetic meter is called caesura, the pure word, the counter-rhythmic rupture— namely, in order to meet the onrushing change of representations at its highest point, in such a manner that not the change of representation but the repre-sentation itself very soon appears" (quoted in WBSW, vol. 1, pp. 340–41).

"According to Hölderlin, the caesura is that place in the Sophoklean tragedies where the seer appears and makes the events transparent according to their background, according to the meeting of the mortals with the gods" (STEIN, p. 70).

kleinen / Gerechten | small / just ones: In his years in Bucharest, Celan translated Paul Éluard's poem cycle *Les petits justes* (The small just ones) as *Die kleinen Gerechten* (BW, p. 876).

aus der Lostrommel fällt / unser Deut | from the lottery drum falls / our doit: Celan to Shmueli: "So make your magic—yes, Ilana, make magic. (I could do it too, once.) And conjure up the word, too, that should fall from the drum with its chances [*Lostrommel*: lottery drum or wheel] choose this word, then I shall set it in place of that 'lot' [*Deut*], which already displeased me when I wrote it. You are cowriting, after all, so come, with it too, with this word. Or should I strike out the drum [*Lostrommel*] and its chances altogether, put it away?" (PC/IS, p. 57). Badiou also points to an unidentified reading note by Celan: "er tat seine Pflicht, aber auch keinen Deut mehr" (he fulfilled his duty, but not a bit more).

Deut | doit: Bernhard Böschenstein comments: "A Deut is a Dutch coin that has no value and simultaneously connects to interpretation (Deutung) while devalorizing it. There are thus two ways of understanding the caesura: it can mark the dividing line between the divine and the human and it can merge with the road that the King of the Jews took before dying." Böschenstein, in a classic gesture of deep Celanian reading, goes on in a near paragrammic way: "If, furthermore, we were to take the first letter of the first verse and the second of the second and so on, we would get INRI, Iesus Nazarenus Rex Iudaeorum. And if we continue that practice from verse five to verse eight, we get the word Niete, also of Dutch origins, and meaning blank ticket in a lottery, thus exactly that Deut that falls from the lottery drum" (C-J, pp. 160–61).

"Es wird" | *"Something shall be"*
December 13, 1969, Paris, avenue Émile Zola.
See commentary on "Vor mein" | "Before my" (pp. 613–14) for connection with a translation of Nina Cassian, whom Celan knew from his Bukovinian days and had met again in December 1969 (and also on the day he wrote the poem) in Paris.

"Das Nichts" | *"Nothingness"*
December 18, 1969, Paris, avenue Émile Zola.

"Im Glockigen" | *"In the bellshape"*
December 29, 1969–January 16, 1970. The following poem was also completed on January 16. Ilana Shmueli was in Paris intermittently from December 23, 1969, to February 3, 1970; Celan gave her a copy of the poems at that time.

"Wie ich" | *"As I"*
January 5–16, 1970.
Ringschatten | ringshadow: See the poem "Du wirfst mir" | "You throw gold" (p. 418), which spoke of the moment Celan took off his wedding band.

"Das Fremde" | *"Strangeness"*

January 20, 1970, Paris, rue d'Ulm. Erich Fried's 1976 essay "Also a Love Poem" in *Die Muse hat Kanten: Aufsätze und Reden zur Literatur*, ed. Volker Kaukoreit (Berlin: Verlag Klaus Wagenbach, 1995) addresses the question of the "comprehensibility" of a late Celan poem, using this poem, which he says is in its language, content, and feeling for life and death unmistakingly Celanian. He writes:

> The first two lines indicate the basic situation: A fate has us in its net. A fate that comes seemingly from outside, that the poet cannot identify and that he cannot completely decipher. Thus, "strangeness." Another power at work in this net is transience, which is our lot and which will eventually destroy us, no matter how we stand in relation to our being in the net, if it remains strange to us, or if we're willing to play along. Transience reaches through us, thus proving that our bodies, and not only them, are not as solid as we sometimes think. This reaching-through-us of transience also has something of the heavy-handed, merciless clampdown of a tyranny or its authorities, the poet feels exposed to in real life. But even this powerful transience (whose power however consists only in passing and in making past [im Vergehen und Vergehenmachen]) has no sense or purpose. It reaches through us "perplexedly." Through us. It is a poem about being exposed, but not a loneliness poem. The "us" does not stand for a collectivity, not for many, but obviously for two. For two deeply connected humans . . .

His analysis of the poem as a complex love poem about a complex, at times contradictory situation goes on for another page or so and concludes: "The poem means so much to me, because it says all this in an incomparably shorter, simpler and more complex way than my explanation is able to do."

zähl meinen Puls | take my pulse: Shmueli indicates that she and Celan had discussed the following lines from the sixth of Elizabeth Barrett Browning's sonnets: "The widest land / Doom takes to part us, leaves thy heart in mine / With pulses that beat double" (1S, p. 56).

"Umlichtet" | *"Illuminated"*
January 22, 1970, Paris, avenue Émile Zola. The last poem written during Ilana Shmueli's stay in Paris, it also concludes the second, or "Jerusalem," cycle of the book.

III

"Fortgesalbt" | *"Salved away"*
February 6, 1970, Paris, rue d'Ulm.

Stein- / weizen | stone- / crop: A mainly Austrian name for various plants of the genus *Sedum*, having fleshy leaves and variously colored flowers, here possibly *sedum acre*, wall pepper.

Skabiose | scabious: *Knautia arvensis*, commonly known as field scabious, a species in the genus *Knautia*, is a perennial plant that grows between twenty-five and a hundred centimeters tall. Its tincture is used in homeopathy as a blood purifier.

"Ortswechsel" | *"Place change"*
February 8, 1970, Paris, avenue Émile Zola.

"Die Welt" | *"The world"*
February 8, 1970, Paris, avenue Émile Zola. Among the last poems Celan sent to Shmueli, writing in the letter of February 16, 1969: "Meanwhile you will have received the poems—all these days I reproached myself for having sent you that terrible poem, 'Welt'; today I know that I was allowed to, that you'd understand it in all its pain, in its full dimension of love" (IS, p. 68).

"Was bittert" | *"What bitters"*
February 7–10, 1970, Paris, avenue Émile Zola.

Hörrinden-Hymnus | auditory cortex-hymn: See reading traces (BW, p. 878) in Reichert/Bleichert book on human physiology, here speaking of the auditory cortex and the neuronal pathways to it.

Daumenschrauben | thumbscrews: See reading traces in the seventeenth-century Spanish baroque writer Baltasar Gracián's writing as translated into German by Schopenhauer, and in which Celan underlined the word *Daumschrauben* in the sentence: "A strange malice often puts such temptations in the path of reason on purpose, to make a voyage of discovery into the interior of the mind, and similarly uses thumbscrews of the secrets [*Daumschrauben der Geheimnisse*] that are able to push even the most reasonable head to extremes."

Zählkammer | counting chamber ... Ringe | rings: Wiedemann locates further reading traces in Reichert/Bleichert, concerning a process of counting blood cells: "A whetted cover glass is pressed on the cleaned counting chamber until at the contact points Newton's rings appear (p. 397)" (BW, p. 878).

"Die gesenkten" | *"The lowered"*

February 20, 1970, Paris, rue d'Ulm. Some of the poem's vocabulary comes from the FAZ of February 18, 1970, where a spread on nature and science was published, including the article "The Dialects of the Elephant Seals," which mentioned *Baumläufer*, "treecreepers," birds of the family *Certhiidae*, small passerine birds, as ellas—in the context of elephant seals, the word *Markierungen*, "markings." Another article, "Universum ohne Anti-Welt" (Universe Without Anti-World) by H. J. Fahr, points to the terms *Strahlengezücht*, "radiationbrood," and *Antimaterie*, "antimatter" (BW, p. 879).

"Krokus" | *"Crocus"*

April 7, 1970, Paris, rue d'Ulm. See the commentaries on the poems "Largo" (pp. 584–85) and "Kalk-Krokus" | "Chalk-crocus" (pp. 606–607).

"Rebleute" | *"Vinegrowers"*

April 1–13, 1970, Paris, avenue Émile Zola.

Paul Celan's last poem.

Select Bibliography

EDITIONS OF PAUL CELAN

SINGLE VOLUMES

Der Sand aus den Urnen. Vienna: Sexl, 1948. Five hundred copies. With lithographs by Edgar Jené.

Mohn und Gedächtnis. Stuttgart: Deutsche Verlags-Anstalt, 1952. Includes twenty-six poems from *Der Sand aus den Urnen*.

Von Schwelle zu Schwelle. Stuttgart: Deutsche Verlags-Anstalt, 1955.

Sprachgitter. Frankfurt am Main: S. Fischer Verlag, 1959.

Die Niemandsrose. Frankfurt am Main: S. Fischer Verlag, 1963.

Atemwende. Frankfurt am Main: Suhrkamp Verlag, 1967. The first cycle of poems, *Atemkristall*, was published in a bibliophile edition of eighty-five copies, with etchings by Gisèle Celan-Lestrange (Paris: Brunidor, 1965).

Fadensonnen. Frankfurt am Main: Suhrkamp Verlag, 1968. The poem "Schlafbrocken," included in this volume, was first published, with an etching by Gisèle Celan-Lestrange, in a bibliophile edition of one hundred copies (Paris: Brunidor, 1967).

Lichtzwang. Frankfurt am Main: Suhrkamp Verlag, 1970. The first fourteen poems in this volume were published under the title *Schwarzmaut* in a bibliophile edition of eighty-five copies, with etchings by Gisèle Celan-Lestrange (Vaduz, Liechtenstein: Brunidor, 1969). The poem "Todtnauberg," also included in this volume, had been published in a bibliophile edition of fifty copies by Brunidor in 1968.

Schneepart. Frankfurt am Main: Suhrkamp Verlag, 1971.

Zeitgehöft. Frankfurt am Main: Suhrkamp Verlag, 1976. (Posthoumous work, this is the one volume not compiled by Paul Celan himself.)

Gedichte 1938–1944. With a preface by Ruth Kraft. Frankfurt am Main: Suhrkamp Verlag, 1986.

COLLECTED VOLUMES

Gedichte in zwei Bänden. Frankfurt am Main: Suhrkamp Verlag, 1975. The first volume of this two-volume edition gathers the books *Mohn und Gedächtnis, Von Schwelle zu Schwelle, Sprachgitter,* and *Die Niemandsrose;* the second volume gathers the books *Atemwende, Fadensonnen, Lichtzwang,* and *Schneepart.* The posthumous volume *Zeitgehöft,* which came out in 1976, was thus not yet available for inclusion.

Gedichte aus dem Nachlaß. Edited by Bertrand Badiou, Claude Rambach, and Barbara Wiedemann. Annotations by Barbara Wiedemann and Bertrand Badiou. Frankfurt am Main: Suhrkamp Verlag, 1997.

Gesammelte Werke in sieben Bänden. Edited by Beda Allemann and Stefan Reichert, in collaboration with Rolf Bücher. Frankfurt am Main: Suhrkamp Verlag, 2000. Volume 1, subtitled *Gedichte 1,* contains *Mohn und Gedächtnis, Von Schwelle zu Schwelle, Sprachgitter,* and *Die Niemandsrose.* Volume 2, subtitled *Gedichte 2,* contains *Atemwende, Fadensonnen, Lichtzwang,* and *Schneepart.* Volume 3, subtitled *Gedichte 3, Prosa, Reden,* contains *Der Sand aus den Urnen, Zeitgehöft, Verstreute Gedichte,* and a number of uncollected poems, consisting of a first section of eleven poems stretching from 1948 to 1967 and a second section, the cycle *Eingedunkelt,* which also contains eleven poems, dating from 1968. The remainder of the volume gathers all the extant prose and speeches. Volume 4, subtitled *Übertragungen 1,* gathers all of Celan's translations from the French. Volume 5, subtitled *Übertragungen 2,* gathers all of Celan's translations from the Russian, English, Italian, Romanian, Portuguese, and Hebrew. (Volumes 4 and 5 gather only the poetry Celan translated, not his prose translations.) Volume 6, subtitled *Das Frühwerk,* gathers chronologically all the early work under the categories "Bukovina," "Bucharest," and "Vienna." Volume 7, subtitled *Gedichte aus dem Nachlaß,* gathers all posthumous poems.

Die Gedichte: Kommentierte Gesamtausgabe in einem Band. Edited and with commentaries by Barbara Wiedemann. Frankfurt am Main: Suhrkamp Verlag, 2003. This is the edition used throughout the present volume. [BW]

Mikrolithen sind's, Steinchen: Die Prosa aus dem Nachlaß. Edited and with commentaries by Barbara Wiedemann and Bertrand Badiou. Frankfurt am Main: Suhrkamp Verlag, 2005.

Paul Celan: Werke: Historisch-kritische Ausgabe. Prepared by Bonner Arbeitsstelle für die Celan-Ausgabe. Frankfurt am Main: Suhrkamp Verlag, 1990–. Fourteen volumes to date. [BA + volume number]

Paul Celan: Werke: Tübinger Ausgabe. Edited by Jürgen Wertheimer. Frankfurt am Main: Suhrkamp Verlag, 2004. Nine volumes. [TA + volume title]

TRANSLATIONS BY PAUL CELAN

The names of the translated authors are given in the German spelling (e.g., Sergej Jessenin, rather than Sergei Yesenin) as used by Celan and the various publications. All of these are gathered in volumes 4 and 5 of the 1983 five-volume collected Celan edition.

Cocteau, Jean. *Der Goldenen Vorhang. Brief an die Amerikaner.* Bad Salzig: Rauch, 1949.

Blok, Alexander. *Die Zwölf.* Frankfurt am Main: S. Fischer Verlag, 1958.

Rimbaud, Arthur. *Das trunkene Schiff.* Wiesbaden: Insel Verlag, 1958.

Mandelstam, Osip. *Gedichte.* Frankfurt am Main: S. Fischer Verlag, 1959.

Valéry, Paul. *Die junge Parze.* Limited edition. Wiesbaden: Insel Verlag, 1960.

Cayrol, Jean. *Im Bereich einer Nacht.* Olten: Walter, 1961.

Jessenin, Sergej. *Gedichte.* Frankfurt am Main: S. Fischer Verlag, 1961.

Shakespeare, William. *Einundzwanzig Sonette.* Frankfurt am Main: Insel Verlag, 1967.

du Bouchet, André. *Vakante Glut.* Frankfurt am Main: Suhrkamp Verlag, 1968.

Supervielle, Jules. *Gedichte.* Frankfurt am Main: Insel Verlag, 1968.

Ungaretti, Guiseppe. *Das verheißene Land / Das Merkbuch des Alten.* Frankfurt am Main: Insel Verlag, 1968.

TRANSLATIONS OF PAUL CELAN INTO ENGLISH

Speech-Grille and Selected Poems. Translated by Joachim Neugröschel. New York: E. P. Dutton, 1971. Contains all the poems of *Sprachgitter* and selected poems from the volumes *Mohn und Gedächtnis* through *Atemwende.*

Nineteen Poems. Translated by Michael Hamburger. Oxford: Carcanet Press; Chester Springs, Penn.: Dufour Editions, 1972. Poems from *Mohn und Gedächtnis* (11), *Von Schwelle zu Schwelle* (3), *Sprachgitter* (1), and *Die Niemandsrose* (4).

Paul Celan: Selected Poems. Translated by Michael Hamburger and Christopher Middleton. Harmondsworth, U.K.: Penguin Modern European Poets, 1972. Includes selected poems from the volumes *Mohn und Gedächtnis* through *Schneepart.*

Breath Crystal. Translated by Walter Billeter. Ivanhoe, Victoria, Australia: Ragman Productions, 1975.

Prose Writings and Selected Poems. Translated by Walter Billeter and Jerry Glenn. Carlton, Victoria, Australia: Paper Castle, 1977.

Poems. Translated by Michael Hamburger. New York: Persea Books; Manchester, U.K.: Carcanet Press, 1980.

65 Poems. Translated by Brian Lynch and Peter Jankowsky. Dublin: Raven Arts Press, 1985.

Last Poems. Translated by Katherine Washburn and Magret Guillemin. New York: North Point Press, 1986.

Paul Celan: Collected Prose. Translated by Rosmarie Waldrop. Manchester, U.K.: Carcanet Press, 1986. [PCCP]

Breathturn by Paul Celan. Translated by Pierre Joris. Los Angeles: Sun & Moon Press, 1995. (Reprinted in 2006 by Green Integer, Los Angeles.)

Glottal Stop: 101 Poems. Translated by Nikolai B. Popov and Heather McHugh. Middletown, Conn.: Wesleyan University Press, 2000.

Selected Poems and Prose of Paul Celan. Edited and translated by John Felstiner. New York: Norton, 2000.

Threadsuns by Paul Celan. Translated by Pierre Joris. Los Angeles: Sun & Moon Press, 2000. (Reprinted 2005 by Green Integer, Los Angeles.)

Fathomsuns / Fadensonnen and Benighted / Eingedunkelt. Translated by Ian Fairley. Rhinebeck, N.Y.: Sheep Meadow Press, 2001.

Lightduress by Paul Celan. Translated by Pierre Joris. Los Angeles: Green Integer, 2005.

Paul Celan: Selections. Edited and with an introduction by Pierre Joris. Berkeley: University of California Press, 2005. [PCS]

From Threshold to Threshold. Translated by David Young. Grosse Point Farms, Mich.: Marick Press, 2010.

The Meridian: Final Version—Drafts—Materials. Edited by Bernhard Bö-schenstein and Heino Schmull; translated by Pierre Joris. Palo Alto, Calif.: Stanford University Press, 2011. [MFV]

Language Behind Bars. Translated by David Young. Grosse Point Farms, Mich.: Marick Press, 2012.

Corona: The Selected Poems of Paul Celan. Translated by Susan Gillespie. Barrytown, N.Y.: Station Hill Press, 2013.

CORRESPONDENCE (IN ENGLISH)

Paul Celan, Nelly Sachs: Correspondence. Edited by Barbara Wiedemann. Translated by Christopher Clark. Rhinebeck, N.Y.: Sheep Meadow Press, 1998. [PC/NS]

Correspondence: Paul Celan and Ingeborg Bachmann. Translated by Wieland Hoban. London/New York/Calcutta: Seagull Books, 2010. [PC/IB]

The Correspondence of Paul Celan and Ilana Shmueli. Translated by Susan Gillespie. Rhinebeck, N.Y.: Sheep Meadow Press, 2011. [PC/IS]

ON PAUL CELAN AND HIS WORK (IN ENGLISH)

BIOGRAPHICAL MATERIALS

Chalfen, Israel. *Paul Celan: A Biography of His Youth.* New York: Persea Books, 1991.

Felstiner, John. *Paul Celan: Poet, Survivor, Jew.* New Haven, Conn.: Yale University Press, 1995.

BOOK-LENGTH CRITICAL STUDIES

Carson, Anne. *Economy of the Unlost (Reading Simonides of Kos with Paul Celan).* Princeton, N.J.: Princeton University Press, 1999.

Colin, Amy D., ed. *Argumentum e Silentio: International Paul Celan Symposium.* Berlin: Walter de Gruyter, 1986. This volume gathers essays on

Celan by Beda Alleman, Jean Bollack, Bernhard Böschenstein, Renate Böschenstein-Schäfer, Rolf Bücher, Amy D. Colin, Jacques Derrida, Hans-Georg Gadamer, Michael Hamburger, Alfred Hoelzel, John E. Jackson, James K. Lyon, Siegfried Mandel, Stéphane Mosès, Rainer Nägele, Elmar Tophoven, Alan Udoff, David E. Wellbery, Bernd Witte, and Shira Wolosky.

Daive, Jean. *Under the Dome: Walks with Paul Celan.* Translated by Rosmarie Waldrop. Providence, R.I.: Burning Deck/Anyart, 2009.

Derrida, Jacques. *Sovereignties in Question: The Poetics of Paul Celan.* Edited by Thomas Dutoit and Outi Pasanen. Bronx, N.Y.: Fordham University Press, 2005.

Fioretos, Aris, ed. *Word Traces: Readings of Paul Celan.* Baltimore: Johns Hopkins University Press, 1994.

Foot, Robert. *The Phenomenon of Speechlessness in the Poetry of Marie Luise Kaschnitz, Günter Eich, Nelly Sachs and Paul Celan.* Bonn: Bouvier, 1982.

Gadamer, Hans-Georg. *Gadamer on Celan: "Who Am I and Who Are You?" and Other Essays.* Translated and edited by Richard Heinemann and Bruce Krajewski. Albany, N.Y.: SUNY Press, 1997.

Glenn, Jerry. *Paul Celan.* New York: Twayne Publishers, 1973.

Hollander, Benjamin, ed. *Translating Tradition: Paul Celan in France.* San Francisco: ACTS 8/9, 1988. This volume, centered around Celan's work as a translator, with special reference to France, gathers essays by Maurtice Blanchot, Dan Blue, Yves Bonnefoy, Bernhard Böschenstein, André du Bouchet, E. M. Cioran, Jean Daive, Robert Duncan, John Felstiner, Joel Golb, Hugo Huppert, Edmond Jabès, Pierre Joris, Robert Kelly, Roger Laporte, Leonard Olschner, and Marc Wortman; it also contains translations of fifteen poems from *Zeitgehöft* by Cid Corman and original writings and artwork by Tom Mandel, Joseph Siman, Claudio Spies, and Tim Trompeter.

Kligerman, Eric. *Sites of the Uncanny: Paul Celan, Specularity and the Visual Arts.* Berlin: Walter de Gruyter, 2007.

Lacoue-Labarthe, Philippe, and Jean-Luc Nancy. *Retreating the Political.* New York: Routledge, 1996.

Lyon, James K. *Paul Celan and Martin Heidegger: An Unresolved Conversation, 1951–1970.* Baltimore: Johns Hopkins University Press, 2006.

————, ed. "Special Issue on Paul Celan." *Studies in Twentieth Century Literature* 8, no. 1 (1983). Contains critical essays on Celan by John Felstiner, Jerry Glenn, James K. Lyon, Nicholas J. Meyerhofer, Joachim Schulze, and Howard Stern, as well as a section titled "Encounters: American Poets on Paul Celan," with contributions by Paul Auster, Cid Corman, Clayton Eshleman, Jack Hirschman, David Meltzer, Jed Rasula, and Jerome Rothenberg.

Szondi, Peter. *Celan Studies.* Translated by Susan Bernofsky with Harvey Mendelsohn. Palo Alto, Calif.: Stanford University Press, 2003.

Tobias, Rochelle. *The Discourse of Nature in the Poetry of Paul Celan: The Unnatural World.* Baltimore: Johns Hopkins University Press, 2006.

SELECTED ESSAYS

Colin, Amy D. "Paul Celan." In *Holocaust Literature: An Encyclopedia of Writers and Their Work*, edited by S. Lillian Kremer, 1:216. New York: Routledge, 2003.

Fries, Thomas. "Critical Relation: Peter Szondi's Studies on Celan." *Boundary* 2 (November 3, 1983): 139–67.

Glenn, Jerry. "A Special Section on Paul Celan." *Sulfur* 11 (1984): 5–99.

————, and Edmund Remys. "Sergej Essenin in German: The Translations of Paul Celan and Alfred Gong." *Germano-Slavica* 5, nos. 1–2 (1985): 5–22.

Hamacher, Werner. "The Second of Inversion: Movements of a Figure Through Celan's Poetry." *Yale French Studies* 69 (1985): 276–314. Reprinted in *Word Traces: Readings of Paul Celan*, edited by Aris Fioretis, 219–63. Baltimore: Johns Hopkins University Press, 1994.

Lyon, James K. "Poetry and the Extremities of Language: From Concretism to Paul Celan." *Studies in Twentieth Century Literature* 8, no. 1 (1983).

————. "Paul Celan's Language of Stone: The Geology of the Poetic Landscape." *Colloquia Germanica* 8 (1974): 298–317.

Melin, Charlotte. "Celan and Enzensberger on an Asian Conflict." *Germanic Notes* 18, nos. 1–2 (1987): 4–5.

Myers, Saul. "The Way Through Human-Shaped Snow: Paul Celan's Job." *Studies in Twentieth Century Literature* 11, no. 2 (1987): 213–28.

Olschner, Leonard. "Anamnesis: Paul Celan's Translations of Poetry." *Studies in Twentieth Century Literature* 12, no. 2 (1988): 163–97.

Petuchowski, Elizabeth. "A New Examination of Paul Celan's Translation of Shakespeare's Sonnet 105." *Jahrbuch der Deutschen Shakespeare-Gesellschaft* (1985): 146–52.

Steiner, George. "A Terrible Exactness." *The Times Literary Supplement*, June 11, 1976, pp. 709–10.

Wolosky, Shira. "Paul Celan's Linguistic Mysticism." *Studies in Twentieth Century Literature* 10, no. 2 (1986): 191–211.

FURTHER RESOURCES USED IN COMMENTARY

Celan-Jahrbuch [CJB]

Frankfurter Allgemeine Zeitung [FAZ]

Paul Celan's Library [LPC]

Celan, Paul. *La bibliothèque philosophique*. Catalogue raisonné annotated by Alexandra Richter, Patrik Alac, and Bertrand Badiou. Lyon: ENS Éditions, 2004. [BPPC]

———, and Peter Szondi. *Briefwechsel*. Edited by Christoph König. Frankfurt am Main: Suhrkamp Verlag, 2005. [PC/PS]

———, and Franz Wurm. *Briefwechsel*. Edited by Barbara Wiedemann, with assistance by Franz Wurm. Frankfurt am Main: Suhrkamp Verlag, 2003. [PC/FW]

———. *Choix de poèmes*. Translated and edited by Jean-Pierre Lefebvre. Paris: Gallimard, 1998.

———, and Gisèle Celan-Lestrange. *Correspondance, 1951–1970*. 2 volumes. Edited by Bertrand Badiou, with the help of Eric Celan. Paris: Seuil, 2001. Simultaneously published in a German translation by Eugen Helmlé as *Briefwechsel* (Frankfurt am Main: Suhrkamp Verlag, 2001). [PC/GCL]

———. *Partie de neige*. Translated from the German and annotated by Jean-Pierre Lefebvre. Paris: Seuil, 2007. [PDN]

———. *Renverse de souffle*. Translated from the German and annotated by Jean-Pierre Lefebvre. Paris: Seuil, 2003. [RDS]

Anderson, Mark M. "The Impossibility of Poetry: Celan and Heidegger in France." *New German Critique* 53 (1991): 3–18.

Baer, Ulrich. *Remnants of Song: Trauma and the Experience of Modernity in Charles Baudelaire and Paul Celan.* Palo Alto, Calif.: Stanford University Press, 2000.

Barnert, Arno Albert. *"Die Insel des zweiten Gesichts von Albert Vigoleis Thelen, gelesen von Paul Celan: 'une vraie oeuvre d'art.'"* *Celan-Jahrbuch* 8 (2001/2002): 175–202.

Benjamin, Walter. *Selected Writings.* 4 volumes. Cambridge, Mass.: Belknap/Harvard University Press, 2003. [WBSW]

Ben-Porat, Ziva. "Forms of Intertextuality and the Reading of Poetry: Uri Zvi Greenberg's Basha'ar." *Prooftexts* 10, no. 2 (1990): 257–81.

Bilz, Rudolf. *Die unbewältigte Vergangenheit des Menschengeschlechts.* Frankfurt am Main: Suhrkamp Verlag, 1967.

Bloch, Ernst. *The Principle of Hope.* 3 volumes. Translated by Neville Plaice, Stephen Plaice, and Paul Knight. Cambridge, Mass.: MIT Press, 1986.

Bollack, Jean. "Pour une lecture de Paul Celan," *Lignes* 1 (November 1987): 147–61.

Bonnefoy, Yves. "Paul Celan." *Translating Tradition: Paul Celan in France.* Edited by Benjamin Hollander. *ACTS, a Journal of New Writing* 8/9 (1988): 9–14.

Böschenstein, Bernhard, and Sigrid Weigel, eds. *Ingeborg Bachmann und Paul Celan: Poetische Korrespondenzen.* Frankfurt am Main: Suhrkamp Verlag, 1997.

Böschenstein-Schäfer, Renate. "Traum und Sprache in der Dichtung Paul Celans." In *Argumentum e Silentio: International Paul Celan Symposium,* edited by Amy D. Colin, 223–36. Berlin: Walter de Gruyter, 1986.

Brinkmann, Roland. *Abriß der Geologie.* 2 volumes. 10th/11th edition, revised by Karl Krömmelbein. Stuttgart: Ferdinand Enke Verlag, 1977.

Broda, Martine. *Contre-jour: Études sur Paul Celan.* Paris: Éditions du Cerf, 1986. [C-J]

Bücher, Rolf. "Erfahrenes Sprechen – Leseversuch an Celan-Entwürfen." In *Argumentum e Silentio: International Paul Celan Symposium,* edited by Amy D. Colin, 99–112. Berlin: Walter de Gruyter, 1986.

Buhr, Gerhard. "Von der radikalen In-Frage-Stellung der Kunst in Celans Rede 'Der Meridian.'" *Celan-Jahrbuch* 2 (1988): 169–208.

Caputo, John D. *The Mystical Element in Heidegger's Thought.* Athens: Ohio University Press, 1978.

Derrida, Jacques. "Poetics and Politics of Witnessing." In *Sovereignties in Question: The Poetics of Paul Celan,* edited by Thomas Dutoit and Outi Pasanen, 65–96. Bronx, N.Y.: Fordham University Press, 2005.

Eckhart, Meister. *Predigten: Die deutschen Werke.* Volume 1. Edited by Josef Quint. Stuttgart: W. Kohlhammer, 1958.

———. *Selected Writings.* Translated by Oliver Davies. London: Penguin, 1994.

Eis, Gerhard, ed. *Wahrsagertexte des Spätmittelalters: Aus Handschriften und Inkunabeln.* Berlin/Bielefeld/Munich: E. Schmidt, 1956. [LPC: acquired May 12, 1959]

Eshel, Amir. "Paul Celan's Other: History, Poetics, and Ethics." *New German Critique* 91 (2004): 57–77.

Faller, Adolf. *Der Körper des Menschen: Einführung in Bau und Funktion.* Stuttgart: Georg Thieme Verlag, 1966. [LPC]

Felstiner, John. "'Ziv, that light': Translation and Tradition in Paul Celan." *New Literary History* 18, no. 3 (1987): 611–31.

Freud, Sigmund. *Beyond the Pleasure Principle.* New York: Bantam Books, 1967.

———. "Das Ich und das Es." In volume 13 of *Gesammelte Werke in Einzelbänden.* 5th edition. Frankfurt am Main: Suhrkamp Verlag, 1967. [LPC: acquired April 1, 1967, Sainte-Anne psychiatric clinic, Paris, "(following an instruction by Frau Fischer)"]

———. *The Ego and the Id.* Translated by Joan Riviere. London: Hogarth Press, 1927.

———. *The Interpretation of Dreams.* Volume 4 of the Pelican Freud Library. Edited by Angela Richards; translated by James Strachey. Harmondsworth, U.K.: Penguin, 1976.

Goßens, Peter, and Marcus G. Patka, eds. *"Displaced": Paul Celan in Wien, 1947–1949.* Frankfurt am Main: Suhrkamp Verlag, 2001.

Hahn, Barbara. *The Jewess Pallas Athena: This Too a Theory of Modernity.* Translated by James McFarland. Princeton, N.J.: Princeton University Press, 2005.

Hamacher, Werner. "Häm: Ein Gedicht Celans mit Motiven Benjamins." In *Jüdisches Denken in einer Welt ohne Gott: Festschrift für Stéphane Mosès,* edited by Jens Mattern, Gabriel Motzkin, and Shimon Sandbank, 173–97. Berlin: Verlag Vorwerk 8, 2000. [WHH]

———. "The Second of Inversion: Movements of a Figure Through Celan's Poetry." In *Word Traces: Readings of Paul Celan,* edited by Aris Fioretis, 219–63. Baltimore: Johns Hopkins University Press, 1994.

Heidegger, Martin. *Holzwege.* Frankfurt am Main: Viktorio Klostermann, 2003.

———. *Unterwegs zur Sprache.* Tübingen: Neske, 1959.

Hellerstein, Kathryn Ann. "Moyshe Leyb Halpern's 'In New York': A Modern Yiddish Verse Narrative." Ph.D. diss., Stanford University, 1981.

Homer. *The Odyssey.* Translated by Charles Stein. Berkeley, Calif.: North Atlantic Books, 2008.

Husserl, Edmund. *Zur Phänomenologie des inneren Zeitbewußtseins (1893–1917).* Edited by Rudolf Boehm. The Hague: Martinus Nijhoff, 1969.

Iiska, Vivian. "Roots Against Heaven: An Aporetic Inversion in Paul Celan." *New German Critique* 91 (2004): 41–56.

Janz, Marlies. *Vom Engagement absoluter Poesie: Zur Lyrik und Ästhetik Paul Celans.* Frankfurt am Main: Athenäum, 1976.

Joris, Pierre. "Paul Celan's Counterword: Who Witnesses for the Witness?" In *Justifying the Margins,* 79–86. Cambridge, U.K.: Salt Publishing, 2009.

Kafka, Franz. *Hochzeitsvorbereitungen auf dem Lande.* Frankfurt am Main: S. Fischer Verlag, 1976.

Kaufman, Walter. "Heidegger's Castle." Translated by Hugo Bergmann. *Iyyun: A Hebrew Philosophical Quarterly* 9, no. 1 (1958): 76–101.

King James Bible. The Official King James Bible Online. 1769 version. Available at www.kingjamesbibleonline.org (accessed May 30, 2014).

Klose, Barbara. "'Souvenirs entomologiques': Celans Begegnung mit Jean-Henri Fabre." In *Datum und Zitat bei Paul Celan,* edited by Bernd Witte and Chaim Shoham, 122–55. Bern/Frankfurt am Main/New York: Peter Lang, 1987.

Kluge, Friedrich, and Alfred Götze. *Etymologisches Wörterbuch der deutschen Sprache*. 16th edition. Berlin: Walter de Gruyter, 1953.

Konietzny, Ulrich. "All deine Siegel erbrochen?" *Celan-Jahrbuch* 2 (1988): 107–20.

Lyon, James K. "Ganz und gar nicht hermetisch: Zum 'richtigen' Lesen von Paul Celans Lyrik." In *Psalm und Hawdalah: Zum Werk Paul Celans*, edited by Joseph P. Strelka, 185–89. Bern/Frankfurt am Main/New York/Paris: Peter Lang, 1987.

———. "Die (Patho-)Physiologie des Ichs in der Lyrik Paul Celans," *Zeitschrift für Deutsche Philologie* 106, no. 4 (1987b): 591–608.

May, Markus, Peter Goßens, and Jürgen Lehmann, eds. *Celan Handbuch: Leben – Werk – Wirkung*. Stuttgart: J. B. Metzler, 2008. [CH]

Mayer, Hans. "Erinnerung an Paul Celan," *Merkur* 24 (1970): 1160.

Mendes-Hohr, Paul. *German Jews: A Dual Identity*. New Haven, Conn.: Yale University Press, 1999.

Nägele, Rainer. *Reading After Freud: Essays on Goethe, Hölderlin, Habermas, Nietzsche, Brecht, Celan, and Freud*. New York: Columbia University Press, 1987.

Oelmann, Ute Maria. *Deutsche poetologische Lyrik nach 1945: Ingeborg Bachmann, Günter Eich, Paul Celan*. Stuttgart: Akademischer Verlag H. D. Heinz, 1980.

Petuchowski, Elizabeth. "Bilingual and Multilingual *Wortspiele* in the Poetry of Paul Celan." *Deutsche Vierteljahrsschrift für Literaturwissenschaft und Geistesgeschichte* 52 (1978): 635–51.

Pöggeler, Otto. "Mystical Elements in Heidegger's Thought and Celan's Poetry." In *Word Traces: Readings of Paul Celan*, edited by Aris Fioretis, 75–109. Baltimore: Johns Hopkins University Press, 1994.

———. "'Schwarzmaut': Bildende Kunst in der Lyrik Paul Celans." In: *Die Frage nach der Kunst: Von Hegel zu Heidegger*, 281–375. Munich/Freiburg im Breisgau: Verlag Karl Alber, 1984.

———. *Spur des Wortes*. Munich/Freiburg im Breisgau: Verlag Karl Alber, 1986. [SPUR]

―――. *Der Stein hinterm Aug: Studien zu Celans Gedichten.* Munich: Wilhelm Fink Verlag, 2000. [STEIN]

Rabinbach, Anson. Introduction to *The Correspondence of Walter Benjamin and Gershom Scholem, 1932–1940,* edited by Gershom Scholem, vii–xxxviii. Cambridge, Mass.: Harvard University Press, 1992.

Rebien, Kristin. "Politics and Aesthetics in Postwar German Literature: Heinrich Böll, Hans Erich Nossack, Paul Celan." Ph.D. diss., Stanford University, 2005.

Reichel, Hans, and Adolf Bleichert. *Leitfaden der Physiologie des Menschen.* Stuttgart: Ferdinand Enke Verlag, 1966. [LPC]

Reschika, Richard. *Poesie und Apokalypse: Paul Celans Jerusalem-Gedichte aus dem Nachlassband Zeitgehöft.* Pfaffenweiler: Centaurus, 1991.

Santner, Eric. *Creaturely Life: Rilke, Benjamin, Sebald.* Chicago: University of Chicago Press, 2006.

Scholem, Gershom. *Major Trends in Jewish Mysticism.* New York: Schocken, 1995.

―――. *On the Kabbalah and Its Symbolism.* New York: Schocken, 1996.

―――. *On the Mystical Shape of the Godhead: Basic Concepts in the Kabbalah.* Translated by Joachim Neugröschel. Schocken, 1997.

―――. "The Tradition of the Thirty-Six Hidden Just Men." In *The Messianic Idea in Judaism and Other Essays on Jewish Spirituality,* 251–56. New York: Schocken, 1971.

―――. *Ursprung und Anfänge der Kabbala.* Berlin: Walter de Gruyter, 1962.

―――. *Von der mystischen Gestalt der Gottheit: Studien zu Grundbegriffen der Kabbala.* Zurich: Rhein-Verlag, 1962.

Schulze, Joachim. *Celan und die Mystiker: Motivtypologische und quellenkundliche Kommentare.* Bonn: Bouvier, 1976.

―――. "Mystische Motive in Paul Celans Gedichten." *Poetica* 3 (1970): 472–509.

Shmueli, Ilana. *Sag, daß Jerusalem ist: Über Paul Celan, Oktober 1969–April 1970.* Aachen: Rimbaud Verlag, 2010. [IS]

Spector, Scott. *Prague Territories: National Conflict and Cultural Innovation in Franz Kafka's Fin-de-Siècle.* Berkeley: University of California Press, 2000.

Speier, Hans-Michael. "Paul Celan, Dichter einer neuen Wirklichkeit: Studien zu *Schneepart*." *Celan-Jahrbuch* 1 (1987): 65–79.

Steinecke, Hartmut. "Lieder . . . jenseits der Menschen?" In *Psalm und Hawdalah: Zum Werk Paul Celans*, edited by Joseph P. Strelka, 192–202. Bern/Frankfurt am Main/New York/Paris: Peter Lang, 1987.

Weidner, Daniel. *Gershom Scholem: Politisches, esoterisches und historiographisches Schreiben*. Munich: Wilhelm Fink Verlag, 2003.

Wiedemann, Barbara. *Paul Celan: Die Goll-Affäre*. Frankfurt am Main: Suhrkamp Verlag, 2000.

Wienold, Götz. "Paul Celans Hölderlin-Widerruf" (Paul Celan's Hölderlin Revocation), *Poetica* 2, no. 2 (April 1968): 216–28.

Witte, Bernd. "Der zyklische Charakter der *Niemandsrose* von Paul Celan." *In Argumentum e Silentio: International Paul Celan Symposium*, edited by Amy D. Colin, 72–86. Berlin: Walter de Gruyter, 1986.

Index of Titles
and First Lines
in German

Index of Titles and First Lines in English

PAUL CELAN, one of the greatest German-language poets of the twentieth century, created an oeuvre that stands as testimony to the horrors of his times and as an attempt to chart a topography for a new, uncontaminated language and world. *Breathturn into Timestead: The Collected Later Poetry* gathers the five final volumes of his life's work in a bilingual edition, translated and with commentary by the award-winning poet and translator Pierre Joris.

This collection displays a mature writer at the height of his talents, following what Celan himself called the "turn" (*Wende*) of his work away from the lush, surreal metaphors of his earlier verse. Given "the sinister events in its memory," Celan believed that the language of poetry had to become "more sober, more factual . . . 'grayer.'" Abandoning the more sumptuous music of the first books, he pared down his compositions to increase the accuracy of the language that now "does not transfigure or render 'poetical'; it names, it posits, it tries to measure the area of the given and the possible." In his need for an inhabitable post-Holocaust world, Celan saw that "reality is not simply there; it must be searched for and won."

Breathturn into Timestead reveals a poet undergoing a profound artistic reinvention. The work is that of a witness and a visionary.

PAUL CELAN was born in Czernowitz, Bukovina, in 1920, and is widely considered to be one of the most innovative poets of the twentieth century. A German-speaking Jew, he was sent to a forced labor camp during World War II. Celan settled in Paris in 1948, where he lived and wrote until his suicide in 1970.

PIERRE JORIS has written, edited, and translated more than fifty books, including poetry, essays, and anthologies. Most recently he published *Barzakh: Poems 2000–2012*, *A Voice Full of Cities: The Collected Essays of Robert Kelly*, and the fourth volume of the anthology *Poems for the Millennium: The University of California Book of North African Literature*. In 2005 he received the PEN Award for Poetry in Translation for Celan's *Lichtzwang | Lightduress*.

FARRAR, STRAUS AND GIROUX
www.fsgbooks.com